Best Places to Stay in the Southwest

Best Places to Stay in the Southwest

Gail Barber Rickey

Bruce Shaw, Editorial Director

Houghton Mifflin Company · Boston

For information about permission to reproduce selections
from this book, write to Permissions, Houghton Mifflin
Company, 2 Park Street, Boston, Massachusetts 02108.

First Edition

ISBN: 0-395-54550-1 (pbk.)
ISSN: 1048-549x

Printed in the United States of America

Illustrations by Chris Schuh
Maps by Charles Bahne

This book was prepared in conjunction
with Harvard Common Press.

HAD 10 9 8 7 6 5 4 3 2 1

To Pat

the best person to be with in a "Best Place"

Author's Note

I guess I'm a collector at heart. Not that I've ever collected anything practical—just things that please my eye. As a child, I collected pretty pictures. I still have some of them, stuck away in an upstairs closet. Every time we move to another house I stumble over them, taking time to flip through the stack of snow-covered mountains and incredibly blue oceans, playful puppies and cuddly kittens, smiling babies and grand-motherly grandmothers.

When I travel I still collect things that please my eye. They don't usually cost much (except for the carpet I couldn't walk away from in Turkey), but they're precious to me. A pastel of a fiord in Norway, tiny figures of Chinese peasants, a minia-ture Thai house, a hand-painted ceramic church from Crete.

There's also something else I collect—hotels. It's a habit that dates back many years, long before I knew there was such a thing as a travel writer. I know it's strange. I can't explain why, but wherever I go, for whatever reason, I have to visit great hotels. I confess it. I'm a dyed-in-the-wool, unreform-able hotel-phile.

Part of the reason I like hotels, I suppose, is that they are often repositories of beauty. Many represent the best of their community, perhaps the best of an age. Architecture, fur-nishings, art work—grand hotels can be better than a museum, for they are filled with life in the here and now.

Also, hotels symbolize joy. They're the places where peo-ple go to celebrate—high school proms, wedding parties, grand receptions. Sometimes the celebration is on a smaller scale—honeymoon, a family vacation, a special getaway.

What makes a hotel great? Setting, sensory appeal, com-fort, tradition—they all enter the formula. But people are at the heart of a hotel's greatness—the service they extend, the feeling their composite efforts project. The way you're greeted when you walk up to the desk, the cordial voice on the phone when you call to request a service, the smile of the waitress, the courteous bellman—those are the things that cre-ate an impression that far outlasts whether your room had one or two TVs.

This book is about bed and breakfast inns, cabins in the woods, guest ranches, grand resorts. But whatever the setting, or the size, the principles of hospitality are the same. And hospitality is what hotels are all about.

One further note about my personal orientation towards selecting the best. From my mother, I inherited a love of beauty. From my father, I acquired a bent toward making money go a long way. I'd like to think that the combination of the two viewpoints has led me to seek value for the money. My husband sees it another way—he says that the combination has created an internal war, with no cease-fire in sight. But no matter—in researching this book, I have judged quality with an eye to price. Outrageous rates, whoever is paying the bill, subtract significantly from my enjoyment. I was so aghast at one price quote during my research that for a moment I though I must be in another country, hearing prices in a currency with a low exchange rate.

I sincerely hope that this guidebook leads you to places of charm and character. I hope that within their doors you find friendly folk who make you glad you're there. And I hope that you return home richer for the experience.

Gail Rickey
Houston Texas

Contents

Introduction

This isn't another "inn book," nor is it an attempt to judge all of the lodgings in Arizona, New Mexico, Oklahoma, and Texas by one rigid criterion. Instead, we have looked at the full range of places to stay in the Southwest and noted first and foremost their astonishing variety, from Grand Old Mansions to National Park Lodges, and we have picked only the outstanding examples. *Best Places to Stay in the Southwest* describes Romantic Getaways, Family Finds, and Gourmet Getaways. It includes Fishing and Hunting Lodges, places to stay and ride horseback, plus inns catering specially to golfers, tennis players, hikers, and birding enthusiasts. It includes elegant small urban hotels and working ranches covering tens of thousands of acres, as well as lake resorts and health spas, outstanding ski resorts, and throughout, lodgings with the historical mix of Southwest Indian, Hispanic, and Anglo-American cultures for which the Southwest is justly famous.

When we are asked for advice on a place "to get away to," we notice that the person asking usually is not set on being in any specific spot, although sometimes there's a desire to be near the great beaches of the Gulf of Mexico or near the incomparable southwestern desert. More often the wish is for outstanding food or a romantic atmosphere, or a special place to go as a family. We know many great places that fit these requirements perfectly but are not listed in any guidebooks; hence our unique system of grouping lodgings by type rather than geographically. In this way we are able to include many wonderful—in some cases one-of-a-kind—places to stay that do not fit other guide books' formats and thus have never before appeared in any book. For maximum ease of use, we include state-by-state maps to help you see at a glance what is to be found near Houston, or Taos, or the Grand Canyon, and thus the book can still be used geographically, just like all the other guidebooks.

Obviously our criteria differ when judging between the best ranches and the best city stops. Our primary standards are cleanliness, palpable presence of a host or, in the case of the larger hotels, a personal style of service, and a conviction that we would like to stay in the place for more than one night. As with all the books in this series, no fees were collected for inclusion—these are not paid advertisements.

Author Gail Rickey joins the *Best Places to Stay* team after 20 years of traveling in the Southwest with and without her family. She journeyed 15,000 miles preparing for this book, and her special interest in the history of her home region is an added bonus we enjoy. Gail understands the distinct traditions of lodging and hospitality that make the Southwest different from, say, New England.

Innkeepers tell us these days that travelers want more and are willing to pay for it. Certainly there are many small places with high prices, but there are also many bargains listed here. The key to planning a trip for yourself, we believe, is value—what you get for your money. For example, we find that families can stay comfortably and economically in many of the new condominium resorts, where the rate is based on per-unit rather than per-person criteria. On the other hand, a number of fine old resorts, large and small, are maintaining the same standards and traditions that have attracted generations of devotees, and many hotels with illustrious histories, previously fallen into disrepair, have been brilliantly refurbished to stand as superior alternatives to the standard (that is, dull) motel.

We have done our very best to provide you with accurate and up to-date information. As is true with any guidebook, certain information changes quickly. Please be sure to call and make reservations, if you can, at these places. And we would suggest that you draw up a list of the four or five points that most concern you when you stay somewhere, and ask the person with whom you are making your reservation about them. If money is important, be sure you know what your room rate will be. If noise bothers you, be sure that you ask for a quiet room. We have found over and over that we get what we ask for.

Maps

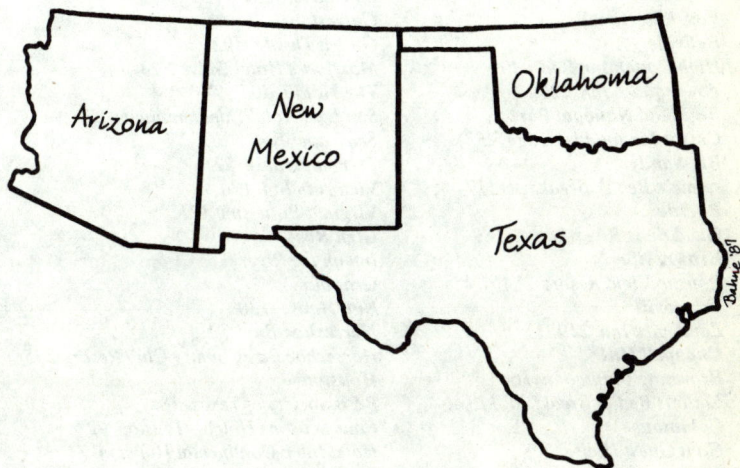

SOUTHWEST

NOTE: The page numbers follow the name of the establishment.

TEXAS

Arlington
Greenhouse 274
Radisson Suite Hotel 131

Austin
Driskill Hotel 48
Four Seasons Hotel Austin 49
La Mansion Hotel Austin 50
Lake Austin Resort 275
Stouffer Austin Hotel 51
Lakeway Inn 236
Wyndham Southpark 52

Bandera
Mayan Dude Ranch 200
Silver Spur Guest Ranch 201

Bastrop
Pink Lady Inn 8

Bellville
High Cotton Inn B&B 303
Townsquare Inn 120

Big Bend National Park
Chisos Mountains Lodge 238

Big Sandy
Annie's Bed & Breakfast 117

Boerne
Guadalupe River Ranch 189

Brownsville
Rancho Viejo Resort 284

Castroville
Landmark Inn 219

Chappell Hill
Browning Plantation 166
Lottie's Bed & Breakfast 113

Columbus
Gant Guest House 208
Montgomery House 210

Corpus Christi
Best Western Sandy Shores 23
Hershey Corpus Christi Hotel 140
Sand Dollar Hospitality B&B 21

Dallas
Adolphus 53
Aristocrat 54
B&B Texas Style (OK) 16
B&B Texas Style (TX) 19
Hotel Crescent Court 57
Loews Anatole Hotel 59
Mansion on Turtle Creek 60
Plaza of the Americas 63
Stoneleigh 63
Stouffer Dallas Hotel 64
Westin Hotel Dallas 65
Fairmont Hotel 56
Omni Melrose Hotel 62

Eagle Lake
Farris 1912 229

El Paso
El Paso Airport Hilton 66
El Paso Marriott 67
Westin Paso del Norte 68

Fort Davis
Butterfields 260
Indian Lodge 129
Prude Ranch 252

Fort Worth
Hyatt Regency Fort Worth 69
Stockyards Hotel 70
Worthington Hotel 71

Fredericksburg
B&B of Fredericksburg 17
Gastehaus Schmidt 21
Landhaus B&B 112

Galveston
Gilded Thistle 302
Marriott's Hotel Galvez 24
The Matali 305
San Luis Hotel/Condominiums 27
Seascape 104
Tremont House 221
Victorian Inn 170
Virginia Point Inn 171

Glen Rose
Inn on the River 7

Granbury
Nutt House 130

Horseshoe Bay
Horseshoe Bay Country Club Resort 235

Houston
B&B Society of Texas 18
Four Seasons Hotel—Houston 72
Hotel Inter-Continental Houston 73
Inn on the Park 74
Lancaster Hotel 76
Phoenix Fitness Resort 276
Remington on Post Oak Park 78
Sara's B&B Inn 41
Warwick 79
Westin Galleria/Westin Oaks 81
Wyndham Hotel Greenspoint 82
La Colombe d'Or 75

Ingram
Lazy Hills Guest Ranch 192

Irving
Dallas Marriot Mandalay Hotel 55
Four Seasons Resort and Hotel 163

Jefferson
Excelsior House 218
Guest House 208
Pride House 9
Stillwater Inn 150
Wise Manor 307
Austin Cottage & Guest Suites 207
The Magnolias 170
McKay House 264

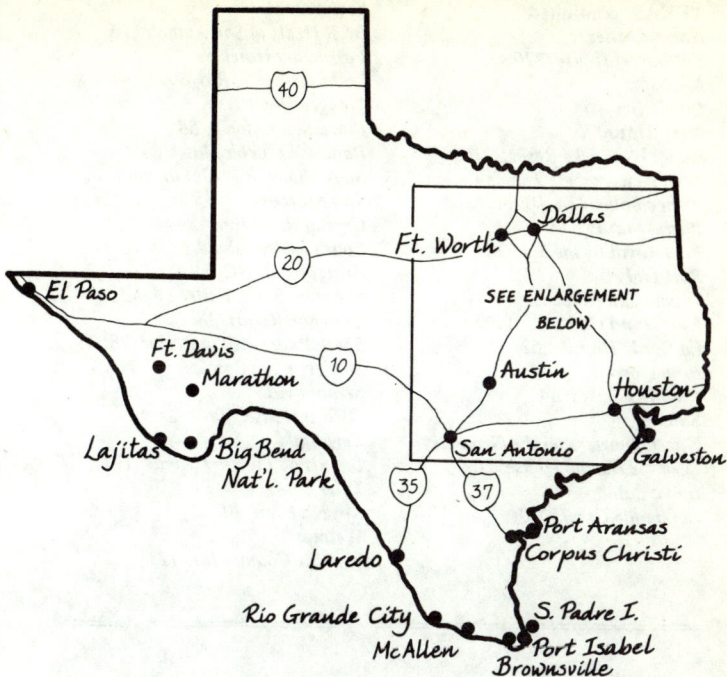

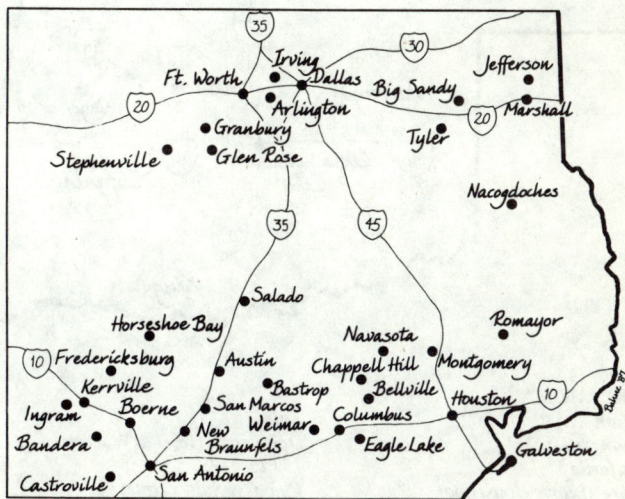

Texas state map with highways and cities:

40
Ft. Worth
Dallas
20
SEE ENLARGEMENT BELOW
El Paso
Ft. Davis
Marathon
10
Austin
Houston
Lajitas
Big Bend Nat'l. Park
San Antonio
Galveston
35
37
Laredo
Port Aransas
Corpus Christi
Rio Grande City
S. Padre I.
McAllen
Port Isabel
Brownsville

Enlargement map:

35
Irving
30
Ft. Worth
Dallas
Big Sandy
Jefferson
20
Arlington
Marshall
Granbury
20
Stephenville
Glen Rose
Tyler
Nacogdoches
35
45
Salado
Horseshoe Bay
Navasota
Romayor
10
Fredericksburg
Austin
Chappell Hill
Montgomery
Kerrville
Bastrop
Bellville
Ingram
Boerne
San Marcos
Weimar
Houston
10
Bandera
New Braunfels
Columbus
Castroville
San Antonio
Eagle Lake
Galveston

Kerrville
Inn of the Hills River Resort 141
Y.O. Ranch Hilton 254
Laredo
La Posada (Laredo, TX) 292
Marathon
Gage Hotel 119

Marshall
La Maison Malfacon 169
Cotten's Patch B&B Inn 301
McAllen
La Posada (McAllen, TX) 293
Montgomery
Del Lago Resort 234

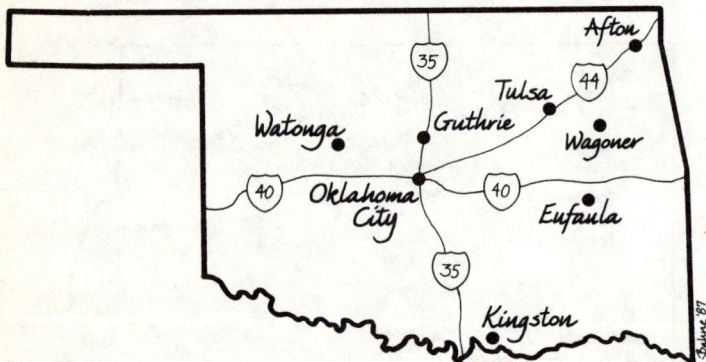

A map of Arizona showing labeled cities: Grand Canyon Nat'l Park, Flagstaff, Sedona, Jerome, Mormon Lake, Prescott, Wickenburg, Carefree, Scottsdale, Litchfield Park, Phoenix, Tucson, Pearce, Sasabe, Bisbee, Apache. Highway markers shown include 89, 40, 17, 10, 8, 19. Signed "Baskin '87".

ARIZONA

Bisbee
Bisbee Inn 123
Copper Queen Hotel 286
Inn at Castle Rock 244

Carefree
Boulders 152

Douglas
Price Canyon Ranch 251

Flagstaff
Little America of Flagstaff 124
Monte Vista Hotel 213

Grand Canyon
Bright Angel Lodge & Cabins 239
Phantom Ranch 242
El Tovar 240

Jerome
Miners Roost Hotel 245

Kitchfield Park
The Wigwam 178

Mormon Lake
Montezuma Lodge 31

North Rim
Grand Canyon Lodge North Rim 241

Pearce
Grapevine Canyon Ranch 256

Phoenix
Arizona Biltmore 174
Pointe at Tapatio Cliff 157
Squaw Park Inn 37

Prescott
B&B Scottsdale and The West 12
Hassayampa Inn 211
Hotel Vendome 212
Lynx Creek Farm 106

Sasabe
Rancho de la Osa 186

Scottsdale
B&B in Arizona 13
Marriott's Camelback Inn 133
Red Lion's La Posada 158
Registry Resort 159
Scottsdale Princess 160
Stouffer Cottonwoods Resort 257
Hyatt Regency Scottsdale at
  Gainey Ranch 154
John Gardiner's Tennis Ranch
  on Camelback 278

Sedona
Garlands's Oak Creek Lodge 115
Graham's Bed & Breakfast Inn 296
John Gardiner's Enchantment 155
Junipine Resort Condo Hotel 99
L'Auberge de Sedona 143
Poco Diablo Resort 135
Sky Ranch Lodge 125

Tempe
Mi Casa Su Casa (AZ) 14
Mi Casa Su Casa (NM) 15

Tucson
Arizona Inn 175
Canyon Ranch Spa 271
Flying V Ranch 203
Hacienda del Sol Guest Ranch
  Resort 177

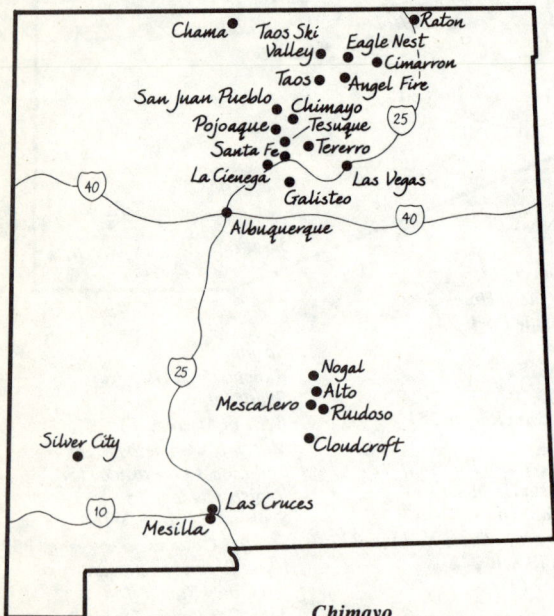

1

B&B Inns

These B&B Inns are some of the most special places in the Southwest. In warmth and personality they are akin to home B&Bs; in operation they are professionally run inns. Some are owner-operated. Others have full-time managers.

NEW MEXICO

El Rincon Bed and Breakfast
110 E. Kit Carson Street
P.O. Box Drawer Q
Taos, New Mexico 87571
505/758-4874, 758-9188
INNKEEPERS: Nina Meyers and Ross Langham
6 rooms (private baths)
$40–$70 double including continental breakfast
American Express, MasterCard, Visa; personal check
Children welcome
Pets with approval
Open year round

Only half a block from the Plaza, El Rincon is a charmingly unusual B&B. Compact in its design, the inn has rooms tucked away on several levels, some opening onto the courtyard.

The six guest rooms offer six different moods—each distinctive within itself. Yet common throughout is an emphasis on visual appeal. The work of local artists predominates—ranging from santos in wall niches to hand-carved doors to intricately crafted furniture. Flowers spill from everywhere, adding color and gaiety.

Most of the building is 100 years old; the "newer" section has been around for only 90 years. Next door is the Original Trading Post of Taos, founded years ago by Indian trader Ralph Meyers, father of today's innkeeper Nina Meyers.

Every guest room at El Rincon has something unexpected—its own surprise. Unit number 1, the most luxurious, has a hot tub below its loft. Unit number 3 is a hideaway reached by two flights of tiny stairs. Everything in the room is diminutive, even the TV. (Beware: Due to the winding staircase, this is not the room for travelers with lots of luggage.) A personal favorite is Unit number 4, or the Sun Room. Decorated in yellow, it shouts cheerfulness. Original art work is in abundance. There's a refrigerator and coffee-maker in the walk-in closet. The bath is small but attractively designed, with a beam ceiling and hand-painted tile. Some of the units have stereos and VCRs. Several have fireplaces. Unit number 6 has a full kitchen, plus washer-dryer.

For families, Unit number 1 on the second floor is probably the best choice. Accommodating six, it has a double bed, queen-size sleeper sofa, and loft with two beds, plus a sun deck and hot tub.

Breakfast at El Rincon is often served on the patio. Guests can choose the time that best fits their own schedule. The menu usually includes fruit, muffins, and cereal.

Grant Corner Inn

122 Grant Avenue
Santa Fe, New Mexico 87501
505/983-6678
INNKEEPERS: The Walter Family—Pat, Louise, and "Bumpy"
13 rooms (6 with private bath)
$45–$50 single, $50–$110 double including full breakfast
MasterCard, Visa; personal check
Children over 5 welcome
No pets
Open year round except January 5 to February 5
   (condominium units remain open)

One of the most delightful inns in all of the Southwest is at the corner of Grant Avenue and Johnson Street in Santa Fe. Walk through the latticed street-side archway to a nostalgic world of pinafores and quilts, warmth and hospitality. Whether your childhood included visits to grandma's house or not, you'll feel as if it did when you visit Grant Corner Inn, a 13-room lodging operated B&B style.

The Colonial manor home situated two blocks from the Plaza was built in 1905 by a wealthy ranching family. In 1982 the Walters renovated the old home and began welcoming guests to their inn.

For both Louise and her husband Pat, the venture was an extension of their personalities. Louise, daughter of Jack Stewart who founded Camelback Inn in Scottsdale in 1936, grew up in the hotel business. Now an interior designer, she also studied at Cornell Hotel School. Pat taught classes in space planning and design—a handy background to have if you want to renovate an old mansion. Nowadays he is likely to be found in the kitchen, overseeing the marvelous fare for which Grant Corner is famed. Who is "Bumpy?" She's the daughter of the family, growing up like Mom at the heart of the hospitality business.

Past the white picket fence and through the etched glass front door, you walk into a living room furnished in antiques. From the Wedgwood blue ceiling and walls to the gleaming wood floors and the Oriental carpets, the house exudes warmth. The adjoining dining room gets lots of use, for not only does the inn serve breakfast to its guests but also to the public. It doesn't take but a moment to start noticing the rabbits—calico rabbits, wooden rabbits, furry rabbits, porcelain rabbits, even rabbit napkin holders on the dining room table. Louise explains that she grew up watching jack rabbits and cottontails on her lawn in Scottsdale, so the creatures have "a place in my heart."

Throughout the house, there are touches, like the rabbits, that give the inn special charm. Hanging on the door of each guest room is a stuffed heart-shaped ornament saying "Welcome." Arriving guests find a small fruit basket with a hand-written note from their hosts.

Eleven guest rooms are on the first through third floors. Each has its own decor; brass and four-poster bed, quilts and tie-back curtains are the featured furnishings. Some rooms have mini-refrigerators, covered in frills. Every room has a private phone, TV, and ceiling fan. Don't expect a large room, but the overall ambience makes up for any loss of space. Adjoining rooms with a shared bath are a good choice for families. Bedrooms range from one twin bed to one king-size and have enough space for a roll-away.

Five blocks away is Grant Corner Inn Hacienda, an adobe-style condominium with two guest rooms upstairs and a living room, dining room, and kitchen downstairs. It has modern decor, cathedral ceilings, and skylights. The entire unit can accommodate up to eight; either of the guest rooms can be rented individually. Both have queen-size beds; one has a beehive fireplace. Rates range from $90 for one room to $250 for eight people renting the entire unit.

Guests in both the main house and the condominium eat a breakfast feast in Grant Corner Inn's dining room or on the front veranda. There's a choice of two entrees—perhaps pumpkin raisin pancakes or artichoke mushroom crêpes with sour cream sauce—plus homemade jellies and breads, fruit frappe, and freshly ground coffee. Brunch is served on Saturdays (7:30 A.M. to noon) and Sundays (8 A.M. to 1 P.M.). So popular are these meals that the inn sells its own cookbook, along with jellies and country crafts. (Whenever you stay in the Santa Fe area, treat yourself to breakfast at the inn. Be sure to make reservations.)

Guests at Grant Corner Inn have use of an area sports club (ten-minute drive away) with tennis, racquetball, indoor and outdoor pools, whirlpool, sauna, and massage.

Pueblo Bonito

138 W. Manhattan at Galisteo
Santa Fe, New Mexico 87501
505/984-8001
INNKEEPERS: Herb and Amy Behm
14 rooms and suites (private baths)
$50-90 double, rooms; $90–$150 double, suites including
    continental breakfast
HIGH SEASON: June to October
MasterCard, Visa; personal check
Children welcome
No pets
Open year round

About a five minute walk from Santa Fe Plaza is Pueblo Bonito, a 14-room B&B-style inn that is well suited to groups as well as individual travelers.

Once the buildings that make up the inn were part of the estate of a circuit judge who raised Arabian horses. Today the century-old adobe home and one-time stables are an inviting inn. There's a sense of privacy at Pueblo Bonito. Flagstone paths lead from the street, and lilacs and apricot trees dot the grounds.

Each guest room is named for an area Indian tribe. As you'd expect, the decor reflects Santa Fe's heritage. All rooms have kiva fireplaces along with Navajo rugs, pueblo and Mexican pottery, woven baskets, and carved santos.

Closets are large, convenient for skiers with their gear. Every room has a private bath and TV. The two suite units, situated in the former stables, each have a living room, bedroom, kitchen, and bath. Although there are no phones in the rooms, pay phones are conveniently located. There are also laundry facilities on the premises.

Breakfast is delivered to guests at the time they request. Billed as "generous continental," it features croissants, muffins, baked or fresh fruit, juice, and fresh-ground coffee.

OKLAHOMA

Harrison House
   124 W. Harrison
   P.O. Box 1555
   Guthrie, Oklahoma 73044
   405/282-1000
INNKEEPER: Phyllis Murray
23 rooms (private baths)
$40–$100 double including continental breakfast
American Express, MasterCard, Visa; personal check
Children welcome
Pets accepted
Open year round

Guthrie, once the capital of the Oklahoma Territory, is a town that celebrates its history every day of the year. Boasting a wealth of Victorian buildings with spindle tops and Romanesque arches, the town is distinctive with its antique shops, turn-of-the-century restaurants, and historic celebrations. One of the best reasons to go to Guthrie is to stay at Harrison House, one of the most charming inns in the Southwest. A collage of quilts and lace, Victorian furniture and colorful accents, it invites you to come in and stay awhile.

Each guest room, clever and inventive in its decor, is named for someone who played a part in the town's history. Carrie Nation's room (she lived in Guthrie for a few months) has a simulated hatchet on the wall. Tom Mix's room (he once tended bar at a nearby saloon) is decorated with blue bandannas. The lobby, originally built as a bank, is grand with its tin ceiling and wall vault. The carved wood check-in desk once stood in the Guthrie Post Office.

Harrison House's history is a story of civic pride in action. In the mid-1980s a group of local citizens decided that the town needed a historic hotel, so they set out to open one. Three downtown buildings dating back to 1890 were combined to form the lodging, and all sorts of folks got involved in developing it. One artisan crafted all of the reproduction light fixtures. Another designed the window coverings. Local women made the quilts (each a different design) and the pillow shams. But it was Phyllis Murray, now innkeeper, who oversaw the entire development, injecting her creativity at every turn. She bought American Victorian antiques (most were found within 100 miles of Guthrie), converting some to meet her needs. Wherever you look, there's an imaginative touch. One lavatory was made from an old chicken incubator. Towel racks were once wagon wheels or even street car steps.

Every room has a private bath and telephone. The only TV is in the upstairs parlor—popular as a gathering place for afternoon refreshments. Breakfast is served continental style on china and silver plates.

Pollard Theatre, built in 1910 and restored in 1987, adjoins the inn. Live productions are presented throughout the year.

TEXAS

Crystal River Inn
  326 W. Hopkins
  San Marcos, Texas 78666
  512/396-3739
INNKEEPERS: Mike and Cathy Dillon
8 rooms (private and shared baths)
$45–$90 double including full breakfast
MasterCard, Visa; personal check
Small children discouraged
Pets and smoking highly discouraged
Open year round

The Texas Hill Country is made for vacationing. Scenic beauty, outdoor recreation, historic sites—it has them all. San Marcos, half way between Austin and San Antonio, is a good hub for experiencing this part of Texas.

In the picture-perfect Crystal River Inn, you're treated to a convivial atmosphere, excellent food, and rooms with exquisite decor. While the four Corinthian columns across the front of the house signal grandeur, the mood of the interior is warm and friendly. Here's an ideal place to sit on the front porch or the second-story veranda and think great thoughts, or at least think about thinking great thoughts.

The bedrooms have charming decor, seeming to spring straight from the pages of a home and garden magazine. Each is named for a Texas river, bearing testimony to the owners' affinity for canoeing. The Frio Room with a queen bed and wicker furniture is in a cool, cool blue. The Medina is especially romantic, with a four-poster queen bed, white shutters, and pink curtains. The Colorado is a good choice for those who aren't partial to ruffles and lace; here symbols of the rugged Southwest predominate.

Five guest rooms are in the main house; three are on the second floor of the Young House across the street. The latter are well-suited to business travelers and to those who want seclusion. Each room in the Young House has its own phone and TV, and breakfast is delivered to the door.

Breakfast at the Crystal River Inn is a headliner event. The menu constantly changes, including such delectables as banana crêpes, stuffed French toast, quiche, and hot breads. Guests choose where they want to be served—in the dining room, on the patio, or in bed. Special events offered seasonally range from historical tours to Super Bowl parties, murder mystery weekends to spa weeks.

Inn on the River

209 Barnard Street
P.O. Box 1417
Glen Rose, Texas 76043
817/897-2101
INNKEEPERS: Steve and Peggy Allman
27 units (private baths)
$70 single, $80–$125 double including full breakfast
MasterCard, Visa; personal check
No children
No pets
No smoking
Open February to November, Tuesday to Saturday only (open Sunday on holiday weekends)

Inn on the River is dedicated to serving up big healthy doses of R&R. Yes, there are some area attractions—Dinosaur State Park, Fossil Rim Wildlife Ranch, and the nearby village of Granbury with its famed opera house—but just outside the lodging's doors is the gentle Paluxy River, and happily, the inn's design takes full advantage of this setting. Its tree-shaded grounds slope down to the river. Several sitting areas are sprinkled over the lawn, and there's a swimming pool beneath the centuries-old live oaks.

In 1919 the inn was built as a health resort, utilizing the area's natural mineral waters. In 1984 Steve and Peggy Allman converted the original structure into an inn with high visual appeal. Peggy, a commercial interior designer, used her talents to create guest rooms with a sense of history coupled with comfort. Overall, the inn has a crisp, clean look—airy and welcoming.

Each room is different—so different that each of the 27 has its own wallpaper design. Many of the beds have upholstered headboards with spreads to match. Private baths, ceiling fans, and individual heating and air conditioning units are in every room. But don't look for TVs or phones, for the inn is truly styled as a getaway.

One of Steve's talents is cooking, and at the inn he practices it with full abandon. He claims that after breakfast—a three or four course gourmet affair—most guests take a nap. The public is invited to the breakfast feast on weekends (reservations are a must). For groups and on special occasions, Steve can cook up a magnificent dinner spread.

Be advised: The hosts are serious about "No Smoking."

The Pink Lady Inn
1307 Main Street
Bastrop, Texas 78602
512/321-6273
MANAGERS: George and Barbara Sutherland
5 rooms (private baths)
$40–$70 double including full breakfast
MasterCard, Visa
No children
No pets
No smoking
Open year round

The name itself is a near-perfect description of this B&B. Yes, the house is pink—pale pink, the color of strawberry ice cream. And yes, she's a lady—gentle, gracious, and lovely.

Bastrop, Texas—a nostalgic village east of Austin—has 131 houses, buildings, and sites listed in the National Register of Historic Places. The Pink Lady, a two-story Victorian built in 1890, is one of them. Since 1984 the home has operated as a B&B-style lodging. Its managers live in a separate cottage on the premises.

Bedrooms are romantic, decorated with antique furnishings, eyelet and lace, and some of the most beautiful fringe lamps imaginable (each one is a work of art). High ceilings, original fireplaces, and period-style wallpaper add to the atmosphere. Every room has a private bath (four adjoin bedrooms, one is across the hall).

Behind the main house is a getaway cottage with stenciled floors and hand-crafted furniture. Once a carriage house, it has the charm of age with the convenience of modern plumbing and air conditioning.

The backyard veranda is a pleasant spot for relaxing. Breakfast is full country fare. If you want to tour Bastrop in a 1929 Model A, the hosts are happy to oblige for an extra charge.

Pride House
409 E. Broadway
Jefferson, Texas 75657
214/665-2675
INNKEEPER: Ruthmary Jordan
10 rooms (private baths)
$60–$75 double including full breakfast
MasterCard, Visa; personal check
Families with children in The Dependency only (see below)
No pets
Open year round

Once guests check into the Pride House, they have trouble ever leaving. Here is the place for a romantic getaway—a true escape from a hurried pace of life. The house itself exudes charm—a two-story Victorian trimmed in gingerbread. Of course there's a wrap-around porch, set with white wicker rockers and a porch swing. And throughout the house there are antique furnishings, swirls of lace, and stained glass windows.

But Pride House has something that no other lodging can boast—Ruthmary Jordan, a delightful lady with a zest for living. She makes the house come alive, creating a sense of warmth and cheer.

Situated in a history-filled East Texas town, Pride House was reportedly the first B&B in Texas, and happily it sets a high standard. In keeping with the getaway atmosphere, the hostess believes in letting guests dine in the privacy of their rooms. Culinary delights appear on the downstairs sideboard about 8 A.M. (look for coffee earlier, if you wish). A restaurateur before she was an innkeeper, Ruthmary is renowned for her cooking. Favorite dishes include apple dumplings with cream sauce, poached pears in cream, and baked grapefruit with pecan praline sauce. You serve yourself on a tray, set with fine china, crystal, and sterling silver.

The six most elegant guest rooms are in the main house; four with a country feel are in a detached building called The Dependency (same vintage as the 1888 main house, but originally the servants' quarters). The beautiful Blue Room is especially comfortable, with a king bed and several easy chairs. The Bay Room is spectacular: its wallpapered ceiling is ablaze with stars. The Golden Era is hard to beat for romance—a half-tester king-size iron bed is set beneath stained glass bay windows, draped in lace. Most of the bathrooms have showers, but the West Room boasts a clawfoot tub, perfectly situated to watch the sunset during a luxurious soak.

Out in the Dependency, the Suite is a top choice, with a wood-burning fireplace, two beds (one queen-size and one hideabed), country furnishings, and a compartmented bath.

All rooms have good lighting, soft sheets, and super-fluffy towels.

Prince Solms Inn
295 E. San Antonio Street
New Braunfels, Texas 78130
512/625-9169
INNKEEPER: Ruth Wood
10 rooms (private baths)
$60–$110 double including continental breakfast
MasterCard, Visa; personal check
Children over 12 welcome
No pets
Open year round

Prince Solms Inn is really special. Historic in character, it's pleasing to the eye, furnished for comfort, and professionally operated. Down in the cellar is one of the best restaurants in the Hill Country, both in cuisine and atmosphere.

Built in 1898, the inn is in a community settled in 1845 by Germans who were led to the new land by Prince Carl of Solms-Braunfels. Among the town's original settlers was the family of the man who built the hotel. Today the trim two-story building, constructed of locally made brick and native timber, is one of New Braunfels' most visible links to its heritage.

The interior, furnished to reflect the inn's history, has delicate charm. On one side of the central hallway is a parlor furnished with antiques, setting the mood for the entire inn. The Princess Sophie Suite across the hall has swags and shutters at the windows, German portraits on the walls, a large sitting room with period furnishings, and a separate bedroom with king-size bed. The bath is small and modern, and there's also a tiny kitchen. Down the hall is the Prince Carl Suite, similarly furnished but more masculine in decor. For guests of these two suites, breakfast is served in the room.

The rest of the bedrooms are upstairs. Furnishings are not luxurious, just tasteful and appropriate to the setting. Cloth-covered tables set with fruit, armoires (thankfully, without TVs inside), wooden beds, and clawfoot tubs are the style. The names of the rooms indicate their decor—Peony and Magnolia, Rose, and Songbird. Each has a private bath, small but conveniently designed. In addition to central air conditioning, there's a ceiling fan in each room. (No phones, just a quiet retreat-like ambience.)

A breakfast of fresh pastries and a choice of coffees and hot teas is laid out on the hall sideboard. Its very style—professional and tastefully elegant—typifies the inn's operation.

Whether you're a guest at the Prince Solms or not, Wolfgang's Keller restaurant down in the cellar is worth a special trip. For inn guests, it's a real luxury to have such a fine dining establishment only a few steps away. The restaurant is named in honor of Wolfgang Mozart, and a specially commissioned portrait of the composer hangs on the landing.

Specialties include chicken Piccata, veal Marsala, and linguini with shrimp and clam sauce. Entrees are priced from $8 to $16. Reservations are recommended.

Behind the inn there's a shaded courtyard and an 1850s house which, like the inn, is a registered historic building. The Prince Solms is an ideal place to begin exploring New Braunfels—the Main Plaza is just down the street. The innkeepers are adept at helping visitors plan their stay.

2

B&B Reservation Systems

By making one phone call, you can have access to as many as 100 lodging choices. Directors of these services pride themselves on matching guests with accommodations that suit their personal preferences. Some services represent inns as well as traditional B&Bs. In keeping with the philosophy of the Best Places guides, the following is a selective list, including only the best reservation services.

ARIZONA

Bed and Breakfast Scottsdale and The West
   P.O. Box 3999
   Prescott, Arizona 86302-3999
   602/776-1102
OWNERS: Joyce and George Thomson
Approximately 35 listings
Accommodations in Scottsdale area, other communities in
   Arizona and New Mexico
From $45 for mini-suites; $50–$150 for guest houses
Cash or traveler's check; no credit cards
Telephone answered 24 hours a day (in person 9 A.M.-6 P.M.)
Children over 12 welcome in some homes
No pets

   B&B Scottsdale and The West has fine lodgings, specializing in mini-suites, guest cottages, and villas. Many have a private entrance, private bath, wet bar, and a southwestern flavor. All hosts live on the grounds.

As a sample, one B&B home is a luxurious, tile-roofed villa in Fountain Hills with walled gardens, pool, and tennis court. The hosts prepare a gourmet breakfast, with homemade sausage, hot breads, and espresso coffee ($90 double).

In the foothills near Scottsdale, the service has a private guest house adjacent to s swimming pool. The hosts' home, a marvelous adobe-style house, is within a few feet. The rolling saguaro-studded desert stretches beyond ($150 per day).

This reservation service also represents inns as well as B&Bs. For example, the Marks House Inn in Prescott is an elegant, intimate hostelry, dating back to 1894. Guests are treated to breakfast served in the parlor, hors d'oeuvres in the afternoon, bed turn-down, and fresh fruit and flowers.

Bed and Breakfast in Arizona
P.O. Box 8628
Scottsdale, Arizona 85252
602/995-2831
OWNERS/OPERATORS: Jo and Jim Cummings
More than 100 listings
More than 20 cities and towns with listings, including:
  Bisbee
  Cottonwood
  Flagstaff
  Jerome
  Lake Havasu
  Mesa
  Payson
  Phoenix
  Pinetop
  Prescott
  Scottsdale
  Sedona
  Sierra Vista
  Sun City
  Tempe
  Tucson
  Wickenburg
$35–$110
American Express, MasterCard, Visa; personal check
Office hours 7:30 A.M. to 2:30 P.M., Monday to Friday
Answering machine during off hours
In-state collect calls accepted from prospective guests
Children accepted at some B&Bs

Pets accepted at a few B&Bs
Handicapped facilities available in one B&B
Some B&Bs designated as non-smoking

Bed and Breakfast of Arizona is true to its name, with listings spread across the state. Not only does it have traditional-style B&B homes with hosts in residence, but also guest houses, lodges, cabins, apartments, and estates.

Some of the B&Bs are in cities, offering intimacy within a bustling metropolis. One listing in Phoenix is a guest house by the hosts' swimming pool, with a fireplace, kitchen, queen hideabed, and private bath. Another in the same city has antiques and stained glass, a heated spa, helpful hosts (one is a gourmet cook), and a central location.

In Tucson, one B&B is a large adobe ranch home on a fenced acre, with views of the Catalina Mountains. Guests have kitchen privileges on weekdays, with groceries provided by the hosts. On weekends, the hostess enjoys cooking breakfast for her guests.

In Prescott, Bed and Breakfast in Arizona has a large Victorian home with a porch swing. In Cottonwood it arranges stays at a ten-acre ranch with horses.

Mi Casa Su Casa

P.O. Box 950
Tempe, Arizona 85281
602/990-0682
OPERATOR: Ruth Young
More than 100 homes, guest houses, ranches, and inns
Listings in 30 cities and rural areas, including:
  Amado Ranch
  Bullhead City
  Chandler
  Cottonwood
  Flagstaff
  Jerome
  Lake Havasu
  Mesa
  Nogales
  Patagonia
  Payson
  Phoenix
  Prescott
  Scottsdale
  Sedona
  Sierra Vista
  Strawberry

Sun City
Tempe
Tucson
Wickenburg
Yuma
$25–$100 single, $35–$125 double
Cash or travelers checks; no credit cards
Telephone answered from 8 A.M. to 8 P.M.
Answering machine during other hours
Children welcome at many B&Bs
Pets accepted at a few B&Bs
Handicapped facilities at several B&Bs

Mi Casa Su Casa's Ruth Young runs a very professional service, taking pride in matching guests with a B&B that suits their needs and preferences. Host families are selected for their warmth and interest in people, says Ruth. Every listing is inspected prior to becoming part of her service. Listings include historic homes, ranches, and small inns scattered across the state. Some are in cities, while others are in mountain and lake country.

In Paradise Valley adjacent to Scottsdale and Phoenix, this B&B reservation system lists a spacious home reminiscent of Seville, Spain, with gardens, pool, lacy white gazebo, and croquet lawn. In central Tucson, there's an adobe mansion listed on the National Register, with courtyards, fountains, and lush gardens.

NEW MEXICO

Mi Casa Su Casa
  P.O. Box 950
  Tempe, Arizona 85281
  602/990-0682
OPERATOR: Ruth Young
Listings include:
  Albuquerque
  Deming
  Las Cruces
  Las Vegas
  Los Alamos
  Santa Fe
Please see under Arizona for details on Mi Casa Su Casa.

Taos Home Bed and Breakfast
P.O. Box 177
Taos, New Mexico 87571
505/758-0287
OPERATOR: Mari Ulmer
Approximately 6 listings
B&B homes in Taos only
Answering machine when no one available to answer phone

Whether you're in Taos as a sightseer or skier, staying in a B&B home is a good alternative to traditional lodgings. Mari Ulmer, owner of Hacienda del Sol (see description in this guidebook), coordinates a reservation system for B&Bs in the Taos area. Listings are limited to homes that operate as B&Bs.

OKLAHOMA

Bed and Breakfast Texas Style
4224 W. Red Bird Lane
Dallas, Texas 75237
214/298-5433, 214/298-8586
OWNER/DIRECTOR: Ruth Wilson
This Texas-based reservation system has several B&Bs in Oklahoma City and Tulsa. See listing under Texas for further information.

TEXAS

Bed and Breakfast Hosts of San Antonio
166 Rockhill
San Antonio, Texas 78209
512/824-8036
OPERATORS: Lavern and Vicky Campbell
Approximately 25 listings
Most listings in San Antonio; some in Canyon Lake, New Braunfels, Seguin, and Utopia
$27 to $105 double
MasterCard, Visa; personal check
Answering service when the Campbells are unavailable to answer phone
Children accepted in some B&Bs

Pets permitted in some B&Bs
Smoking permitted in some B&Bs
Policies: Payment refunded, minus a $5 processing fee, with
three-day notice of cancellation

Bed and Breakfast Hosts of San Antonio is a well-run reservation service with listings ranging from hosts who welcome guests into their own home to B&B inns run by a full-time staff. Owner Lavern Campbell is known for her hospitable and efficient service.

In San Antonio, a popular tourist city with lots of hotels, B&B Hosts offers lodgings with intimacy. Locations are scattered across the city. Some are in the historic King William residential area near downtown. Others are close to Sea World, Fort Sam Houston, or the airport.

For example, there's a Cape Cod guest house decorated in antiques in Alamo Heights near McNay Art Museum. Its large sun deck overlooks landscaped grounds and a swimming pool. Guests have use of the entire house, including the kitchen and fireplace. The bed is a four-poster queen-size with canopy. For musicians, there's a grand piano in the main house.

In the King William area, B&B Hosts lists a new guest house that includes a downstairs bedroom with double bed, loft bedroom with twin beds, and a sofa bed in the living room. The adjacent hosts' home dates back to 1871. Bikes are available for exploring the surrounding area ($50–$60).

In New Braunfels, guests can choose a tree-shaded cottage on the Comal River ($70). In Canyon Lake, the service lists a three-bedroom home on the lake ($120 for up to 6).

Also available through the service are several well-known lodgings. The Norton-Brackenridge House in San Antonio, winner of awards for its restoration, is a Victorian house with four guest rooms ($50–$105). Terrell Castle, also in San Antonio, is fanciful and fun. Built in 1894 to resemble a mix of European castles and French chateaux, it's furnished in antiques. Nine guest rooms are spread over the second and third floor; a loft-style room is on the fourth floor ($59–$79).

Bed and Breakfast of Fredericksburg
102 S. Cherry
Fredericksburg, Texas 78624
512/997-4712
OWNER: Kathy Kopp
Approximately 25 listings
All listings in Fredericksburg area
$49–$71

MasterCard, Visa; personal check
Telephone answered from 8 A.M. to 10 P.M.
Children accepted in some B&Bs
Pets accepted in some B&Bs
No B&Bs with handicapped facilities
Smoking okay in some; most prefer non-smokers

Founded in 1982, B&B of Fredericksburg was the first such reservation service in the state. "Come as a guest, leave as a friend," is its motto. Listings, all in the Fredericksburg area, range from owner-in-residence homes to self-catered styles of lodging. Country cottages, "Sunday Houses," guest houses, rock barns, Victorian homes—all are excellent options.

Owner Kathy Kopp sends prospective guests a delightful booklet describing each accommodation in detail. Like a treasure chest, it overflows with wonderful little gems. In addition to 20-plus lodgings, it lists such extras as an antique toy tour, photographic tours (offered by a B&B situated on 2,000 acres of ranchland with camera blinds set up where wildlife is fed), and picnic basket lunches (packed with smoked ham, pumpernickel bread, cheddar cheese, homemade pickles, pretzels, German sour cream twists, and homemade brownies).

A sample listing is a two-story Victorian cottage with two bedrooms and private baths, renting for $49 per night. The host likes to cook and will fix picnic baskets upon request.

For guests who want privacy, B&B of Fredericksburg can arrange a stay in a 130-year-old stone house one block off Main Street, decorated in antiques. Guests have use of the living room and kitchen as well as the bedroom and loft sleeping area ($71).

Note that Fredericksburg is a popular tourist destination, and special events are scattered throughout the year. Kathy advises that you make reservations several months in advance, especially for weekends and holiday periods.

Bed and Breakfast Society of Texas
921 Heights Blvd.
Houston, Texas 77008
713/868-4654
OWNER: Marguerite Swanson
Approximately 100 listings
Accommodations in about 50 locations including Houston, other Texas cities, and popular vacation spots throughout the state
$35–$125 double
MasterCard, Visa; personal check

Telephone answered 8 A.M.-5 P.M.; answering machine at
   other times (telephone is often answered during off-hours)
Children accepted at a few B&Bs
No pets
Handicapped guests can be accommodated in some B&Bs
   with first floor guest rooms
No smoking at most B&Bs, smoking permitted at a few

A well-managed service, Bed and Breakfast Society of
Texas has private homes, bungalows, waterfront cottages,
country cabins, condos, Victorian mansions, and antebellum
plantations. Owner Marguerite Swanson is adept at matching
guests with appropriate hosts.

Her own home, a beautifully restored Victorian house in
Houston's Heights residential area, sets the tone. Once an antique dealer, Marguerite has decorated the home with turn-of-
the-century treasures from china dolls to a player piano. One
of her guest rooms is a confection of blue, with lace curtains
and a white iron bed topped with a comforter. The second
bedroom has an antique bed set beneath bay windows. Breakfast is hearty, including hot breads and fresh fruit.

In Houston, Marguerite has B&Bs scattered throughout the
city, including ones in River Oaks, Memorial, Montrose,
Meyerland, Sharpstown, and Spring Branch. B&B homes are
available near the Galleria, Medical Center, and Astrodome.

For vacationers who want a place in the country, this service
offers lots of choices. One is on a 175-acre working ranch
northwest of Brenham. When bluebonnets are in bloom, the
front lawn of the ranch house is carpeted in blue. The hospitable hosts enjoy sharing their farm life with guests, taking
them across the fields to see their cattle, or down to the ponds
to fish. Eating is important at this B&B. Breakfast is country-
hearty, and gourmet lunches and dinners are served upon request.

In Utopia near Kerrville, Blue Bird Hill B&B has a hideaway cabin accommodating up to eight, and several guest
rooms in the main house.

Popular for birdwatching and wild life observation, this
B&B is also an excellent getaway spot.

Marguerite keeps close contact with the B&Bs she represents, making sure that a high level of quality is maintained.
Guest fees are paid directly to her in advance.

Bed and Breakfast Texas Style
   4224 W. Red Bird Lane
   Dallas, Texas 75237
   214/298-5433, 214/298-8586

OWNER/DIRECTOR: Ruth Wilson
Approximately 100 listings
Accommodations in about 50 cities, towns, lake areas, and
    farm areas in Texas
$25–$60, some special listings of up to $200
MasterCard, Visa; personal check
Telephone answered 8 A.M.-5:30 P.M., Monday-Friday
Answering machine on weekends (Reservations can some-
    times be handled on weekends)
Children welcome in many B&Bs
Pets accepted in some B&Bs
Some listings with handicapped facilities

Not only are Bed and Breakfast Texas Style's listings
widespread, but they also offer lots of variety. Some are on
the National Historic Register while others are sparkling new
metropolitan homes. Some have hosts in residence; others are
unoccupied guest houses offering complete privacy.

The service represents inns with their own identity as well
as homes with one or two guest rooms. As a result, Ruth can
help guests choose a lodging that is best for their individual
needs and preferences.

Accommodations range from budget to super-luxurious. In
addition to listings in Dallas and other major metropolitan areas, Bed and Breakfast Texas Style represents accommodations near Palo Duro Canyon and at Lakeway, Brownsville,
Bryan (home of Texas A&M University), Granbury, Midland,
Palestine, Port Isabel, Waco, and Wichita Falls. More than 50
locations are represented state-wide.

Durant Star Inn, east of Dallas, is an especially interesting
choice. Built in the 1930s, the house has five guest rooms, a
formal living room with wind-up Victrola, and tree-shaded
patio. Furnishings are exquisite. There's usually a Durant or
Star car from the 1920s at the door to give guests a ride
through the woods to the nearby Auto Museum.

One of the most unusual accommodations that can be
booked through this reservation service is a yacht on Lake
Texoma. A moonlit cruise, gourmet dinner, overnight stay,
and brunch the next day costs $250 for two.

Owner Ruth Wilson asks guests to fill in evaluation forms
on B&Bs that she books. Through such feedback, she's able
to keep close tabs on the many lodgings she represents.

A current list of Bed and Breakfast Texas Style's offerings
is available for $3.

Gastehaus Schmidt
  501 W. Main
  Fredericksburg, Texas 78624
  512/997-5612 Monday to Friday 10 A.M.-5 P.M.; Saturday
  1-5 P.M.
  512/997-3234 after 5 P.M.
PROPRIETORS: Dr. Charles and Loretta Schmidt
Approximately 35 listings
All listings in Fredericksburg and nearby area
$39–$85
American Express, MasterCard, Visa; personal check
Children welcome at many B&Bs
Pets accepted in some
Smoking and non-smoking accommodations available

Gastehaus Schmidt has a rich variety of lodgings, many reflecting the historic character of Fredericksburg. Guests can
choose from farms, "Sunday Houses" (built by pioneer farmers as a place to spend the night when they went to town for
church), log cabins, and modern homes. Some accommodations are in owner-in-residence homes; in others, guests have
the entire lodging to themselves.

Upon request, the Schmidts will send you an in-depth description of their listings. Browsing through the choices is
pleasurable in itself, presenting a well-rounded view of the
community settled by German farmers.

Wunderlich Log Cabin, built in 1883, was the first home of
Adolph Wunderlich and his family. The downstairs bedroom
is "a bedroom-of-the-past with its wooden floor, quilt coverlet
on the bed, and handmade closets." Up the narrow stairway is
another bedroom sleeping three. The kitchen, plastered and
whitewashed, has handmade chairs with heart cut-outs
matching the Dutch blue shelves. The host family who lives
next door provides continental breakfast ($60 for two).

Other historic homes include a rock house built in the early
1850s and a barn of the same era converted into an antique-
furnished guest house.

Sand Dollar Hospitality Bed and Breakfast
  3605 Mendenhall
  Corpus Christi, Texas 78415
  512/853-1222
OPERATOR: Pat Hirshbrunner
Approximately 15 listings
Accommodations in Corpus Christi area and Rockport
$27–$57
No credit cards

Telephone answered or answering machine 8 A.M.-9 P.M.
Children welcome in some B&Bs
No pets
No B&Bs with handicapped facilities

Pat Hirshbrunner's goal is to offer guests a "taste of the South" with host families who exemplify high standards of hospitality. In a popular coastal region she has a variety of lodgings, including in-town homes and seaside cottages.

Blue Heron in Corpus Christi, for example, is three blocks from the bay. Accommodating five, the home has a backyard pool and a whirlpool. "These hosts go the extra mile," says Pat.

Other samples include a private guest cottage with pool, and condos on Corpus Christi Beach or Padre Island.

3

Beachside

The Texas coast is a 624-mile crescent of shoreline, fronted with a ribbon of barrier islands. Galveston, Corpus Christi, and South Padre are the centers of activity. Here are some of the best places to stay along the coast. (See also chapters on Condominiums, Grand Old Mansions, Historic Hostelries, Village B&Bs.)

TEXAS

Best Western Sandy Shores
3200 Surfside Boulevard
Corpus Christi Beach
Corpus Christi, Texas 78403
512/883-7456
800/528-1234
OWNER: Stern Feinberg
253 rooms
$29–$59 single, $39–$79 double
HIGH SEASON: summer
American Express, Amoco, Carte Blanche, Diners Club,
   Discover, MasterCard, Visa; personal check
Children welcome
Pets $6 extra per day
Open year round

Corpus Christi Beach is a mile-long stretch of sand on Corpus Christi Bay, about a five minute drive across Harbor Bridge from downtown. Best Western Sandy Shores, directly on the beach, is a good choice for those who want an upbeat environment at moderate prices.

The hotel has a nice size pool, a sauna and hot tub in a cute pagoda-style building, and an activities director who arranges everything from bike rental and volleyball to fishing and golfing.

Throughout the hotel there's a spirit of creativity. The Espresso Coffee Shop has a good choice of fresh ground coffees. The Pantry will deliver pizza to your room or let you pick it up. Wine tasting, free to the public as well as guests, happens every afternoon at Calypso Restaurant and Bar, and from 10 P.M. to midnight there's a Viennese dessert buffet. And how many other hotels do you know that have a kite museum? Sure, it's small, but there's an adjoining kite shop and the whole concept adds interest. Joggers will appreciate that the owner, a jogging enthusiast himself, has devised a brochure detailing several routes as well as jogging tips. Overall, there's the feeling that this is a hotel where somebody cares about more than profit margins.

A composite of a motel section built in the 1960s and a 1980s five-story hotel building, Sandy Shores has more than 250 guest rooms, some with bay views. Rooms are comfortable but not luxurious. Some open onto the pool deck, a pleasant, family-oriented area.   Top-of-the-line accommodations are corner rooms in the hotel building.

The beach in front of the hotel is wide, but the sand is fairly coarse. Be advised that jellyfish are prevalent during some seasons. Area attractions are plentiful, including North Padre Island's beaches, city museums, and a wildlife refuge.

Marriott's Hotel Galvez
2024 Seawall Boulevard
Galveston, Texas 77550
409/765-7721
800/231-6399 US, 800/392-4285 TX
GENERAL MANAGER: George VanEtten
228 rooms and suites
$56–$109 single or double
HIGH SEASON: May to mid-September
American Express, Carte Blanche, Diners Club, Discover,
    MasterCard, Visa
Children welcome
No pets

Open year round

Galveston is a city with a dual personality, for it is both a beach destination and a historic town. Hotel Galvez —Galveston's only beachfront lodging listed in the National Register of Historic Places—links the two sides of its character.

In 1911 the Spanish-style stucco hotel rose proudly as the Queen of the Beach. Eleven years earlier a devastating storm had permanently altered the city's history, killing 6,000 people and virtually leveling the one-time Wall Street of the Southwest. Hotel Galvez, built with funds raised from the community, was the island's first opulent beach attraction—symbolizing a reborn city. In that era, Galveston was known as a gambling center, attracting big name entertainers who performed in its casinos. Hotel Galvez was their hotel, for not only was it the finest lodging around, but also one of the two best casinos in town was right across the street.

The Galvez's Spanish architecture reflects the island's heritage. The hotel is named for the island's namesake, Bernardo de Galvez—an 18th century Spanish colonial governor and general. Galvez never saw Galveston, but the island was named for him by a chart maker whom he commissioned to explore the Texas coast. As governor of Louisiana and Florida, Galvez fought with the colonials against the British in the American Revolution.

In 1980 the Hotel Galvez was restored, acting as a spark for historic preservation throughout the city. While room floors were totally redesigned, the lobby was refurbished to its 1911 charm. Graceful arches, a handsome wood ceiling, and chandeliers create a nostalgic mood. The Galvez Dining Room, just off the lobby, has historic ambience. Potted palms line the hall walkway to the Veranda Bar (light and airy) and the Galvez Lounge (dark and masculine, with live entertainment).

The hotel's main entrance is on the north side, away from the beach. Through the lobby and overlooking the Gulf is an indoor pool and hot tub. Beyond is the outdoor pool, fairly small for a beachside resort but well-landscaped and appealing.

Guest rooms are ordinary and rather small, with tiny bathrooms. Furnishings are tasteful but uninspired. Views are less than you might expect, with the ocean in the distance fronted by a parking lot.

The service attitude throughout the hotel is definitely above average, however. While there are no such amenities as valet parking, the staff is friendly and truly hospitable. Parking is free.

The Galvez is convenient to area attractions (historic structures, The Strand entertainment area, Sea-Arama) as well as to the beach itself, which is just across Seawall Boulevard. Following the 1900 storm, a massive seawall was built along the island's shores. As a result, all structures along its 10.4 mile length are behind the seawall instead of directly on the beach.

Port Royal by the Sea
P.O. Box 336
Port Aransas, Texas 78373
512/749-5011
800/847-5659 US, 800/242-1034 TX
GENERAL MANAGER: Michael Kennedy
200 condos
1 bedroom: $59–$130 (1 to 4 persons)
2 bedroom: $79–$190 (1 to 6 persons)
3 bedroom: $125–$265 (1 to 8 persons)
American Express, Diners Club, MasterCard, Visa
Children welcome
No pets
Open year round

On Mustang Island right on the Gulf of Mexico, Port Royal is a resort set apart from the crowd. Beautiful grounds, upscale condos, and a service-oriented staff make it an excellent destination. Port Aransas, also on the island, is seven miles north. Corpus Christi on the mainland is a ten-mile drive away.

Condominiums are in four buildings arranged around one of the best water extravaganzas in Texas. A composite of four pools, waterfalls, swim-up bar, and a waterslide, it's the focal point of the resort. Beyond it, boardwalks lead over the dunes and onto the wide beach.

Although Port Royal's condos are individually owned, the resort is operated as a hotel, with a full range of services and planned activities during high seasons. One-, two-, and three-bedroom units are all spacious and nicely appointed. Extra touches include built-in stereos, whirlpool tubs, and washers and dryers. All condos have private patios or balconies. The three-bedroom units are the most luxurious; the only units that directly front the ocean, they have lots of extra goodies including balcony whirlpools.

Royal Beachcomber Restaurant, decorated Kon-Tiki style, serves all three meals. Happily, seafood gets top attention, but there are also beef and chicken entrees. Smaller portions at much cheaper prices are offered not only for children but senior citizens as well.

The San Luis Hotel and Condominiums
  5222 Seawall Boulevard
  Galveston, Texas 77550
  409/744-1500
  800/445-0090 US, 800/392-5937 TX
GENERAL MANAGER: Ron Vuy
244 hotel rooms; approximately 150 condos
$66–$126 single, $76–$140 double; $84–$295 condos
HIGH SEASON: May to early September
American Express, Diners Club, MasterCard, Visa
Children welcome
No pets
Open year round

There's a touch of the Caribbean about the San Luis. Perhaps it's the free-form pool with palapa swim-up bar, tropical gardens, waterfalls, and bridges. Or maybe it's the breezy lobby with its wicker furniture and casual atmosphere.

The San Luis is two lodgings in one. The hotel is a 15-story building with restaurants and 244 guest rooms overlooking the Gulf. Adjacent to it is a sister building with privately-owned condominiums, most of which are available for rent. Opened in 1984, the San Luis has set a new standard for Galveston beach resorts. It has two restaurants, a lounge with live entertainment, and a beachfront activity center with rental equipment.

The beach is across the street from the hotel, since a seawall extends along most of Galveston's beachfront. The hotel sits on a hill overlooking the ocean.

Rooms are large and tastefully decorated. All have narrow balconies. Bathrooms are small but adequate.

Condos range from hotel-style rooms to large two-bedroom units with kitchens. Access to the condo area is by security key.

Sheraton South Padre Island Beach Resort

310 Padre Boulevard
South Padre Island, Texas 78597
512/761-6551
800/325-3535
GENERAL MANAGER: Bill Donahue
252 rooms and condos
$70–$140 single or double; $150–$230 condos
American Express, Carte Blanche, Diners Club, Discover, MasterCard, Visa
Children welcome
No pets
Open year round

Opened in 1986, the Sheraton is a 12-story hotel right on the beach. Every guest room has a balcony and an angled view of the ocean. Decorated in cool colors and rattan furniture, the accommodations are both attractive and comfortable.

King parlors are worth the extra charge: sleeping and sitting areas are separated by a floor-to-ceiling armoire housing a TV that swivels. Both king and king parlor rooms are furnished with sleeper sofas. Rooms have air-conditioning units (king parlors have two).

The beachside pool and deck area is a social center, with a grill, small outdoor/indoor pool, outdoor hot tub, and lots of lounge chairs for sunbathing. Tennis courts are also on the grounds.

Brandi Renee's Café fronting the ocean is the fine dining room. Pepper's Lounge has dancing and live entertainment. Be sure to watch your step in the High Tide Bar, for it adjoins the indoor pool.

South Padre Hilton Resort

500 Padre Boulevard
P.O. Box 2081
South Padre Island, Texas 78597
512/761-6511
800/292-7704
GENERAL MANAGER: Mark Hamner
353 units
$65–$150 single or double; $155–$195 condos

HIGH SEASON: late May to early September, spring break
American Express, Carte Blanche, Diners Club, Discover,
   MasterCard, Visa
Children welcome
Pets with approval
Open year round

For a fun-filled roster of activities, excellent swimming
pools, and a festive atmosphere, Hilton Resort is the best
choice on South Padre. A composite of cabana, hotel, and
condo units, its accommodations range from modest to luxurious. Best of all, the staff is enthusiastic and personable.

Whatever your mood, choose from five pools, seven
whirlpool spas, eight tennis courts (in excellent condition),
and rental of all sorts of water toys, from aqua-cycles to sailboards. The activities director always has something zany
going on—pool volleyball, crab races, sandcastle building,
scavenger hunts, beach games for the kids, Me Tarzan You
Jane parties, lollipop licking contests. When you're ready to
explore past the hotel, you can arrange fishing, sailing, boat
charters, and tours to Mexico at the activities desk.

Out on multi-level Quarterdeck Lounge, there's live entertainment and lots of socializing beneath the stars. Windjam-
mer's Beachfront Café serves fresh seafood and Mexican
dishes.

Cabana rooms have poolside balconies and fairly standard
furnishings. Royale parlor suites are akin to condos, with
kitchens, good-size living room, and one or two bedrooms.

Condos in a separate tower are top-of-the-line. Especially
spacious, they have well-decorated living rooms and bedrooms, kitchens with all you could want on a vacation, and
washers/dryers. Unlike most condo complexes there's no
compromise here—you get lots of space, great decorating, and
excellent views.

Sunset on the Bay
   5100 Laguna Boulevard
   P.O. Box 2171
   South Padre Island, Texas 78597
   512/761-1177
MANAGER: Elizabeth Arrambiden
28 units
2 bedroom: $90–$175, 3 bedroom: $120–$225, 2-day mini-
   mum
HIGH SEASON: April to early September
MasterCard, Visa; personal check
Children welcome

No pets
Open year round

Sunset is a 16-story condo unit that overlooks not the Gulf of Mexico, but Laguna Madre, the two-and-one-half-mile-wide bay separating Padre Island from the mainland. The ocean is only a few blocks away, just across South Padre Island. Staying at Sunset is the best of two worlds—a bay setting with private marina, plus quick access to the beachfront.

The condos have large balconies overlooking the bay—a truly restful setting. There's a choice of two- and three-bedroom units. Living rooms and bedrooms are huge. Kitchens have a microwave as well as dishwasher; master baths have whirlpool tubs.

One of the most outstanding features of Sunset is its health and fitness club, which condo guests can use free of charge. Not only does the club have extensive facilities (tennis and racquetball courts, exercise room, weight room, indoor spa, steam room and cold plunge, sauna, masseuse), but it also has a convivial atmosphere with pleasant areas for socializing. Outside, beside the bay, there's a small recreational pool, lap pool, and heated hot tub. And next door (but under different ownership from Sunset) is Scampi's Restaurant and Bar, one of the best dining establishments on the island.

4

Cabins

When you're in the mood for simplicity, a cabin is the perfect spot. Outside is nature in all her glory waiting to be explored.

ARIZONA

Montezuma Lodge
P.O. Box 483
Mormon Lake, Arizona 86038
602/354-2220
OWNER/MANAGER: Cathy Palmer
20 units (private baths)
$49–$55 single or double
Two-night minimum stay
MasterCard, Visa; personal check
Children welcome
No pets (no exceptions)
Open May 1 to November 1

Montezuma Lodge is an assortment of rustic cabins scattered in the pines near Mormon Lake. Set in Coconino National Forest at an elevation of about 7,000 feet, it's a peaceful retreat from urban life. Flagstaff is 25 miles northwest.

Originally built for hunters, each of the cabins is different in size and design. The largest accommodates up to ten people. All are "tooth-brush clean," to use the term of the lady who wields the toothbrush. The waxed wood floors sparkle, and the cedar closets gleam. Kitchens have full-size stoves and re-frigerators, and the cabinets nearly overflow with pots and pans. Every unit has its own bathroom with a shower. There is no daily maid service.

In this wooded retreat vacationers can fish in Mormon Lake (renowned for its northern pike), ride horses at nearby facili-ties, and stroll in the woods. There's also wildflower gather-ing and chipmunk watching. In September and October hunters are drawn to the area for elk and deer hunting; permits are assigned by Coconino National Forest by "draw." One of the largest archery shoots in the nation takes place in Septem-ber.

Nearby, Mormon Lake Lodge Western Steak House is a good alternative to cooking. Diners come from miles around for its excellent food and western flavor. Montezuma Lodge will make special eating arrangements for groups of 20 or more, providing home-cooked meals at a fixed price. Meals are served in the main lodge building.

NEW MEXICO

Los Pinos Guest Ranch
  Rt. 3, Box 8
  Tererro, New Mexico 87573
  505/757-6213
HOSTS: Bill and Alice McSweeney
4 cabins
$60 per adult, $45 per child age 6-13 (all meals included)
3 night minimum
Personal checks; no credit cards
Children over 5 welcome
No pets
Open Memorial Day weekend to mid-September

If you truly want to get away, Los Pinos may suit your fancy. From Santa Fe, head east on U.S. 85 to Glorietta. Then take the road to Pecos and turn north on SR 63 to Tererro—and you're not even close yet. The road is dirt from here on. It follows the Pecos River (here it's a mountain stream instead of a full-fledged river) up the canyon, through forests of aspen, spruce, and fir. When you get to Cowles (a sign lets you know it's a town), go past two ponds and turn left toward Panchuella Campground. Los Pinos is up the narrow dirt trail about one-quarter mile.

Here in the Pecos Wilderness Area you're in camping country. Los Pinos lets you enjoy the surroundings in comfort, with home-cooked meals and hosts who can arrange anything from fishing to exploring. If you have a yen to see the countryside on horseback, then this is indeed the place. Guided trail rides go out according to guest demand, with up to eight riders in a group. The rate is $20 to $40 for a three- to eight-hour expedition.

Los Pinos is surrounded by a national forest, with mountain lakes and peaks as high as 13,000 feet. On a ride to Glass Mountain, the trail leads through aspen forests, ending at the top of the mountain with a panoramic view of the Pecos Wilderness.

Make no mistake about it—the accommodations at Los Pinos are rustic, and therein lies the charm. Four log cabins, sleeping up to six, are scattered among the trees. Interiors are clean and cozy. Sit on the front porch, look out the bedroom windows to watch nature's showcase. The cabin named Mañana is the only one with a fireplace.

Dining is in the hosts' rambling old house just a few steps away. Guests gather around the table to feast on such dishes as Irish pork chops, sauerbraten, turkey, or salmon. Usually guests show up ahead of time just to visit with other vacationers on the big screened-in porch.

Favored pursuits in addition to horseback riding are trout fishing, hiking, and just plain relaxing. The hosts enjoy taking guests on trips to nearby historic areas upon request.

Story Book Cabins
  P.O. Box 472
  Ruidoso, New Mexico 88345
  505/257-2115
OWNERS: Bob and Joan Bailey
10 cabins
$59–$90, dependent on size of cabin (cabins sleep 2-6)
Reduced rates in spring and fall

MasterCard, Visa; personal check
Children welcome
No pets
Open year round

Story Book Cabins are certainly not hidden away within the woods. Indeed, they are one of the many groups of cabins that line Upper Canyon Road just off Highway 70, which runs through the center of Ruidoso. But if you're looking for a pleasant place to stay in the Ruidoso area, then the cabins are a good choice.

Accommodating from two to six people, they come in one-, two-, and three-bedroom varieties. Interiors are country cozy, with large stone fireplaces and comfortable furnishings. The roof is tin, adding a romantic touch when it rains.

Kitchens have gas ranges and full-size refrigerators. Bathrooms, while not large, are nicely decorated. There's a color cable TV in the sitting room, a swing or rocker on the porch, and an outdoor grill.

Only a few steps away from the cabins is the Rio Ruidoso, popular for trout fishing. Ruidoso Downs is a major tourist attraction, with quarter horse racing from May through early September. During winter months, Ski Apache 16 miles to the northwest draws skiers of all abilities. (No lodgings are at the ski basin.)

TEXAS

Chain-O-Lakes
P.O. Box 218
Romayor, Texas 77368
713/592-2150
OWNERS: Jim and Beverly Smith
8 cabins (accommodating up to 10)
$95–$125 double including breakfast
Lower rates on weekdays, excluding summer season
American Express, MasterCard, Visa; personal check
Children welcome
No pets
Open year round

You can find a little bit of everything at Chain-O-Lakes. Camp sites and a gourmet restaurant, pedalboats and horse-drawn carriages, a rollicking waterslide and quiet nature trails—all are part of the mix.

It's the cozy log cabins, smelling of cedar and sprinkled among the trees, that make Chain-O-Lakes a "Best Place." There's a wood-burning fireplace, antique furnishings, and maybe a loft bedroom hide-away to add to the charm. Central heating and air conditioning enhance the comfort, but the best is yet to come: In the morning, just as the mist is rising from the trees, a horse-drawn carriage arrives at your door to take you to a country inn nestled in the woods. There awaits a gourmet breakfast, prepared just for you.

Chain-O-Lakes is a series of 13 small lakes, most interconnecting, set in the piney woods of East Texas 18 miles east of Cleveland. Since the 1930s it has a been a campground. On weekends and during the summer it is popular with campers and day visitors who come to frolic on the swimming beach, go boating and fishing, and ride horses. In the mid 1980s the Smiths revitalized the campground, adding romantic cabins in the woods. (Older cabins, more rustic and less atmospheric, are also part of the resort.)

Hilltop Country Inn, operated by a family with a distinguished reputation for cooking (especially with herbs), opened as part of the complex in 1986. Owner Madalene Hill has served as president of the Herb Society of America, and she and her daughter Gwen have written a book on growing herbs. The inn is open to the public from 11:30 A.M. to 10 P.M. Sunday buffets are especially popular.

Chain-O-Lakes' huge party barn, equipped with food service sections, entertainment areas, and an upstairs dormitory, is excellent for groups.

5

City B&Bs

In the midst of a city, a B&B can be a warm, personable place to stay. Hosts often take pleasure in introducing guests to their home town—recommending sights to see, restaurants to try, and cultural events not to be missed. By the time you leave, you'll feel as if you've seen the city through an insider's eyes instead of only as a visitor. (See also chapter on B&B Reservation Systems.)

ARIZONA

La Posada Del Valle
  1640 N. Campbell Avenue
  Tucson, Arizona 85719
  602/795-3840
INNKEEPERS: Debbie and Charles Bryant
5 rooms (private baths)
$75–$95 single or double including full breakfast
MasterCard, Visa; personal check
Children over 13
No pets
No smoking
Open year round

  In a fine residential section of Tucson there stands a pristine white adobe with a red tile roof. A fountain adds grace to its courtyard, and the manicured grounds are sprinkled with orange trees. A white stucco wall separates the tranquil scene from the street beyond. Designed in 1929 by a renowned Tucson architect, the home exemplifies the early Santa Fe style of architecture. Inside, it sparkles with Art Deco furnishings.

In 1987 La Posada del Valle opened as a B&B, one of the city's first, setting a high standard for other B&Bs sure to follow. It's the extra touches that make this place special, from stained glass art to peach potpourris. Guests gather for afternoon tea in the living room. Turndown service is provided in the evening. Breakfast is in the dining room or patio, featuring stewed fruit, fresh bread, eggs, and French toast or waffles. Art work by Arizona artists is displayed throughout the home, much of it for sale.

Each room honors an illustrious woman of the 1920s. Isadora's room is decorated in pale green, with swirls of geometric designs. Claudette's is mauve, featuring a maple burl king-size bed. Sophie's is one of the prettiest, decorated in peach and furnished with a Victorian bedroom suite, fainting couch, and an 1818 king-size bed. (The bedroom suite was once owned by a fan dancer at the notorious Crystal Palace in Tombstone.) Every room has a private bath, and four have private entrances.

The University of Arizona and University Medical Center are within walking distance of La Posada.

Squaw Peak Inn
4425 E. Horseshoe Road
Phoenix, Arizona 85028
602/998-4049
INNKEEPERS: Bill and Ann Epley
3 rooms, 1 guest house (private baths)
$55–$125 double for rooms, $125 for guest house including breakfast
Cash preferred, personal check accepted; no credit cards
Children welcome
No pets
Open year round

In a city known for its glitzy resorts, Squaw Peak Inn is a good alternative, with convivial hosts and comfortable rooms plus a sense of history. The inn is actually a home, set within a modern residential neighborhood north of downtown Phoenix. Just to the west is Squaw Peak Mountain Preserve.

The B&B long predates its neighbors, for it was built in 1929-30. Frank Lloyd Wright, the architect who inspired the famed Arizona Biltmore nearby, is said to have taken his students to see the adobe structure, labeling it as "authentic territorial style." From the late 1930s to the early 1950s the building operated as an inn, counting among its guests such notables as Mamie Eisenhower, Clark Gable, and Robert Taylor.

In 1979 Bill and Ann Epley discovered the then-dilapidated structure and undertook its salvation. Their task was enormous, starting with replacing 500 window panes. Ann, who is a potter as well as a natural hostess, made the thousands of tiles for the floors and counters. (Ann also loves to cook, often greeting guests with an apple pie and serving pastries for breakfast.) The huge "great room" is wonderfully romantic, with a high beamed ceiling, arched entranceways, and Southwest antiques.

Three guest rooms are in the main house, each with a private entrance, bath, limited cooking facilities, and a TV. Several have balconies. Furnished with some antiques, rooms are homey and casual.

A separate adobe-style guest house has a living room, three bedrooms, two baths, full kitchen, and native stone fireplace.

NEW MEXICO

Inn of the Arts Bed and Breakfast
618 S. Alameda
Las Cruces, New Mexico 88005
505/526-3327
INNKEEPERS: Linda and Jerry Lundeen
7 rooms (private baths)
$28–$65 single or double including continental breakfast
American Express, MasterCard, Visa; personal check
Children welcome
Pets with approval
Open year round

You don't have to be an art expert to stay at this B&B. But if you are, you won't be disappointed. And if you aren't, you can enjoy being surrounded by the work by numerous contemporary artists.

Linda Lundeen runs an art gallery; in fact, it's in the same adobe building that houses the B&B and the Lundeen residence. Art is everywhere, creating a look of vivacity and beauty.

The living room is fresh and modern, setting just the right tone for a stay in this B&B. Each guest room is named for an artist, with furnishings designed to reflect that artist's style. The Georgia O'Keeffe Room, decorated in blacks, grays, and whites, has an antique bed and a private balcony. The Olag Wieghorst Room, with blue quilts and red accents, has two double beds and a red clawfoot tub.

In the afternoons guests gather for hors d'oeuvres and apple cider. At breakfast, the Lundeens serve continental style, perhaps blueberry muffins or cinnamon swirls, accompanied by fruit, herb tea, and coffee.

Catering to groups as well as individuals, the hosts can coordinate such special functions as theater nights. They also schedule events of their own—art seminars, watercolor workshops, mystery weekends, archaeological digs, even trips to the nearby Deming Duck Races.

William E. Mauger Estate

701 Roma Avenue NW
Albuquerque, New Mexico 87102
505/242-8755
OWNER: Richard Carleno
8 rooms (private baths)
$45–$70 single, $50–$75 double including continental breakfast
American Express, MasterCard, Visa; personal check
Children welcome
Pets accepted
Open year round

On the corner of a residential neighborhood between Old Town and downtown Albuquerque, there's a three-story brick B&B inn with charm and sophistication. Built in 1896, it's a stately Queen Anne, ideal for putting you in touch with history yet imbued with modern-day comfort.

The William E. Mauger opened for guests in late 1987. Its beautiful restoration is the work of owner Richard Carleno. Great effort has been taken to preserve as much of the original home as possible. Decorated with period-style furnishings, guest rooms have an air of elegance. Each has a modern private bath. The Victorian, one of two rooms on the ground floor, has a brick fireplace original to the house, flanked by large oval windows. The two garret-like rooms on the third floor have special appeal. Most rooms have a double bed and a sleeper sofa.

Breakfast, a continental-style affair, includes fresh baked breads and seasonal fruits.

Although the inn was still being restored when visited, all the raw materials of a high-quality hostelry are here, from the impressive house itself to the owner's commitment to hospitality. This unique spot should offer a good alternative to the city's traditional lodgings.

TEXAS

Rosevine Inn
  415 S. Vine Avenue
  Tyler, Texas 75702
  214/592-2221
INNKEEPERS: Bert and Rebecca Powell
5 rooms (private baths)
$50–$75 double including full breakfast
Personal check; no credit cards
No children under 12
No pets
No smoking
Open year round

Rosevine Inn combines the best qualities of B&Bs, offering hospitality, comfort, convenience, and a sense of history. Tyler's first B&B, it gives travelers an excellent alternative to the run-of-the-mill motels and hotels which predominate in this city.

Situated on a hill overlooking a brick-paved street, the Rosevine has a residential feel with its white picket fence and tastefully small sign. The Vine Avenue area in which it is located is an emerging visitor attraction, with specialty shops and restored homes. Nearby is the Azalea District, notable for its variety of architectural styles representing many periods in Tyler's history.

On this site once stood the home of Dr. Irwin Pope, the son of one of Tyler's first doctors. Although the original home was destroyed by fire, the Powells have replicated its 1930s style, building the present home over the foundation of the old one. Unlike most B&Bs, from its inception the Rosevine Inn was designed to accommodate guests, and Bert and Becca Powell chose its site because of the beauty and spaciousness of the grounds as well as its convenience to city attractions.

Don't expect a grand old mansion—instead, enjoy the comfort of a well-planned new home. The living areas are cozy and intimate. Guest rooms (all but one on the second floor) are cheerful. Each has a private bath, small but modern. Three rooms have double beds; one has twin beds. The downstairs bedroom, with the lowest tariff in the house, has a daybed. Furnishings range from antiques to country collectibles, many of which are for sale. There's a touch of lace at the windows, flowers on the dresser, and a handy digital clock radio on the bedside table.

Breakfast—a grand affair with quiches, hot breads, and fresh fruits—is served in the dining room. For socializing, guests can gather in the outside patio, the living room, or the den-like setting at the top of the stairs—furnished with couches and a TV.

The innkeepers are a bright energetic couple, convivial and eager to please. They'll happily direct you to area attractions, make suggestions about day trips, even cook your favorite breakfast food upon request. In the evenings they serve wine and cheese, or if you prefer, a cup of hot chocolate by the fire.

Sara's Bed and Breakfast Inn

941 Heights Boulevard
Houston, Texas 77008
713/868-1130
INNKEEPERS: Donna and Tillman Arledge
12 rooms (most with shared baths)
$46–$96 double including breakfast
American Express, Carte Blanche, Diners Club, MasterCard, Visa
Children accepted in only one unit
No pets
Smoking in designated areas
Open year round

Downtown Houston is four miles away—you can see the skyscrapers on the horizon. But here in the Heights, a community born in the 1880s as one of Texas' first professionally planned suburbs, you relive the days of lemonade and cookies, almost forgetting that the glistening modern city exists. Here Victorian-style structures predominate; 90 of them are on the National Register. There's a central boulevard set with trees, a park with a lacy gazebo, and a public library that makes you want to curl up for hours.

Right on Heights Boulevard is Sara's Bed and Breakfast Inn, a wonderful two-story Victorian confection of ginger-bread with a wrap-around porch, turret, and widow's walk. In truth, the entire structure is not as old as one would guess from its architecture. The core of the house—a one-story cottage—was indeed built in 1898. But the flourishes were added much more recently, in 1980.

In 1983 along came the Arledges, who spent three years renovating the structure. The inn is fanciful and fun, offering lots of diversity. If you've never been to Texas, then Sara's is a good place to start, for each of the ten guest rooms in the main house is decorated to reflect a Texas town or city. Get a quick tour of the state while choosing a room for the night. Dallas is sophisticated; Galveston has a nautical theme. Fredericksburg has German-style hand stenciling. Paris has French furniture. Tyler, a city famed for its roses, is remembered in the Tyler room, decorated in a rose motif. Austin, with its white iron and brass bed and its bay window, is the prettiest.

Jefferson, on the first floor, is furnished with a trundle bed. It's the only room in the main house with a private bath. Shared baths have showers in lieu of tubs. In a separate building on the second floor there's a balcony suite with two bedrooms, two baths, kitchen (only light cooking allowed), and living area. Well-suited for families, it is the only unit accommodating children.

Adjoined to the main house is a large deck with a hot tub. Since most of the inn's interior is dedicated to guest rooms, the deck is the primary gathering spot.

Breakfast is served in a small dining room. The hostess' specialties are hot breads and creamy scrambled eggs with cheese.

6

City Stops

City hotels are rich in variety. Some are grand and glorious, putting you in touch with the city's history. Others are newcomers on the scene, basing their reputations on exemplary service. Still others are the best places to take a family, offering high value at an economy price. For vacationers, weekend stays at downtown hotels are often the best buy in town. Here you can get luxury at a bargain rate, for many first class downtown hotels cut their weekday rate by as much as half during the weekend.

ALBUQUERQUE

Albuquerque Marriott
  2101 Louisiana Boulevard NE
  Albuquerque, New Mexico 87110
  505/881-6800
  800/228-9290
GENERAL MANAGER: Thomas Chase
414 rooms
$97 single, $110 double
American Express, Carte Blanche, Diners Club, Discover,
  MasterCard, Visa; personal check
Children welcome
Pets accepted
Open year round

From the outside, the 16-story Marriott looks like hundreds of other hotels. Its location right off I-40 is convenient but not particularly romantic. Yet there's an air of excitement about this hotel that makes you want to stay.

The lobby is a friendly place, abuzz with activity. Herbs and Roses restaurant has a country-French look, set with flowers and baskets and lots of private dining nooks. Nichole's is the fine-dining restaurant. Decorated in rich greens and brass, it's elegant and inviting.

Guest rooms aren't the typical hotel design, but are odd-shaped, creating visual interest. Some look down onto enclosed gardens. All were refurbished in late 1987, now featuring soft colors and plush fabrics. Bathrooms are nicer than those in ordinary city hotels, with marble vanities and appealing wall coverings.

The indoor/outdoor pool is particularly pleasant, larger than average in this city. Adjacent to the inside pool is a large hot tub. The health club has seven types of equipment, including exercise bikes. For a more relaxed approach to vacationing, there's backgammon, checkers, chess, even audio head sets and tapes.

Barcelona Court All Suite Hotel
900 Louisiana NE
Albuquerque, New Mexico 87110
505/255-5566
800/222-1122
GENERAL MANAGER: Joe Frampton
164 suites
$80–$90 single, $90–$100 double including full breakfast;
    $10 each additional person
American Express, Diners Club, Discover, MasterCard, Visa;
    personal check
Children welcome
No pets
Open year round

Clear your mind of all the other all-suite hotels you've seen. This one is different, both in layout and in atmosphere. From the outside, it's not particularly impressive, but the front doors open onto a gracious Spanish-style lobby with Mexican tile floors, Oriental rugs, and curved staircases trimmed in wrought iron.

Once the hotel was a cluster of apartments. In 1984, open areas were enclosed and the complex was converted into a hotel, hence its sprawling nature and unusual use of space.

Suites, which are larger than those in most all-suite hotels, are on the first and second floors. Decorated in Southwest-style, they're inviting and comfortable. Living rooms have a hideabed sofa, easy chair with ottoman, and game table. Bedrooms are furnished with two queen- or one king-size bed, and marble vanity alcove. The kitchenette is geared to light meals, equipped with a microwave, refrigerator, cooking utensils, and tableware. Two TVs and three telephones add to the convenience. Four "special occasion" suites, priced at $181 for two, have such extras as fireplaces and whirlpool.

At the center of activity is Fountain Court, a huge enclosed atrium. Cooked-to-order complimentary breakfast is served here. So are free cocktails in the afternoons; guests have the privilege of inviting friends or associates. Although no restaurant is on the premises, room service is offered through a nearby restaurant. Other services include free enclosed parking, free limousine transport to and from the airport (also to area malls and restaurants Mondays through Thursdays), and valet service.

There's an indoor pool with whirlpool and sauna, small outdoor pool, and laundry facilities.

Set on the edge of a residential area in uptown Albuquerque, Barcelona is convenient to Coronado and Winrock Shopping Malls and the New Mexico State Fairgrounds. The University of New Mexico is about ten minutes away.

La Posada de Albuquerque

125 Second Street NW at Copper
Albuquerque, New Mexico 87102
505/242-9090
800/621-7231 outside NM
GENERAL MANAGER: Theresa McFerrin
114 rooms
$56–$78 single, $66–$88 double; $80–$200 suites
American Express, MasterCard, Visa; personal check
Children welcome
No pets
Open year round

In 1939 Conrad Hilton built his first hotel in New Mexico, his native state. Now named La Posada de Albuquerque (and no longer a Hilton), the restored Southwest-style hotel has character and charm. The lobby recalls colonial Mexico, with arched doorways, Mexican tile floors, tin chandeliers, and tiled fountain. The lobby bar is popular with locals and guests alike, acting as a downtown gathering spot.

Upstairs the guest rooms, redecorated in 1984, reflect their southwestern heritage: furnishings are beautiful in their simplicity. Wooden shutters cover the windows, regional art accents the walls, and touches of Mexico such as hammered tin light switch covers add interest. Standard, mini-suite, and deluxe units differ primarily in size.

Eulalia's Restaurant has earned a reputation as one of the finest places to dine in Albuquerque. Dinner entrees include southwestern fare such as blue corn enchiladas and pork tenderloin roasted in a chile apple sauce. Pheasant, salmon, and veal are featured as well as more standard offerings. Prices range from $8 to $16.

Guests can use the facilities of Executive Sports Club across the street, including indoor pool, racquetball, and exercise equipment ($5 fee). Room service, free airport transportation, and free parking are nice amenities.

Situated across the street from Albuquerque's convention center, La Posada is about five minutes from Old Town (a historic shopping area) and ten minutes from the University of New Mexico.

The Pyramid Holiday Inn
I-25 North at Paseo del Norte
5151 San Francisco Road NE
Albuquerque, New Mexico 87109-4641
505/821-3333
800/HOLIDAY
GENERAL MANAGER: Russell Steele
311 rooms
$66–$84 single, $72–$90 double; $125–$250 suites
American Express, Diners Club, Discover, Holiday Inn,
    MasterCard, Visa; personal check
Children welcome
Pets accepted
Open year round

Opened in 1987, the Pyramid is set within the Journal Center business complex about seven miles north of downtown. True to its name, the hotel is a modern-day version of Mexico's pyramids, reflecting Albuquerque's heritage.

Inside, the hotel gleams with modernity, centering around a ten-story atrium and a tiered 50-foot waterfall. Guests ride up glass elevators to rooms decorated in upbeat tones, such as peach and blue. Furnishings are traditional.

Room types, beginning with standard, include queen suites, king rooms (king-size bed, living area, desk), king executive rooms (larger living area than king rooms), king suites (large living/dining room, wet bar, separate bedroom), and deluxe suites (upgraded version of king suite). The presidential suite has a large living room, dining room, and a whirlpool.

The Gallery restaurant serves continental cuisine, while the atrium Terrace Café offers casual dining. The Pyramid Club is a contemporary dance lounge.

In addition to the small indoor/outdoor pool, there are two indoor hot tubs and an exercise room. Jogging trails wind through the 313-acre Journal Center.

Upscale shops are off the lobby, there's a concierge on duty, and parking is free. Best of all, the staff is cordial and eager to please. The hotel is owned and operated by locally-based John Q. Hammons Hotels.

Ramada Hotel Classic

6815 Menaul NE
Albuquerque, New Mexico 87110
505/881-0000
800/2-RAMADA
GENERAL MANAGER: John Conner
297 rooms
$68–$88 single, $78–$98 double
American Express, Carte Blanche, Diners Club, MasterCard,
    Visa; personal check
Children welcome
Pets with approval
Open year round

From its public areas to guest rooms, the Ramada Hotel Classic is visually pleasing. The lobby and adjoining areas—decorated in peach, mauve, and green—have skylights and lots of plants, creating a cool, soothing environment in Albuquerque's uptown business district. Built in the mid-1980s, this hostelry was the dream of an Albuquerque businessman who died soon after it opened. His portrait hangs in the entranceway.

Take time to see the ornate white pipe organ with five keyboards and 27 sets of pipes. A true showpiece, it originally was used to entertain audiences at a New York theater.

Outside, the hotel is surrounded by activity. The city's largest mall, Coronado, is across the street. Winrock Shopping Center is one-half mile away, and numerous corporate addresses are within a few miles.

Here in the hotel, guests have easy access to the city yet can relax in calming surroundings.

Guest rooms, situated on the second through eighth floor, have an air of sophistication. Colors are soft and warm.

Their design emphasizes comfort, with such extras as small refrigerators. The 24 suites have deluxe whirlpools.

The upscale Café Fennel serves all three meals. Chardonnay's serves dinner only; the Quest lounge is adjacent to it. Parking is free, and there's complimentary transportation to and from the airport.

AUSTIN

The Driskill Hotel
Sixth and Brazos
P.O. Box 1528
Austin, Texas 78767
512/474-5911
800/252-9367
GENERAL MANAGER: Mike Kolanek
183 rooms and suites
$59–$79 single, $89–$99 double; $99–$400 suites
American Express, Carte Blanche, Diners Club, Discover,
    MasterCard, Visa
Children welcome
No pets
Open year round

Built in 1886 by a Texas cattle baron, the Driskill has a history intertwined with that of the Lone Star State. Walk through its doors and you know you're in Texas. Behind the registration desk there's an expansive painting of the Texas range. Overlooking the lobby is a massive bronze sculpture depicting a dramatic moment in the lives of two cowboys. Portraits of the state's governors line the walls of the handsome lobby bar. The wall outside the LBJ Suite exhibits photographs of the president who often made the Driskill his headquarters during his political career.

Situated in the heart of downtown Austin, the Driskill is an architectural treasure, with an immense arched entrance, ornamented balconies, and a column-studded lobby. A bust of the hotel's builder, Colonel Jesse Driskill, is perched on top of one exterior wall and stares southward; busts of his two sons look to the east and west.

Throughout the hotel there's a feeling of openness and space, a fitting style for the Texas-to-the-core hostelry. Guest rooms are arranged in two connecting buildings: the 1880s hotel with high ceilings and an assortment of room configurations, and the 1930s tower with lower ceilings and a more uniform room design.

Rooms in both sections are spacious. Baths in the tower rooms are especially convenient, with an adjacent dressing area. Tastefully decorated, all of the rooms have touches of grandeur, from wall border designs to crystal drawer pulls on the period furniture.

Speaking of grandeur, one of the hotel's banquet rooms is designed around eight mirrors framed in gold leaf that were the wedding gift of Mexico's Maximillian to his bride, the Empress Carlota of Belgium.. Atop each mirror is a gilt medallion likeness of the Empress, said to be the most beautiful woman in Europe.

The Driskill Dining Room, romantically decorated with mirrors and a carved white ceiling, serves nouvelle American cuisine. House specialties show a Southwestern bent, from pheasant to wild boar.

Hotel guests have privileges at a health club across the street. Facilities include a workout area with Universal and Nautilus equipment, racquetball courts, lap pool, whirlpool, and sauna.

Located a few blocks from the state capitol and the University of Texas, the Driskill opens onto Sixth Street, a lively entertainment area with restaurants, bars, and specialty shops. In front of the hotel you can climb aboard trolleys that stop at most area attractions.

Four Seasons Hotel Austin

99 San Jacinto Boulevard
Austin, Texas 78701
512/478-4500
800/332-3442
GENERAL MANAGER: John Indrieri
308 units
$98–$180 single, $118–$180 double; $180–$650 suites
American Express, Diners Club, EnRoute, MasterCard, Visa;
    personal check
Children welcome
Small pets on leash
Open year round

On the shores of Town Lake, ten blocks south of the state capitol, the Four Seasons Austin is a first class hotel with Southwest flair. Opened in 1987, it's a bright new star in the capital city, setting a new standard for downtown lodgings.

When you walk into the lobby, set with a stone fireplace and leather chairs, you feel that you're visiting the home of a wealthy Hill Country rancher instead of staying in a city hotel. Southwestern art, tastefully arranged, accentuates the residential feel.

Luxury is the tone here—extra touches like terry robes and hair dryers in the rooms, attentive service such as pressing within an hour and twice-daily maid service. More importantly, the staff is genuinely friendly and eager to please. Guest rooms are attractive, decorated in soft earth tones. Although not especially large, they bespeak comfort, equipped with such conveniences as three phones and digital clocks. Rooms designated as "Four Seasons" are more akin to suites than to standard hotel rooms.

The hotel's lakeside locale is used to full advantage. Whether you're eating in the café, lounging by the pool, or working out in the health club, the lake is the focal point. Jogging trails lead along its banks. The health club is far above average, with good exercise machines, nicely appointed locker rooms, saunas, and a whirlpool. Riverside Café serves southwestern cuisine with an emphasis on freshness and innovative combinations.

Self-service parking is free; valet parking is also available.

La Mansion Hotel Austin
6505 I-35 North
Austin, Texas 78752
512/454-3737
800/531-7208 US, 800/292-7300 TX
GENERAL MANAGER: Mark Fallon
350 rooms and suites
$90–$110 single, $110–$130 double; $295–$395 suites
American Express, MasterCard, Visa; personal check
Children welcome
Pets accepted
Open year round

A Spanish colonial-style lodging on the northern edge of Austin, La Mansion has quiet charm. While its sister hotel in San Antonio, La Mansion del Rio, is housed in a historic building dating back to the 1850s, La Mansion Austin is of modern vintage, built in 1984.

The focal point of the hotel is a peaceful inner courtyard with waterfalls, fountains, and a shell-shaped swimming pool. Nearly half of its guest rooms, arranged on the second through sixth floors, open onto galleries overlooking the courtyard—a sanctuary from the bustling city beyond.

Rooms are spacious and comfortably furnished. Some have French doors opening onto small balconies. All have dressing areas adjacent to the bathroom and bath telephones. Two styles of suites are on the Premier Floor, where guests are pampered with continental breakfasts and afternoon cocktails.

The second floor fitness room has a sauna and exercise equipment including a treadmill. In addition to the outdoor pool, there's a whirlpool spa.

La Mansion's most distinctive dining room is La Talavera, serving classic and contemporary dishes. Lovers of Mexican art will appreciate the museum-quality display of 18th-century Talavera pottery, complemented by hand-thrown copies used in the restaurant's table service. You can also dine well at Las Ventanas, an informal restaurant with southwestern fare. Rio Brazos is a cozy bar with stone fireplace, dance floor, and live entertainment.

Guests can park free in the hotel's garage; valet parking is also available. Free transportation is offered to both the airport and downtown Austin. And on top of the hotel is a heliport for those quick arrivals and departures.

Stouffer Austin Hotel

9721 Arboretum Boulevard
Austin, Texas 78759
512/343-2626
800/HOTELS-1
GENERAL MANAGER: Jacques Van Seters
478 units
$94–$114 single, $104–$124 double; $175–$225 suites
American Express, Carte Blanche, Diners Club, MasterCard,
   Visa; personal check
Children welcome
Small pets accepted
Open year round

In the rolling countryside north of downtown, Stouffer Austin is a retreat from the city while offering easy access to numerous business addresses, most notably the high tech companies for which Austin is now known. The hotel is part of the Arboretum, a 95-acre development with upscale shops and restaurants as well as sleek office towers. The entire complex sits on a hillside overlooking the Texas Hill Country, with its cedar forests and limestone cliffs.

An atrium-style hotel, the Stouffer has a different look from others of this design. At its center is an expansive marble plaza set with sculptures, dining kiosks, and sitting areas. Off to one side is The Overlook restaurant, a truly grand dining room with excellent food and service with a flair. True to its name, it has a great view of the scenic terrain.

Guest rooms, decorated in Queen Anne furniture and oriental art, are luxurious and large (some of the largest in the city). Ask for a wake-up call and you get complimentary coffee and a newspaper delivered to your door.

For relaxation, there's a wider range of choices than expected from a city hotel—an outdoor pool (especially appealing due to its hillside setting), indoor pool, well-equipped exercise room, jogging path, short nature trail, and picnic tables tucked away within the trees. Adjacent to the hotel are the Arboretum shops (several cuts above average, from Banana Republic to fancy boutiques), a four-screen movie theater, and the hotel-operated club, Tangerines.

Stouffer Austin is about 15 minutes from the state capitol and downtown Austin and about 20 minutes from the airport. Transportation to the airport and hotel parking are free.

Wyndham Southpark

4140 Governor's Row
(I-35 and Ben White Boulevard)
Austin, Texas 78744
512/448-2222
800/822-4200
GENERAL MANAGER: Jack Highsmith
312 rooms and suites
$82–$92 single, $92 double
American Express, Carte Blanche, Diners Club, Discover,
    MasterCard, Visa
Children welcome
No pets
Open year round

Situated south of downtown Austin, Wyndham Southpark has a relaxing atmosphere, outstanding recreational features, and a hospitable staff.

The 14-story hotel, opened in 1983, is contemporary in design. Just outside the lobby is a Texas-size indoor/outdoor pool and recreation area. A bridge leads across the pool and into the fitness center with its attractive deck area, whirlpool, sauna, and weight and exercise room. Nearby is the hotel's sports court (basketball or volleyball), jogging track, and shuffleboard.

Room furnishings are luxurious and modern, with rich fabrics, plush carpeting, and colorful artwork. Rooms have comfortable seating, TVs with in-house movies, and digital clock radios. Executive suites have a parlor with conference table, sitting area with fold-out bed, and one or two connecting bedrooms. Both the Presidential and the Governor's suites have a large parlor and two bedrooms; the Presidential has a whirlpool tub.

Onion Creek Grill, a casual dining room, has all-day service. Pasta and pizza are featured on the bill of fare, as well as steak and seafood. Sweetwaters Lounge has nightly entertainment.

Van transportation (between the hotel and the airport) and hotel parking are free.

DALLAS

The Adolphus
1321 Commerce
Dallas, Texas 75202
214/742-8200
800/221-9083 US, 800/441-0574 TX
GENERAL MANAGER: Jeff Trigger
435 rooms and suites
$160–$205 single, $185–$230 double; $425–$1,000 suites
American Express, MasterCard, Visa; personal check
Children welcome
No pets
Open year round

The Adolphus is a grand and glorious hotel. Built in 1912 by beer baron Adolphus Busch, Dallas's landmark hotel was totally renovated in 1981. Today guests can enjoy the grandeur of an earlier era coupled with the comforts of a modern-day luxury hotel.

The exterior is an extravagance of ornamentation—sculptures, bas-relief figures, gargoyles, heraldic characters, even a beer stein-shaped corner turret. Inside there's a wealth of antiques from Europe and Asia as well as the United States.

Public areas have a museum-like quality, with such treasures as two huge 1660s Flemish tapestries, a six-foot tall portrait of Napoleon dressed in coronation robes, and carved English Regency oak furniture. So extensive is the collection that there's a 22-page guidebook describing the lamps, clocks, carvings, furniture, and paintings that adorn the Adolphus.

The hotel's centerpiece is the richly ornamented French Room, a dining room with vaulted ceiling, columned walls, and rococo murals. On the ceiling, cherubs holding floral garlands fly beneath a pale blue sky.

Unlike new hotels, guest rooms in the Adolphus come in 30-plus configurations. Retaining their original high ceilings, they are warm yet elegant, decorated in reproduction antique furniture, matching draperies and bedspreads, and touches of lace. All have refrigerators, multiple phones, and TVs enclosed in armoires. Goosedown comforters and terry cloth robes add an extra dollop of luxury.

·Terrace suites have an expansive sitting area, two baths, and a large terrace. Skylight suites on the 19th floor are especially appealing, with their slanting glass exterior walls, large wet bar, and Asian accents intermingled with reproduction period furniture. The penthouse, accessible by private elevator, was once the residence of Adolphus Busch. From its antique canopied bed to baby grand piano, it is truly special.

A service-oriented hotel, the Adolphus has a concierge, multilingual staff, 24-hour room service, and valet parking ($8.50 fee).

Dining choices include The French Room (dinner only), Bistroquet (country-French decor, continental fare, open for all three meals), and Lobby Living Room (afternoon tea).

Adjoining the hotel is the Clark Hatch Physical Fitness Center with weight room, whirlpool, sauna, and steam room. One block away is the Texas Club with indoor lap pool, racquetball, squash, indoor track, gym, Nautilus equipment, and steam room. Guests have privileges at both facilities (charge of $8 to $10).

The Aristocrat
   1933 Main Street
   Dallas, Texas 75201
   214/741-7700
   800/231-4235
GENERAL MANAGER: Tony Salazar
173 units
$65–$125 single, $75–$135 double including continental
   breakfast
American Express, Diners Club, MasterCard, Visa; personal
   check
Children welcome
No pets
Open year round

A chic downtown hotel, The Aristocrat is personable, cozy, smartly decorated, and convenient. Most of its guest units are suites. Though designed for the corporate traveler, it's a good lodging choice whatever the reason for traveling. Through an extensive skywalk and tunnel system it's linked to ten or so office buildings. The historic Majestic Theater, home of Dallas Ballet and Opera, is around the corner, and the Dallas Museum of Art is within walking distance.

Built in 1925 by Conrad Hilton, it was the first hotel to bear his name. Since the nearby Adolphus was already the recognized luxury hotel in town, Hilton designed a no-frills property for traveling salesmen. In 1938 Hilton sold his hotel, and over the years it suffered a decline. In late 1985 it was restored under the guidance of the Texas Historical Commission. Now The Aristocrat is a gem well worth discovering. Luxurious suites were formed by combining pairs of original rooms. Architectural features such as ornate trim and ceiling plaster were preserved, as were public areas decorated with wood paneling, etched glass, and period furnishings.

The suites trade off spaciousness for intimacy. Cherry furniture, sophisticated colors and fabrics, and lots of amenities combine to create a feeling of warmth. Each unit has a mini-refrigerator, remote control TV, three phones (one in the bath), and a separate vanity area. Beds are queen-size.

The hotel's small restaurant is a convivial spot, serving full breakfasts, lunch, dinner, and late-evening snacks. It features varietal wine by the glass, espresso, capuccino, and premium liquors. Room service is also available. Complimentary continental breakfast is served in the cozy Club Room downstairs.

Parking in a covered garage across the street is free—a real plus for a downtown Dallas hotel. Valet parking is not offered.

Dallas Marriott Mandalay Hotel

221 E. Las Colinas Boulevard
Irving, Texas 75039
214/556-0800
800/228-9290
GENERAL MANAGER: Lew Sherer
421 rooms
$120 single, $135 double; $300–$1,200 suites
American Express, Diners Club, Discover, MasterCard, Visa; personal check
Children welcome
Pets accepted
Open year round

West of Dallas there's a master-planned community called Las Colinas, a world of its own set apart from the Dallas/Fort Worth metroplex. Amid the office towers, residential villages, and green space is the Dallas Marriott Mandalay.

The hotel is adjacent to Lake Carolyn and the Mandalay Canal, a mini-version of San Antonio's Riverwalk. Lined with 30 or more shops, it has cobblestone lanes and a covered bridge spanning the waterway. Water taxis stop at the hotel's mini-wharf, taking guests sightseeing or to office building destinations.

Despite the Marriott Mandalay's size—27 stories and 421 guest rooms—it has the feel of a more intimate lodging. The low-ceilinged lobby is sophisticated and gracious, with sumptuous furnishings and a profusion of greenery. One of the focal points of the hotel is its attractive outdoor pool adjacent to the lake. The hotel also has a fitness area with whirlpool, saunas, exercise equipment, and massages. Jogging trails wind along the shores of the lake.

Guest rooms are decorated with traditionally styled furniture and rich fabrics. All have remote-control TVs, digital clock radios, and multiple phones.

Rooms designated as "Mandalay Rooms" are especially appealing, with lots of space and bay windows opening onto private balconies. Situated at the four corners of the building, they're triangular in shape, allowing for non-typical use of space. Bathrooms are particularly luxurious. The king-size bed is recessed into an alcove, creating a feeling of separation from the sitting area. Two concierge floors offer special services, such as continental breakfast and afternoon hors d'oeuvres.

Café D'Or, overlooking Lake Carolyn, serves American cuisine. Rhapsody specializes in light lunches and Sunday brunch. On the lobby level in a lush garden-like setting, Les Jardins is a peaceful spot for cocktails. Nearby Aperitif has a wine and champagne bar.

From the moment you enter Enjolie, the gourmet restaurant, you can tell that it's really special. The decor is dramatically elegant, and the cuisine lives up to the quality suggested by the setting.

The hotel is approximately 12 minutes from D/FW International Airport, 15 minutes from downtown Dallas, and 40 minutes from downtown Fort Worth. Self parking is free; valet parking is also available.

Fairmont Hotel
   1717 N. Akard Street
   Dallas, Texas 75201
   214/720-2020
   800/527-4727 US, 800/492-6622 TX
GENERAL MANAGER: Howard Connor

551 rooms
$140–$190 single, $165–$215 double
American Express, Diners Club, MasterCard, Visa; personal
  check
Children welcome
No pets
Open year round

A sophisticated downtown hotel adjacent to the Dallas Arts
District, the Fairmont has sweeping public areas and one of
the best known restaurants in town.   The lobby lounge is
dominated by an eye-catching contemporary work of art celebrating Cabeza de Vaca as the first European to see the interior of Texas, New Mexico, and Arizona. The Venetian Room
is dramatic—a supper club with Spanish arches, wall sconces,
and red chairs. The Pyramid Lounge is also distinctive, decorated with a bright mural depicting events and figures of the
1960s.

But it's the Pyramid restaurant that draws the most attention.   The award-winning cuisine has a southwestern flair.
Entrees, priced from $20 to $25, include such creations as
sauteed snapper with tomatillo, eggplant, and red pearl onions;
grilled bobwhite quail with wild mushrooms on yellow corn-
cake; and marinated rack of lamb with herbs and spicy mus-
tard.

Guest rooms are situated in two glass towers. Furnishings
are upscale but not particularly distinctive. Amenities include
round-the-clock room service and twice daily housekeeping.
The rooftop garden swimming pool is a real plus—attractive
and inviting.

Valet parking is $8.50 per day.

Hotel Crescent Court
400 Crescent Court
Dallas, Texas 75201
214/871-3200
800/654-6541
GENERAL MANAGER: Jean Mestriner
218 rooms
$180–$235 single, $210–$265 double
American Express, Diners Club, MasterCard, Visa; personal
  check
Children welcome
Pets with approval
Open year round

Staying at Hotel Crescent Court is an immersion in beauty. Every sense is stimulated from the time you enter the lobby. Arched windows and marble floors, Louis XV furnishings and European art, massive floral arrangements and airy palms set the tone. In the background, classical music plays. The bell-man, the desk clerk, and the concierge are more than attentive; they seem dedicated to satisfying guests' needs. Before you know it, you've forgotten the traffic, the work-day hassle, the phone calls you intended to make. You can relax. Somebody else will take care of everything.

Make no mistake—this is not a retreat. Indeed, there's a sense of vibrancy about the place, a mood that flows from the lobby to the restaurant to the courtyard beyond. The Beau Nash restaurant and bar, named for the arbiter of taste in 18th century England, is truly outstanding. Popular with Dallasites as well as travelers, it has a lively atmosphere and excellent food. Southwestern and California cuisine predominate.

Opened in late 1985, Hotel Crescent Court is a Rosewood Hotel, sister to the Mansion on Turtle Creek (also located in Dallas), the Bel Air in California, and Hotel Hana Maui in Hawaii. Crescent Court differs from the other Rosewoods because it's geared to the business traveler. But whatever your reason for being in Dallas, it is a hotel well worth discovering.

Guest rooms are just as beautiful as the public areas would promise. Residential in feel, they're spacious and aesthetically pleasing. French windows open to a view of the court-yard below. Furnishings are comfortably elegant—easy chairs and sofas with goosedown cushions, armoire desks, and original works of art.

Above all, it is attention to detail that sets this hotel apart. In your room, expect fresh flowers, three phones, newspapers, terry cloth bathrobes, and high quality bath amenities. If you want to be pampered, a maid will unpack your luggage. When you need a torn hem repaired, a seamstress will come to call. Laundry comes back in a lined wicker basket. Turndown service includes placing a homemade chocolate truffle by your bed. Hotel Crescent Court's swimming pool fits into the overall mood of distinction. Its hand-railing is made of brass—and is polished to a gleam.

The hotel is part of a mixed-use project named The Crescent. From the lobby you can walk through a courtyard and into a tri-level marketplace of upscale shops and galleries. On the other side of the hotel are three 18-story office towers. The Spa at The Crescent, a private membership health and fitness club for men and women, is also part of the complex. European treatments are combined with America's zest for fitness. Lancaster Beauty Farms beauty treatments, water therapy and massage, exercise facilities and equipment, and nutrition are all emphasized. Hotel guests have spa privileges, but services do not come cheap. Use of the workout area is $45 per hour (participants work with a private trainer). Wet area usage is $25. A one-hour European facial is $50. Spa packages which include a multiple-day stay are available.

Situated north of downtown, Crescent Court is convenient to the Arts District, Dallas Market, and West End Historical District. D/FW Airport is a 20 minute drive; Love Field Airport is a ten minute drive. Free transportation to the downtown business district aboard The Crescent Trolley is available every day but Sunday.

Loews Anatole Hotel

2201 Stemmons Freeway
Dallas, Texas 75207
214/748-1200
GENERAL MANAGER: Randy Gantenbein
1,620 units
$105–$145 single, $125–$165 double
American Express, Carte Blanche, Diners Club, MasterCard,
    Visa; personal check
Children welcome
No pets
Open year round

Loews Anatole is the kind of hotel in which you need a map to get around. Spread over 45 acres, it's a city unto itself, with nine restaurants, eight lounges, a dozen or so shops, and a huge health spa. Downtown Dallas is about a five-minute drive away.

The largest hotel in the Southwest, the Anatole is primarily geared to conventions. But groups of all sizes as well as individual vacationers can enjoy its wealth of services. It's worth a stop just to see the public areas. Parking is free, so at least pull off Stemmons Freeway and take a look. Two enormous elephants, carved from monkey pod wood by entire villages in Thailand, stand guard inside the tower section. Behind them is an 18th century white marble Hindustani Pavilion, originally housed in a royal palace in India. Inside Atrium II hang five fantastic batik banners, created in Ceylon especially for the hotel. The Jade room, used for receptions, has a magnificent collection of jade artistry. Outside the Wedgwood Ballroom, with its collection of pieces dating back to the 18th century, is a rare Wedgwood vase nearly five feet tall.

And so the collection continues—much of it inspired by Trammell Crow, who developed the hotel as well as the innovative Infomart across the freeway.

Behind the hotel in a Southern mansion-style building is The Verandah Club, a health spa with indoor and outdoor jogging tracks; indoor and outdoor swimming pools; tennis, racquetball, and squash courts; full-size basketball court; exercise rooms; and a sauna, steam room, whirlpool section. A membership club, Verandah is available to guests for about $11 a day. Extra fees are charged for racquetball. Outdoor swimming is free.

Guest rooms are in two atrium highrises and a 27-story tower. Furnishings are traditional in style—comfortable and yet not particularly distinctive.

The 70 tower suites have small parlors and upgraded baths (marble vanities, phones, extra amenities). A variety of other suites are also available. And there are two concierge floors with such services as continental breakfast, afternoon wine and cheese, and a full-time concierge.

The Mansion On Turtle Creek
2821 Turtle Creek Boulevard
Dallas, Texas 75219
214/559-2100
800/527-5432 US, 800/442-3408 TX
GENERAL MANAGER: Atef Mankarios
143 rooms and suites
$170-$$235 single, $200–$265 double; $575–$870 suites

American Express, Diners Club, MasterCard, Visa; personal
  check
Children welcome
No pets
Open year round

The only problem with staying at The Mansion is that it
spoils you for staying anywhere else. Inside its doors there's a
world of quiet opulence—a combination of aesthetic beauty
and attentive service. Beginning at registration, guest preferences for everything from newspapers to wine are noted and
attended to, with records kept on file for future visits. Best of
all, the hospitality extended by the staff seems genuine.

The hotel is indeed a mansion, set on a terraced hillside in
one of Dallas's most prestigious residential areas. Once it was
the home of millionaire Sheppard King. Built in 1925, it has a
16th-century Italianate design with imaginative spires and tur-
rets. In 1981 Rosewood Hotels restored the original building,
converting it into a fine restaurant and constructing an adjacent hotel tower to complement the mansion itself.

At this hotel the concierge wears a suit, not a uniform.
There are no shops off the lobby, no hints of commercialism.
Instead, there's soft music, fresh flowers, and a bevy of em-
ployees to satisfy every whim. The lobby resembles a fine
living room, accented with antique mirrors and an English
Chippendale breakfront.

Guest rooms are exquisite. Decorated in peach, gold, or
beige, they have four-poster beds, overstuffed chairs with ottomans, love seats, armoires with TVs, and French doors
opening onto small balconies. Bathrooms are not only luxurious but pleasing to the eye, decorated in marble and brass.
Terry robes, bathroom telephones, and turndown service add
to the feeling of luxury. In the evening, a special treat is delivered, perhaps hot spiced tea or cookies and milk.

One of the highlights of staying at The Mansion is dining at
its restaurant, an architectural treasure as well as a culinary
delight. Much of the grandeur of the original mansion has
been retained in its restoration. A dramatic wrought-iron
staircase spirals up from the foyer. The ceiling of the main
dining room is a composite of 2,400 pieces of enameled and
inlaid wood. A set of stained-glass windows depicts British
barons signing Magna Carta, and two pairs of early 19th century Spanish cathedral doors open to one of the dining areas.

The cuisine does justice to its rich surroundings. Nouvelle
American dishes with a Southwestern flair are well-prepared
and   attractively   presented.   Service   is   polished   but

unpretentious. Elaborate brunches on Saturday and Sunday are popular with Dallasites as well as hotel guests. Breakfast and afternoon tea are served in the cheerful Promenade.

Located about five minutes from downtown Dallas, The Mansion is convenient to numerous business, cultural, and shopping areas. D/FW International Airport is a 30-minute drive. Valet parking costs $8.50. No self parking is available.

Omni Melrose Hotel
  3015 Oak Lawn
  Dallas, Texas 75219
  214/521-5151
  800/527-1488 US, 800/635-7673 TX
GENERAL MANAGER: Tom Gaskill
185 rooms
$110 single, $125 double; $125–$195 suites
American Express, Carte Blanche, Diners Club, MasterCard,
  Visa
Children welcome
No pets
Open year round

The Melrose is grandeur on a small scale. It's a visit to another era, with tall arched windows and stately white columns, lunch in the Library Restaurant, and afternoon lemonade and cookies. Situated in the Oak Lawn area north of downtown, the hotel is convenient to WestEnd Marketplace, the Arts District, Dallas Market Center, and the central business district. The Melrose opened in 1924 as an apartment hotel. Restored in late 1982, it's now a small luxury hotel with real warmth.

Since the guest rooms were once apartments, they are more spacious than average. All are truly charming, furnished with antique reproductions. Each room is different, both in size and decor. Four-poster beds, overstuffed chairs, and dressing tables with stools set the tone. Beds are dressed with comforters and bed-ruffles. The concierge level provides continental breakfast as well as turndown service with milk and cookies.

The Garden Court restaurant is splendid with its Art Deco setting. Its enticing menu features such dishes as roast breast of duck with pecan truffle stuffing, served with scallions and plum wine sauce. Or you can opt for Cajun seasoned trout, blackened and served with lime and fresh chive butter and New Orleans crawfish cream sauce. Entrees are priced from $15 to $24. The elegant but cozy Library restaurant, doubling as a piano bar, serves lunch and late evening fare.

Hotel parking is free. Complimentary transportation is available to Dallas Love Field.

Plaza of the Americas
650 N. Pearl Street
Dallas, Texas 75201
214/979-9000
800/225-5843
GENERAL MANAGER: W. Von Baumbach
445 units
$140–$175 single, $160–$195 double; $300–$375 suites
American Express, MasterCard, Visa; personal check
Children welcome
No pets
Open year round

Fourteen-story Plaza of the Americas, situated in downtown Dallas within the financial and arts district, is a hotel plus shops, restaurants, and offices. In contrast to hotels that are an adjunct to a mall or mixed use center, this center is an integral whole, with hotel restaurants situated across the atrium-centered mall from the lobby and guest rooms.

A hospitable staff, genteel environment, and rich mix of facilities make this hotel special. Step into the lobby to refinement. The furnishings are traditional but not opulent. The mood is tranquil. Past the front desk and into the atrium, there's a change of mood. An ice-skating arena is the focal point. Two levels of specialty shops circle round it.

Café Royal, open for lunch and dinner, is the fine restaurant, specializing in French nouvelle cuisine. Next door is casual Le Relais with all-day service including a Sunday brunch. Passarelle Bar overlooks the skating arena. Afternoon tea is served in the lobby.

Guest rooms are some of the nicest in the city, decorated with soothing colors, Oriental art, and modern furnishings. Rooms and baths are both spacious.

Services include a concierge, 24-hour room service, twice daily housekeeping, and complimentary limousine within downtown. The hotel's athletic club has tennis, racquetball, jogging, sauna, whirlpool, and Nautilus equipment (fees charged).

The Stoneleigh
2927 Maple Avenue
Dallas, Texas 75201
214/871-7111
800/255-9299 US, 800/336-4242 TX

GENERAL MANAGER: Gary Bruton
158 rooms
$75–$95 single, $89–$109 double; $115–$250 suites
American Express, Carte Blanche, Diners Club, MasterCard,
    Visa; personal check
Children welcome
Pets accepted
Open year round

Classical music plays in the background. Antique furniture, marble columns, and fresh flowers grace the lobby. The Stoneleigh is a gem, hidden away within a residential neighborhood on the edges of the prestigious Turtle Creek area. In 1923, the 11-story hotel opened as a hostelry of distinction. While its doors never closed in the decades that followed, the hotel suffered a definite decline. In 1986-87 the Stoneleigh was gloriously reborn, with refurbished interiors and a renewed emphasis on service.

Beautiful guest rooms are set with armoires, chintz-covered overstuffed chairs, matching drapes and bedspreads, and brass light fixtures. Rooms have different shapes and sizes and are individually decorated. Some suites have kitchens.

In the morning there's a paper at the door. Maid service is twice a day, and turndown service includes a cookie. Room service is available until 10 P.M., and a concierge meets special guest requests.

Ewald's restaurant serves all three meals. Seafood and continental dishes are the dinner highlights. Prices are from $13 to $22. The cozy Lion's Den Lounge serves cocktails, lunch, and appetizers.

Unusual for a hotel of its type, the Stoneleigh has excellent recreational facilities. The apartment building next door, also restored, is owned by the same family, and on its grounds there's a beautiful tree-shaded swimming pool and tennis courts hidden away in a garden-like setting. There's also a wonderful rock garden and lily pond—a tranquil spot seemingly far removed from the city beyond.

At this writing, the exterior of the hotel has not been renovated. Its somewhat shabby appearance belies the beauty within the hotel doors.

Stouffer Dallas Hotel
    2222 Stemmons Freeway
    Dallas, Texas 75207
    214/631-2222
    800/HOTELS-1
GENERAL MANAGER: Anthony Stewart-Moore

542 units
$104–$124 single, $119–$139 double
American Express, Carte Blanche, Diners Club, MasterCard,
   Visa; personal check
Children welcome
Pets with approval
Open year round

Stouffer Dallas is a sleek 30-story pink ellipse, distinctive in its architecture and its service. A wide spiral staircase winds from the center of the lobby to the mezzanine, flanked by a spectacular curved chandelier that is reportedly the longest chandelier in the world (140 feet long, with 7,500 Italian crystals). Works of art from the orient add aesthetic interest.

But distinctive architecture and art alone do not make a hotel great. Indeed, it's the people at Stouffer Dallas that make it a "Best Place to Stay." Throughout the hotel, the staff is hospitable and attentive, making you feel that they're glad you're there. Despite its near-500 guest rooms, the hotel has a feeling of intimacy. Public areas are small—almost residential in style. Bay Tree Restaurant is cozy and elegant. The Café is casual, serving all three meals.

Hotel guests are primarily business travelers. Dallas Market Center, the largest wholesale merchandise market in the world, is next door, with Infomart, the country's first information processing mart, as part of the complex. Downtown Dallas is to the southeast, about a five-minute drive.

Guest rooms are refreshingly different in their look, styled with an oriental theme. For example, one king-size room is decorated in jade green, accented with oriental prints and an apricot-colored lamp. Bathrooms, compartmental in design, are also well-decorated.

On top of the hotel there's an open-air swimming pool and a health club with exercise equipment, whirlpool, sauna, and steam room. Ask for a wake-up call and you get coffee and a morning paper delivered to your door. Parking is free—an extra not to be discounted in this metropolitan area.

The Westin Hotel Dallas
   13340 Dallas Parkway at LBJ Freeway
   Dallas, Texas 75240
   214/934-9494
   800/228-3000
GENERAL MANAGER: J. Pat Burton
434 rooms and suites
$120–$165 single, $145–$190 double; $260–$1,000 suites
American Express, Diners Club, Discover, MasterCard, Visa

Children welcome
Pets with approval
Open year round

The 21-story Westin Dallas sparkles with liveliness. It adjoins the Galleria in North Dallas, a sophisticated shopping and entertainment mall with Macy's, Saks Fifth Avenue, Marshall Field's, Tiffany's, and a host of specialty shops, restaurants, and cinemas. At the center of activity is an ice-skating rink, adding to the festive atmosphere.

Rooms are well-appointed and have traditional-style furniture. The Clark Hatch Health Club within the hotel is a real plus, with a one-half mile rooftop jogging track, exercise facilities, saunas, and massage. (Hotel guests pay less for usage of the facilities than the general public.) A small outdoor swimming pool is also within the hotel complex.

Zucchini's Sidewalk Café adjoining the Galleria is informal. The Grill, handsome in its dark woods and club-like atmosphere, serves fish and beef prepared on an open port broiler. Blom's, elegant in style, serves nouvelle American cuisine. Visions lounge has great rooftop views.

Services include a concierge and valet parking. Self parking is free.

EL PASO

El Paso Airport Hilton
  2027 Airway Boulevard
  El Paso, Texas 79925
  915/778-4241
  800/HILTONS
GENERAL MANAGER: Rich Cane
272 rooms
$69–$95 single, $79–$105 double
American Express, Carte Blanche, Diners Club, Discover,
  MasterCard, Shell, Visa; personal check
Children welcome
Pets with approval
Open year round

Soothing colors and plashing waters greet your senses when you enter the El Paso Airport Hilton. Comprising five buildings, most of which face onto the pool, it is an attractive, low-key place to stay.

El Paso International Airport is only 200 yards from the hotel's front door, making it very convenient when traveling by air. Flight crews account for a significant portion of the hotel's guest list.

Rooms are especially comfortable. Mexican fabrics and art create a friendly atmosphere. Beds have mirrored headboards. Over half of the guest rooms are suites, with a small parlor with refrigerator, sofabed, bedroom, two TVs, and two phones. A few suites have whirlpool tubs; others have wide screen TVs and whirlpool baths.

Magnim's Restaurant, fresh and airy, is delightfully arranged, with lots of intimate dining rooms. Steak, veal, chicken, and seafood dishes are priced from $11 to $16 on the dinner menu. If you would rather eat poolside (El Paso is dubbed Sun City, boasting sunshine almost every day of the year), you can pick up a poolside phone and order lunch.

The hotel staff is hospitable and helpful. Extra touches include free van transportation within a two-mile radius, non-smoking rooms, hot tub, and sauna.

El Paso Marriott
1600 Airway Boulevard
El Paso, Texas 79925
915/779-3300
800/228-9290
GENERAL MANAGER: Mike Shoffit
297 rooms
$86–$99 single, $98–$115 double (Monday to Thursday)
$59 double (Friday to Sunday) including full breakfast
American Express, Carte Blanche, Diners Club, Discover,
    MasterCard, Visa; personal check
Children welcome
Pets accepted
Open year round

Situated right at the entrance to El Paso International Airport, the El Paso Marriott exudes Texas-style friendliness. The outside of the six-story rectangular building is not distinctive, but its service and hospitality are. The fountain-centered lobby is fairly small. Off to one side, La Cascada restaurant has all-day service, specializing in South of the Border dishes. Dinner entrees are from $5 to $13. Chatfield's Restaurant, behind beveled glass doors, is more intimate. Entrees are priced from $14 to $18.

Guest rooms were completely refurbished in mid-1987. Sporting matched-fabric drapes and bedspreads, plush carpet, and local artwork, they are fresh and inviting. On the concierge level, continental breakfast and afternoon cocktails are served at no extra charge. "Executive" rooms are larger than standard, equipped with a work desk and two phones.

The indoor/outdoor pool is attractive, and an exercise area adjoins it. A putting green is just outside the back doors.

The hotel has non-smoking rooms, video check-out, handicapped facilities, and most notably, rooms specially designed for the hearing impaired. Parking is free.

The Westin Paso del Norte
101 S. El Paso Street
El Paso, Texas 79901
915/534-3024
800/228-3000
GENERAL MANAGER: Doug Hales
365 rooms
$69–$114 single, $79–$124 double; $195–$950 suites
American Express, Carte Blanche, Diners Club, Discover,
   MasterCard, Visa; personal check
Children welcome
Small pets accepted
Open year round

Staying at the Westin Paso del Norte puts you in touch with El Paso's history and at the same time immerses you in beauty. Built in 1912, the hotel is centered with an exquisite Tiffany stained-glass dome that sets a tone of grandeur. Apricot-colored scagliola columns and walls, crystal chandeliers, and tall arched windows combine to create a true aesthetic delight.

Tradition has it that Pancho Villa wined and dined at Paso del Norte between skirmishes across the border. The restored hotel, along with a new adjoining 17-story tower, opened in 1986. The environment is refined, the staff is Texas-friendly; together they equal a top-quality hotel.

Rooms are decorated in Queen Anne furniture, with two-poster beds and mirrored armoires (truly functional, for they replace closets). Baths are large and have lots of amenities.

Off the lobby beneath the famed dome is a massive bar matching the dome in circumference. It's a great place to soak up the ambience of the hotel. Adjoining it is The Dome Grill, decorated in soft yellows and elegant with its high ceiling, octagonal columns, and mirrored walls. Dinner entrees feature fresh seafood as well as beef. Appetizers are especially imaginative, with such choices as wild rice crêpes filled with julienne of duck. Entrees range from $10 to $15.

Café Rio has a Mexican theme, specializing in regional dishes. It opens onto a courtyard pre-dating the original hotel. A plaque commemorates the spot where "four men were shot dead in about five seconds" in 1881 when El Paso was "the wildest 24-hour town in the Old West."

The hotel has a swimming pool, whirlpool tub, steam bath, and exercise complex. Mexico is seven blocks away, an easy walk if you're so inclined. The city's civic center is next door. Parking at the hotel is free.

FORT WORTH

Hyatt Regency Fort Worth
815 Main Street
Fort Worth, Texas 76102
817/870-1234
800/228-9000
GENERAL MANAGER: Steven Millard
530 rooms
$95–$115 single, $105–$125 double
American Express, Carte Blanche, Diners Club, Discover,
    MasterCard, Visa; personal check
Children welcome
Pets accepted with deposit
Open year round

Today's Hyatt opened in 1921 as the Hotel Texas. Situated at one end of downtown Fort Worth, it reigned for years as the city's social center. Big dance bands played in its ballroom, and the rich and famous stayed in its guest rooms. One of its most noteworthy guests was President John F. Kennedy, who spent his last night in the hotel before going to Dallas.

In 1979 the Hotel Texas closed, re-opening in 1981 as Hyatt Regency Fort Worth. By then it had been named to the National Register of Historic Places. The 14-story hotel, rectangular in design, is built of red brick and terra cotta. While its exterior went virtually unchanged in Hyatt's renovation, the interior was gutted and is now totally modern. The lobby is soothing, with its waterfalls and reflecting ponds. There are two restaurants: the Café Centennial is casual and relaxed; Crystal Cactus is the fine dining room.

Guest rooms, traditionally furnished, are spacious. The concierge level has such extras as continental breakfast and afternoon hors d'oeuvres.

The health club in an adjacent office tower has a pool, sauna, and exercise room.

Self-service parking in an underground garage costs about $5. Valet parking is also available. Since the hotel is within a few blocks of I-30, it is easily accessible to all area attractions.

Stockyards Hotel
  Main and Exchange
  P.O. Box 4558
  Fort Worth, Texas 76106
  800/423-8471 US
  817/625-6427 TX
GENERAL MANAGER: Barbara Burch
52 rooms
$89 single, $99 double; $125–$300 suites
American Express, Diners Club, Discover, MasterCard, Visa;
  personal check
Children welcome
No pets
Open year round

The Stockyards Hotel lives up to the expectations of many first-timers to Texas, for they find at the hotel what they imagine the whole Lone Star State to be. Situated in the Stockyards National Historic District in a city affectionately referred to as "Cow Town," it is a slice of history, reflecting the world of affluent cattlemen of the early 1900s who dealt at the livestock markets just down the street.

Dating back to 1907, the hotel building was transformed in 1983 into a gem of a luxury hotel. Not intended as a historical reproduction, it is inventive and vivacious, capturing the spirit of the era it portrays.

Outside its doors, western-style shops, restaurants, and saloons line the streets in the area which was once the cattle center of the Southwest. Today it supports a thriving cattle-auction business.

The hotel lobby is decorated with leather sofas, carved-wooden chairs covered with animal hides, bronze sculptures, and western art. One of the most eye-catching pieces is a mirror framed in doeskin and topped with antlers.

Guest rooms are on the second and third floors. Take a choice of Indian, Western, mountain man, and Victorian decor—each beautifully executed. Decorating touches are indeed unique, such as deerskin headboards and ram's skull chandeliers. Victorian rooms are soft and feminine, with white wicker furniture, lace curtains, and fringed lamps. Rooms have king-size beds, baths with chain-pull

waterclosets, and wardrobes that conceal TVs. Nightly turndown service includes a gold nugget candy and a copy of a
cowboy's prayer on the pillow. ("Give me a saddle and blanket for a bed/Out where the stars shine and twinkle overhead...").

The Bonnie and Clyde Suite, reportedly frequented by the
infamous twosome, has appropriate memorabilia: Bonnie
Parker's gun, newspaper clippings of their escapades, and
vintage photographs. The Celebrity Suite (with a celebrity
price of $350) has a living area with fireplace, private deck
with hot tub, and a private entrance.

Downstairs in Booger Red's Saloon you can order a drink
while sitting on a saddle mounted on a bar stool. The adjacent
restaurant serves home-style cooking with a Southwestern flavor. Hotel parking, valet style, is $4.

The Worthington Hotel

200 Main Street
Fort Worth, Texas 76102
817/870-1000
800/433-5677 US, 800/772-5977 TX
GENERAL MANAGER: Robert Jamison
509 rooms and suites
$107–$118 single or double, $128–$650 suites
American Express, Carte Blanche, Diners Club, MasterCard,
   Visa
Children welcome
No pets
Open year round

A hospitable staff, good location, and excellent fitness club
combine to make The Worthington a top-notch hotel. It occupies three city blocks at one end of downtown Fort Worth,
across the street from Sundance Square, a turn-of-the-century
style shopping and entertainment area. For a romantic tour of
the city, you can climb into a horse-drawn carriage right at the
hotel's doors. Area attractions as well as numerous business
addresses are a short drive away.

The Worthington's fitness club has an indoor pool, outdoor
tennis courts, sundeck, sauna, whirlpool, and exercise room
with free weights, Lifecycles, and treadmills. The club has a
welcoming tone, from a sociable staff to such extras as a comfortable sitting area with magazines and newspapers, baskets
of fruit, and a big screen TV. Use of the pool and whirlpool is
free to hotel guests; the rest of the facilities can be used for a
daily fee of $5.40 per guest room.

Dining gets lots of emphasis at this hotel. In addition to elegant Reflections restaurant and the casual Brasserie, it operates Winfield's '08 family restaurant and the Houston Street Bakery, both across the street, and Firehall Marketplace Deli in Sundance Square. The room service menu is several cuts above average, featuring delectables from the bakery as well as the hotel's own kitchen. Afternoon tea and lavish Sunday brunches are Worthington traditions.

The Worthington is distinctively contemporary in design. Its marble lobby is softened by gentle waterfalls and lots of greenery. Guest rooms are modern and sleek, with especially comfortable sitting areas. Prints in the rooms are from original works in Fort Worth museums. For an extra-special splurge, terrace suites have expansive balconies overlooking the city, separate living and bedrooms, and lots of amenities.

Throughout the hotel, the staff is Texas-friendly. A concierge is on duty for special requests. Valet parking costs $5.40; self parking is $3.75.

HOUSTON

Four Seasons Hotel–Houston Center
1300 Lamar Street
Houston, Texas 77010
713/650-1300
800/332-3442
GENERAL MANAGER: Wolf Hengst
300 rooms and suites
$115–$155 single, $140–$180 double; $325–$600 suites
American Express, Carte Blanche, Diners Club, MasterCard, Visa
Children welcome
Pets accepted with $50 deposit
Open year round

For the traveler who values quality and aesthetics, the Four Seasons Houston is worth a special trip. Opened in 1982 in downtown Houston, it is truly grand—a combination of classic European style and Texas hospitality. The 30-story hotel occupies a city block in the downtown business district. It's connected by skywalk to The Park, a three-tier shopping mall with boutiques and restaurants. The George R. Brown Convention Center, a state-of-the-art facility which opened in late 1987, is two blocks away.

A grand staircase spirals up from the hotel's lobby, joining three floors of public space. On the fourth floor is a garden with one of the most attractive swimming pools in the city. A whirlpool, sauna, and game room are adjacent. Guests also have use of the Houston Center Athletic Club (accessible by indoor walkway) with racquet sports, jogging, and exercise equipment.

Guest rooms, decorated with custom-designed furniture, have a residential feel. Bathrooms are stylishly decorated. All of the rooms are spacious and luxurious, but the ones designated as "Four Seasons" are especially so. The sleeping area is in an alcove, and there's a separate sitting area.

Service is more than perfunctory at the Four Seasons. Bed turndown, 24-hour room service, complimentary shoe shines, and one-hour pressing service are all standard. There's also free limousine service within downtown (even on weekends). Most important, it's all performed with professionalism.

Maison de Ville is an outstanding restaurant, headed by a bright young chef bursting with creativity. Entree choices for the evening might include broiled red snapper with a corn and truffle risotto, hickory crisp duck and orzo-black bean salad, and charbroiled veal chop with country ham and mozzarella cheese. Entrees range from $13 to $18. The Terrace Café serves lighter fare.

Hotel Inter-Continental Houston
At the Galleria
5150 Westheimer
Houston, Texas 77056
713/961-1500
800/327-0200
GENERAL MANAGER: John Sutherland
518 rooms and suites
$120–$150 single, $140–$170 double; $255–$1,000 suites
American Express, Carte Blanche, Diners Club, EnRoute,
   JCB, MasterCard, Visa
Children welcome
No pets
Open year round

Just across the street from the Galleria shopping mall is a sophisticated hotel with international flair. One of 95 Inter-Continental Hotels in 45 countries, it reflects its international heritage simultaneously with seeming at home in this Texas city.

The lobby of the 23-story hotel gleams with marble, brass, and crystal. Chic shops line a side hallway. Les Continents restaurant serves classic continental cuisine; in its dining rooms decorated with crystal chandeliers, peach damask-covered walls, and fresh flowers, you dine on Rosenthal china. Casual dining is in The Brasserie, decorated with rare pre-Columbian artifacts. In contrast, Pete's Pub has a Roaring Twenties speak-easy theme.

Guest rooms are among the most tastefully decorated and comfortably appointed in the Southwest. Art was specially commissioned from Houston artists. Furniture is refined. There's a sitting area with small couch, armoire with TV, and a convenient desk. Bathrooms have phones, mini-TVs, and built-in hair dryers. Terry cloth robes are a nice added touch.

The hotel's recreational facilities and health club are a real plus. The fifth-floor indoor/outdoor pool, although small, is a convivial gathering spot; a food-service bar is adjacent to the indoor portion. The health club has racquetball and tennis ($3 per hour), aerobics ($5), co-ed sauna and steam room ($5), and extensive workout equipment ($10 daily).

The Inter-Continental has a concierge, round-the-clock room service, and valet parking. Self parking is free.

Inn on the Park
(A Four Seasons Hotel)
Four Riverway
Houston, Texas 77056
713/871-8181
800/332-3442
GENERAL MANAGER: Peter O'Colmain
383 rooms and suites
$120–$500 single; $135–$500 double; $400–$500 suites
Weekend packages
American Express, Diners Club, MasterCard, Visa; personal
   check
Children welcome
Small pets (under 10 lbs.)
Open year round

A tranquil oasis within the bustling city, Inn on the Park is only a few minutes' drive from the Galleria and numerous business addresses. Its park-like setting, nestled among gleaming office towers, is unexpected. The wooded banks of Buffalo Bayou are on the eastern perimeter, and there's a reflection pond surrounded by weeping willows to the west.

Just inside the hotel's doors, the Palm Court Lounge sets the tone. A lush tropical garden, it soothes with a gentle waterfall, soft piano music, and views of the hotel's pools and fountains. The colors of the garden are repeated throughout the hotel, with a profusion of green marble in the lobby accented with Asian screens and modern paintings. Indeed, the entire hotel has a garden-like atmosphere, bringing the outdoors inside with lush plants, while affording expansive views of the landscaped grounds.

Guest rooms have a view of the grounds or the bayou. Furnishings are modern in design, luxurious in quality. All rooms have overstuffed chairs, remote control TVs, stocked minibars, and bath telephones. Terry robes add to the feeling of luxury.

A good choice for a weekend retreat as well a city stop, Inn on the Park is geared to recreation. Its two swimming pools are heated (one has underwater music), four tennis courts are on top of the parking garage, and bikes are available for rent, with trails easily accessible in nearby Memorial Park. The health club has extensive exercise equipment and a whirlpool.

Dining choices are all good. Café on the Green, open from 6:30 a.m. to midnight, has a sumptuous Sunday brunch. La Reserve is the gourmet restaurant, serving French, American, and regional dishes. Downstairs is the Black Swan, a pub named in honor of the hotel's mascots. Offering over 100 brands of beer, it serves light evening fare and has live entertainment. Afternoon tea, Saturday night "breakfast," and Viennese dessert bars are all part of Inn on the Park's bill of fare.

Parking is free, unless you opt for valet service. Free limousine service is available to the Galleria and to a shuttle terminal where you can catch a bus to either Intercontinental or Hobby Airports. Downtown Houston is about ten miles east of the hotel.

About Inn on the Park's mascots: Two beautiful black swans glide across the pond, adding to the tranquil mood. But if you get too close, their docile nature disappears and you may find yourself running from an irate swan. Staffers explain that the birds, prolific producers of offspring, are suspicious of intruders since fledgling swans are often given up for adoption.

La Colombe D'Or
3410 Montrose Boulevard
Houston, Texas 77071
713/524-7999
INNKEEPER/PROPRIETOR: Steve Zimmerman
6 suites
$150–$400 single or double including continental breakfast
American Express, MasterCard, Visa; personal check
Children welcome

No pets
Open year round

A stay at La Colombe d'Or combines the style of a country manor with the convenience of a city hotel. Small and intimate, it's also elegant and grand. Once it was the home of a wealthy Houston family; today it plays host to guests from around the world.

Here you are treated as a valued house guest. Personalized service is the pervading tone. Expect a bottle of French wine and a basket of fruit when you arrive. Luxuriate in a breakfast of fresh croissants and fruit served in your suite each morning.

The three-story yellow brick inn has a welcoming front porch, residential style lobby decorated in treasures from Europe, a cozy bar, and a library for cognac-sipping. While some of the architectural components come from around the world, the mahogany staircase and the decorated ceilings are original to the 1920s home.

Five guest suites are on the second floor. Each is unique—artfully decorated and unusual in use of space. All have a king-size bed, sitting area, separate dining room, and bath. Phones, clock radios, and ceiling fans are in each. The Renoir, although the smallest, is a personal favorite. Its dining area is separated from the bedroom with interior columns and draped fabric, yet the theme is oriental, with a carved screen for a headboard, oriental rugs and chest, and a glass-topped dining table. The Cezanne, once a master bedroom, is boldly decorated in bright green and orange. The Degas is contemporary, highlighted by a bed with a glass headboard, and an airy dining room.

The third-floor penthouse is even larger. Its antique furnishings in the bedroom, dining area, and sitting room are no surprise; the luxurious bathroom with an elevated whirlpool tub is.

Downstairs there's a fine restaurant, popular with locals and inn guests alike. Decorated in soft pinks and mauves, it's sophisticated and grand on a small scale. With an emphasis on regional products and fresh herbs, the cuisine is French, inspired by the Provence region. (Open for lunch Monday through Friday, dinner Monday through Saturday).

La Colombe d'Or is about a five-minute drive from downtown and within easy access of the Galleria, Texas Medical Center, Alley Theater, Wortham Center, and Jones Hall. The University of St. Thomas is a block away.

The Lancaster Hotel
  701 Texas Avenue
  Houston, Texas 77002
  713/228-9500
  800/231-0336 US, 800/392-5566 TX
  GENERAL MANAGER: Roberta Sroka
  93 rooms
  $130–$155 single, $155–$180 double; $275–$725 suites
  American Express, Carte Blanche, Diners Club, MasterCard,
    Visa
  Children welcome
  No pets
  Open year round

In the midst of downtown's cultural district, The Lancaster is a small elegant hotel with European style a la Texas. Its service is spelled with a capital "S". Its look is polished and refined. The lobby, like the rest of the hotel, is intimate, more akin to a parlor than a standard hotel lobby. Handsome elevators, decorated with mirrors and polished wood, take guests to rooms on the second through tenth floors. No more than nine rooms are on each floor, adding to the sense of intimacy.

In truth, the hotel hasn't always been so fine. Built in 1926 as the Auditorium Hotel, it has a colorful and varied history. Gene Autry once rode his horse into the Stage Canteen in the basement. Symphony musicians and circus performers, wrestlers and ice skaters stayed at the Auditorium. So did young Clark Gable, who had to leave his trunk as ransom until he could pay his bill.

In 1982 the building was transformed into a gem of a luxury hotel. Guest rooms, intimate in size as well as styling, have a British theme, with imported English fabrics and wallpapers, prints depicting the English countryside, overstuffed chairs with foot stools, and carved poster beds. Bathrooms are sleek with their white marble and brass.

Multiple phones, remote-control TVs in armoires, terry robes, and such unexpected extras as umbrellas enhance the feeling of luxury. Expect a newspaper at your door in the morning and bed turndown at night.

Club-like Lancaster Grill serves breakfast, lunch, dinner, and late-night fare. For recreation and fitness, hotel guests have privileges at the Texas Club one-and-a-half blocks away. Facilities include a rooftop pool, Nautilus equipment, squash and racquetball courts, and a gym.

If the performing arts are high on your list of things to do in the city, there's hardly a better place to stay in Houston. The

Lancaster is next door to the Alley Theater, across the street from Jones Hall, one block from Wortham Center, and within a few blocks of the Music Hall.

The hotel has a concierge, complimentary downtown limousine service, and 24-hour room service. Of special interest to business travelers, portable cellular telephones are available for rent.

The Remington on Post Oak Park
1919 Briar Oaks Lane
Houston, Texas 77027
713/840-7600
GENERAL MANAGER: Alexander de Toth
248 rooms and suites
$155–$280 single, $185–$280 double; $430–$1,500 suites
American Express, Carte Blanche, Diners Club, Discover,
  MasterCard, Visa
Children welcome
Pets with approval
Open year round

The Remington is a gleaming palace, combining sophistication with hospitality. Despite its size, it has a residential feel. No large lobby yawns at its front door; instead, guests sign in at an unimposing hall desk. Public space is high on aesthetics—skylighted rotundas, alcoves with comfortable chairs, arched corridors with greenery.

Best of all, the hotel has a service attitude to match its classic architecture. Guests are treated as honored visitors. Personal preferences are noted and attended to, and staff members call guests by name. Valet parking, round-the-clock room service, and complimentary transportation to nearby shopping are all available.

The Living Room is the setting for tea, served to the strains of harp music. Nearby is the handsome bar, resembling an English men's club with couches and a fireplace.

Guest rooms are pleasing to the eye as well as comfortable. Deluxe rooms are especially large, with bay windows and separate sitting areas. Baths are warmly decorated with colored marble vanity tops and brass fixtures. Suites have canopied beds, expansive wet bars with refrigerators, and large bathtubs with Jacuzzi jets. Terry cloth robes, a choice of goosedown or synthetic-filled pillows, three phones, and remote controlled TVs are appreciated amenities. When you walk into your room you feel expected—the thermostat is set, lights are on, and soft music is playing.

The second-floor swimming pool is a tranquil hideaway. While the pool itself is small, the setting is garden-like, far removed from the city streets beyond. Guests also have access to the fitness and recreational facilities at the nearby Houstonian Hotel. The Remington provides free transportation.

Dining is a stellar event. Choose from the formal Garden Room, airy Conservatory, and the handsome Bar and Grill. Cuisine is new American; service is impeccable. The kitchen staff does everything from scratch, not just bread-baking but sausage-making and salmon-smoking.

Located within Post Oak Park off Loop 610 West, the Remington is a few blocks from the Galleria and is easily accessible to most business addresses, including downtown. Overnight valet parking costs $9.

The Warwick
  5701 Main Street
  Houston, Texas 77005
  713/526-1991
  800/231-5701
GENERAL MANAGER: Heinrich Lutjens
300 rooms and suites
$90 single, $110 double; $125–$1,000 suites
American Express, MasterCard, Visa
Children welcome
No pets
Open year round

In a fast-paced city where change is the norm, The Warwick is a welcome link to the past. Not that the hotel itself is particularly old: True, the original structure was built in 1926, but its opulence only dates back to 1964 when the hotel was totally renovated and refurbished by oilman John Mecom, Sr.

That refurbishment is the reason for the Warwick's historic character. The furnishings are far from ordinary. A virtual museum of European treasures, they include ornate pilasters and exquisite paneling from the Murat palace in France, 18th-century statues from Italy, Baccarat crystal chandeliers, an Aubusson tapestry, and a profusion of art works—all collected by the Mecoms.

As an oilman, John Mecom was a visionary, striking oil where others swore there could be none. He also had an eye for beauty. Mecom's business took him around the world, and wherever he went he added to his collection. While overseeing the renovation of the hotel (its purchase was sentimental as well as an investment, for Mecom had stayed in the hotel with his mother as a youth, and she had later taken an apartment there when he was a student at nearby Rice University), Mecom instructed his wife to use any color she wanted—as long as it was blue. Why blue? "Green is beautiful too," he said. "But you look down at the grass to see green. You look up to see blue."

Situated in Houston's museum district—within a few blocks of the Museum of Fine Arts, Cullen Sculpture Garden, Contemporary Arts Museum, and the Museum of Natural Science—the Warwick is surrounded by beauty. Just outside its doors is one of Houston's favorite landmarks, the Mecom Fountains.

In recent years the hotel has gone from having a rich mature look to getting a little worn around the edges, in contrast to the burst of sparkling luxury hotels that opened in Houston in the early 1980s. And yet the Warwick is still a very elegant lodging. At this writing, the King and Queen of Spain, accompanied by their retinue, had just occupied several floors of the hotel including the Presidential and John Mecom suites. The list of notables who have stayed at the hotel is truly impressive, including royalty, heads of state, entertainment stars, and an array of other luminaries.

Guest rooms at the Warwick vary in size and decor. Most are furnished in the style of Louis XV, with custom designed furniture, marble-topped dressing tables, and a choice of king or twin beds. Bathrooms have phones. Lanai rooms, situated in a separate wing of the hotel, face the swimming pool and its terrace. Having a curved shape to allow maximum exposure to the exterior view, their configuration adds interest as well as convenience. All have two baths and a balcony or patio, with easy access to the men's and women's saunas. One of the best room choices is a junior suite; some have full kitchens. Most of the hotel's 50 suites are one-of-a-kind. Some have outstanding views of the city to the south (Bob Hope once labeled this view as the prettiest sight in the world).

Staying at the Warwick enables you to dine at the 12th-floor Warwick Club, open only to members and hotel guests. Here is where Houston's "Old Guard" gathers. The setting is superb, a combination of decor (European antiques and a blue-on-blue color scheme) and the southerly view. Downstairs the Hunt Room is handsome with its rich woods and fireside setting. Its menu has depth and excitement. Entrees range from $15 to $20. The informal Café Vienna serves breakfast and lunch.

Hotel services include valet parking, courtesy limousine to major points in the city during the business week, bed turn-down, and a multi-lingual concierge.

The Westin Galleria and Westin Oaks

Westin Galleria: 5060 W. Alabama
713/960-8100
Westin Oaks: 5011 Westheimer
713/623-4300
Houston, Texas 77056
800/228-3000
GENERAL MANAGER: Bob Hawes
491 rooms in Galleria, 406 rooms in Oaks
$130–$210, $160–$240; $350–$1000 suites
Weekend: 50% of weekday rates
American Express, Carte Blanche, Diners Club, Discover,
  MasterCard, Visa
Children welcome
Small pets on leash
Open year round

Houston has not one but two Westins, each offering luxury coupled with vivacity. Both are part of a "city under glass," the Galleria Mall inspired by Galleria Vittorio Emanuele in Milan, Italy. Houston's Galleria has more than 300 shops and restaurants, an Olympic-size ice-skating rink, and several cinemas as well as two excellent hotels.

The 21-story Westin Oaks was the first of the two, opening with the enclosed mall in 1971. The 24-story Westin Galleria opened in 1977. Situated about a five-minute walk from each other, the two complement each other in style and mood.

Guest rooms, furnished in contemporary decor, are large and well-appointed. Each has a stocked bar and refrigerator, multiple phones, and walk-out balconies. Rooms have either one king- or two queen-size beds. Cable TV and movies are complimentary.

For dining and entertainment, there's a total of six choices. (Guests at either hotel can charge services to their room at the sister hotel.) Delmonico's at Westin Galleria is the fine dining restaurant. Shucker's Sports Bar at the Oaks serves seafood and casual fare. Both hotels have an informal restaurant. Annabelle's at the Oaks and The Roof at the Galleria have live entertainment and happy hour buffets.

For recreation, you can swim at either hotel, play tennis at the Galleria, and jog at the Oaks. Guests also have use of the University Club within the mall, with ten indoor tennis courts

($3 to $8 per hour), tennis ball machine, whirlpools and saunas, and massage.

Hotel services include a concierge, 24-hour room service, express check-in and -out, and valet parking. Self parking is free.

Wyndham Hotel Greenspoint

12400 Greenspoint Drive
Houston, Texas 77060
713/875-2222
800/822-4200
GENERAL MANAGER: Patrick Lupsha
473 rooms
$81–$115 single, $91–$125 double; $150–$375 suites
American Express, Diners Club, MasterCard, Visa
Children welcome
No pets
Open year round

Ten minutes west of Houston Intercontinental Airport and 20 minutes north of downtown Houston, Wyndham Greenspoint is Houston's best near-airport hotel. Greenspoint Mall with 150 stores is right across the street. I-45 is a few blocks away.

Opened in late 1984, the hotel has eye-catching architecture—a marked departure from standard glass towers. On the outside, it has sharp-peaked dormers roofed in green-tinged copper, truly distinctive on the horizon. The front doors open onto a mammoth atrium lobby built to resemble a European urban marketplace, with street lanterns, trees, and marble floors. The lobby serves as the hotel's center of activity, and it's set with numerous areas for socializing, including a sunken lounge. As you might expect, there's a "sidewalk Café" (open round the clock); unexpectedly, there's an elegant Northern Italian restaurant off to one side.

Rooms are more akin to suites than to standard hotel rooms. Decorated in soft green, they're convenient and comfortable, with remote control TVs and clock radios.

The outdoor pool is large and attractive. Hotel guests also have use of the Greenspoint Club, a private membership health club in an adjoining building. Facilities include racquetball and squash courts, a basketball court, indoor jogging track, Nautilus equipment, saunas and whirlpool ($10 charge per day).

Hotel services include free transportation between the hotel and the airport, a concierge, and 24-hour room service. Covered parking is free.

OKLAHOMA CITY

Oklahoma City Marriott
  3233 Northwest Expressway
  Oklahoma City, Oklahoma 73112
  405/842-6633
  800/228-9290
GENERAL MANAGER: Ned Shavely
354 rooms
$93–$99 single, $105–$111 double; $175–$350 suites
American Express, Carte Blanche, Discover, MasterCard,
  Visa; personal check
Children welcome
Small pets accepted
Open year round

  The Marriott is conveniently located, has attractive guest rooms, and offers good recreational facilities. Located northwest of downtown off Northwest Freeway, it's across the street from the Baptist Medical Center. Area attractions and business centers are easily accessible.

  Guest rooms, traditionally styled, are comfortably furnished and well-decorated. Executive suites are especially nice, with large sitting areas, private balconies, and bedrooms sectioned off with curtains. A concierge floor offers special services, continental breakfast, and afternoon hors d'oeuvres.

  The indoor/outdoor pool is larger and more appealing than many versions of this combo. The inside portion functions as a social center. Board games and FM cassette headsets are available for the asking. There's also an exercise room, adjoined by a sauna and locker rooms.

  Beechwood's Restaurant is popular, well suited for families. Russell's Lounge is light and airy—a pleasant, convivial spot. Hotel parking is free.

The Waterford Hotel
  6300 Waterford Boulevard
  Oklahoma City, Oklahoma 73118
  405/848-4782
  800/992-2009 US, 800/522-9440 OK
GENERAL MANAGER: J. Randal Kolls
197 rooms
$79–$104 single, $89–$113 double; $99–$230 suites
American Express, Carte Blanche, Diners Club, MasterCard,
  Visa; personal check

Children welcome
No pets
Open year round

The Waterford is a class act—an elegant hotel with all the attributes that term connotes. Guests sit at a desk to check in. A concierge is ready to meet special requests. There's a fine restaurant down the hall, plus dining in a veranda café. Set in one of the finest residential neighborhoods in the city, it's eight miles northwest of downtown.

Rooms are well-appointed, set with a sofa, writing desk, and armoire with concealed TV. You can almost imagine that you've stepped into a fine home instead of a hotel. Baths are decorated with Italian marble and have separate dressing areas. In suites, the sleeping and parlor areas are completely separated, creating a sense of spaciousness. There's a concierge floor with such extras as morning coffee or tea delivered to the room along with a newspaper.

Some rooms overlook the landscaped swimming pool (unusually attractive for an in-city hotel). The fitness center has a great whirlpool, locker rooms with saunas, and excellent exercise equipment. There are also two hard-surface tennis courts and two squash courts. All of the recreational facilities are used by members of an associated athletic club as well as by hotel guests.

The Waterford Restaurant, with entrees from $13 to $24, serves such dishes as grilled salmon with ginger cream sauce, or filet of sauteed veal loin in a white wine cream with golden chanterelles and angel hair pasta.

SAN ANTONIO

The Fairmount Hotel
401 S. Alamo Street
San Antonio, TX 78205
512/224-8800
800/642-3363 US, 800/642-3339 TX
MANAGING DIRECTOR: J.P Horst
37 rooms and suites
$95–$145 single, $115–$165 double; $200–$325 suites
American Express, Diners Club, MasterCard, Visa
Children welcome
Pets with approval
Open year round

If you like class and can afford to pay for it, then pack your bags and head for The Fairmount. To label this gem of a hotel as "service-oriented" is an understatement. From the minute you drive up until you leave, you're pampered by a warm, friendly staff. The only bad thing about staying at The Fairmount is driving away.

Built in 1906 in Italianate Victorian style, the hotel operated until the 1960s and then was boarded up. In 1985 it made headlines when it was moved six blocks, becoming the largest building ever moved in one piece. The new owners transformed the structure into a luxury hotel, constructing an addition that complements the original building.

The Fairmount is next to San Antonio's La Villita Historic District, a picturesque assortment of shops and restaurants within a few steps of the famed Riverwalk. Across the street from the hotel are Hemisfair Plaza and the city convention center.

Guests have a choice of 20 rooms and 17 suites, each with a different design. Common to all are high ceilings, reproduction antiques, bleached wood floors and muted colors. Bathrooms are appointed with Italian marble and solid brass. Luxury abounds: terry robes, bath telephones, make-up mirrors, remote control TVs, twice daily maid service, bed turndown, complimentary shoe shine.

Some rooms are designed for families, with two queen-size beds. (Children get milk and cookies.) Veranda suites have separate living and sleeping areas, canopy beds, stereos, and video cassette players. There's a library of free movies downstairs, including a tape of The Fairmount's move.) The master suite is the largest, with all of the features of Veranda suites plus a whirlpool tub, wet bar, and separate dressing area.

Wherever you're staying, or even if you're just passing through San Antonio, treat yourself to a meal at Polo's at The Fairmount. Chef Bruce Auden is a master. His menus are intriguing, his presentations are works of art, and the food is as delectable as it sounds. The menu changes continually, but on an evening in September here were some of the choices: grilled venison and wild sheep on guajillo pepper sauce, grilled redfish with fiesta lime butter and crab, stir-fry shrimp and scallops on tomato mint vinaigrette, charred filet of Chianina beef with sweet shallot sauce.   Starters are exotic; desserts are memorable. Entrees range from $7 to $24.

La Mansion Del Rio
112 College Street
San Antonio, Texas 78205
512/225-2581
800/531-7208 US, 800/292-7300 TX
GENERAL MANAGER: Mark Fallon
337 rooms
$95–$150 single, $115–$170 double; $275–$1,100 suites
American Express, Discover, MasterCard, Visa
Children welcome
Small pets accepted
Open year round

At the heart of this popular tourist city is the Riverwalk, a gentle canal-like river flanked by shops and restaurants. The most charming hotel along its expanse is La Mansion del Rio, a quiet retreat that is within a few steps of the Riverwalk's vivacity.

The Spanish colonial-style building dates back to 1852 when it opened as a Catholic school. A hotel since 1968, La Mansion is a composite of classical arches, wrought iron, and red tile. At its cedar-shaded Riverwalk entrance, a profusion of greenery cascades from stone walls, and an arched bridge spans the waterway. A rambling hotel due to sections added over its years as a school, La Mansion has guest rooms spread over seven floors. Many overlook the river. Others open onto two inner courtyards, one with an attractive swimming pool.

Spanish in decor, rooms have luxuriant bedspreads and plush carpets. All have beamed ceilings. While some are rather small, all are attractive and comfortable. Every room has a dry bar with refrigerator and a remote-control TV enclosed in an armoire.

Restaurante Capistrano serves Southwestern cuisine, with an emphasis on authentic Mexican dishes. Romantic Las Canarias overlooking the river is the fine-cuisine restaurant. Paella, poached salmon, mesquite smoked steak, and veal scaloppini are typical entrees, ranging from $16 to $20.

Hotel guests have privileges at two health clubs. One has tennis courts, an indoor/outdoor pool, and exercise equipment (no fees for usage); the second has racquetball, squash, handball, Nautilus equipment, and an indoor pool ($10 fee). Hotel services include a concierge, 24-hour room service, and valet parking.

San Antonio is a romantic city with a Spanish heritage. La Mansion del Rio is the essence of the city, enveloping you in its charm.

Menger Hotel

204 Alamo Plaza
San Antonio, Texas 78205
512/223-4361
800/345-9285
GENERAL MANAGER: Art Abbott
383 rooms
$55–$70 single, $68–$90 double; $95–$275 suites
American Express, Carte Blanche, Discover, MasterCard,
   Visa; personal check
Children welcome
Small pets accepted
Open year round

The Menger claims to be the oldest continuously operating hotel west of the Mississippi. When German brewer William Menger built it in 1859, he had a practical purpose in mind: patrons of his brewery frequently needed a place to spend the night, and he was tired of converting bar tables into beds. San Antonio was still a frontier town (the Battle of the Alamo had taken place only 23 years earlier). William Menger added a strong dose of refinement to the town, building a fine lodging with beautiful furnishings. Throughout the years the Menger has played a part in Texas history. During the Spanish American War, Teddy Roosevelt recruited his Rough Riders in the hotel's bar. The lodging was long popular with cattlemen visiting San Antonio. Today, with its centralized location and moderate prices, it attracts families and other vacationers as well as business travelers.

The Menger is a hotel that continues to grow, sprawling out from its original design to include a motor inn. In early 1988, 33 rooms were added as part of a major refurbishment undertaken in conjunction with the creation of a new section of the city's Riverwalk, joining the Menger to the new Rivercenter Mall.

Despite these new additions, there's a strong sense of history about the hotel. The rotunda is spectacular, with a stained-glass ceiling and two oval-shaped mezzanine floors overlooking the antique-studded lobby.

If you yearn to savor history, opt for a one-of-a-kind suite such as the Devon Cattle or the King Suite. Both have a large carved bed with canopy and a parlor with antique furnishings. The Roy Rogers Room was decorated to accommodate Roy and Dale when they visited HemisFair in 1968. All of these suites open onto the mezzanines. Other lodging choices include the new guest rooms (top-of-the-line), standard rooms (completely refurbished in late '87), and motel rooms (fairly ordinary).

The hotel's pool, surrounded by lush landscaping, is especially attractive. The Patio restaurant serves lunch and dinner; the coffee shop serves breakfast and lunch. The Menger Bar, decorated with photos of Teddy Roosevelt and the hotel's early years, is well worth a visit.

Plaza San Antonio

555 S. Alamo
San Antonio, Texas 78205
512/229-1000
800/421-1172
GENERAL MANAGER: R. Eric Beltelheim
250 rooms and suites
$97–$127 single, $117–$147 double; $250–$470 suites
American Express, Carte Blanche, Diners Club, MasterCard,
   Visa
Children welcome
Pets accepted
Open year round

The Plaza San Antonio is a hacienda hideaway, only a few blocks from the Riverwalk and yet far removed in its tranquility. Here you can get to a multitude of attractions within minutes, retreating to the hotel's grounds in between sightseeing jaunts. A swimming pool surrounded by gardens, two tennis courts, a croquet lawn, and a health club are all on the premises.

The mood is Old Mexico—perfect for enjoying San Antonio with its missions, Mexican markets, and La Villita Historic District. The entrance to the lobby is through a small courtyard centered with a fountain. Also on the grounds are remnants of early Texas. Three historic cottages, each representative of a different style of architecture, serve a practical purpose as well as add character. Both the Alsace-Lorraine bungalow and the Victorian cottage are used for private groups. The restored German-style house is the site of the health club, with sauna and exercise facilities. Next door to the main hotel is the 19th-century school built for children of the German settlers. Today it's the hotel's conference center.

Guest rooms are arranged in two connecting wings of the six-story hotel. Many have balconies overlooking the lush gardens below. Junior suites have seating areas with TVs and an additional TV in the bedroom. Bathrobes, hairdryers, and cable TV with a movie channel are in every room.

Staffed by a concierge, the hotel has 24-hour room service and lots of special touches, from complimentary shoe shines to bed turndown. Bicycles are available free of charge. Complimentary limousine service is offered on weekdays.

The Anaqua Restaurant serves regional cuisine, and The Arbor (outdoor setting) and Palm Terrace restaurants have lighter fare.

Radisson Gunter Hotel
205 E. Houston Street
San Antonio, Texas 78205-1897
512/227-3241
800/228-9822
GENERAL MANAGER: E.J. Schanfarber
326 rooms and suites
$79–$99 single, $89–$109 double; $100–$575 suites
American Express, Diners Club, Discover, MasterCard, Visa;
     personal check
Children welcome
No pets
Open year round

San Antonio is a city that values history. The Gunter, built in 1909, is a classic, mirroring an earlier, grander era. Its expansive lobby, set with columns and chandeliers, is topped with a molded ceiling. Throughout the 12-story hotel are marble floors and walnut paneling dating back to the days when the Gunter was the largest building in San Antonio. Rooms are decorated with Queen Anne furniture and matching drapes and bedspreads. There's a look of subdued plushness here, accented with tradition—from high ceilings to heavy wooden doors.

Unlike some historic hotels, the modern-day bent toward recreation and fitness is well recognized. The second floor hide-away swimming pool, and an exercise room with Nautilus equipment, add just the right touch of modernity.

Just off the lobby, Café Suisse serves European fare in a convivial setting, decorated with rich woods and soft lighting. Entrees such as lamb, duck, and prime rib range from $16 to

$21. Muldoon's is a multi-level bar, adjoined by a glass enclosed terrace.

Service is important at the Gunter—valet parking, round-the-clock room service, bed turndown. Two floors function as concierge levels. Shops within the hotel include a deli, barber shop, and upscale gift shop. Parking is in an adjacent garage.

The Gunter is in the heart of downtown, one block from the Riverwalk and five blocks from the Alamo.

St. Anthony Inter-Continental
300 E. Travis
San Antonio, Texas 78205
512/227-4392
800/327-0200
GENERAL MANAGER: R. Schuster
362 rooms
$85–$115 single, $85–$130 double; $175–$225 suites
American Express, Carte Blanche, Diners Club, MasterCard, Visa
Children welcome
Pets with approval
Open year round

St. Anthony Inter-Continental is a grand lady, reflecting the sumptuous grace of an earlier age. Built in 1909, the hotel is European in design and decoration yet pure Texan in tradition and hospitality.

Owned and managed by Inter-Continental Hotels since 1983, it is one of nearly a dozen Inter-Continentals in the U.S.

For many years the St. Anthony was owned by a wealthy railroad builder and rancher, becoming a showcase for the art objects that he collected in his travels. Today its public areas are a treasure house of fine furnishings.

The center of attention is a rosewood-and-bronze Steinway piano dating from the czarist Russian embassy in Paris. French Regency couches, 19th-century Chinese urns, and oil paintings decorate the lobby. Empire chandeliers hang from the coffered ceiling, Venetian mosaic tiles cover the floors, and puffed Austrian curtains frame the arched windows.

Take time to see the Anacacho Ballroom where Prince Ranier and the late Princess Grace were once entertained. The Navarro Room has a huge mural-like painting of cowboys on the range (as earlier stated, despite its Old World grandeur, this is a Texas hotel at heart).

Peacock Alley, a local meeting place since the 1930s, overlooks Travis Park, a gem of green set in the city's downtown.

The Alamo is four blocks from the hotel; the Riverwalk is three blocks.

Guest rooms have a sense of refinement, decorated with traditional furniture, matched draperies and bedspreads, and brass accessories. Even though there are 362 guest rooms, no two are alike; many have antiques and art objects. Doorbells are a nice touch.

Hotel guests may dine at the St. Anthony Club, a prestigious private membership club with nationally known entertainers and politicians on its membership roster. The informal Brasserie is open all day, and Pete's Pub (lunches, snacks, cocktails) is open until 2 A.M.

Unusual for a hotel of its vintage, the Inter-Continental has a rooftop swimming pool and sun deck. Hotel services include a concierge, 24-hour room service, and valet parking. Self parking in an outdoor lot is also available.

Of special interest is the chance to hear about the hotel's history from someone who talks about it from experience. Longtime concierge Dick Kinnally, now retired, started working at the hotel as a bellman in 1943. Enraptured with the St. Anthony—its history and romance—he enjoys telling guests about the celebrities who have passed through its doors. So popular are his stories that he hosts weekly dinners in the Brasserie. Ask at the desk if you want to join the party.

SANTA FE

The Inn At Loretto
211 Old Santa Fe Trail
Santa Fe, New Mexico 87501
505/988-5531
800/528-1234
GENERAL MANAGER: Jim Bagby
135 rooms
$85–$108 single, $97–$120 double; $135–$300 suites
American Express, Amoco, Carte Blanche, Diners Club, Discover, MasterCard, Visa; personal check
Children welcome
No pets
Open year round

Resembling a pueblo-style village of its own, The Inn at Loretto stands at the corner of Old Santa Fe Trail and Alameda Street. All around it spreads Santa Fe, cultural capital of the Southwest. Canyon Road, known for its art galleries, stretches to the east. The historic Plaza is two blocks north.

Next door to the inn—in fact, attached via an enclosed walkway—is the Chapel of Loretto, built between 1873 and 1878 at the request of Archbishop Jean Baptiste Lamy. The first Gothic building west of the Mississippi, the chapel is best known for its choir loft staircase, composed of two complete spirals and no center or side supports. According to tradition, the masterpiece was built by an unknown carpenter who mysteriously appeared and offered to do the work, accepting no pay and then disappearing when he had completed the task.

A girls' school dating back to 1850 was on the site of today's inn. After the school burned, the land was purchased for a hotel. Loretto Chapel is owned by The Inn of Loretto and managed by a historical foundation. Although the inn itself is a relative newcomer to the centuries-old city, being adjoined to the chapel gives it a strong historic flavor. A popular visitor attraction, the chapel is open to the public.

Unfortunately, the lobby of the inn does not do justice to this lodging's overall character. Look past its darkness to the genuine hospitality extended by the inn's personnel.

Guest rooms themselves are fairly ordinary. A few have fireplaces. Air conditioning, cable color TV, and phones are standard. Ask for a room with a balcony to get good views of downtown Santa Fe. Some of the guest-room floors have appealing common-area patios, good for group gatherings.

There's a small heated pool, lots of interesting shops and galleries, a good wine shop, and a beauty salon. Footsteps Across New Mexico Theater and Book Store presents a high-quality slide presentation about New Mexico and has an excellent selection of books on the area.

Los Rincones restaurant serves regional specialties as well as more standard fare. Entrees range from $7 to $17.

The Inn of the Governors

234 Don Gaspar
Santa Fe, New Mexico 87501
505/982-4333
800/234-4534
GENERAL MANAGER: Charlotte Hall
99 rooms
$55–$135 single or double
HIGH SEASONS: May to October; December
American Express, MasterCard, Visa; personal check
Children welcome

Pets accepted
Open year round

Three blocks from Santa Fe's famed Plaza, The Inn of the Governors has touches of Old Santa Fe coupled with modernity. Rooms are situated in three low-rise sections: the main building, referred to as "Senators"; the motel wing, called "Representatives"; and the new wing, or "Governors."

The lobby is small, and functional rather than social in nature. In the courtyard just outside its doors there's a small swimming pool, pleasant and inviting. The Forge Restaurant and Lounge adjoins the lobby. Decorated with a rustic theme, this low-ceilinged dining room has an air of warmth, making it a cozy retreat from the busy city beyond.

Guest rooms, more spacious than average, have lots of variety. Some rooms have corner fireplaces. Others have patios or balconies. Common to all are stocked refrigerators, coffee-makers, lots of lighting, and comfortable sitting areas. Furnishings are Spanish Colonial style, with hand-painted headboards and window valences.

The inn's location makes it convenient for both vacationers and business travelers. During the winter, a shuttle bus (Shuttlejack) connects it to Santa Fe Ski Basin.

La Fonda
On the Plaza
100 East San Francisco Street
Santa Fe, New Mexico 87501
505/982-5511
GENERAL MANAGER: Mickey Stewart
125 rooms
$75–$90 single, $85–$100 double; $110–$295 suites
HIGH SEASONS: July to mid-October; late December
American Express, Carte Blanche, Diners Club, MasterCard, Visa; personal check
Children welcome
Pets accepted
Open year round

If you like to be at the center of activity, La Fonda is the place. Situated right on the Plaza, it's a nucleus for tourists. Step outside the doors to an ongoing Indian market. Walk a half block to St. Francis Cathedral. Cross the Plaza to Palace of the Governors and the Museum of Fine Arts.

Inside the hotel you can sign up for area sightseeing tours, river rafting, the Cumbres and Toltec Scenic railway, even trips to the Grand Canyon. You can also start your Santa Fe shopping close at hand, with an art gallery and a host of shops right in the hotel.

While town records show that Santa Fe has had a "la fonda," or inn, since the town was founded in 1610, the present La Fonda was built in 1920, occupying the site of an earlier hotel. Today's La Fonda is a rambling adobe filled with local flavor and a festive spirit.

Guest rooms spread over four floors come in standard, deluxe, mini-suites, and suites. Color spills from the rooms in the form of gaily painted headboards and hand-decorated Spanish colonial furniture. Stand in the hallways and you'll swear that a band of elves got hold of paint brushes and had a marvelous time decorating everything in sight. Look one direction to see a flock of birds in mid-flight. Turn the other way and the air-conditioning vents are trimmed in bright designs. Even the entrance to the elevator didn't escape the painters' attention.

Downstairs off the lobby, La Plazuela restaurant is set in a festive enclosed courtyard and serves three meals a day. There's also a French pastry shop and crêperie, plus seasonal dining on the rooftop.

An indoor swimming pool, two hot tubs, and a cold plunge pool are on the first floor. Massages (15 therapists on duty) start at $12 for 20 minutes.

TUCSON

Hotel Park Tucson
 5151 E. Grant Road
 Tucson, Arizona 85712
 602/323-6262
 800/257-7275 US, 800/344-0189 AZ
GENERAL MANAGER: Charles Gray
217 rooms and suites
$55–$95 single, $55–$105 double
HIGH SEASON: mid-January to mid-May
LOW SEASON: mid-May to mid-September
Children welcome
Pets accepted
Open year round

In a city rich in resorts, Hotel Park Tucson is a good alternative, whether you're in town for business or sightseeing.

Opened in mid-1985, the hotel is distinctive with its lush landscaping and arched passageways. The V-shaped complex has rooms and suites spread over four floors, all opening onto the open-air courtyard and pool. Rooms have modern decor and are larger than average. Suites have a bedroom, living area, and wet bar. About half of the rooms are non-smoking. Some rooms are specially furnished for women. An exercise room (fairly well-equipped), sauna, and steam room are nice amenities.

Services include a concierge, transportation to and from shopping (two regional shopping centers within ten minutes) and University Medical Center. Tucson Medical Center is next door.

The Brass Eagle Restaurant, having an identity of its own separate from the hotel, is elegant and features a seafood bar and a gourmet room.

TULSA

Doubletree Hotel at Warren Place
  6100 S. Yale
  Tulsa, Oklahoma 74136
  918/495-1000
  800/528-0444
  GENERAL MANAGER: Tom Butters
  371 rooms
  $99 single, $106 double
  American Express, Diners Club, MasterCard, Visa; personal
    check
  Children welcome
  Pets accepted
  Open year round

One of the most outstanding hotels in Oklahoma, the Doubletree is beautiful and gracious. Its primary business is the corporate traveler, but whatever your reason for being in Tulsa, this hotel is an excellent choice.

Doubletree, built in 1985, is part of the Warren Place office park development in southeast Tulsa, about a 20 minute drive from downtown. St. Francis Hospital is across the street. Yet despite the surrounding development, there's almost a pastoral feel to the hotel's setting. Some rooms and public areas overlook rolling, well-landscaped grounds. Covered hotel parking is free.

A one-and-a-half mile jogging track threads through the property. The indoor pool is several cuts above average—adjoined by a whirlpool, steam room and sauna. This is a good place to relax, with views of the grounds adding to the mood. Guests also have use of the Physical Performance Center across the street. Part of St. Francis Hospital, it has an indoor jogging track, aerobic classes, and weight equipment. Nearby LaFortune Park has tennis and golf.

Rooms in the 10-story hotel are well-appointed. On the Executive Level there are such extras as robes, continental breakfast, evening cocktails, newspapers, and free local phone calls.

Greenleaf's on the Park is an airy café; Encounters lounge has dancing. Whether you stay at the hotel or not, try Warren Duck Club restaurant, known for its duck dishes as well as rotisseried meats. Sophisticated and club-like, it has an appetizer bar and a dessert buffet. (Open for lunch and dinner Monday to Saturday.)

Embassy Suites Hotel

3332 S. 79th East Avenue
Tulsa, Oklahoma 74145
918/622-4000
800/EMBASSY
GENERAL MANAGER: Doug Lawrence
248 suites
$57–$76 single, $57–$86 double including full breakfast
American Express, Carte Blanche, Diners Club, MasterCard, Visa; personal check
Children welcome
Pets accepted
Open year round

There's a friendly feel when you walk through the hotel doors at the Embassy Suites. People are socializing in the greenery-bedecked atrium, the piano player is playing a festive tune, and the bellmen are truly hospitable. Adding to its desirability, the hotel is conveniently located right off I-44.

An all-suite hotel, Embassy has one- and two-bedroom units, all similarly designed. Suites are intended to seem like home, equipped for comfort and arranged to allow privacy. They each have a living room with pull-out couch, TV, and phone; kitchenette with microwave, refrigerator, and sink; and bedroom with such conveniences as remote control TV, digital clock, and vanity with lavatory. Furniture, traditionally styled, is upscale in quality.

Breakfast comes with the price of a room, and pleasingly enough, it's much better than it needs to be, with a cooked-to-order format. For a family, it's an especially good deal. (Children under 12 stay free.) Everybody in the family can go downstairs when they want and order a full breakfast including eggs, bacon, sausage, pancakes, muffins, fruit, and cereal.

Cattleman's Steakhouse and Chocolate Factory is right off the lobby. So is Harvey's Lounge. Despite the fact that both are popular in the evening and that the hotel has an open-atrium design, you can't hear the festivities once you're in the sleeping portion of your suite.

An indoor pool and hot tub are also off the lobby.

Tulsa Marriott
  E. 41st Street and S. Garnett
  Tulsa, Oklahoma 74146
  918/627-5000
  800/228-9290
GENERAL MANAGER: Mike Kondrat
336 rooms
$90–$96 single, $102–$-$106 double
American Express, Carte Blanche, Diners Club, MasterCard,
  Visa; personal check
Children welcome
Small pets accepted
Open year round

The 11-story Marriott, situated on the outskirts of Tulsa about eight miles southeast of downtown, is a pleasant stop. Lowkey in style, it's a good place to relax. Numerous business addresses and several shopping malls are within a few miles. Business travelers account for nearly 80 percent of the hotel's guests. The lobby is welcoming, like a fresh bouquet. There's an outdoor pool, an adjoining indoor pool with nearby hot tub, and a health club with exercise equipment and tanning beds. And if you want more, there is table tennis, volleyball, basketball, board games, and headsets.

Guest rooms have contemporary-style furnishings. The top-floor concierge rooms are worth the difference in price, with such extras as continental breakfast, newspapers, and bathrobes.

Two restaurants give you a choice of formal or casual dining. One has a waffle dessert bar for Sunday brunch. Bronson's lounge is lively, with dancing, a wide-screen TV, and Las Vegas-style black jack ("no gambling: for amusement, entertainment, practice, and instruction").

To arrange a candlelight dinner in your room, call the hotel direct (ext. 6619) prior to check-in. The restaurant staff is ready to accommodate.

The Westin Hotel, Williams Center
10 East Second Street
Tulsa, Oklahoma 74103
918/582-9000
800/228-3000
GENERAL MANAGER: Michael Deighton
450 rooms
$89–$130 single, $109–$150 double; $250–$875 suites
American Express, Carte Blanche, Diners Club, MasterCard,
    Visa; personal check
Children welcome
Small pets acceptable
Open year round

Not only is the Westin a luxurious hotel with top service and extra flourishes, but it's joined to a shopping mall centered with an ice skating rink, and it's next door to Tulsa's Performing Arts Center. In short, it's the place to be.

Guest rooms have a classic look, decorated in rich colors and furnished for comfort. All have armoire-concealed TVs with Home Box Office, stocked minibars, and large desks. "Premier" rooms have two TVs (one in the bath), three phones, minibar, terry cloth robes, and extra services such as fresh fruit and flowers.

Tucked away on the third floor is an outdoor pool overlooking the city, and an adjoining indoor pool with nearby hot tub. Happily, guests can get to the pool without going through the lobby or other public areas, making it almost a hideaway. Indoor tennis courts and exercise equipment are available at a health club adjacent to the hotel.

Dining choices are plentiful. Fine dining is at Montagues, Glass on the Green is informal (all-day service and special Sunday brunches), and Le Bistro serves Northern Italian fare, with an antipasto bar and make-your-own-sundaes. Barristers lounge has live entertainment. Through the glassed skywalk and into Williams Center, there's a profusion of small eateries.

Across the outside square, set with gardens and pools, is the Performing Arts Center that is home to Tulsa Ballet Theatre, Tulsa Opera, and Tulsa Philharmonic. The center also has several small stages used by theater companies and performing artists.

Hotel parking, a choice of valet or self-service parking, is in a covered garage. The fee is $5 per day.

7

Condominiums

Not only do condos offer space and privacy, but they can be the most economical lodging for a family or a group of friends. Condominiums selected for this chapter are spread across the Southwest, from the seashore to the mountains. (See also chapters on Beachside, Family Resorts, Lakeside, Ski Lodging, Sports Lodges.)

ARIZONA

Junipine Resort Condo Hotel
   8351 N. Highway 89A
   Sedona, Arizona 86336
   602/282-3375
   800/542-8484 US, 800/842-2121 AZ
GENERAL MANAGER: Mary Fuller
35 units
1 bedroom: $68–$138 for 2 people (available Sunday-Thursday only)
2 bedroom: $99–$196 for 4 people
Minimum of two nights during weekends
HIGH SEASON: May to October
LOW SEASON: January to February
American Express, MasterCard, Visa; personal check
Children welcome
No pets

Open year round

Oak Creek Canyon north of Sedona is one of the area's top scenic attractions—a combination of evergreen forests and rugged mountain vistas. Junipine Resort, nestled among huge trees on the banks of Oak Creek, provides spaciousness and comfort in a beautiful setting.

Families with children will appreciate the fact that there's plenty of room to "go out and play," with wooded hillsides to run up and down and trails to explore. Travelers seeking seclusion will find what they're looking for here, with condo units well-designed for privacy.

Junipine's management points out that the condos are the most expensive accommodations on the creek between Sedona and Flagstaff, differing greatly from some of the tacky lodgings on this stretch of road. All privately owned, the condos were built in 1985. Upscale natural-wood structures, they blend well with the surrounding forests. Interiors are modern and plush, accented with southwestern art. Happily, the outdoor setting is emphasized; each unit has a large deck, accessible from both the living and sleeping areas through sliding glass doors.

Kitchens are straight out of upper-class suburbia, complete with all you need, including table settings. Bathrooms are divided into sections, providing convenience. Some units have lofts.

NEW MEXICO

Fort Marcy Compound
320 Artist Road
Santa Fe, New Mexico 87501
505/982-9480
800/552-0070

MANAGERS: John and Amy Smallwood
67 units
$60–$150 single, $10 for each additional person
Two-night minimum during most of the year
Four-night minimum in August and Christmas holidays
American Express, MasterCard, Visa; personal check
Children welcome
No pets
Open year round

Just a short drive from Santa Fe's Plaza is Fort Marcy Compound, a 100-unit complex of one-, two-, and three-bedroom condos set in a residential neighborhood. While all of the units are privately owned, 67 of them are in a rental pool, offering vacationers a spacious accommodation within easy access of area sights.

The condos are 15 miles from Santa Fe Ski Basin, which boasts a 12,000 foot summit and a vertical descent of 1,650 feet. There are seven lifts and 32 runs at the ski mountain, plus a certified ski school.

Fort Marcy Military Reservation was once on the land where the condos stand. According to some archaeologists, an Indian pueblo may have been on this site much earlier, as in 1000 A.D. (pre-dating Santa Fe by more than 500 years).

The condo complex, built in 1975, spreads over ten acres dotted with cedars and willows. An enclosed pool and hot tub as well as a full laundry are attractive amenities. Condo units, some situated on hillsides, include one-bedroom flats, two-bedroom flats and townhouses, and three-bedroom townhouses. Interiors reflect Santa Fe style, with kiva fireplaces and Mexican tile. Kitchens are well-equipped; microwaves, toasters, and coffee makers are standard to each unit. In addition to the expected cable color TV, the condos also have stereo/cassette systems. A VCR library is in the main office.

Daily maid service is available for an extra charge. Fort Marcy personnel take care of personal requests, from stocking guest refrigerators to making dinner reservations. Trolleys connect the compound to numerous points within Santa Fe.

Otra Vez

Galisteo at Water
P.O. Box 1754
Santa Fe, New Mexico 87504
505/988-2244
PROPERTY MANAGER: Patsy Block
18 units
1 bedroom: $85–$125

2 bedroom: $100–$150
Children welcome
No pets
Open year round

For small groups traveling together, either for skiing or enjoying Santa Fe, Otra Vez condominiums offer convenience and spaciousness. One and two-bedroom units are available, situated in a three-story building about three blocks from the Plaza.

The emphasis is on modernity and comfort versus area flavor. Living rooms have fireplaces and TVs. Kitchens are well-equipped—dishwashers, coffee makers, and blenders, plus place settings for six people. Units are arranged around a second-floor open-air area with a hot tub. There's a washer and dryer on each floor of the condominium complex. Daily maid service is included in unit rates, and parking is free.

An attendant is on duty to check guests in between 8 A.M. and 5 P.M., seven days a week. Later check-ins can be arranged, with guests admitted by the security guard. No weekly rates are available.

TEXAS

Bridgepoint
333 Padre Boulevard
P.O. Box 3590
South Padre Island, Texas 78597
512/943-7969
800/531-7383 US (ext. 2126), 800/292-5098 TX (ext. 2126)
PROPERTY MANAGER: M. David Tiedt
Approximately 30 units
2 bedroom: $150–$250, 1 bedroom: $100–$175, 3-4 bedroom: $200–$400
HIGH SEASON: late May to early September
American Express, Discover, MasterCard, Visa; personal check
Children welcome
Pets accepted
Open year round

For luxurious vacationing high above the crowds, Bridgepoint is the place. The sleek 29-story beachfront condominium tower opened in 1984. Approximately 30 of its

114 privately owned units are available for rent. While each is individually decorated, all are super-luxurious retreats.

Differing from standard condos in floor plan, units are especially spacious, airy, and inviting. (One-bedroom units have 1,400 square feet; 2-bedroom have 1,800 square feet.) Most rooms within each unit have ocean views. Penthouses (4 bedrooms) are truly exquisite, with sweeping views. Kitchens are well-equipped, and there are washers and dryers within each unit.

Guests can enjoy the attractive outdoor area with its children's pool, sunken whirlpool tub, adult pool with diving board, and palapa snack bar; there are also a well-equipped exercise room and two lighted tennis courts. Of course the beach itself is right outside the front door. Beach umbrellas and chairs are free.

Not only is the property itself top-notch, but also the condo manager operates the rental units with a hotel attitude. In short, you're treated like a valued guest instead of a person who's allowed to stay in someone else's condo. There is a security gate to go through—just be sure that you're expected.

Condos are not rented to students. (South Padre is a popular spring break destination.) A $100 telephone deposit is required of all guests, returnable after the monthly telephone bill reaches the manager.

Camp Warnecke Resorts
P.O. Box 310620
New Braunfels, Texas 78131-0620
512/625-3710
800/292-1167
MANAGER: Sharon Handrick
56 condos
$70–$130 double
Minimum stay of two nights
HIGH SEASON: mid-May to mid-September
MasterCard, Visa; personal check
Children welcome
No pets
Open year round

The gently-flowing Comal River springs up from natural rock formations within New Braunfels and then flows through town to join the rambunctious Guadalupe. Along the Comal's tree-lined banks are the condos of Camp Warnecke, a peaceful retreat within themselves and yet only steps from the fun of New Braunfels.

Camp Warnecke has long been one of the most popular places in town, attracting fun-loving types with its inner tubing park. The condos, situated across the street from the park and older motel units, were built in the mid-1980s. The high-quality, spacious condos are a great hub for vacationing in the New Braunfels area. In addition to inner tubing on the river, there's a swimming pool and hot tub on the grounds, plus lots of sightseeing and water fun within a few miles.

Individually owned and decorated, the condos are well furnished and are equipped with microwave ovens, cookware, telephones, TVs, and washers and dryers. Some have fireplaces. There's a choice of one-, two-, and three-bedroom units. Two-story designs have outdoor terraces on both levels. Be sure to ask for a unit directly on the river.

Seascape

10811 San Luis Pass Road
Galveston, Texas 77551
409/740-3561
800/392-0075 TX only
PROPERTY MANAGER: Bob Wickham
Approximately 50 condos
1 bedroom: $84–$124 (accommodating 4 adults, 2 children)
2 bedroom: $114–$164 (accommodating 6 adults, 2 children)
HIGH SEASON: May to early September
American Express, MasterCard, Visa
Children welcome
No pets
Open year round

On Galveston Island's West Beach, just past the seawall, Seascape condominiums are directly on the beach. (Most area condos are behind the 10.4 mile long seawall.) Units are attractive and well-furnished, there's a pool and tennis court on the grounds, and the management is efficient and accommodating.

Condos come in a choice of five designs. All have well-equipped kitchens (full-size refrigerator, dishwasher, two-burner range-top, microwave, cookware, and tableware). These privately owned condos are individually decorated. Out of 135 total units in the complex, about 50 are in the rental pool. One-bedroom units sleep up to six; two-bedrooms, up to eight. In addition to sleeping accommodations in the bedrooms, living rooms have pull-out couches and entry halls have two built-in bunk beds. Bathrooms are divided into three components, with a total of two toilets, two lavatories, and one tub/shower.

If you like privacy, then pay the extra charge and get one of the beachfront units. While all of the condos have their own ocean-view balcony, they also look onto neighboring balconies. In contrast, the beachfront units look straight out to sea, offering a definite sense of privacy.

Boardwalks lead over the dunes and onto the beach. Seascape is adjacent to a public beachfront park, but security within the complex is excellent, limiting usage of its pool and surrounding deck to condo owners and guests only. Covered parking is free. There's a laundry on the premises and some units have their own washer and dryer.

8

Country B&Bs

Country B&Bs are small retreats far off the beaten path. All give you a taste of country life, whatever part of the Southwest they are in. Their hosts let you set the pace, whether you want to visit or be left alone.

ARIZONA

Lynx Creek Farm
  P.O. Box 4301
  Prescott, Arizona 86302
  602/778-9573, 257-4210
HOSTS: Greg and Cathy Temple
2 rooms (private baths)
$60 single, $75 double including full breakfast
MasterCard, Visa; personal check
Children welcome
No pets
No smoking in guest rooms
Open year round

One of the most delightful B&Bs in all of the Southwest is seven miles east of Prescott. A sign points to Lynx Creek Farm, Orchards and Bed and Breakfast. Drive down a farm road through the orchards to the home of Greg and Cathy Temple. In the mid-1980s this energetic young couple from Phoenix bought the 20-acre hillside orchards on Lynx Creek.

From the outset, they intended to operate a B&B. It opened in mid-1987, offering guests a country getaway amid beautiful surroundings.

The two guest rooms are housed in a wooden building situated about 50 feet from the host's country-style home. A wonderful cedar deck with a large hot tub and chaise lounges looks down on the creek below. The rooms themselves are like a fairy-tale come true. Victorian antiques, country crafts, and imaginative decorating equal romantic, enchanting interiors. Everywhere you look there's something special—an old-fashioned school desk, antique quilts, decades-old Farmers Almanacs, framed pages from old Prescott newspapers.

More akin to mini-apartments than bedrooms, the units are spacious and well-designed for comfort. The Sharlot Hall room (named for Arizona's first state historian) has a king bed and a loft that sleeps two. The Margaret McCormick room (she was the wife of the first territorial governor) has a queen bed and day bed.

Breakfast is geared to suit the tastes of in-house guests, whether it's fresh fruit (from the orchards, of course) and homemade granola, or heartier fare such as huevos rancheros and handmade tortillas.

After breakfast, you can hike by the creek, pick fruit in the orchard, and enjoy the seclusion. If you yearn for more activity, the hosts will arrange for horseback rides or mountain bike rental. Nearby Prescott is a historic town with museums, antique shopping, and a host of festivals.

Catering to families, this B&B has a playground and sandbox, plus an attitude that truly means, "Children Welcome." Baby sitters are arranged upon request.

NEW MEXICO

Chinguague Compound
  Box 1118
  San Juan Pueblo, New Mexico 87566
  505/852-2194
INNKEEPERS: Phil and Joan Blood
3 guest houses
$55–$150 double including full breakfast
HIGH SEASON: October to April
Minimum of 2 nights during high season
MasterCard, Visa; personal check
Children accepted

Pets with approval
Open year round

North of Santa Fe between the Sangre de Cristo Mountains and the Jemez Mountains is the "cradle of New Mexico," so called because of the three cultures that have shaped it—Indian, Hispanic, and Anglos—as well as the confluence of two rivers—the Rio Chama and Rio Grande.

On the banks of the Rio Grande two miles north of San Juan Pueblo is Chinguague Compound—an eight-acre estate with a private home and three guest houses. Huge cottonwoods shade the grounds, and fruit trees and grape arbors invite you to stay and enjoy the country setting. Chinguague (ching-wah-yea) is the San Juan Indians' word for "wide place," referring to the arroyo that visitors cross to reach the compound. In this secluded setting you can relax undisturbed, and when you're ready for activity, you can make day trips to nearby attractions.

San Juan Pueblo, minutes away, is known for its decorated pottery and wood carvings. Other pueblos in the vicinity include Picuris, Santa Clara, San Ildefonso, Pojoaque, Nambe, and Tesuque, as well as Taos.

Taos is 42 miles north; Santa Fe, 30 miles south; and Los Alamos, 28 miles southwest.

The hosts at Chinguague are affable people, knowledgeable about the area and conversant on many subjects. The compound once belonged to host Phil Blood's aunt, a concert violinist who used it as a retreat as well as a place to entertain friends. Her collection of classical records remains in one of the houses, available to today's B&B guests.

The guest houses, varying from one to two bedrooms, are reminiscent of the 1930s. All have TVs and kiva fireplaces, but there the similarity ends. Ann's Place, the smallest of the three, has a large brick-floored living room, bedroom with double bed and rocking chair, and a small kitchen. This cottage's focal point is the screen porch which the hosts refer to as a bird-watching cage: guests are enclosed, while the birds fly freely around them. Aztec, offering more privacy due to its location, is spacious and has a living room with kiva fireplace, bedroom with double bed, bath (shower only), and full kitchen.

The Studio, which can be used as either a one- or two-bedroom accommodation, is by far the most spacious of the three guest houses. Well-suited for families or for friends traveling together, it has a fireplace, full kitchen, and a washer and dryer. Its large front porch is set with chaise lounges, and there's a flagstone terrace as well. The front entry leads to a huge living room (16 feet x 30 feet).

Breakfast has a genuine personal touch at this B&B. The hosts make their own bread, granola, yogurt, and jellies. Honey comes from their hives; fresh fruit comes from their orchards. They even grind blue corn meal for pancakes.

Two Dobermans are part of the host family—Hildy (short for Brunnhilde) and Cleo (Cleopatra).

La Posada de Chimayo

P.O. Box 463
Chimayo, New Mexico 87522
505/351-4605
INNKEEPER: Sue Farrington
2 suites (private baths)
$65 double including breakfast
Reduced weekly rates during winter
MasterCard, Visa; personal check
Children over 12 welcome
Pets with approval
Open year round

The tiny village of Chimayo, renowned for its weavers and their masterful creations, is not exactly on the beaten path. To get to Santa Fe, 25 miles to the south, you wind through wide-open countryside before reaching the main highway. Taos via the High Road, which passes through the craft villages of Cordova and Truchas, is 45 minutes north.

But even more off the beaten path than Chimayo is La Posada de Chimayo, a two-suite B&B with Southwestern charm. You turn off Highway 76 onto a narrow dirt road that twists past El Chimayo Weavers, then ambles by such landmarks as "building with the colorful roof" and "house with blue trim." Just as you think you must have missed it—or maybe you're on the wrong road altogether—there it is, with a sign in front to prove it.

La Posada is a "new old adobe," says innkeeper Sue Farrington, who lives in an adobe house next door. Built in 1981, it blends beautifully into the surroundings—quite a trick when you realize that the ancient settlement of Chimayo dates back to 1598.

A traditional adobe structure, La Posada has viga ceilings, brick floors, and corner fireplaces. The furniture is comfortable and the decorations are pure Southwest, with Mexican rugs and handwoven bedspreads as accents. The house has two separate apartments. Each consists of a sitting room with

"Taos bed" (sleeps one), small bedroom with double bed, and private bath.

Breakfast at this B&B is not for the faint-hearted, the innkeeper warns. Come with a big appetite, for a typical menu includes scrambled eggs, locally made sausage, bread pudding, juice, and coffee. Stuffed French toast, corn muffins, and cheese and egg casserole are other house specialties. When the weather permits, breakfast is served on the deck. When the air gets nippy, guests dine in their private sitting room.

In addition to visiting local sights, most notably the shops of the weavers and a historic church where miraculous cures are said to have taken place, there are day trips to several Indian pueblos, Bandelier National Monument, Santa Fe, and Taos.

Skiers wanting to avoid the crowds can head to Sipapu Ski Area. For hikers, there are trails in nearby desert country and alpine forests.

Monjeau Shadows
  Highway 37
  (3 miles north of Highway 48 junction)
  Nogal, New Mexico 88341
RESIDENT MANAGERS: Howard and Pauline Skeean
6 rooms, some with private bath
$35–$40 single, $50–$60 double (includes continental breakfast)
MasterCard, Visa; personal check
Children over 12 welcome; younger children not encourages
No pets
Open year round

The highway leading to Ruidoso is only a few hundred feet below. But at this hillside guest home you feel are removed from the crowds. From any of the home's three porches you look upon miles of wooded terrain. To the northeast is Capitan Mountain where a frightened bear cub was found after a devastating forest fire in 1950, inspiring a national awareness of forest conservation under the name Smokey the Bear.

Monjeau Shadows, built as a home in 1980 and transformed into a B&B four years later, is an excellent hub for a New Mexico mountain vacation any time of the year. Ski Apache, with eight lifts including a four-passenger gondola, is 18 miles away. Hiking and fishing enthusiasts can find plenty of opportunities to enjoy the outdoor life. One of the most popular tourist attractions in the area is Ruidoso Downs where horse racing is held from May to September.

Setting is certainly not Monjeau Shadows' only attribute. If you think you could get addicted to watching hummingbirds, this is the place to start. Blacktail and Rufous hummingbirds are constant visitors to the second-floor balcony, lured by the feeders kept filled by the managers. Howard and Pauline vow that when the syrupy fluid runs low, the birds let them know by flying against the kitchen windows.

Not to be discounted at this mountain hide-away is the cuisine. Continental breakfast comes with the room rate, but for an extra charge, Howard cooks up a country feast. With advance notice, he'll also serve you dinner. A five-course dinner, priced at $25 for two, features such entrees as chicken breast in white wine or barbecued brisket with pasta salad. Every dinner includes a soup matched to the entree, perhaps fresh mushroom or chili bean chowder. Bananas Foster is one of Howard's specialties. Even if you dine at Monjeau Shadows every night for a week, your dinner will be served on different china each night. Whether you dine with the hosts or not, you will still enjoy their hospitality, beginning with hors d'oeuvres and wine upon check-in. Visiting with guests is important to these B&Bers. In the living room there's a photo album featuring everyone who has stayed with them.

Guest rooms are situated on four levels of the home, from the basement to the loft. Each is named for the one-time resident children and is decorated accordingly. Bryan's rooms has a masculine look, with deep blue carpet, wallpaper featuring ships, and carved wooden toys. The adjoining bath has several surprises—wallpaper that you can read (advertisements from a Victorian-era catalog) and a red clawfooted tub. Elaina's and Lisa's rooms, feminine in decor with touches of lace, share a bathroom. The two bedrooms can be shut off from the rest of the house, creating a suite. Every bedroom has a TV, digital clock, and well-matched furnishings.

Throughout the house there's a look of orderliness and beauty. In the living room, distinctive with its apricot carpet and yellow walls, a stained-glass skylight is the focal point.

There's lots of public space available to guests. Especially popular in winter is the basement game room, with a tournament-size pool table, dart board, jukebox, and sitting area beside the fireplace.

Flexibility and creativity are keynotes of Monjeau Shadow's hosts. Inquire about their Murder Mystery weekends and tennis packages. For groups (the house can accommodate up to 16), the managers will make special arrangements upon request, including meals and entertainment. For games like badminton, croquet, and horseshoes, you don't have to go any farther than the front lawn.

TEXAS

Landhaus Bed and Breakfast
P.O. Drawer E
Fredericksburg, Texas 78624
512/997-4916, 997-9624
OWNER: Maria McDonald
4 bedrooms, 1 bath (house rented as a whole)
$115 for 2, $180 for 8 including cook-your-own breakfast
Minimum of 2 days preferred
Personal checks; no credit cards
Children welcome
Pets outside only
No smoking
Open year round

If you yearn for your own place in the country, you can have it at Landhaus. A small one-story house, built circa 1880, it sits on a 170-acre ranch about ten miles northeast of Fredericksburg. The owners. who live in a separate house almost out of sight, give their guests the privilege of hunting (wild turkey, quail, dove, and deer) and horseback riding. Fishing in the creek is another favored pursuit.

Unimposing on the outside, the Landhaus is a glistening treasure inside. The decorating scheme is charm with a country flair. There's warmth and softness in this house—a composite of quilts, soft cushions, and lush carpeting. With a total of four bedrooms and one large bath, the house is leased to one group at a time. There are six beds: two doubles, one three-quarter size, and three singles. One bedroom, sunken below the main level, is excellent for children.

The country kitchen, adjoined by an especially comfortable den, is the focal point of the house. The refrigerator is stocked with breakfast food, including locally made sausage and jams. Guests can cook other meals if they wish; the kitchen is fully modernized—even a microwave and dishwasher.

There's also a living room at Landhaus, as well as a TV and telephone. If you have requests such as flowers or a special-occasion cake, the owner enjoys catering to individual needs.

If anybody in your group begins to tire of the country life, nearby Fredericksburg, settled by Germans in the mid-1800s, has lots of historic sites and country-style shops to explore. Enchanted Rock State Park is also worth a side trip.

Lottie's Bed and Breakfast
Main at Chestnut
P.O. Box E
Chappell Hill, Texas 77426
409/836-9515
OWNERS: Mr. and Mrs. Harvin Moore
2 bedrooms, 1 1/2 baths (house rented as a whole)
$55 per room including breakfast
Personal check; no credit cards
Children over age 5 welcome
No pets
No smoking
Open year round

Chappell Hill, Texas, may not be a large town (fewer than 400 residents), but it's definitely big on history. More than 25 homes and buildings wear historical markers. The most renowned is the beautifully restored Stagecoach Inn, built in 1850. Maintained as a residence, the house is open for tours, not for lodging. But right across the street is a casual B&B where guests can spend the night—and have a tour of the grand house thrown in as an extra.

Lottie's B&B is a cozy five-room cottage furnished in Texas antiques and heirlooms. (It's named for the woman who owned the Stagecoach Inn from 1851-1858.) One of the bedrooms has a double bed and a youth bed; the second bedroom has two twins. There's also a sofa bed in the living room.

The tone at Lottie's is informality. It's a good place for a vacationing family or a group of friends traveling together. The house is rented as a whole, which means that you have use of two bedrooms, living room, dining room, kitchen, and one-and-a-half baths.

9

Country Inns

Country inns are slow-paced sorts of lodgings that invite you to come in and stay awhile. Larger than country B&Bs, they are still small, having a sense of intimacy. Most (but not all) serve meals.

ARIZONA

Garland's Oak Creek Lodge
  P.O. Box 152
  Sedona, Arizona 86336
  602/282-3343
INNKEEPERS: Mary and Gary Garland
15 cabins
$85–$105 single, $115–$135 double including breakfast and
  dinner); minimum stay of 2 nights
MasterCard, Visa; personal check
Children welcome
No pets
Open April to mid-November (Closed on Sundays)

To get to Garland's Lodge you turn off Highway 89A at the Banjo Bill Campground about eight miles north of Sedona. Then you drive through the campground, over the creek, and onto Garland's property. All of a sudden, you're in a private world—peaceful and serene, far removed from the tourists in Sedona. Garland's Lodge is situated right on Oak Creek, the same creek that created the surrounding canyon renowned for its beautiful views. The Garland family's orchards surround the lodge—a total of about 200 fruit trees including apples, pears, peaches, and cherries.

The main lodge is a rambling log building that functions as office, dining room, and social center. Set with rustic wood furniture, a piano, and a stone fireplace, its casual atmosphere is inviting.

Fifteen log cabins are scattered over the grounds, each with a porch overlooking the creek or the gardens. Large cabins have a combination bedroom/sitting room and a fireplace. Beds are either one king, two double, or one double and one twin. Small cabins have one double bed. Truly this is a retreat, for the cabins do not have TVs, radios, or phones.

Operating under its present owners since 1972, the lodge is so popular that guests make reservations a year ahead. Note that Garland's is unusual in several ways. First of all, there's a two-day minimum stay. Second, the lodge is closed on Sundays, meaning that guests stay Monday and Tuesday, Wednesday and Thursday, or Friday and Saturday. Of course you can stay longer than two nights, provided that your stay doesn't include Sunday.

Both breakfast and dinner are included in a stay at Garland's. Breakfast features homemade breads, eggs from the farm's chickens, and fruit from the orchard. Dinnertime is a fancy affair. That doesn't mean you have to dress for dinner, just that you dine versus eat. A typical meal starts with French onion soup, followed by Caesar salad, shrimp with garlic red sauce, linguini with creamy basil sauce, carrots and cauliflower (fresh from the garden), and Kahlua cheesecake. The wine list, featuring California wines, has about twenty choices, plus wine by the glass.

When guests aren't enjoying the seclusion amid the forest, they have lots of choices: fishing in Oak Creek, hiking, browsing in Sedona, and day trips to numerous sights, especially the Grand Canyon (100 miles north).

NEW MEXICO

Galisteo Inn
  Box 4
  Galisteo, New Mexico 87540
  505/982-1506
INNKEEPER: Elizabeth Luster

9 rooms (some with shared baths)
$50–$115 single, $65–$115 double including breakfast
HIGH SEASON: mid-May to mid-June
MasterCard, Visa; personal check
No children under 15
No pets
Open year round

A sleepy cat curls up on top of the guest register. Travelers sit on the carved bench outside the front door and talk about their day. Out back, the energetic types are swimming in the pool or working out in the exercise room.

About 250 years ago what is now Galisteo Inn was built as a Spanish homestead. Today, centuries-old trees shade its grounds, and there's a picturesque stone fence around it. The road out front is dirt. Santa Fe is 23 miles away.

Here is a historic inn offering tranquillity, built hacienda-style and decorated with a modern eye. The living room has a big fireplace, leather couches, and contemporary art. Guest rooms—all named for trees—are airy, fairly spacious and set with Mexican furniture. Several have kiva fireplaces. Two rooms have private baths; the other seven share three community baths—especially attractive with viga ceilings and lots of tile.

Breakfast comes with the room rate, featuring home-baked blue corn muffins and scones, fresh fruit, juice, and coffee.

The inn has its own horses, and guided rides can be arranged upon request.

TEXAS

Annie's Bed and Breakfast
   Highway 155 North
   P.O. Box 928
   Big Sandy, Texas 75755
   214/636-4355
INNKEEPERS: Les and Martha Lane
13 rooms (some with shared bath)
$38–$105 single, $48–$115 double including full breakfast
Reduced rates for combined Friday/Saturday stay
American Express, MasterCard, Visa; personal check
Children including infants welcome
No pets
No smoking

Open year round

Folks driving through the East Texas countryside, do a double-take when they get to the little town of Big Sandy. Unexpectedly, they come upon a trio of brightly painted houses clearly kin to Victorian days.

Anita Gentry is the creator of this tranquil getaway destination. It all started with the headquarters for Annie's Attic—Anita's mail order needlecraft business. Very quickly the operation grew to include a conglomerate of businesses. Now there's Annie's Tea Room, Needlecraft Gallery, Gift Shop, and The Pantry.

When customers repeatedly asked for a place to spend the night, the Gentrys decided to open Annie's Bed and Breakfast across the street, enlarging a turn-of-the-century home into a 13-room inn. A house of seven gables, the lodging has definite charm.

The smallish living room with Empire furniture and lace curtains is the place to meet fellow guests. A wide staircase, excellent for making dramatic entrances, leads to most guest rooms. But two of the most elegant rooms are on the first floor. The Queen Victoria is truly romantic—all burgundy and pink, with a bed sized for a queen and a private bath. The Prince Albert with its masculine air adjoins.

Upstairs rooms are smaller, ranging from the Garden View (twin beds, shared bath) to the Garret (double bed, private bath with clawfoot tub, private balcony). Some rooms have lofts, making them excellent for families. Every room has a telephone and a small refrigerator, disguised as an old-fashioned safe.   Quilts, needlework, and soft-colored wallpaper add to the feeling of coziness. All bathrooms, including those that are shared, are well-decorated and modern. The third-floor Queen Anne, by far the highest-priced room, has a queen bed and private balcony. A spiral staircase leads to its loft, which is furnished with twin beds.

Sunday through Friday, guests eat a bounteous breakfast across the street at Annie's Tea Room, a cheery place with waitresses in period costume. Saturday breakfast is continental-style in the guest rooms.

Special offerings at Annie's B&B include a gourmet picnic brunch (packed in a wicker basket with china and glassware), weekend packages, and special events such as murder mystery weekends and craft festivals.

Gage Hotel
   Marathon, Texas 79842
   915/386-4205
INNKEEPER: Giddings Brown
19 rooms (some with shared bath)
$30–$50 double
MasterCard, Visa; personal check
Children welcome
Pets okay
Open year round

Welcome to West Texas—both in location and flavor. Situated in Marathon, one of the major gateways to Big Bend National Park, the Gage is an oasis. No matter what direction you approach from, civilization stops at least 100 miles before you reach its doors.

In 1928 the hotel was built by Alfred Gage, a prosperous banker and rancher from San Antonio. Since there were few places to stay when he visited his 500,000-acre ranch near Marathon, Gage built the hotel to serve as his operations headquarters. In 1982 the once-grand hotel was restored, and today it offers an atmosphere reminiscent of turn-of-the-century West Texas.

The Gage sits right on the edge of U.S. 90. A rather plain yellow-brick building on the outside, it opens onto a treasure of unusual furnishings and artifacts, most with a historical tie to West Texas. There are tools crafted by the Tarahumara Indians (now settled in northern Mexico, they once lived in West Texas), a table designed for shearing sheep, and tiles representing some of the oldest cattle brands in the county. A Spanish Colonial trunk came from Peru; the large breakfront was originally in the Gage Inn in England.

The barroom is delightful. The bar itself was once an altar in a Mexican church; the wine rack was the original post office for a nearby town. You can't help but be fascinated by the chusa table, a roulette style game (circa 1890) from Chihuahua, Mexico.

Meals are served in a western dining room, decorated with Indian artifacts. The innkeeper is the chef; border cuisine is his style. Feast on red snapper sauteed in ranchero sauce, fajitas and enchiladas, or good ole chicken fried steak. Entrees range from $6 to $15.

The 19 guest rooms, named for area landmarks, are spread along hallways on two floors. Some are rather plain in furnishings, but all are appealing, with their primitive western atmosphere. Each has a lavatory, air conditioning unit, and ceiling fan. In keeping with Old West flavor, there are no such modernities as phones or TVs. Several rooms are very special. Persimmon Gap has an 1840's four-poster bed plus a day bed; it's decorated with 19th-century santos and a black cross crafted by the Mennonite colony in Mexico. This room shares a bath with Stillwell's Crossing, set with a handsomely unique brass bed and Indian rugs. Jacal de Luna, one of the four rooms with a private bath, is more spacious than the rest and has two double beds.

In planning a trip through West Texas, note that the busiest seasons at the Gage are spring and holidays; slow season is mid-July through October.

Townsquare Inn
21 S. Bell
Bellville, Texas 77418
409/865-9021
INNKEEPERS: Deborah and Bob Nolen
9 rooms (most with shared baths)
$40–$65 double including continental breakfast
American Express, MasterCard, Visa; personal check
Children welcome
No pets
Open year round

In the town of Bellville, population 2,500, Townsquare Inn is at the center of activity. Part of a composite of businesses operated by the same owners, it's on the second floor of a building that also houses the Tea Rose restaurant, Tap Room Pub, and Timeless Interiors design shop. Several antique shops (one of Bellville's claims to fame) are within a few blocks. And as promised by its name, the inn is indeed on the town square, overlooking the county courthouse.

Interior designer and inn owner Deborah Nolen used her skills to convert the second-story space into a lodging of beauty. Chintz, stained glass, and greenery play a large part in the decorating scheme. Comfort is the keynote, from spacious living quarters to such conveniences as digital clock radios. More flexible than most accommodations of this genre, Townsquare has two three-bedroom suites, two adjoining rooms, and a grand suite. Guests staying in the three-bedroom suites, ideal for small groups, share a parlor with TV and game table, and a bathroom with clawfoot tub and shower. (One, two, or three bedrooms can be rented.)

The Court (queen bed) and the Chambers (twin beds) adjoin and can be rented separately or jointly. Baths are across the hall—one for men and one for women. The Bell Suite is worth its $65 price tag. Not only is it spacious, with a parlor and private bath, but also its decor is decidedly romantic. The king-size bed is canopied in lace. The elegantly styled bathroom has a clawfoot tub, toilet with pull-chain, and dressing table.

Continental breakfast, included in the price of an overnight stay, is placed in the kitchenette at the end of the hall, long before most guests awaken. But beware—the aroma of country cooking at the Tea Rose may entice you to skip the muffins and head downstairs.

Weimar Country Inn
101 Jackson at S. Center
P.O. Box 782
Weimar, Texas 78962
409/725-8888
INNKEEPER: Nancy Trojecek
9 rooms
$30–$65 double including continental breakfast
American Express, MasterCard, Visa
No children
No pets
Open year round

A few miles away motorists zoom along on I-10 between San Antonio and Houston. This rambling old country inn in quiet Weimar is an excellent stopping point, offering a pleasing alternative to interstate motels.

The restored frame lodging has inherent charm, with pressed tin ceilings, polished wood floors, and an ambience of warmth. Downstairs is a restaurant serving country fare and a saloon offering small-town entertainment, such as dominoes and checkers, as well as drinks. Live entertainment on weekends adds a festive air.

A talented decorator's touch is in evidence throughout the inn, especially in the guest rooms. Victorian furniture and handmade quilts create a sense of history. There's a Laura Ashley feel to the decor, with fine fabrics and wallpaper. But never for a moment do you doubt that you're in Texas. Rooms are dubbed Sam Houston, San Jacinto, Longhorn, and Lone Star—each with a stained-glass transom bearing an appropriate motif. The extra-spacious Bluebonnet room with a king-size bed is a personal favorite.

Breakfast is served continental-style in the upstairs parlor. Kolaches (Weimar is famous for them) prompt a chorus of praise from the guests. If you prefer, you can order a full country breakfast by requesting it the night before (about $4).

10

Family Finds

Family Finds focuses on lodgings that save you money, enabling you to get the most out of a family trip. All are located in areas well suited for family vacations.

ARIZONA

The Bisbee Inn
45 Oklahoma Street
P.O. Box 1855
Bisbee, Arizona 85603
602/432-5131
OWNERS: John and Jay Timbers
18 rooms (shared baths)
$22 single, $34–$39 double including full breakfast; $5 for additional person
MasterCard, Visa; personal check
Children welcome
Pets acceptable
No smoking
Open year round

On one of the steepest streets in a town known for steep streets is The Bisbee Inn, an 18-room B&B inn with very affordable prices. In 1917 it opened as the LaMore Hotel. Across the street was Brewery Gulch, lined with bars.

A certified historic restoration, the inn reflects its history yet gleams with freshness. Many of the furnishings have a history of their own. The iron beds, recently sandblasted and re-painted, date back to the original hotel. The oak tables and chairs came from the old Brooks Apartments next door.

Each guest room is different, both in decor and configuration. All have period wallpaper, perhaps deep blue with flowers or another dainty design. Bed arrangements include one double, two doubles, or one double and one twin. Central air conditioning and heat inject the right touch of modernity. No TVs are in the guest rooms, but a tiny TV room and lounge are at the top of the stairs. A lavatory is in each room, and bathrooms are down the hall. Guests share seven toilets and five tiled showers. Also on the premises is a coin-operated washer and dryer.

In the mornings guests gather around oak tables for a full breakfast, dining on fresh fruit, honey wheat pancakes, bacon and eggs, and homemade bread. Then it's time to explore Bisbee. Tours of the Queen Mine, narrated by ex-miners, lead visitors through an old copper mine with turn-of-the-century mining demonstrations. Area excursions include Chiricahua National Monument, Fort Huachuca, and the western town of Tombstone.

Little America of Flagstaff

I-40 at Butler Avenue
Box 850
Flagstaff, Arizona 86002
800/443-6406 US, 800/FLAG-FUN AZ
GENERAL MANAGER: Robert Button
248 rooms
$52–$62 single, $58–$72 double; $125–$165 suites
American Express, MasterCard, Visa; personal check
Children welcome
No pets
Open year round

Set on 400 acres of pine forest on the outskirts of Flagstaff, Little America is a hospitable, family-oriented lodging. It has a large attractive pool surrounded by trees, a cheerful casual restaurant (open round the clock) as well as a fine dining room, and some of the best guest rooms in the area.

Spread out in two-story brick buildings, the rooms are spacious and truly beautiful. The look is 1950s, freshly re-done. Velvet drapes, French provincial furniture, marble counter tops—all add grace. Big bathrooms and in-room vanities make the rooms especially appealing for families.

"King petites" (priced from $62 to $77) are huge, featuring a nice sitting area that can be separated from the sleeping area by a curtain. Some rooms have private saunas and fireplaces. Many have two entrances, opening onto the manicured lawns adjoining the pool. All have TVs.

Other features include a lounge with live entertainment, a jogging trail, and a 24-hour service station and garage.

Centrally located amid an array of attractions, Little America is an ideal hub for day trips, especially to Grand Canyon (80 miles), Montezuma Castle Indian ruins (40 miles), Sunset Crater (15 miles), and Snow Bowl skiing (15 miles).

Sky Ranch Lodge

Airport Road
P.O. Box 2579
Sedona, Arizona 86336
602/282-6400
OWNERS: John and Isabel Joynt, Gary and Sheri Graham
76 rooms; 2 cottages
$40–$65 double rooms; $100 double cottages; no charge for children under 12
MasterCard, Visa; in-state personal check only
Children welcome
Pets accepted, $5 fee
Open year round

On Table Mountain about two miles from downtown Sedona is a family-operated motel offering comfort and serenity at value-for-the-dollar prices. Highway 89A into Sedona is one mile below. Tiny Sedona Airport (one 5,100-foot runway) is a few hundred feet up the road at the top of the mesa-like mountain.

Built in 1982, the motel is spread over six acres, with units in 17 wood buildings. Most are one-story. The prime location is on the mountain rim, with views of the Red Rock country for which Sedona is famed. Rim Rooms open onto wood decks, where nothing other than an occasional cedar tree is between you and the valley below.

Room interiors are not fancy but are thoughtfully decorated. Some have fireplaces and small kitchenettes. Sleeping accommodations include a choice of one king, two queen, or two double beds. Air conditioning, electric heat, color TV, and phones are in every unit. The two rim cottages, accommodating two, have a kitchenette, fireplace, and deck.

The grounds are well-tended. Obviously this is a place with a sense of pride. The pool and separate spa are inviting. There's no restaurant at Sky Ranch, but hot coffee is always brewing in the lobby and a family-style restaurant is at the airport, which is within walking distance.

NEW MEXICO

El Rey Inn
   1862 Cerrillos Road
   P.O. Box 130
   Santa Fe, New Mexico 87504-0130
   505/982-1931
   OWNER/MANAGER: Terrell White
   56 rooms
   $37–$90 single or double including continental breakfast;
      children free
   American Express, MasterCard, Visa
   Children welcome
   No pets
   Open year round

When you first drive up to El Rey, you may think that it is just another motel. But as soon as you check in, you know that it's far from ordinary. The grounds, dotted with spruce and elm trees, are well groomed. Extra touches are everywhere, from porch swings to potted plants. Indeed, there's a look of TLC about the place. The swimming pool is set amid trees. The children's playground looks as if it were designed for beloved grandchildren.

Owned by the same family since 1973, El Rey is an accommodation with high value for the money. When you leave you feel that you have gotten more than your money's worth.

Surprisingly for a motel-type lodging, rooms have lots of variety. All have air conditioning, color TV, AM/FM radios, and phones. Interiors are definitely Southwestern, with foot-thick adobe walls, and either viga-and-latilla or wood-beamed ceilings. But there the similarities end. Such features as brass or wooden carved beds, kiva fireplaces, tile murals, and sky-lights add individual personality. Bathrooms are adorned with colored tile. Apartments, accommodating up to six people, have kitchenettes or kitchens. Some have fireplaces.

The lobby, with its fireplace and game tables, is a good gathering place for groups. There's a hot tub to add to the fun and a guest laundry to add to convenience. While El Rey does not have a restaurant of its own, a café is two doors away. No need to look for somewhere to eat breakfast, however—continental breakfast is included in the room rate.

OKLAHOMA

Roman Nose Resort
  Box 161
  Watonga, Oklahoma 73772
  405/623-7281
  800/654-8240 AR, CO, KS, MO, NM, TX (except 512)
  800/522-8565 OK
MANAGER: Pam Rickey
47 rooms
$40–$55 double; $100–$150 suite
HIGH SEASON: mid-May to mid-September
American Express, Carte Blanche, Diners Club, MasterCard,
  Visa; personal check
Children welcome
Kennels for pets
Open year round

Southern Cheyenne Chief Henry Roman Nose once settled his tribe in the canyon where the state park named for him now stands. At Roman Nose Resort, waiters wear buckskin, Indians perform native dances, and folk legends come alive around the campfire.

There's an upscale air about Roman Nose Lodge. With only 47 guest rooms, it's never crowded. Best of all, it's well-managed and well-maintained. Recreational facilities—swimming pool, nine-hole golf course, paddleboats, and canoes—are used by lodge guests and park campers alike. The lodge has its own small pool, plus a recreation staff that plans such activities as tram tours, games, arts and crafts, nature hikes, and trips to nearby sites. Trout fishing is popular from November through March. Overall, the mood is relaxed and laid back.

From April through November, the lodge presents Indian Adventure packages celebrating the area's heritage. Included are an Indian cookout, native arts and crafts workshops, Indian cooking lessons, and an outdoor interpretive program, plus two nights' lodging. You can even spend the night in a tepee if you wish. (Tepees accommodate up to eight.)

Accommodations in the main lodge are nicer than expected in a state-operated lodge, with pleasant furnishings. Some have two queen beds, others have one king. Many have private balconies overlooking the cedar-studded hills.

Western Hills Guest Ranch

P.O. Box 509
Wagoner, Oklahoma 74477
918/772-2545
800/522-8565 OK
800/654-8240 AR, CO, KS, MO, NM, TX (except area code 512)
MANAGER: Steve Flaming
156 units
$38–$75 rooms, cottages; $100–$175 suites
HIGH SEASON: mid-May to mid-September
American Express, MasterCard, Visa; personal check
Children welcome
Kennels (all pets must be boarded)
Open year round

As soon as you turn off the main highway and head toward Western Hills Guest Ranch, the rolling countryside, lush with pine forests, entices you to stay. Here in Sequoyah State Park are the ingredients of a great vacation—lots of recreational choices, comfortable lodging, extra-friendly staff, and affordable rates.

The "Howdy" sign over the lobby entrance sets the tone. Western flavor is at the heart of this destination: the staff dress in cowboy gear, the salad bar is inside a chuck wagon, the lodge itself is shaped like a horseshoe. Most importantly, there's always something Western going on—trail rides, cookouts, hayrides, square dancing, and even Western movies shown poolside.

For those who are serious about learning cowboy skills, the lodge packages five-day adventures with lessons in roping, sharpshooting, riding, and horse care. A Wild West Show is the grand finale. Shorter versions of the package are also offered. One of the most delightful aspects of Western Hills is the flexibility of its program. Just ask the recreation department and they'll try to accommodate your interests. Several times a week they organize Little Wrangler Outings for 6- to 16-year-olds, and such activities as archery, fishing, and sharpshooting. For groups, whether it's a family reunion or a corporate meeting, they custom-design anything from square dance parties to stagecoach rides (even supplying the bad guys for mock hold-ups).

But you don't have to yearn for the Old West to enjoy Western Hills. Situated on a 19,000-acre lake, it has lots of water activities. The marina rents sailing, fishing, and pontoon boats. There's also an 18-hole golf course, outdoor pool, tennis courts, and miniature golf.

Your dollar buys lots of recreation at Western Hills. Horseback riding is $5 an hour. The greens fee is $9.

Nature observation is a special plus of a visit here. Depending on the season, the resident park naturalist leads pelican, eagle, and wildflower tours. A truly talented professional with an obvious love for his work, he always has something interesting to offer—pontoon boat excursions along the shoreline, walks along fossil trails, campfire programs. Be sure to visit his nature center to see what animals are in residence—maybe a mother opossum with her young, a beaver, or some newborn deer.

Accommodations are in the main lodge (101 rooms) or in duplex-style cottages designed for two to six. Some cottages have small kitchens (half-size stove, refrigerator; no table or cooking ware). All units have TVs and telephones. Lodge rooms are brightly decorated and comfortable; baths are small but adequate. Cabana units, connected to the lodge, are smaller but more private. Cottages, clustered near the lodge, are plainly furnished.

The most upscale accommodations are the three suites. Miss Kitty is a personal favorite. Fun/Gaudy is the decor, with burgundy velvet upholstered furniture in the parlor and a king-size brass bed. (Surely the Long Branch Saloon is downstairs.) The rate ($100 in winter, $125 in summer) includes breakfast in bed and a bottle of champagne.

The main lodge has a restaurant serving home-style cooking, moderately priced.

TEXAS

Indian Lodge
  P.O. Box 786
  Fort Davis, Texas 79734
  915/426-3254
  MANAGER: Jane Russell
  39 rooms
  $30 single, $35–$45 double
  Personal check written on Texas bank; traveler's check; no
    credit cards
  Children welcome
  No pets

Open year round except 2 weeks in mid-January

Indian Lodge sits nestled in a valley in the Davis Mountains. The mountains themselves are rugged, distinctive with their rock outcroppings tempered with lush green foliage. The air is fresh with cedar at this tranquil retreat, elevation 5,000 feet.

The white adobe-style lodge, built on multiple levels, is a visual treat. All of its rooms open to the outdoors, some opening onto verandas with excellent views of the canyon. Part of Davis Mountain State Park, the lodge is operated by Texas Parks and Wildlife. But make no mistake—this is not an ordinary state park accommodation. No, there are no luxuries such as room service, but the overall atmosphere is upscale. Rooms are well-furnished, each with carpeting, TV, phone, and central air conditioning. Beds are decorated with Indian-theme stenciling, adding to the overall flavor.

The 15 rooms in the original building (with numbers in the 100s) are the most desirable, varying in size and design. Built by the Civilian Conservation Corps in the 1930s, the building's adobe walls are 18 inches thick. Room 121 is the largest, more akin to a suite than a standard hotel room. The 24 newer rooms, built in 1967, are of average size. Interior walls are cinder block.

The lodge's restaurant serves three meals a day. Dinner entrees range from $5 to $7. There's a heated pool down below the lobby, but the top attractions are in the scenic countryside. In Davis Mountains State Park there are miles of hiking trails. Campfire programs are presented during the summer. Old Fort Davis is four miles away; McDonald Observatory (12th largest telescope in the world, visitors center, tours) is 13 miles from the lodge.

The Nutt House
Town Square
Granbury, Texas 76048
817/573-5612
MANAGER: Madge Peters
15 units (some with shared baths)
$35–$45 single or double for room; $60–$85 for apartment
American Express, MasterCard, Visa; personal check
Babies not encouraged; children welcome
No pets
Open year round

Granbury calls itself "a door to yesterday." Its town square was the first in Texas to be listed on the National Register of

Historic Places. Lining its streets are a bevy of antique stores, gift shops, and restaurants. The restored Granbury Opera House, one of the region's most popular attractions, overlooks the square. So does the Nutt House hotel and restaurant, housed in a two-story stone building dating back to 1893.

Downstairs is an old-fashioned restaurant serving "dinner" in the middle of the day Tuesday through Sunday and "supper" on weekends. An all-you-can-eat buffet, the food is country-good (hot water cornbread and buttermilk pie are two of its specialties), and the price is a true bargain ($5 during the week, $7 on weekends).

Upstairs is a hotel straight out of 1919. A socializing nook at the top of the stairs is set with a coffee pot—the first guest up in the morning makes coffee. Guest rooms have screen doors (there's a curtain behind the screen), iron beds, simple furnishings, and lavatories. The bath is down the hall; nine rooms share three baths. The one apartment unit is perfect for a family, with one double and two twin beds, full kitchen, sitting area, and private bath. Don't expect phones or TVs, but the hotel is centrally air-conditioned and heated.

About a block away is the Nutt House Annex, built as a law office in the 1890s. Here the look is entirely different—somewhat modern and with more conveniences, even TVs. Choose from suites or single rooms. All have private baths. The single rooms can all connect. (Unfortunately they are not soundproof.)

Radisson Suite Hotel
700 Avenue H East
(Northeast corner of I-30 and Highway 360)
Arlington, Texas 76011
817/640-0440
800/228-9822
GENERAL MANAGER: Mike Fett

203 suites
$79–$95 single, $89–$105 double; children 17 and under free
    (suites accommodating up to 6)
American Express, Carte Blanche, Diners Club, MasterCard,
    Visa; personal check
Children welcome
No pets
Open year round

Six Flags Over Texas, Wet n'Wild waterpark, and Arlington Stadium (home of the Texas Rangers baseball team) are only a shuttle bus ride away. Cooked-to-order breakfast comes with the price of a room. And children under age 17 stay free in family-size suites accommodating up to six people.

The all-suite Radisson opened in 1986. Its night-lit exterior arches have a high-energy look. Inside, the lobby is airy and refreshing. Adjoining it is a seven-story atrium—not massive and overpowering as atrium-style hotels tend to be, but almost intimate. Suites all open onto the atrium. Their sitting areas are fairly small but well-equipped, with a pull-out couch, TV, phone, and wet bar with refrigerator. Bedrooms, decorated in soothing colors, have two double or one king bed and a remote control TV. Baths are larger than average but do not have separate vanities. Downstairs there's an oval swimming pool, hot tub, and sauna.

Mandolins Restaurant is definitely upscale, with etched glass at the entrance, soft music in the background, and a menu with such dishes as veal Marsala, shrimp scampi, and grilled lamb. Prices for adults range from $12 to $15; children's prices are from $4 to $5. Sunday brunch is a champagne-style affair, with a buffet featuring everything from fresh fish to eggs Benedict. A special selection is available for children. Mandolins Lounge has live entertainment Tuesday through Saturday.

Hotel parking is free.

11

Family Resorts

Family Resorts have a wealth of recreational offerings, making them good destinations for families or groups of friends with differing interests. (By the way, having children along isn't required for enjoying these playgrounds.)

ARIZONA

Marriott's Camelback Inn
  5402 E. Lincoln Drive
  Scottsdale, Arizona 85253
  602/948-1700
  800/228-9290
GENERAL MANAGER: Wynn Tyner
423 units
$75–$220 single, $85–$230 double; $120–$450 suites; no
  charge for children under 18 (up to 5 people per unit)
HIGH SEASON: January to mid-May
American Express, Carte Blanche, Diners Club, Discover,
  MasterCard, Visa; personal check
Children welcome
No pets
Open year round

  Camelback Inn dates back to 1936, when it was built by
Jack and Louise Stewart. With their hospitality and dedica-
tion, they wrote a romantic chapter in the story of American

resorts. Their inn attracted notables from around the world, many of whom returned year after year to the popular desert resort. "In all the world, only one," was the Stewarts' guiding principle as they molded a lodging of rare charm, where attention to detail and personalized service were the pervading tone.

In 1967 the Stewarts sold the resort to the Marriotts, a family who had been guests at Camelback over the previous 14 years. Today's resort is greatly expanded from the one the Marriotts bought. But you don't have to look far to sense the tradition—a true plus in an area now overgrown with posh new playgrounds.

Spread over 125 acres of beautiful desert terrain, Camelback has two highly acclaimed 18-hole championship golf courses, 10 tennis courts, two pools, and seven restaurants and lounges. Its front lawn is an 825-yard executive golf course. Stables with horseback riding are nearby (the inn has free transportation). Hiking trails lead up Mummy Mountain at the resort's back door. There's a playground for kids, rental bikes, shuffleboard, and lots of space to roam. Social programs during holiday seasons reflect the spirit of the Stewarts' resort.

Guests stay in low casa-style rooms scattered over the rolling grounds, which are studded with citrus, olive, and mesquite trees and more than 40 varieties of cactus. Lodgings include single rooms, sun deck rooms (decks adjoin room), and a variety of suites (some with private pools). All have refrigerators and small cooktops. Even rooms designated as "standard" are spacious, having such extras as two phones and remote control TV. Decor is modern Southwest—and distinctly luxurious.

The main lodge, small for a resort of its size, looks like a real lodge should. Decorated with an Indian theme, it has wonderful hand-painted beams, Navajo rugs, and light fixtures formed from arrows. The lobby is listed on the National Register of Historic Places.

Dining offers lots of choices, both in cuisine and prices. Adults and children (even finicky ones) should be able to find dishes to suit their tastes and mood. MAP, FAP, and CAP ("Camelback American Plan" with breakfast and lunch) are available.

Poco Diablo Resort

P.O. Box 1709
Sedona, Arizona 86336
602/282-7333
800/528-4275 US, 800/352-5710 AZ
GENERAL MANAGER: Stan Martin
111 rooms; 33 villas
$75–$150 single or double; $10 for each additional person; no charge for children under 12
American Express, Carte Blanche, Diners Club, MasterCard, Visa; personal check
Children welcome
No pets
Open year round

Sedona is an excellent family destination, a something-for-everybody kind of place. First of all, there's the natural setting. Outdoor enthusiasts can enjoy Oak Creek Canyon (multi-colored cliffs and wooded mountainsides) and the famous Red Rock country. Hiking, fishing, horseback riding, jeep tours, scenic plane rides—all offer ways to enjoy the countryside. Also known as a center for the arts, Sedona has numerous galleries, an arts and crafts village, and an arts museum. On top of all that, the town acts as a hub for exploring nearby attractions, everything from Indian ruins to ghost towns to the Grand Canyon.

Where for a family to stay in Sedona? Poco Diablo Resort offers recreational variety of its own. Spread over 25 acres, it has two heated pools, four tennis courts, two racquetball courts, and a nine-hole par 3 golf course, plus three outdoor hot tubs. The grounds are overhung with willow trees, backed by beautiful mountains in the distance. Many of the guest rooms look onto the golf course.

Guest rooms are extra-large, have refrigerators and wet bars, and are adjoined by patios or balconies. Bathrooms are also spacious, with vanities and lavatories separated from the main bath—a convenient design for families. Some rooms have hot tubs and fireplaces. In addition to the motel-style rooms, which are spread over the grounds in one-story buildings, there's a villa complex at the back of the resort with its own pool. For both types of accommodations, parking is within a few steps of guest rooms, particularly good for family travel.

Willow's Dining Room is well-appointed, offering indoor and outdoor seating, but is a bit pricey for families. Its Sunday Champagne Brunch is popular among locals as well as vacationers.

Westward Look Resort

245 E. Ina Road
Tucson, Arizona 85704
602/297-1151
800/722-2500 US, 800/624-5317 AZ
GENERAL MANAGER: John Dailey
244 rooms
$55–$140 single, $65–$145 double
HIGH SEASON: mid-January to mid-April
LOW SEASON: mid-May to mid-September
American Express, Carte Blanche, Diners Club, MasterCard,
    Visa; personal check
Children welcome
Pets accepted
Open year round

Westward Look, about eight miles north of Tucson's center, glistens on the high desert landscape. Its attributes are a wide assortment of sports, a highly-rated restaurant, and well-designed lodging, plus a friendly atmosphere conducive to family vacationing.

Spread over 84 acres, the resort has three swimming pools and hot tubs, eight Laykold tennis courts, basketball, volleyball, fitness center, and exercise trail, plus such extras as horseshoes and shuffleboard.   Tennis gets lots of attention right at Westward Look. There's a pro shop, clubhouse, and a viewing deck. The cost for play is $8 per court per hour. Tennis packages are frequently offered. There is not a golf course at the resort, but the staff can arrange for you to play at any one of seven area courses.

The Gold Room restaurant specializes in seafood, veal, and continental dishes. For light meals, there's the lobby café.

Lodgings are sprinkled over the grounds, with nearby parking for each unit. The decor is pure Southwest, from exposed beam ceilings to desert art. Each unit has a private balcony or patio, mini-refrigerator, coffee maker, wet bar, cable TV, and a choice of one king or two double beds. Baths are attractive, decorated in such colors as yellow or terra cotta and accented with hand-painted tiles.

Wickenburg Inn

P.O. Box P
Wickenburg, Arizona 85358
602/684-7811
800/528-4227 outside AZ
GENERAL MANAGER: Charles Brinkman
47 rooms
$80–$170 single, $130–$260 double including all meals, horseback riding, tennis; extra person age 2-12: $25; age 13 and up: $40
HIGH SEASON: mid-February to mid-April, Christmas, Thanksgiving
LOW SEASON: June to mid-October
MasterCard, Visa; personal check
Children welcome
Pets with approval
Open year round

About eight miles north of Wickenburg is a resort with an innovative mix of attractions, especially well-suited for families. Tennis, horseback riding, nature observation, and arts and crafts are the star events.

Spread over gently rolling desert landscape studded with saguaro cactus, Wickenburg Inn is made up of a ranch-style lodge, luxurious adobe casitas, and a host of recreational features. The inn's 11 acrylic tennis courts are among the best resort courts in the state. Its instruction center is equipped with automatic ball machines, strategy boards, fixed targets, and practice walls. Clinics and individual lessons are easy to arrange.

Over at the stables are 40 to 60 horses during the winter months, 15 or so in the summer. Rides go out daily, with special cookout, breakfast, and moonlight rides according to season. You can also take private lessons or enroll in horsemanship clinics.

The arts and crafts center, unusual for a resort of this type, has excellent programs for all ages, including leather work, stained glass, pottery, and weaving. Sometimes local artisans are on hand to demonstrate their craft.

Want even more? One of the most imaginative offerings of Wickenburg Inn is its nature program. A resident naturalist introduces guests to the Sonoran Desert through interpretive walks and slide presentations as well as exhibits and a natural history library in the nature center. Surrounding the resort is a 47,000-acre wildlife preserve, home to more than 200 species of animals and 300 kinds of plants. The nature program is geared toward helping guests understand the desert. Special desert ecology programs and desert study weekends are scheduled during the year. Day-long guided excursions to Grand Canyon, Oak Creek, Sedona, and Prescott are also offered (check with the inn prior to arrival).

Of course there's a pool at this resort, along with a hilltop outdoor spa, archery, and jogging trail.

Meals, included in the cost of a stay, are served in the main lodge's dining room. Saturday nights are special, with western cookouts and maybe a hay ride.

Most accommodations are in the 15 casita complexes scattered over the grounds. (A few guest rooms are in the main lodge.) There's nothing rustic about these accommodations, despite the fact that Wickenburg Inn is often referred to as a ranch. Well-decorated and spacious, the casitas have modern southwestern furnishings and such amenities as fireplaces, color TVs, and wet bars equipped with a two-burner range top and refrigerator. Deluxe suites are definitely deluxe, with their own rooftop decks.

NEW MEXICO

Inn of the Mountain Gods

P.O. Box 269
Mescalero, New Mexico 88340
505/257-5141
800/545-9011 outside NM
GENERAL MANAGER: William F. Smith, Sr.
250 rooms
$75–$110 single, $70–$120 double
American Express, MasterCard, Visa; personal check
Children welcome
No pets
Open year round

High in the Sacramento Mountains, The Inn of the Mountain Gods sprawls along the shores of Lake Mescalero. Although the tourist center of Ruidoso is only four miles north, this resort is a world of its own, beautiful in its seclusion. Owned and operated by the Mescalero Apache Indian Reservation, it sits at the heart of their forested land.

The inn, built in 1975, is made up of a series of rambling buildings connected by enclosed walkways. There's an air of informality about the place—no pretension, just relaxed fun.

Every room has a balcony or patio, and all overlook the lake or the mountains. The decor is modern with some accents of Indian art. These accommodations rank high in spaciousness and convenience; bathrooms are compartmentalized, with vanities and mirrors separated from the rest of the bath. Tower rooms are the most deluxe.

The inn has three restaurants, five lounges, and a poolside hot dog stand specializing in international versions of the snack food. The finest restaurant, Dan Li Ka Room (Mescalero Apache for "good food"), has excellent fare with such choices as fresh snapper stuffed with a Southwest pesto, chicken breast stuffed with cilantro and piñon nuts, and sauteed tournedos finished in cream, brandy, mushrooms, and dijon. Wild game is also offered. Entrees range from $11 to $15.

Golfing, boating, tennis, fishing, horseback riding, archery, and trap and skeet shooting are enough to keep most vacationers happy. In the winter, shuttle buses connect the resort to Ski Apache, and big game hunting is offered between mid-September and December. The inn's 18-hole championship golf course is one of the most outstanding in the Southwest. Scenic, challenging, and well-maintained, it's a prime drawing card for the resort. The greens fee for hotel guests is $20; cart rental is $18.

Tennis is also important at this resort, with six outdoor and two "bubble-enclosed" courts, a pro shop, and viewing deck. (Fee is $10–$15 per court hour.) Boat rental choices include canoes, rowboats, and pedalboats; no motor boats are allowed. For anglers, the lake is stocked with rainbow and cutthroat trout, and there's a bait and tackle shop by the pier. The horse stables, about one-and-a-half miles from the inn, offer one-hour to all-day rides.

For hunters, the inn operates a hunting program September through December. The reservation abounds with trophy-size elk, whitetailed deer, and pronghorn antelope herds. Black and brown bear, turkey, and mountain lions are also featured game.

The inn operates bus service to Ski Apache (also owned by the Mescalero Apache tribe) during ski season and to Ruidoso Downs Race Track on race days.

TEXAS

The Hershey Corpus Christi Hotel

900 N. Shoreline
Corpus Christi, Texas 78401
512/887-1600
800/533-3131
GENERAL MANAGER: William O'Boyle
474 rooms
$82–$90 single, $90–$98 double, $120 concierge floor; ages
    17 and under free in room with parents
Special packages from $69 per room
American Express, Carte Blanche, MasterCard, Visa; personal
    check
Children welcome
No pets
Open year round

There's nothing remarkable about the Hershey from the outside. It's sleek and modern, a white 19-story rectangle juxtaposed against the blue bay beyond. But on the inside, there's an attentive staff that is Texas-hospitable, an excellent health club, a rooftop restaurant with romantic view, and a children's program to please the whole family.

Opened in 1985, the hotel is part of Hershey Hotels and Resorts. (The grande dame of the family is The Hotel Hershey in Hershey, PA.) Guests are handed a Hershey bar on check-in, chocolate kisses are usually within reaching distance, and the hotel hosts a Chocolate Festival in December, with chocolate buffets, demonstrations, and exhibits. (You might as well get it over with and go to the Glass Pavilion as soon as you check in to eat a piece of The-Devil-Made-Me-Do-It Devil's Food Cake. The chocolate chip pecan pie laced with bourbon is also hard to ignore.)

Throughout the hotel, there's a recognition of the bayside setting. Colors and designs tend to bring the outdoors in. Guest rooms, angled to have a glimpse of Corpus Christi Bay, are furnished with traditional furniture, two double beds (some have a queen-size bed with settee and lounge chair), TVs, and clock radios. Rooms on the concierge floor, dubbed the Mainline Club, have special touches (robes, refrigerator, extra goodies in the amenity basket) plus an inviting lounge where guests are served hors d'oeuvres and continental breakfast. The concierge is unusually helpful, acting as a personal valet.

At the second floor recreational area there's an expansive sunbathing deck, outdoor and indoor pools, large whirlpool, racquetball courts, and a weight room. (Make time to try out the micro massage machine, a 15-minute computerized massage for $5.) You can rent bikes and fishing equipment at this center, which is staffed all day.

Within the center is the hotel's Leave the Children to Us Playmates Program. Available at no extra charge, it has an enthusiastic staff who make both you and your children feel good about leaving them. For young children, there's a nursery with toys and games. Older children can enjoy scavenger hunts, supervised water games, and pinball tournaments. The staff will also take children to lunch and dinner, if you wish.

Self parking in the hotel's covered garage is free; valet parking is $5. During some seasons, trolleys connect the hotel to shopping centers. Throughout the year the Hershey has an array of innovative packages, making it even more of a good buy.

Inn of the Hills River Resort

1001 Junction Highway
Kerrville, Texas 78028
512/895-5000
800/292-5690
GENERAL MANAGER: Charlotte Thompson
150 rooms; 68 condos
$40–$55 single, $50–$75 double; $75–$150 condos
American Express, Amoco, Carte Blanche, Diners Club, Discover, MasterCard, Visa
Children welcome
Small pets accepted
Open year round

Set in the Texas Hill Country, this resort has a wide range of offerings, both in style of accommodations and in recreation. Inn of the Hills began welcoming guests in the early 1960s. In the mid-1980s a luxurious condominium complex on the banks of the Guadalupe River was added, greatly enhancing the lodging's appeal. Guests now have a choice of motel rooms, cabanas, junior suites, and executive suites—all in the older section, and of riverfront condos with or without kitchenettes.

The motel centers around a swimming pool and playground area; the new complex provides a river view for every unit. While the original motel reflects its age, there's a look of TLC about the place. Rooms are pleasantly decorated, and the grounds are well-maintained. The elegant high-rise condos, ranging in size from 700 to 1500 square feet, are a decided contrast to the older lodgings.

Wherever guests stay, they have full use of all the resort's facilities. That translates to two outdoor pools, lighted tennis courts, and nine-hole putting green; a boat marina on the river bank with canoes, and paddleboats; fishing pier; rental bikes; and use of the sports center next door with racquetball, handball, exercise room, indoor pool, and bowling.

The Guadalupe River Club, part of the condo complex, is an excellent place to dine in elegance, with the river itself as the background. Two casual restaurants are also on the grounds. Both the River Club and the Sports Center are private clubs; Inn of the Hills guests have temporary memberships.

12

Gourmet Getaways

Beautiful surroundings, excellent food, and someone to enjoy it all with—what more could you ask for in a getaway? The following entries will help you find the first two. For the third, you're on your own.

ARIZONA

L'Auberge de Sedona
  301 Little Lane
  P.O. Box B
  Sedona, Arizona 86336
  602/282-1661
  800/272-6776 US, 800/331-2820 AZ
GENERAL MANAGER: Eric Umstattd
95 units
The Orchards: $60–$110 double
Lodge: $85–$120 double
Cottages: $175–$300 double including gourmet breakfast and
  dinner; special prices for a 2-night, 1-dinner stay sometimes
  available
Children welcome
No pets
Open year round

L'Auberge de Sedona is the definition of a gourmet getaway, a total aesthetic experience. Lodging is on the banks of

Oak Creek in a country-French cottage. On the outside, it's a cozy log cottage with a porch entwined in wisteria. On the inside it's a confection of romance, with a brass canopy bed, overstuffed chairs, and a stone fireplace. Designer fabrics and country crafts add just the right touch.

All this and dining too. L'Auberge Restaurant, also set in a creekside cottage, is a collage of greens and pinks, with a fabric-covered ceiling and tiny lamps on each table. Le Diner begins with a choice of hors d'oeuvres, perhaps sauteed Pacific seafood with white mushrooms on a nest of fettucini mantled with a tarragon sauce, or grilled scaloppini of Swedish reindeer with diced apples and Marsala wine sauce. Then on to the soup course, maybe chilled pineapple rum bisque or cream of broccoli. Les Salades of the evening may be mixed greens with mandarin oranges, water chestnuts, and a tomato basil vinaigrette.

There are five entrees to choose from, and what a choice—sauteed grenadines of veal mantled with a chanterelle mushroom sauce; roasted breast of Long Island duckling laced with a brandied peach sauce; grilled California king salmon complemented with a kiwi papaya sauce. Dessert includes an assortment of pastries, but the bananas Foster is personally recommended (one of the best renditions I've ever experienced).

The menu changes nightly. Service is hospitable and professional. For non-guests, dinner is a fixed price, approximately $30 on weekdays and $33 on weekends. Reservations are definitely recommended.

L'Auberge de Sedona is a resort with three different lodging styles. It all started in 1984 when Jean Rocchi built the cottages and the restaurant, fulfilling his dream of a French country inn in the Red Rock Country. Two partners joined him in 1986, and together they built a 20-room lodge and more cottages down by the creek (now there are 32). Additionally, they bought an existing motel on top of the hill behind their resort, extensively remodeling it and installing an outdoor "hillavator" to connect the two portions.

The hilltop rooms, or The Orchards at L'Auberge, have a fresh country look, with tie-back curtains and carved wooden beds. Though not as elaborate as the creekside rooms, they are a good alternative, given their lower rates. All open onto a patio or balcony. The lodge is romantic, all done up in bows and country crafts. Lodge rooms, situated on two floors, are similar to the cottages in their decor. Opening the door to each is like unwrapping a present. All are spacious and have king-size canopied beds, French provincial chairs, armoires, and a small patio or balcony. Often used by groups (especially for conferences), the lodge has several meeting rooms. Two guest houses, each with three bedrooms and a full kitchen, are part of the resort.

On top of the hill there are two swimming pools and a chic restaurant, The Orchards Grill, serving light American cuisine. Winding pathways and flower gardens tie the various segments of the resort together.

When you want to leave the tranquil grounds and explore the Sedona area, the desk personnel can arrange tennis, golf, jeep tours, or horseback riding.

NEW MEXICO

Hacienda Rancho de Chimayo
P.O. Box 11
Chimayo, New Mexico 87522
505/351-2222
OWNERS: The Jaramillo Family
7 rooms (private baths)
$39–$66 single, $49–$76 double including continental breakfast
American Express, MasterCard, Visa; personal check
Children over age of three welcome
No pets
Open year round except January

Heading north from Santa Fe, the road to Chimayo turns east at Pajoaque. Once you leave U.S. 285 connecting Santa Fe and Taos, you're definitely on "the road less taken." Highway 4 is a beauteous stretch, rising and dipping over the wide-open countryside, with expansive views of the Sangre de Cristo Mountains in the distance.

Chimayo, population approximately 1,500, is an old Spanish settlement, dating back to 1598. Today renowned for its weavers, it is one of New Mexico's most famed craft villages. The Ortega family started the tradition eight generations ago. Area shops include Ortega's Weavers and Art Gallery, Trujillo's Weavers, and El Chimayo Weavers. Visitors come from all parts of the country to buy their work, especially blankets, rugs, curtains, and place mats.

Another longtime Chimayo family, the Jaramillos, have created their own tradition in recent years. Today they have two hospitality operations—a large restaurant serving native cuisine and a seven-room inn across the street. The family traces its roots to the area's first Spanish settlers. In the 1880s, two Jaramillo brothers helped each other build family homes, now separated by the little road leading into town. In 1965 their descendants restored one of the homes and converted it into a hacienda-style restaurant.

Highly popular despite its remote location, Restaurante Rancho de Chimayo is a festive getaway. Interior dining areas are authentic Southwest with their hand-stripped vigas and white-washed walls. Terraced patios spill down the hillside. Everybody has a great time, developing a sense of camaraderie in this off-the-beaten-track restaurant.

Comidas Nativas (native dishes) are all tempting: chicken breasts topped with red chili and melted cheese; sopaipillas stuffed with beef, beans, and Spanish rice; pork cutlets marinated and cooked in a red chili sauce; and more than a dozen other choices. (For those in your group who yearn for more traditional fare, such dishes as hamburgers and trout amandine are on the menu.)

Usually open from noon until 9 P.M., the restaurant closes on Mondays during part of the year, and is completely closed during January. Whatever the season, be sure to make reservations (505/351-4444).

So successful was the restaurant that the Jaramillo family restored the second family home across the road, opening it as an inn in 1984. Now travelers can dine at the restaurant and extend their stay in the charming village by spending the night at Hacienda Rancho de Chimayo. (Again, be sure to make reservations.)

The 100-year-old brown stucco home, trimmed in white, has a wreath of dried peppers on the front door. The atmosphere is casual—definitely a country feeling. All of the guest rooms open onto a central courtyard. Stepping into any of the rooms is a beautiful surprise. Not reminiscent of Santa Fe or Taos-style decor, they are country Victorian. Antique mahogany beds, Queen Anne chairs, touches of lace—all combine to form a look of casual elegance.

Uno, which can adjoin Dos (both have private baths), is a large high-ceilinged room with king-size bed, marble-top dresser, couches, and private balcony. Even the bath has high visual appeal, with a wooden vanity and a water closet-style toilet. Siete is delightfully exquisite—double four-poster bed, fireplace, and such furnishings as a Queen Anne chair and antique mirror.

Most rooms can be joined with at least one other. Cuatro can adjoin Tres to form a two bedroom/living room suite. Guests have a choice of twin, double, queen, and king beds.

Continental breakfast—served either in your room, the lobby, or the courtyard—is likely to be croissants and fresh fruit. You can spend the morning visiting the weavers' shops and also El Santuario, a church where miraculous cures are said to have taken place since it was built in the early 1800s. At lunchtime, head to Restaurante Rancho de Chimayo.

Meson de Mesilla
  1803 Avenida de Mesilla
  P.O. Box 1212
  Mesilla, New Mexico 88046
  505/525-9212
INNKEEPERS: Chuck Walker
13 rooms (private baths)
$45–$75 double including full breakfast
American Express, Diners Club, MasterCard, Visa; personal
  check
Children accepted based on prior agreement
Pets with approval
Open year round

Mesilla was once the largest town in the southern part of the New Mexico Territory. During the Civil War it was declared Confederate Capital of a territory that extended to California. Billy the Kid stood trial in Mesilla, and the Gadsden Treaty, transferring 45,000 square miles of land that is now southern Arizona and New Mexico, was signed on Mesilla's plaza. Now a village of about 2,000, Old Mesilla is known for its galleries, shops, and restaurants, while neighboring Las Cruces, population 45,000, is economic leader of the region.

About six blocks from Mesilla's plaza is an inn well worth discovering. Its style is classic adobe, but its vintage is 1985.

From the outset, Meson de Mesilla was designed as an inn—hence the large airy rooms, each with private bath, and the spacious restaurant.

Guest rooms, all on the second floor, open onto a porch that leads down to the pool and covered patio. Honeysuckle twines down the wrought iron stairway. Beyond the pool, past the backyard, stretch miles of cotton fields. Every guest room at Meson de Mesilla is different. With names like Yucca and Roadrunner, their decor reflects the inn's locale. Brass beds, southwestern art, and handsome vertical blinds at the windows combine to provide comfort, beauty, and seclusion. The three suites have kiva fireplaces and a sitting area. No phones or TVs are in the rooms, but TVs are available for the asking.

Breakfast is beautifully served in the restaurant downstairs. Through the windows you look upon a landscaped cactus garden. Inside you dine on such dishes as eggs Creole or orange yogurt pancakes, served with panache. But the best is yet to come—at dinner time.

The menu for the evening includes seven or eight choices, such dishes as redfish Sicilian, veau Rachel, frog saute Provencale, and steak a la Meson. You might begin the feast with escargot a la Bourguignonne followed by soup, salad, and then the main course served with wild rice pilaf. The price of the entire meal, including dessert, ranges from $14 to $17. A wine connoisseur, host Chuck Walker offers guests a wide selection of California, Spanish, Italian, German, and New Mexican wines.

The restaurant is open for dinner Tuesday through Saturday, for lunch Wednesday through Friday. Sunday brunch is a weekly highlight.

Reservations, whenever you choose to dine, are recommended.

St. James Hotel
Route 1, Box 2
Cimarron, New Mexico 87714
505/376-2664
INNKEEPERS: Ed and Pat Sitzberger
8 rooms (some shared baths)
$40–$75 single or double
MasterCard, Visa
Children welcome
No pets
Open year round

In the dusty little town of Cimarron about an hour's drive southwest of Raton is a historic hotel with delightfully different rooms and a restaurant guaranteed to please.

It all started back in 1873 when the man who had been personal chef to Abraham Lincoln headed west. Henri Lambert, a French immigrant, never found the gold he left home for, but he bought some land at a stop along the Santa Fe Trail and built a saloon. In 1880 he added a hotel, building it of thick adobe.

Back then Cimarron was a tough kind of place—a hangout for desperados and horse thieves, mountain men and traders. The hotel, being the center of local social life, ended up being the last stop for some of its patrons. Twenty-six men were killed within its walls. Bullet holes in the tin ceiling of the one-time bar (now the restaurant) bear testament to the violence that became legendary. Outlaws like Blackjack Ketchum, Jesse James, and Clay Allison (a notorious gunman) stayed at the St. James. So did lots of respected folks. Annie Oakley met with Buffalo Bill Cody here and joined his Wild West show. Zane Grey wrote a novel here. Frederic Remington stayed at the hotel while he sketched nearby scenes.

In 1985 the charmingly restored St. James opened its doors. Its saviors were Pat and Ed Sitzberger, who lovingly nursed it back to health. Pat is an artist; Ed, a native of Cimarron, grew up behind the hotel. Furnished throughout with period pieces, the hotel is a showcase of Western history. The Jesse James Room has red brocade wallpaper, red velvet chairs, a red quilt-covered brass bed, and a cranberry lamp. The Thumbelina Room, named for Tom Thumb and his wife, who performed in the Wild West show, is especially attractive, with its fabric-draped ceiling and white fireplace. Buffalo Bill's room is the largest. Next door is a tiny poker playing room—past and present.

Most guest rooms have a private bath. Some have tubs with hand-held showers. There are no TVs or phones in the rooms but both are available in the lobby and the lounge.

It's only fitting for a classic hotel to have a fine restaurant. The setting is elegant; the food is the best for miles around. Feast on stuffed flounder Florentine, filled with crab meat and fresh vegetables and topped with veloute sauce. Or pollo Gismonda—breaded chicken breast in a spiced spinach ring, covered with fresh sauteed mushrooms. Broiled swordfish steak, shrimp Diablo, veal Marsala, tournedos of beef, pasta carbonara, plus a dozen or more entrees give you plenty of choices.

Unexpectedly for a historic hotel, the St. James has a swimming pool. It was built to accompany a next-door motel, which is now operated as an annex for the main hotel (rooms are about half the rate of those in the hotel).

Across the street is Old Mill Museum, filled with history (open late spring to early fall). A National Historic District, Cimarron has other sites to visit. Two miles down the road is the Philmont Scout Ranch, national camp grounds for the Boy Scouts of America. Fishing, hunting, and skiing are popular area attractions.

By the way, St. James is known for having ghosts. But the Sitzbergers are excellent hosts, the setting romantic, and the food fantastic, so have an extra glass of wine and enjoy.

TEXAS

Stillwater Inn
   203 E. Broadway
   Jefferson, Texas 75657
   214/665-8415
INNKEEPERS: Bill and Sharon Stewart
3 bedrooms (private baths)
$60–$75 single or double including full breakfast
MasterCard, Visa; personal check
Children usually not accepted (negotiable)
No pets
No smoking on second floor
Open year round

In a historic town chock full of charming B&Bs, Stillwater Inn is refreshingly different. Downstairs is a refined restaurant (one of the best in town) with the air of colonial Williamsburg. In contrast, the three bedrooms upstairs are strikingly contemporary—cheerful lodgings converted from former attic space, accented with skylights as well as stained glass.

A white picket fence surrounds this residential-style inn on Broad Street. Diners come from miles around to eat at its restaurant, renowned for French-American cuisine. Owners Bill and Sharon Stewart moved to Jefferson from Dallas where Bill was a sous chef at the famed Adolphus Hotel. The standards of this family-run operation are high. Herbs are plucked from the garden outside; all of the dishes are prepared from scratch. Fresh seafood is always prominent on the menu

(Bill has to drive to a neighboring town to pick it up). Of special note, wine aficionados will be pleased at the selections available.

Overnight guests have the convenience of a private entrance at the rear of the inn. Stairs lead to a sitting area on the second floor, informal and relaxing. Use of space throughout this floor is whimsical and imaginative. The three bedrooms vary in size; each has a TV appropriate to the size of the room. Furnishings are modern, featuring bare-wood poster beds, brass fixtures, and cool colors. A handsome stained-glass window is the focal point of one guest room. Another, perhaps the best choice for a romantic getaway, has an oversized tub.

Guests are treated to coffee upstairs before descending to the dining room for a full breakfast. Since the restaurant is open to the public only for dinner (Wednesday through Sunday), lodging guests dine at breakfast in privacy.

13

Grand New Resorts

Sparkling new resorts that glisten with excitement. Like gems in a treasure chest, each has special charm.

ARIZONA

The Boulders
  34631 N. Tom Darlington
  P.O. Box 2090
  Carefree, Arizona 85377
  602/488-9009
  800/223-7637 outside NY, 800/442-8198 NY state
GENERAL MANAGER: Richard Holtzman
120 casitas
$200–$305 single, $250–$380 double including 2 meals
American Express, Diners Club, MasterCard, Visa; personal
  check
Children welcome
Pets accepted
Open early September to late June

About 30 minutes north of Scottsdale on the first plateau out of the desert, there's an exclusive resort hidden away in the foothills. Huge boulders dominate the landscape, like toys haphazardly strewn by a wayward giant as he ambled through the countryside. Aptly enough, the resort is named The Boulders. It's a retreat from the city, a refuge from the masses. At first glance, you have to look twice to distinguish casitas from the surrounding rock formations. A wonderful free-form pool set amid the rocks looks almost natural.

To be sure, The Boulders is pricey. It is part of the Rockresort family, which includes Caneel Bay, Little Dix Bay, and Carambola Beach in the Caribbean, Woodstock Inn in Vermont, and Jenny Lake Lodge in the Grand Tetons.

There's plenty to do at The Boulders, but not so much that you have to schedule your day frantically to get it all in. A residential community as well as a resort, it has 27 holes of golf and six plexi-cushioned tennis courts, all set against spectacular desert scenery. Through the concierge you can arrange such things as horseback riding, jeep tours, hot air ballooning, and flights to the Grand Canyon.

The main lodge is a stone extravaganza, and entering it is like stepping into a science fiction movie. Circular in shape, it has boulder-like doors, polished stone floors, and unusual use of space. Not only does its architecture reflect the outdoor setting, but also the interior design reflects the area's Indian heritage. For instance, the Latilla Dining Room represents the inside of a Hopi kiva.

Casitas are large, luxurious, and visually interesting—wooden beamed ceilings, adobe walls, and fireplaces (winter evening temperatures drop to the 40s). Baths have step-in showers as well as large tubs. Continental breakfast—white linen style—is served in your room upon request. Breakfast and dinner are included in the cost of lodging, and there's a choice of three dining areas. Evening dining is formal, with jackets required for men.

Transportation can be arranged between the resort and Sky Harbor Airport in Phoenix. Rental cars are available on the property.

Hyatt Regency Scottsdale at Gainey Ranch

7500 E. Doubletree Ranch Road
Scottsdale, Arizona 85261-6211
602/483-3388
800/228-9000
GENERAL MANAGER: Edward G. Sullivan
497 rooms
$85–$265 single or double
HIGH SEASON: late December to early May
LOW SEASON: mid-June to mid-September
American Express, Carte Blanche, Diners Club, MasterCard,
    Visa; personal check
Children welcome
Open year round

Hyatt Regency Scottsdale is the Caribbean in the midst of
the desert, a true oasis with a water playground extravaganza
far surpassing anything else in the Southwest. And there's
more—27 holes of golf, health and fitness center, eight tennis
courts, lawn croquet, and jogging and cycling trails. As part
of the Gainey Ranch complex, which includes residential and
retail development, the hotel opened in late 1986. Set with
hundreds of palm trees and other lush foliage, it's an elegant
resort, a virtual destination within itself.

The water playground is truly dazzling. Built on multiple
levels, it has 28 fountains, ten pools, and a three-story waterslide—but statistics don't tell the story. It's a water fantasy, a
quasi-Roman-Grecian creation with a pure American sandy
beach.

The hotel lobby, decorated with international art, leads
down to two dining rooms. The Normandie (like the pools, a
seeming transplant from the Caribbean) has all-day service
with both indoor and outdoor dining. The more formal
Golden Swan restaurant overlooks the resort's lake.

Guest rooms, average in size, are decorated in cool colors
and have private balconies and stocked minibars. Regency
Club rooms on the third floor have complimentary breakfast,
afternoon hors d'oeuvres, and upgraded amenities. Several
deluxe casitas (living room, two to four bedrooms) are on the
lake.

The fitness center far surpasses that of a typical hotel facility. In addition to exercise equipment, saunas, massage
rooms, and herbal wraps, it has the Mollen Clinic—a physical
fitness and medical facility which offers personalized health
evaluations and health programs.

Sample fees for recreational facilities are $10 per court per hour for tennis, $10 per person daily for the health club, $31 in summer and $59 in winter for 18 holes of golf, and $10 per person golf cart rental.

John Gardiner's Enchantment
P.O. Box 2549
Sedona, Arizona 86336
602/282-2900
800/826-4180
GENERAL MANAGER: Paul Pastoor
120 units
$160–$445 double with no meals; $225–$545 double including breakfast and dinner
American Express, MasterCard, Visa; personal check
Children welcome
Pets acceptable
Open year round

Without a doubt, Enchantment lives up to its name. Deep in Boynton Canyon—mystically beautiful with red rock boulders and spires—the resort snuggles into the cliffsides. A composite of casitas, clubhouse, tennis courts, and spa, it spreads over 70 secluded acres about eight miles from Sedona.

Enchantment opened in 1987 as the third of John Gardiner's resorts. But unlike Gardiner's tennis ranches in Scottsdale, Arizona and Carmel Valley, California, you don't even need to pick up a tennis racket at this resort.

Of course if you want to play tennis, there's hardly a better place. Twelve championship Plexi-Pave courts are at the heart of the resort's design, and guests can play at no extra charge. Tennis clinics and lessons are also available.

The spa and fitness center has exercise facilities, steam and inhalation rooms, saunas, whirlpools, and tanning beds. Spa packages and wellness packages are available at selected times. Both offer something no other resort can—hikes into incredibly beautiful Boynton Canyon.

Also on the grounds are two regulation croquet lawns (tournaments are held several times during the year), three swimming pools, outdoor whirlpool spas, pitch-and-putt golf, and jogging and hiking trails.

Within the clubhouse there's lots of public space, including an elegant dining room with picture windows. (The evening dress code is jackets for men and "evening attire" for women.)

Lodging is in casita rooms and suites tucked into the hillsides. Whether you opt for a one-bedroom unit or the entire suite (living room with fireplace, bedroom, kitchenette), you get a large private balcony—perfect for canyon-gazing. Interiors are plush, with wood-beamed ceilings, easy chairs, two queen-size beds, southwestern art, and lots of windows. Kitchenettes have all of the essentials plus a microwave oven. Balconies are equipped with grills. A few casitas have their own pools.

Loews Ventana Canyon Resort

7000 N. Resort Drive
Tucson, Arizona 85715
602/299-2020
800/223-0888 US, 800/522-5455 NY State
GENERAL MANAGER: John Thacker
392 units
$65–$190 single or double
HIGH SEASON: mid-January to mid-May
American Express, Carte Blanche, Diners Club, MasterCard,
     Visa; personal check
Children welcome
No pets
Open year round

The setting could hardly be more dramatic. Ventana Canyon, centered with an 80-foot waterfall, is the natural backdrop for this resort, built of gray block to blend with the mountains behind.

Loews Resort with its 94 acres of facilities is part of a 1000-plus-acre planned community. Adjacent to the hotel is Lakeside Spa and Tennis club, with ten championship tennis courts, lap pool, fitness trail, exercise center, and spa facilities. Also nearby is Ventana Canyon Golf and Racquet Club, featuring a 27-hole Tom Fazio-designed PGA golf course. Loews guests have privileges at both clubs.

Behind the hotel itself there's a large attractive pool, croquet lawn, and shallow lake at the mountain's base. Best of all, there's a path leading to the waterfall—an invitation to explore the mystical desert landscape just beyond the hotel.

Guest rooms, with views of either the mountains or the city, have private balconies or terraces, minibars, and armoires with concealed TVs. Bathrooms, accented in marble, feature double whirlpool tubs.

Art is integral to the hotel's interior decor, from Arizona landscapes in the foyer to original lithographs in guest rooms. Ventana Restaurant, serving dinner only, specializes in new American cuisine. Canyon Café has all-day service. The Flying V Bar and Grill serves lunch and dinner; after 9 P.M., it's transformed into a video disco.

The Pointe at Tapatio Cliffs
  11111 N. Seventh Street
  Phoenix, Arizona 85020
  602/997-6000
  800/528-0428
GENERAL MANAGER: Rita Wheeler
591 suites
$60–$195 single, $70–$195 double
HIGH SEASON: January to May
LOW SEASON: June to mid-September
American Express, Carte Blanche, Diners Club, Discover,
  MasterCard, Visa; personal check
Children welcome
No pets
Open year round

The mood is festive at The Pointe. With pool parties and a host of special activities, it's like a giant cruise ship, moored at an inland shore.

Spread over 400 acres, The Pointe is huge. It's a complete vacationland with a number of sports (five pools, 15 tennis courts, four racquetball courts, horseback riding), three major restaurants, a spa, and nearly 600 suites arranged in Spanish-styled buildings with arches, courtyards, and fountains.

Suites, all similarly arranged, have a sitting room with wet bar and refrigerator, bedroom with armoire for a closet, bath divided into sections, and a small balcony.

The tennis courts are excellent; not only is the court quality good, but extensive landscaping between courts also adds appeal (extra fee for tennis). Horseback rides are by the hour or half-day; special rides include breakfast, lunch, and pony rides for children younger than seven.

Pointe In Tyme restaurant evokes a spirit of fun. Its interior is glitzy; its menu is enticing, featuring dishes made famous at restaurants across the country. There's pasta jambalaya from Mr. B's in New Orleans, veal Oscar from the Waldorf Astoria in New York, raisin rice pudding from King's Arms in Williamsburg, plus dozens more. Reading the menu is half the fun.

But the creme de la creme is Etienne's Different Pointe of View on top of the mountain. A silver stretch limousine provides transportation. Etienne's bursts with energy, created by its innovative architecture, decor, and setting. Boasting a mile-long list of awards, the restaurant has one of the most impressive wine lists in the country—more than 20 pages of unusual wines, including an extensive list of California Cabernets. Entrees range from $22 to $26.

Located at the base of North Mountain Desert Park, The Pointe at Tapatio Cliffs is one of three Pointe hotels in Phoenix. All are similar in layout and facilities. The Pointe at Squaw Peak is several miles south. The Pointe at South Mountain, the newest and the only one with a golf course, is south of downtown.

Red Lion's La Posada

4949 E. Lincoln Drive
Scottsdale, Arizona 85253
602/952-0420
800/547-8010
GENERAL MANAGER: Chuck Freije
264 rooms
$75–$200 single or double
HIGH SEASON: mid-January to mid-May
LOW SEASON: mid-May to mid-September
American Express, Carte Blanche, Discover, MasterCard,
   Visa; personal check
Children welcome
Pets accepted
Open year round

Red Lion's La Posada brings water to the desert and adds an extra dollop of glitz to Scottsdale's hotel row. In a lobby more kin to Las Vegas than the Southwest with its profusion of fuchsia, gold, and sparkle, you can tell this is no ordinary lodging. It's a lively place, a resort where the staff greets you with a smile and the tone is definitely upbeat.

Out back there's a half-acre swimming pool, actually more of a lagoon, with a manmade boulder mountain, splashing waterfalls, and a half-hidden grotto bar. Directly behind the hotel is the area's most distinctive landmark—Camelback Mountain. The Garden Terrace Restaurant is a great place to dine while overlooking the pool and the mountain. Like the lobby below, it is refreshingly energetic in its decor. The adjoining Terrace Lounge has live entertainment.

Guest rooms are in 16 long buildings arranged over the resort's 32 acres. Inside they are opulent, decorated with brocades, formal furniture, and mirrors. The smallest room is large by hotel standards, measuring 450 square feet. Cabanas are 759 square feet, casitas are 950 square feet. All rooms have mini-refrigerators, honor bars, TVs hidden away in armoires, and patios or balconies.

La Posada has six tennis courts, racquetball, fitness center, massage, putting green, and hot tubs. There's concierge service, car rental, and airport limo transportation. A shopping plaza on the grounds has two restaurants of its own—Guadala-Harry's with Mexican dishes (what else?) and Mancusco's, serving Northern Italian food.

The Registry Resort

7171 N. Scottsdale Rd.
Scottsdale, Arizona 85253
602/991-3800
800/247-9810
GENERAL MANAGER: Rick Dumos
318 rooms
$85–$225 single or double
HIGH SEASON: January to mid-May
LOW SEASON: mid-May to early September
American Express, Diners Club, MasterCard, Visa; personal
  check
Children welcome
No pets
Open year round

One of the resorts set along Scottsdale Road, The Registry stands apart from its neighbors with its abundant tennis and golf and its varied dining. The Registry is part of McCormick Ranch development comprising residential, office, and recreational facilities. The development's two golf courses, one adjacent to the hotel, are 18-hole, par 72 championship courses. The resort's tennis courts are exceptionally fine, accompanied by a small grandstand. The main swimming pool is one of the best in the area; not only is it large, but it also has a three-meter and a one-meter diving board and a lifeguard on duty. Several smaller pools are also on the grounds.

The lobby has an elegant tone, set with fine furnishings. La Champagne restaurant is formal (entrees $18–$22); Café Brioche is casual. Kachina Lounge has live entertainment. The Phoenician Room, used for special functions as well as Sunday brunch, is opulent, a step back into supper club days, with a stage for live entertainment.

About one-third of the guest rooms are attached to the main building. Casitas are spread over the grounds, charmingly interspersed with courtyards and flowering shrubs. Modern in decor, they have all the expected amenities. Casita accommodations are by far the most appealing.

Scottsdale Princess

7575 E. Princess Boulevard
Scottsdale, Arizona 85261
602/271-0001
800/255-0080
GENERAL MANAGER: Manfred Gerling
525 rooms and casitas
$180–$230 single, $190–$250 double
American Express, Diners Club, Carte Blanche, MasterCard,
  Visa
Children welcome
No pets
Open year round

Opened in late 1987, the first Princess Hotel in the U.S. has
sister hotels in Acapulco (Acapulco Princess and Pierre
Marques), Bermuda (Southampton Princess and The Princess
Hamilton), and Grand Bahama Island (Bahamas Princess
Resort and Casino).

The estate-like resort, spread over 450 acres several miles
north of other Scottsdale resorts, is a destination within itself.
Built in Mexican colonial style, it is truly grand. Guest rooms
are in the sprawling main building; casitas are clustered near
the tennis courts.

Recreation choices spill cornucopia-like over the grounds:
two 18-hole golf courses (designed by Jay Morrish and Tom
Weiskopf), 12 tennis courts (including a 10,000-seat stadium
court), three swimming pools, and a health club and spa
(racquetball and squash courts, health and beauty treatments).
Adjacent to the hotel, the City of Scottsdale has built a 400-
acre horse park with nine equestrian arenas, two stadium arenas, polo field, grand prix field for jumping, and 500 stables.

Guest rooms are large and have interesting configurations.
All have big terraces and wet bars with refrigerators. Bathrooms are luxurious and extra large, with separate tub and
shower. Casitas have microwave ovens.

Restaurants such as La Hacienda and Chula Vista reflect the
resort's international pedigree. There's a total of four dining
areas, three lounges, and two swim-up bars.

Sheraton Tucson El Conquistador Golf and Tennis Resort

10000 N. Oracle Road
Tucson Arizona 85704
602/742-7000
800/325-3535
GENERAL MANAGER: Irving Hutsen
440 rooms

$55–$160 single or double; $85–$750 for suites
HIGH SEASON: January to late May
LOW SEASON: late May to late September
American Express, Carte Blanche, Diners Club, MasterCard,
   Visa; personal check
Children welcome
Pets accepted
Open year round

Spread over 150 acres of high rolling desert about ten miles north of Tucson, the Sheraton El Conquistador looks up at the cliffs of the Santa Catalina Mountains directly beyond. A self-contained resort with a colonial Mexican theme, it's a composite of one- to three-story lodging buildings. Guest rooms have traditional furniture and southwestern decor. All have private patios or balconies. The most luxurious are the casita units.

There is a variety of recreational facilities. With a nine-hole golf course of its own and use of the 27-hole Canada Hills Country Club six miles away, it offers guests 36 holes of championship golf. El Conquistador's 16 tennis courts are excellent. There's a stadium court, pro shop, and tennis instructors. About 20 horses are stabled on the grounds, with trail rides into the foothills of the nearby mountains. Cookout rides and sunset champagne rides are sometimes scheduled. For groups, hayrides, barbecues, and square dances can be arranged. Of course there's a large swimming pool, along with such extras as racquet ball courts, a fitness center, and jogging paths.

Summertime is an excellent time to get top value for your dollar, with prices not only substantially lower for rooms but also for recreation. For example, tennis fees which are $10 per hour during the winter season drop to $5 in the summer. Greens fees drop significantly as well; during some periods, they are waived entirely.

The Sundance Café (casual, serves all meals), The Last Territory (rustic steakhouse with entertainment and dancing), and The White Dove (gourmet dining) give dimension and variety to the dining choices.

Westin La Paloma
   3800 E. Sunrise Drive
   Tucson, Arizona 85718
   602/742-6000
   800/228-3000
GENERAL MANAGER: Andy MacLellan
487 rooms

$70–$215 single, $75–$250 double; $465–$1,200 suites
HIGH SEASON: January to mid-May
LOW SEASON: mid-May to mid-September
American Express, Discover, JCB, MasterCard, Visa;
    personal check
Children welcome
No pets
Open year round

The Westin La Paloma is a pink palace set within the desert. Its facilities are first class—some of the best in the Southwest. And its staff is hospitable, making the near-500 room resort seem almost intimate.

The resort's 27-hole championship Jack Nicklaus-designed golf course is challenging, unusual in its layout, and highly scenic. The course takes advantage of its Sonoran Desert setting while making a minimal impact on it. (Indeed, so sensitive were the developers to the landscape that with careful planning they were able to save more than 7000 of the 8000 saguaro cacti on the resort site.)

The tennis courts (10 hard surface, 4 clay) are top quality, scenic in their setting, and adjoined by a good pro shop. La Paloma's free-form pool with its bridges, waterfalls, and lagoons is more akin to pools at Caribbean resorts than those in the Southwest. Hot tubs are tucked away invitingly among the shrubs. And there's more—a health club with racquetball, Nautilus equipment, and aerobics; a spa with massage, facials, waxing, and body wraps; a game area with croquet, volleyball, and bike rentals; and hot air balloon rides.

At mealtime, choose from the graciously elegant La Paloma Dining Room (part of the private membership La Paloma Country Club), La Villa (set in a charming hacienda), and Desert Garden (in the main building, affording views of the mountains beyond the resort). Entrees at La Paloma range from $17 to $21 and feature such delectables as escalope of duck breast with apples, Dover sole with avocado and crayfish, and grenadins of lamb with asparagus and morels.

Throughout the resort, the look is refined Southwest with a modern flair. Accommodations are in 27 two- and three-story buildings arranged in a semi-circle facing the mountains. All are painted "La Paloma rose," a color intended to suggest the sunset. Interior colors reflect the desert—sage green, cobalt blue, mauve, and gray.

While rooms tend to be small, they are cleverly decorated and arranged. Each has a patio or balcony, refrigerator, and remote controlled TV within an armoire. Bathrooms are especially luxurious, with separate tub and shower, phone, and robes.

Of special interest to families, day care is provided for children ages six months to 12 years.

TEXAS

Four Seasons Resort and Hotel
(Las Colinas Inn and Conference Center)
4150 N. MacArthur Boulevard
Irving, Texas 75062
214/570-0800
800/332-3442
GENERAL MANAGER: Jim Fitzgibbon
315 rooms
$120–$155 single or double
American Express, Diners Club, En Route, MasterCard, Visa;
personal checks
Children welcome
Small pets on a leash
Open year round

Hidden away between Dallas and Dallas/Fort Worth International Airport is a sparkling new community named Las Colinas. A composite of office and residential development, it's an innovative master-planned town.

Four Seasons sits on a hill overlooking Tournament Players Golf Course. The hotel opened in mid-1986. It was pre-dated by a sophisticated fitness center and spa, now operated by Four Seasons. The combined facilities give vacationers a multi-faceted resort with lots of appeal. (Incidentally, it's also a fine conference center, but that doesn't interfere with a leisure traveler's enjoyment.)

The roster of activities is enticing, a something-for-everyone kind of resort. The 18-hole golf course is the only TPC course in northern Texas and provides elevated areas for tournament-watching.

Racquet sports include indoor and outdoor tennis, squash, and racquetball. The fitness section has Nautilus equipment, treadmills, bicycles, rowing machines, and a gym. There's an outdoor and indoor pool, jogging tracks, and aerobics classes.

The spa is one of the best equipped in the Southwest. Herbal wraps and loofah scrubs, facials and pedicures, tanning beds and massages are all included.

A preventive medicine center is also part of the complex. Health-care professionals perform diagnostic testing geared toward achieving optimum health through exercise and nutrition.

Use of the sports and spa facilities doesn't come cheap ($67 for 18 holes of golf with cart rental, $20 per hour for tennis; $40 for a Swedish masssage), but lots of cost-saving packages are available combining lodging with sports and spa services.

Throughout the hotel there's a sense of spaciousness. Public areas and guest rooms overlook lush grounds. Café on the Green is casual. Other dining areas include Alternatives, a restaurant featuring dishes low in calories, sodium and cholesterol.

Accommodations get high marks for comfort and luxury—overstuffed chairs with ottomans, three phones, large tub and separate walk-in shower, and balconies.

Shuttle service is available to Dallas/Fort Worth Airport. Hotel parking is free.

14

Grand Old Mansions

Grand old homes that beg you to come inside and savor their charm—these are the Grand Old Mansions of the Southwest. Each has a story to tell, and you're invited to hear it first hand.

NEW MEXICO

Preston House
   106 Faithway Street
   Santa Fe, New Mexico 87501
   505/982-3465
OWNER: Signe Bergman
9 rooms (2 with shared baths)
$45–$115 double including breakfast
American Express, MasterCard, Visa; personal check
Infants, children over 12
Pets with approval
No smoking
Open year round

The Victorian house on Faithway Street is a refreshing change from the adobe structures characteristic of Santa Fe. Built in the 1880s, it reflects an important segment of the capital city's history.

The house was elegant from its inception. Intricately crafted wooden trims are the work of Oriental workers brought to the area to build railroads. Fireplaces throughout the house, each different from the others, add visual interest.

There's an inviting porch at the front of the blue and white house, and a huge bell to summon the innkeeper. Guests enter an 1880s parlor and find tea and fruit awaiting their arrival.

Six guest rooms are within the main house, situated on the first through third floors. Number 1 on the first floor is a romantic escape—it has a king-size white iron and brass bed, a beautiful fireplace encased in wood trim, and a carved wooden armoire. Even the ceiling has aesthetic appeal, with peach and white borders. The bath has a wonderful stained glass window, carved cabinet, and delicate wallpaper. And so the beauty continues—up the stairs past the landing (one of the spots where coffee is served) to rooms doused in romance. Number 3, the least expensive room and one of the two with a shared bath, has a brass double bed.

Outside the house, right past the back patio, are two Queen Anne-style cottages built in 1987. Lace curtains, mauve wallpaper with delicate designs, alcove seating with lots of frilly pillows, white Queen Anne chairs, and a gleaming brass bed combine to form a superior getaway. There's sherry on the bedside table, a dimmer control on the lights, and a ceiling fan overhead.

What's for breakfast at Preston House? Guests dine on bread pudding, muffins, fruit tarts, fresh fruits, and cereal, all served buffet style.

Four managers rotate duties at this B&B, and one of the four lives on the premises. The owner, Signe Bergman, is an artist and designer who moved to Santa Fe in 1974. Commissioned to paint murals for the Santa Barbara Biltmore Hotel in 1978, she decided to operate a hotel of her own. Preston House, which opened in 1981, is her creation.

TEXAS

Browning Plantation
Route 1, Box 8
Chappell Hill, Texas 77426
409/836-6144
Also 713/626-9592 for reservations
INNKEEPERS: Dick and Mildred Ganchan
Main house: 4 rooms (shared half bath), separate baths for
men and women on third floor
Detached building: 2 bedrooms (private bath)

Main house: $110 to $150 double including full breakfast
Detached building: $70 double including continental breakfast
Personal check; no credit cards
No children under 12
No pets
No smoking in main house
Open year round

Welcome to Tara in the Texas Hill Country—a grand old mansion set on sprawling grounds, reminiscent of a bygone era. Drive up the gravel road to a world conducive to relaxation: here you can relive the life of Southern gentry, sipping cool drinks on the veranda and luxuriating in oversized guest rooms.

Listed on the National Register of Historic Places, the Browning Plantation home was built in 1857. Dick and Mildred Ganchan discovered the deteriorated structure in 1980 and decided "somebody had to do something." For the next three years they painstakingly restored it, retaining the historical integrity of the building and transforming it into a magnificent house.

Although set with antique furnishings, the Greek Revival home has comfort more than elegance. The four guest rooms, all on the second floor, are enormous. In addition to the expected plantation and tester beds, there are specialty pieces such as a "mammy bench," designed for rocking babies. One doorway still bears marks designating the height of children who stood against it in 1872.

The third floor is a delight. Throughout the rest of the home the Ganchans remained true to the original design, but since this floor was originally attic space, they gave their imagination full rein. To supplement the half-baths adjacent to each guest room on the floor below, they created two bathrooms with whimsical decor. For ladies, the theme is Victorian bordello—chandelier, mirrored wall, fuzzy rug, even a stained-glass skylight. The men's bathroom shouts masculinity—rough cedar walls, pine dressing table, zebra-skin rug, and antlers doubling as towel racks. Climb the stairs from this floor to a rooftop observation deck, which affords an excellent view of the surrounding farmland.

A swimming pool in the backyard keeps you from losing touch with the 20th century. Also on the grounds is a restored log cabin, now serving as an antique and crafts shop (a low-key operation, open only on special occasions or when guests request it).

Breakfast is served in the dining room at an antique table seating up to 18. The fare is bounteous—a full country breakfast. Stained-glass doors lead to the modern kitchen, built over the site of the original one.

So popular is the plantation-home accommodation that another building has been added, housing two guest rooms. Resembling a 19th-century train depot, it's adjacent to a scaled-down model train; the pet project of "a railroad nut" in the Ganchan family. Guests staying in the "depot" are served a continental breakfast.

The Castle Inn
  1403 E. Washington
  Navasota, Texas 77868
  409/825-8051
INNKEEPERS: Tim and Helen Urquhart
4 bedrooms (private baths)
$66 single or double including continental breakfast
Personal check; no credit cards
Children over 13 welcome
No pets
Open year round

Step into the Victorian era at The Castle Inn in this quiet East Texas town, about one-and-a-half hours northwest of Houston. The 1890s mansion is indeed a castle, complete with turret. Every room is exquisitely decorated with American antiques, making this lodging especially appealing to history aficionados.

The house sits on two acres overlooking one of the main streets of Navasota. You enter a world of elegance through a porch enclosed with 110 panes of beveled glass. Built by German craftsmen, the house is made up of nine-and-a-half bays, resulting in octagonal rooms. Now-extinct curly pine is used throughout the home. So are carved wooden trims and ornate brass hardware. Every room is thoughtfully furnished with articles of beauty as well as special meaning to the owners. China dolls are dressed in Victorian baby clothes handed down through the family. Two child-size dolls wear costumes that Helen Urquhart and her brother once wore for a tap-dance performance. The music room, where socially prominent ladies used to gather for their bridge luncheons, is decorated with musical instruments, including a player piano.

Sliding doors 14 feet tall open into the most beautiful room in the house, the dining room. Its ornately decorated ceiling, hand-painted borders, and tiger oak walls combine to form a work of art. Upon request, the hosts serve gourmet dinners, dressing in period clothes of course. (Available when all four bedrooms are reserved by one party; approximately $20 per person.)

Bedrooms are on the second floor. A spool staircase leads past a 20-foot stained-glass window (original to the house) to a parlor and adjoining balcony where continental breakfast is served. This is also the gathering spot for wine and cheese service in the evenings. Bed choices are a rosewood Louisiana plantation, a half-tester, or a carved highback bed. Marble-top dressers, accent pieces such as fainting couches, and memorabilia, including quilts handed down through the family, complete the feeling of Victorian elegance. The Bridal Suite is especially eye-catching—decorated in fuchsia and pink, with an alcove bed and a clawfoot tub. Each room has a private bath.

So completely do the owners carry out the theme of old-time living that they give guests a ride in a 1930 Ford coupe with rumble seat. In addition to being used as a B&B, the home hosts luncheon tours and private parties.

La Maison Malfacon

700 E. Rusk Street
Marshall, Texas 75670
214/935-6039
INNKEEPERS: Jim and Linda Gililland
5 rooms (shared bath)
$55 single or double including breakfast
MasterCard, Visa; personal check
Children welcome
Pets with approval
Smoking only on veranda
Open year round

One of the warmest and most thoughtfully decorated B&Bs in the Southwest is La Maison Malfacon. The historic house reigns with dignity over a quiet street in Marshall—a sleepy East Texas town that was once the fourth largest city in the Lone Star State, and today boasts nearly 60 historical markers.

The first floor of the Greek Revival house was built circa 1866; the second story was added in 1896, resulting in a mix of architectural styles. Today's home is rich and intriguing. The wide front porch is straight out of the pages of a Southern novel. Handsome woods, hand-crafted trims, and antique furnishings abound throughout the house. Look for the gentleman's drinking chest, courtship mirror, and signed pieces of china.

It's the finishing touches that make this house special—an open 1920s suitcase packed with a gentleman's suit from Saks Fifth Avenue, a turn-of-the-century curling iron, a trunk with long-time family treasures. The hosts dress in Victorian clothing on special occasions. Ask for a ride on their bicycle built for two.

The Gilillands, an enthusiastic young couple with a bent for the dramatic, entertain their guests royally, serving such breakfast specialties as herbal eggs, eggs La Maison, and French pastry toast (all their own recipes). Sunday's fare is a champagne breakfast. Guests dine on a hand-carved table made of golden tiger oak, set with Royal Doulton china and Waterford crystal.

Bedrooms are a visual feast. There's the Shakespeare Room with an 1870s hand-carved bed and dresser, each topped with a carved bust of the playwright. The Plantation Room has a 200-year-old bed from a Marshall-area plantation, covered with a 100-year-old quilt. The Children's Room is decorated with antique children's clothing and toys. There's even a bassinet for babies who visit. Christine's Room is the most elegant, set with a 200-year-old canopied bed once owned by royalty.

Since there's only one guest bath (separate rooms for the toilet and the tub), the hosts restrict their guest list to three couples at a time.

The Magnolias
209 E. Broadway
Jefferson, Texas 75657
214/665-2754
INNKEEPER: Diane Elliott
3 rooms (2 with private bath)
$70 single or double including breakfast

Personal check
Children welcome
No pets
Open year round

A giant magnolia tree shades the lawn of this Greek Revival Mansion. In 1867 it was built by one of the town's early settlers as a dowry gift for his daughter. Today the home is open for tours as well as for bed and breakfast guests.

The Magnolias conjures up romantic images of the Old South. The wide front porch with its white columns invites you in. Walk into a guest room and you almost expect to see Scarlett and Rhett. Furnishings are Victorian antiques. Two guest rooms with private baths are on the second floor. The downstairs bedroom shares a bath with the innkeeper. Guests have lots of places to relax and play Southern plantation. Sit in the formal living room for a while, then move on to the music room or study. For less romantic types, there's also a sitting room with TV.

Breakfast with quiche, fresh fruit, and hot breads is served in the dining room at 9:30 A.M.—giving you time to awaken slowly, Southern style.

Listed in the National Register of Historic Places, The Magnolias is one of 70 structures in Jefferson with Texas State Historical Survey Medallions.

The Victorian Inn
  511 17th Street
  Galveston, Texas 77550
  409/762-3235
INNKEEPER: Wilma Jordan
5 rooms (some shared baths)
$45–$125 double including breakfast
HIGH SEASON: June to August
American Express, MasterCard, Visa; personal check
Children 13 and over
No pets
Open year round

This stately two-story brick mansion has stood since 1899. So sturdy is its construction that it has served as a sanctuary from storms hitting this coastal city. Today it's a sanctuary for travelers, offering an escape from the ordinary. Resident managers oversee the inn, welcoming guests to the spacious lodging. A beautifully designed home, its interior illustrates artistic craftsmanship of the late 1800s—spindled fretwork, floors of inlaid maple, bird's eye maple wainscoting, a handsome staircase of stained oak, and Belgian tiled fireplaces.

Four guest rooms are on the second floor. Maury's Room is cheerful, with a brass king-size bed dressed in yellow, white wicker chairs, and a wonderful semi-circular porch. Amy's Room, furnished with a king-size bed, has a small adjoining room with a twin bed. All of the guest rooms share a bath with a neighboring room; some have private porches while others share. Access to the porches is by walk-through windows, delightfully reflective of the local architectural style. Zachary's Room, actually a three-room suite, is on the third floor. Modern in decor, it has one large bedroom, another small bedroom with daybed, sitting room and private bath, but alas—no porch. (If a private bath or total privacy isn't your prime consideration, choose a second floor room. The porches are a real plus.)

Breakfast, served at the dining room table, is hearty continental. Snacks and beverages are kept on hand at the hospitality bar just off the dining room.

From the inn you can walk to The Strand entertainment district. The beach is a short drive.

The Virginia Point Inn
2327 Avenue K
Galveston, Texas 77550
409/763-2450
INNKEEPERS: Tom and Eleanor Catlow
5 rooms (some with shared baths)
$60–$125 double including full breakfast
American Express, Diners Club, MasterCard, Visa
Children over 12 welcome
No pets
No smoking
Open year round

There's no doubt about it: As soon as you walk in the door, you know that the Virginia Point Inn is as much a home as a guest lodging. And therein lies its charm. Warm and homey, it's welcoming—even comforting. Surely this is another era, you think, reminiscing about grandmother's house or some long-forgotten place from your childhood.

The Catlows bought the tree-shaded, early-1900s house with B&B in mind. Owned by the same family throughout its history, the attic was crammed with treasures. After restoring the house and beautifying its grounds (the house sits on three city blocks), the Catlows opened it for guests in mid-1985.

Virginia Point is a sprawling stucco two-story with arches, wide porches, and an expansive interior. Furnished in antiques, it has Catlow family memorabilia as well as pieces from the original owners. On display is a letter written by Tom Catlow's great-grandfather in 1864 when he was stationed at a Confederate army fort at Virginia Point, a spit of land in Galveston Bay overlooking the city. The letter ties the Catlows' venture to the past and the present, serving as their inspiration for Virginia Point Inn.

Bedrooms are on the second floor. Each opens onto a marvelous private screened porch accessed by walk-through windows. The master bedroom, decorated in pink and lace, has a king-size bed, working fireplace, and private bath. Rooms 2 and 3 share a bath; so do 4 and 5. Bed arrangements include twin, three-quarters, double, and king. Sarah's Room has a special warmth.

Guests can enjoy the inn's spacious grounds (room enough for croquet or badminton), and the Catlows provide bicycles free of charge. Virginia Point is seven blocks from The Strand entertainment district and one block from Ashton Villa, one of the city's most popular historic homes open for touring.

One important note: Eleanor Catlow loves to cook. Typical breakfasts start with fresh fruit and include coddled eggs, homemade breads, and Scottish marmalade. The cookie jar usually bulges with chocolate chip cookies. At this writing, once-a-month theme dinners were being planned. Guests at the inn will have priority in making reservations. Meals are served at a dining room table seating up to 20.

15

Grand Old Resorts

These are lodgings with character and style. Each has stood the test of time—and come up a winner. You feel a link to the past here, sensing tradition and becoming a part of it. When you leave, you feel richer for the experience.

ARIZONA

Arizona Biltmore
  24th Street and Missouri
  Phoenix, Arizona 85016
  602/955-6600
  800/528-3696
GENERAL MANAGER: Cecil Ravenswood
500 rooms
JUNE TO AUGUST: $70–$125 single, $80–$135 double
SEPTEMBER TO MAY: $150–$260 single, $170–$280 double
American Express, Carte Blanche, Diners Club, Discover,
  MasterCard, Visa; personal check
Children welcome
No pets
Open year round

  The grande dame of Phoenix area hotels, the Arizona Biltmore has more to recommend it than its long and distinguished history. Spread over 39 acres, it's rich with recreational features—two championship 18-hole golf courses,

17 tennis courts, several swimming pools, health club, game lawns, and jogging trails. Two of its restaurants, Orangerie and Gold Room, have identities of their own, garnering awards for their cuisine and decor. Best of all, the hotel has a staff that works hard at pleasing guests, not only offering a full range of services but doing so with a smile and a high degree of professionalism.

Few hotels can claim a totally distinctive look, both inside and out; the Arizona Biltmore can. Built in 1929, it was inspired by Frank Lloyd Wright. Pre-cast concrete blocks, molded on site using Arizona sand, are the primary building material. Interiors are wonderfully vibrant with Wright's geometric designs. Guest room furnishings are far from ordinary. Not only are the colors bright and the designs eye-catching, but the furniture itself has an individualistic flair. Mirrors, stained glass, and tile designs are generously woven into the decor.

Rooms come in all sizes, situated in one of five buildings or in cottages spread over the lush grounds. Designated as traditional, classic, resort, and premier, they range from moderate-sized with a minibar to extra-large units with a bedroom and sitting room, minibar and refrigerator, large bath with separate shower and bath stall, and private balcony or patio. All rooms have views of the golf courses, mountains, or the beautifully landscaped gardens. Set within the gardens is an Olympic size pool, evocative of an earlier era with its private poolside cabanas.

Indeed, the entire hotel seems transported from a slower-paced, more gracious time. Extensive renovation in 1987 further enhanced an already top-quality hotel. The Arizona Biltmore is managed by Westin Hotels.

Arizona Inn
2200 E. Elm Street
Tucson, Arizona 85719
602/325-1541
800/421-1093 outside Arizona
GENERAL MANAGER: Robert Minerich
85 rooms
JUNE TO DECEMBER: $52–$95 single, $62–$106 double; suites from $120
JANUARY TO MAY: $92–$115 single, $102–$125 double; suites from $134
American Express, MasterCard, Visa; personal check
Children welcome
No pets

Open year round

A mourning dove sits on the tennis court net and watches two players approach down the hedge-lined walkway. Beyond the first row of hedges, near the flower-decked fountain, a young couple sits sipping coffee. Palms and oleander, cypress and citrus trees grace the grounds of this estate.

The Arizona Inn is a lady—classic in her beauty and refined in her taste. She wears an air of maturity, having acted as grand hostess of the Southwest for nearly six decades. Many of the 125 employees are college students from nearby University of Arizona. Their youth and enthusiasm add vivacity to the lady.

From the very beginning, the inn was designed to have a residential feel and a sense of privacy. It opened in 1931 as the creation of Mrs. Isabella Greenway, a sophisticated, dynamic community leader. (Her accomplishments include being elected as Arizona's only congresswoman, serving from 1933 to 1936, and establishing a company to employ disabled servicemen, enabling them to make and sell furniture. One of the original intents of the inn was to provide a market for their furniture.)

The inn is still owned by the same family, and Mrs. Greenway's philosophy is still at the heart of its operation—a commitment to quality and service. Most of the furnishings were selected by the founder herself, some coming from her personal collection, and many originating in the servicemen's workshop.

The pink adobe-style inn is surrounded by vine-covered walls. Low residential buildings sprawl over 14 acres of grounds, connected by winding pathways.

Public rooms are grand and gracious. The library, with its vaulted ceiling and polished wooden floors, comfortable seating and shelves of books, has a lodge-like feel. The Audubon Bar, set with a white piano and a vine-encircled skylight, is decorated with 19th century Audubon prints. One of the dining rooms is hung with George Catlin hand-colored lithographs from Mrs. Greenway's collection. The African Room is studded with animal figures and weapons that she acquired while on safari.

But the guest rooms themselves are at the heart of Arizona Inn's charm. Spacious and well-furnished, they feel like home. Since furnishings were individually selected and many were hand-crafted, each room has its own character. Rooms are designated as standard, mid-range, and deluxe. Some have fireplaces, most have patios, and all have TVs, radios, and air conditioning.

As an example, one deluxe room, 25 feet by 25 feet, has a king-size bed, couch, and overstuffed chair, plus 15 other assorted pieces of furniture—and it still has the feeling of spaciousness. There's lots of light (nine lamps plus an overhead light), a small but convenient 1940s-look bath, and bounteous closet space. Its room-sized patio, set with yellow and white chaise lounges, is wonderfully secluded. Standard rooms, also well furnished, are nearly twice as large as typical hotel rooms.

The inn's swimming pool is a private world, adjoined by glassed gardens and a pool bar beneath vine-covered arbors. The tennis courts are Har-Tru clay, giving an extra touch of class to an already classic inn.

Hacienda del Sol Guest Ranch Resort

5601 N. Hacienda del Sol
Tucson, Arizona 85718
602/299-1501
INNKEEPER: Frank Fine
48 units
$50–$225 single or double
HIGH SEASON: mid-September to April
American Express, MasterCard, Visa; personal check
Children welcome
Pets accepted
Open year round

Hacienda del Sol recreates the vacationing style of the 1930s and '40s. Situated on a hillside within Tucson, yet seemingly far removed, its mission-style gates open onto a gentle scene of grounds set with date palms, orange trees, prickly pears, and saguaro cactus. The hacienda sprawls out in all directions, with low adobe casitas as well as the main lodge building. The city has grown up all around, but within its walls, Hacienda del Sol is a world of its own.

Guests come to the resort for its ambience and personalized service. Make no mistake, there's plenty to do here—horseback riding, tennis, swimming, croquet, shuffleboard, and daily tours. But somehow it's all secondary to the feel of the inn itself—relaxed elegance, combined with conviviality.

During the winter season (beginning in mid-September and extending through April), there's a bevy of daily activities. Starting with "coffee for early birds" at 6 a.m., there's a morning trail ride, a talk about desert ecology, aerobics classes, tours to area attractions, family volleyball game,

Cowgirls Only Trail Ride—and it's only mid-afternoon. Every day is chock full of choices—Roy and Dale Trail Ride (couples only), decathlon (an all-day event competing in table tennis, shuffleboard, croquet, putting, and badminton), cocktail parties, movies on the big screen TV, chuckwagon barbecue and show, plus dozens of others.

The living room is a delightful gathering spot. At one end is a large library. The focal point is the pale blue adobe fireplace—distinctive and beautiful.

Guest rooms come in all shapes and sizes, adding to the charm. (Built in 1929, the hacienda was originally an elite girls' school.) Each room has a phone and a private bath with tub and shower. Furnishings date back to the 1930s. Some rooms open onto courtyards; others have mountaintop views. At the high end of the scale are large suites with bedroom (king bed), full kitchen, fireplace, private patio, and excellent views of the valley below. Decorated with a Southwestern theme, they have Mexican tile floors and huge carved doors.

Hacienda del Sol's restaurant deserves special mention. The food is outstanding (lots of tableside cooking), the service is gracious, and the sunset view is spectacular.

The Wigwam
Litchfield Park, Arizona 85340
602/935-3811
800/327-0396
GENERAL MANAGER: Bill Hall
225 rooms
$145–$215 single, $178–$248 double including breakfast and
    dinner
HIGH SEASON: January to April
American Express, MasterCard, Visa; personal checks
Children welcome
Pets accepted
Open mid-September to May 30; beginning September 1988
    open year round

The Wigwam dates back to 1929. With its three championship golf courses and high service standards, the resort has long been a top choice for golfers. In 1987 it underwent extensive renovation, promising to be better than ever before.

The resort sprawls over 75 acres in Litchfield Park, a small community 17 miles west of Phoenix. Its history is unique. In 1915 the vice president of Goodyear, Paul Litchfield, developed a revolutionary tire, one that required fabric woven from staple cotton. The special cotton was grown in only two places—the Sea Islands off the Georgia coast and the Nile

Valley in Egypt. Both sources were threatened, one by boll weevils and the other by the eruption of World War I. When Goodyear found that an area in southern Arizona approximated the Nile's climate, it brought thousands of acres and began producing cotton.

And so it all started. Goodyear developed a community to support its operation. To accommodate business visitors, it built a lodging house. The accommodations got so popular that Goodyear opened them to the public. Over the years, the Wigwam helped establish the Phoenix area as a winter vacationland.

Goodyear sold the resort to SunCor Development in late 1986. SunCor's expansive renovation project ranged from the guest rooms to the famed golf courses themselves.

The Gold and the Blue Courses were designed by Robert Trent Jones, Sr., and the West Course was designed by Robert Lawrence. The Gold Course is labeled as one of the 100 best in the country.

The estate-like resort is also known for its tennis (eight Plexi-Pave courts) and its Western-style program. There's a stable of horses on the grounds, and special events include stagecoach and haywagon rides, even desert steak broils. An activities director arranges something for everyone, including children.

The main lodge is pure Southwest, decorated with Indian rugs and pottery. The huge dining room overlooks a swimming pool. All stays at the Wigwam include either two or three meals. Breakfast and lunch are served buffet-style.

Lodging is in 15 low-rise casas spread residential-style over the grounds. Interiors are extra-large; the decorating scheme is contemporary with some southwestern flavor. All have a refrigerator, TV, phone, and private patio or terrace. Most units can sleep four people. Some have Murphy beds.

NEW MEXICO

The Bishop's Lodge
  Box 2367
  Santa Fe, New Mexico 87504
  505/983-6377
INNKEEPERS: Jim and Lore Thorpe
65 rooms
JULY 1 TO LABOR DAY, MAP only: $115 single, $165–$285
  double including breakfast, dinner, and children's program

APRIL THROUGH JUNE, SEPTEMBER THROUGH OCTOBER:
  from $70 single, from $90–$195 double
15% service fee added to all services (room, restaurant, sta-
  bles)
Personal check; no credit cards
Children welcome
No pets
Open April 1 to October 30

Downtown Santa Fe—with its galleries and shops, museums and historic churches—is only five minutes away, but
here at The Bishop's Lodge amid the foothills of the Sangre
de Cristo Mountains, guests find a quiet retreat far from the
crowds.

The lodge's grounds sprawl over 1,000 acres at the head of
the Tesuque Valley. Guests can go horseback riding over
miles of trails, play tennis on five championship courts, enjoy
trap and skeet shooting, hike through the juniper-studded red
hills, and relax by the pool, in between jaunts into Santa Fe,
the cultural capital of the Southwest.

Retreating to these foothills is not without precedent. In
fact, at the heart of the lodge's charm—its gentleness and hospitality—is the man for whom it is named. Archbishop Lamy
of Santa Fe (he was the model for the main character in Willa
Cather's novel *Death Comes to the Archbishop*) came to this
very spot about a century ago for rest and eventually retirement. Over a span of years he planted an orchard, supplementing the fruit trees already in the valley planted by
Franciscan Fathers during the early 17th century. Remnants
of the orchard are still sprinkled over the grounds.

Adjacent to his adobe home the Archbishop built a private
chapel—a simple structure with vaulted ceiling and painted-
glass windows to simulate the stained glass of cathedrals in
his native France. The tiny chapel still stands, creating an
atmosphere of warmth and peacefulness.

Only a few steps away down a foliage-lined pathway is the
lobby of the Bishop's Lodge. Here guests can sign up for
some of the resort's numerous activities, dine in the central
dining room, and enjoy spectacular sunsets from the terrace
bar. Life is casual at the lodge. While male guests are asked
to wear jackets at dinner and women are requested "to dress
accordingly," there's an informal air throughout the resort.
Breakfast and lunch are served buffet-style. Cocktails are
served in El Charro lounge as well as on the terrace.

Guest rooms are spread out in several one- and two-story
buildings, all reflecting their New Mexico heritage. Interiors,

which come in a wide assortment of sizes and configurations, are especially spacious, well-lit, and well-furnished, translating into lots of comfort. The decor is Southwest Ranch—kiva fireplaces, simple wooden furniture, earth-tone fabrics with splashes of color. Some rooms have beamed ceilings. Bathrooms are larger than average and designed for convenience. Air conditioning, TVs, and telephones are standard features.

Compared to all area accommodations, The Bishop's Lodge gets an A+ for recreational offerings. Not only does it have ample facilities for horseback riding, tennis, swimming, and skeet shooting, but it also has lots of extras, such as a fishing pond for children (stocked with trout), maps with hiking trails, and lists for birdwatchers (over 110 species can be observed on the grounds). Golfers can play at any of three private courses in the area. Whatever the season, the lodge offers an abundance of special activities as well—newcomer's cocktail party hosted by owners Jim and Lore Thorpe, exercise classes, fashion shows, storytelling on the front lawn, steak fries, children's cookout—the list goes on. In addition to its own activities, the resort keeps guests informed of area events.

The lodge has an excellent program for children ages 4-12 during the summer months, with counselor-supervised activities such as hiking, swimming, pony rides, and arts and crafts. The cost is included in the Modified American Plan during July and August, and is available for an extra fee in June.

Teens get special attention at Bishop's Lodge. During the summer months there's a dining table designated for them. Events such as swim parties are planned, depending on the guests in-house.

Horseback riding is important here. Approximately 80 percent of the guests ride, whether they have ever mounted a horse before or not. With more than 60 horses, the resort offers daily guided rides ($17 per person) plus special breakfast and picnic rides.

Three generations of the Thorpe family have owned and operated the lodge, beginning with James R. Thorpe, who developed it as a ranch resort in 1918. Previously the property had belonged to Joseph Pulitzer of Pulitzer Prize fame.

The Lodge
P.O. Box 497
Cloudcroft, New Mexico 88317
505/682-2566
OWNERS: Carole and Jerry Sanders
47 rooms
$55–$70 single or double; $95–$120 suites

American Express, MasterCard, Visa; no personal check
Children welcome
No pets
Open year round

Even in July the air is cool high in the Sacramento Mountains. Walk into the lobby of The Lodge to find a crackling fire, while folks down at the mountains' base 15 miles away swelter in the desert heat.

The Lodge, intimate and secluded, is a romantic escape. Here you can play golf or hike during the summer, ski or snuggle by the fire in the winter. The original lodge, built in 1899, was destroyed by fire in 1909. Two years later the current lodge was constructed. Over the years the hotel has undergone numerous renovations, but its Bavarian-style exterior has remained essentially the same.

You might as well know ahead of time that the hotel has a ghost. Her name is Rebecca, and reportedly she's friendly. According to local legend, many years ago beautiful Rebecca was a chambermaid at The Lodge. One day her lumberjack lover found her in the arms of another man, and after that Rebecca mysteriously disappeared. Some people swear that they see her ghost from time to time, wandering the halls of the old inn.

So popular is the legend, that The Lodge's restaurant is named for the raven-haired beauty, and her portrait hangs at the entrance. Follow the legend at least as far as the restaurant—renowned for its continental cuisine. Shrimp Diablo, rack of lamb, peppercorn tournedos—the menu is a feast in itself. For dessert, there is crêpes Suzette or bananas Foster. Entrees range from $12 to $18.

One of The Lodge's most distinctive features is its five-story copper tower. Judy Garland wrote her name on the wall here. So did Clark Gable. For a romantic tête-à-tête (more than one couple has gotten engaged here), reserve the tiny parlor at the base of the tower. Climb up the tower stairs to the summit and look out over miles of alpine scenery. White Sands National Monument glistens 40 miles in the distance. On a clear day, you can see much farther than that—150 miles, so they claim.

Down in the basement is Red Dog Saloon with a history of its own (ask about the dollar bills encased in glass). And upstairs is a Victorian-style bar from Al Capone's home.

The lobby of the hotel looks like a lodge, with leather couches, bear skins, even a stuffed bear. Guest rooms are much more romantic, decorated French-country style with antique furniture, matched bed and drapery fabrics, and accents of brass. As you might expect, every room in this personable inn has its own decorating scheme. Commonalities are high ceilings, clicking steam radiators, down comforters and French eyelet linens, along with private baths, TVs, and phones. Family Rooms, sleeping up to four, are especially spacious. King Rooms tend to be dormer style, with four-poster beds, dormer seating, and shutters with fabric insets.

The honeymoon suite undoubtedly has no equal. Decorated in bordello red, it features a gold-crowned, mirror-topped bed (you have to see it to believe it). The Governor's Suite (a real bargain at $120) has a brass bed backed by blue swags, sitting area with antique furniture, antique-style phone, and oriental rugs. Supposedly, this room is Rebecca's favorite.

The Lodge's nine-hole golf course, elevation 9,200 feet, is among the highest in the world. Golfers can pause between holes to enjoy the spectacular scenery punctuated with blue spruce and ponderosa pine. The outdoor pool, kept at 80 degrees year round, and the outdoor hot tub are attractive amenities.

A family-oriented hostelry, The Lodge will arrange for baby sitters upon request. Nearby family activities include skiing at Cloudcroft (25 runs), outdoor fun in Lincoln National Forest, and seasonal festivals.

Rancho Encantado
  Route 4, Box 57C
  Santa Fe, New Mexico 87501
  505/982-3537
  OWNERS: Betty and John Egan
  22 ranch rooms, 27 condos
  Ranch: $95–$170, single or double
  Condos: $168–$185, double (low season: January to March)
  American Express, MasterCard, Visa; personal check
  Children welcome
  No pets
  Ranch open mid-March to early January
  Condos open year round

When Rancho Encantado opened as a resort ranch in 1968, it was the realization of a dream for Betty Egan and her family. In the intervening years the Egans' lodging has earned an enviable reputation, playing host to the rich and famous. Guests return year after year, charmed by the resort's quiet and privacy.

The ranch nestles within the rolling hills of Tesuque (teh-soo-key) about eight miles north of Santa Fe. The surrounding countryside is a blend of juniper, piñon, and cactus—just the right setting for an exclusive getaway. The Santa Fe Opera is also in Tesuque, only a ten minute ride from the ranch.

Guests can play tennis, swim, or hike at Rancho Encantado, with time out for relaxation. Of course there's horseback riding, but it's not an all-consuming activity. Two trail rides go out a day. All 11 of the resort's horses are gentle, and the gait of rides is geared to the least experienced rider.

One of the most favored pursuits at Rancho Encantado is dining. The restaurant, open to the public as well as to guests, has a classy menu. Entrees, priced from $12 to $19, include poached salmon with hollandaise sauce, filet of sole stuffed with mushrooms, and pâté baked in puff pastry with sauce beurre blanc. Due to the restaurant's popularity, guests are advised to make reservations well in advance of their arrival.

The flavor of the ranch is casual southwestern, but with elegance and style. More like visiting in the ranch home of well-to-do friends than staying at a hotel, the lodge has no bellman at the door, no shuttle connecting it to town, no room service.

Accommodation choices include main lodge rooms (first and second floor bedrooms), cottage rooms (large bedrooms with fireplaces), and casitas (bedrooms and living rooms with fireplaces and refrigerators). Two luxury suites have fireplaces and refrigerators.

Guests can also stay in Pueblo Encantado condominiums, just across the road from the ranch. All of these adobe-style cottages are privately owned; 27 are in the ranch's rental pool. One-bedroom condos have a bedroom with king or twin beds, living room with queen sleeper sofa, kitchen, and dining area. Two-bedroom units, accommodating up to six people, have fireplaces. Master bedrooms are sometimes available as individual units, renting for $95.

16

Groups

Not only do these lodgings have sufficient space to accommo-date groups, but they're willing to gear their program to suit group needs.

ARIZONA

Rancho de la Osa
  P.O. Box 1
  Sasabe, Arizona 85633
  602/823-4257
HOSTS: The Davis Family
20 rooms (accommodating up to 40)
$75–$90 per person including meals, riding
MasterCard, Visa; personal check
Children welcome
No pets
Open September to mid-June (individuals or groups), August
  for groups only

About 65 miles southwest of Tucson, near the border of Mexico and far from the resorts in the city, there's a ranch that dates back to the 1730s. Here you can retreat into an earlier era, simultaneous with riding horses, studying nature (especially birds), and taking excursions to nearby Arizona sites as well as into Mexico.

The Davis Family has been operating the ranch since 1982. Their program is flexible, and their facilities are well-suited to groups. The adobe cantina was built as a mission about 1737 by Franciscan monks. Still retaining a feeling of history on the outside, it's definitely modern on the inside, set with pool tables, a big screen TV with VCR, and a bar.

The rambling adobe hacienda, or main house, was built in 1860. Today vacationers gather in it for hearty ranch meals. The dining room is open to the public for lunch every day and for dinner on Friday through Sunday. Special arrangements for groups include outdoor cookouts under the trees.

Guest rooms are in low adobe block buildings with walls up to three feet thick. While far from plush, they have lots of southwestern character—handpainted furniture, Mexican pigskin chairs, and Indian throw rugs. Fires (every room has a fireplace) are lit twice a day. There are electric blankets on the beds for the winter and ceiling fans overhead for the warmer months (no air conditioning). Bathrooms, remodeled in the mid-1980s, have showers and tubs.

Wrangler-led horseback rides go out twice a day. Since the ranch raises its own quarter horses, there are always plenty of horses to go round. Rides are leisurely, and riders are grouped according to ability.

The swimming pool and spa, shaded with palm trees, are good for relaxing. Of special interest is Buenos Aires National Wildlife Refuge (more than 200 bird species sighted) a few miles away. Other nearby attractions include Kit Peak Observatory, Tubac, Tucson, and Nogales, Mexico.

NEW MEXICO

La Junta
  Box 139
  Alto, New Mexico 88312
  505/336-4361
OWNERS: The Finley and Dunstan families
11 units, total of 27 bedrooms (shared baths)
Group rates: from $15 per person
Personal check; no credit cards
Children welcome
Pets acceptable
Open year round

La Junta means "meeting place," and that is exactly what this lodging offers—an informal gathering spot for groups of up to 60, whether they want to ski at nearby Ski Apache Resort or enjoy the wooded surroundings any time of year. The atmosphere is camplike and lowkey, giving groups a chance to create their own mood.

Spread over seven acres of beautiful countryside six miles north of Ruidoso, La Junta has a central recreation room and guest rooms in five assorted buildings. Picnic tables and grills are scattered amongst the trees. Best of all, the managers are willing to work with groups to meet their specific needs.

The owners are transplanted Louisianians, and happily they have brought a touch of their native state to this part of New Mexico. Each room has the name of a Louisiana parish, and interiors reflect the Finley's penchant for Cajun country. For example, tucked into the basket of goodies awaiting guests—items such as coffee, tea, and catsup—is a bottle of Trappey's pepper sauce.

Each of the buildings is a different design, offering a wide variety of sleeping accommodations. There's a well-equipped kitchen in each building. Several buildings have fireplaces. Vermilion and St. Charles can be rented as separate or adjoining units. Together they can accommodate 12. The two units, situated on top of the recreation building, have a wide upstairs porch and two living room/kitchen combinations in addition to bedrooms.

Orleans, the most private of the buildings, has two bedrooms and a deck overlooking the woods. Acadia has four bedrooms; the other two buildings have three bedrooms each.

OKLAHOMA

Lake Texoma Resort
Box 248
Kingston, Oklahoma 73439
405/564-2311
800/654-8240 AR, CO, KS, MO, NM, TX (except 512)
800/522-8565 OK
MANAGERS: J.W. and Rolla Wright
97 rooms; 69 cottages
$45–$75 single or double
American Express, Carte Blanche, Diners Club, MasterCard, Visa; personal check
Children welcome

Pets in cottages only
Open year round

Operated by Oklahoma Tourism and Recreation Department, Lake Texoma Resort has a long roster of activities, a casual setting, and bargain rates, making it a good destination for groups and families. Most important, the staff is enthusiastic and proud of their program.

Boating, fishing, horseback riding, golf, tennis, hiking, and biking are all available. The recreation department, housed in a well-equipped facility, offers all kinds of team sports as well as a game room with video games, pool, and table tennis. Its daily menu of activities has such choices as water aerobics, ski instruction, arts and crafts, and nature hikes. Family dances or theme parties are held on Saturdays. Most activities have minimal charges or are free. Also in the recreation building is an impressive array of exercise equipment geared toward fitness instead of muscle building. Special fitness packages are scheduled throughout the year.

For the fishing enthusiast, there's a year-round striper guide, and Striper Camps offered seasonally. Camps include guides, boats, equipment, lodging, and meals. Two days of fishing for striped bass in Lake Texoma's abundant waters climax with a tournament.

Guest rooms in the main lodge have a choice of two twin, one queen, one king, or one double plus one twin bed. Furnishings are simple; cabana rooms are the most spacious (king bed, queen sleeper sofa, mini-refrigerator, patio doors opening to pool). Most of the cottages, more modestly furnished than the lodge rooms, have two-bedrooms. All have kitchens (bring your own cookware), dining tables, and TVs. For groups, Bayview unit accommodates up to 40.

The lodge's dining room is cheerful, and food is reasonably priced.

TEXAS

Guadalupe River Ranch
P.O. Box 929
Boerne, Texas 78006
512/537-4837
MANAGERS: Mike and Maggie Ezzell
36 units
$60–$150 per person including all meals

MasterCard, Visa; personal check
Children welcome
No pets
Smoking in designated areas only
Open mid-January to Christmas

Built in the late 1920s as a country showcase, the 360-acre ranch stretches along a high bluff overlooking the cedar-lined Guadalupe River. The setting is pastoral, peaceful, and secluded. Here you can hike in the scenic Hill Country, float along the river in an inner tube, play tennis, swim in two pools, go horseback riding, get a massage at the spa center, or lie in a hammock and feel the quiet.

Well-suited for groups, families, and anyone who enjoys the outdoors, the ranch has accommodations in cottages and a dorm-style building. Meals, more akin to fine restaurant cuisine than standard ranch food, are included in the price of a stay. The menu is chef's choice, with an emphasis on fresh ingredients and healthful eating. Homebaked breads and desserts get rave reviews.

The ranch gears its facilities to meet group needs. Because of its physical layout, the ranch can accommodate several small groups simultaneously, and each can have a sense of privacy. Lodging is sufficient for up to 75 guests. Guadalupe River Ranch is also a great romantic getaway destination. The best lodging choice is one of the newer two-room suites with balconies overlooking the river. Spacious and modern, they're also cheerful and well-furnished. The cluster of stone cottages is another appealing spot. Some have big porches. Once used as an artists' colony, they have names like Georgia O'Keeffe and Albert Einstein. Dorm rooms in a separate building are well-decorated and upbeat.

The ranch opened a spa facility in 1987. Still in an embryonic stage at this writing, it is oriented to fitness with a program that includes aerobics, water exercise, therapeutic massages, and nutritional counseling.

Lajitas on the Rio Grande

Star Route 70
Box 400
Terlingua, Texas 79852
915/424-3471
800/527-4078
MANAGER: Regina Worster
100 units
$52–$111 for 2, $56–$123 for 4
American Express, MasterCard, Visa; personal check
Children welcome
Pets accepted
Open year round

There's no doubt about it: Lajitas is a world apart. First of all, it's not near anything, unless you count Big Bend National Park, which isn't near anything either. Alpine is 90 miles north, El Paso is 310 miles to the northwest, and San Antonio is 430 miles to the northeast.

Not only is Lajitas physically remote, but it also belongs to an earlier era, a time when army troops chased Indians and rustlers holed up in desert hideaways. A virtual Williamsburg of the Old West, Lajitas is a great place for families or groups.

The entire town is a development of the Mischer Corporation. It all started with a real trading post on the banks of the Rio Grande. Now Lajitas is a tourist attraction as well as a small residential community, complete with condos and a few houses. It boasts a nine-hole golf course, swimming pool, tennis courts, livery stable, desert museum, restaurant, saloon, and a handful of shops. Each lodging reflects a different aspect of the region's history. The Badlands Hotel is straight out of a cowboy movie. The Cavalry Post Motel is built on the site of a real cavalry post where General "Black Jack" Pershing housed his troops in the early 1900s. Over at the Officers' Quarters (the exterior is a replica of the officers' quarters in old Fort Davis), guests are housed in style. Then there's the Spanish-style motel La Cuesta, mirroring the area's proximity to Mexico (it's just across the river).

Make no mistake: this is desert country. The river, lined with graceful salt cedars, marks the southern perimeter. Rugged mountains are in the distance. The landscape is a composite of prickly pear and ocotillo, yucca and scrub mesquite. Spring and fall are the prime seasons to visit, but the town never closes its doors.

Since all lodgings are owned by the same company, reservations are handled centrally. The four hotels/motels have similar quality furnishings but different environments. Air conditioning, phones, and TVs are in all units. Upstairs rooms at the Badlands Hotel open onto a long porch overlooking the town. The Officers' Quarters is the most modern, but seems out of step with the old-timey mood. Some units in Cavalry Post have fireplaces.

One- and two-bedroom condos are also a good option. Adobe-style on the outside, they have stone fireplaces, good kitchens, big bedrooms, and larger-than-average baths. Clustered together in a separate section of the town, they resemble a little village.

For small groups or large families, several houses are also available, each with a dramatic setting overlooking the desert terrain. At the other end of the spectrum, there are two bunkhouses right across from the Badlands Hotel. Each has two sleeping sections accommodating seven persons each, baths adjoining the sleeping areas, and a central sitting area.

The area is rich in recreation, including excursions into Big Bend, hiking and backcountry trips, and river rafting. Rockhounds, birdwatchers, history buffs, and outdoor enthusiasts can luxuriate in the abundance of choices.

Lazy Hills Guest Ranch

Box G
Ingram, Texas 78025
512/367-5600
HOSTS: Bob and Carol Steinruck
25 units
$45–$65 per adult per day for stays of 3 nights or more including meals
Reduced rates for children in same room as adults
$450 per week including meals, 6 rides
Stays of 1 or 2 nights allowed when space available; $10 extra per night
MasterCard, Visa; personal check
Children welcome
No pets
Open year round

Spread over 750 acres in the Texas Hill Country, family-run Lazy Hills Guest Ranch offers friendliness and fun. The pace is slow, providing time for strolling and relaxing. Horseback riding fits the mood in this pastoral setting. Guests choose one of four hour-long rides a day. (The price of a week-long stay includes six rides.) There's also a large swimming pool, tennis, and volleyball, plus exploring along the creek and hiking in the woods.

Catering to groups, especially during the non-summer months, the hosts are happy to arrange activities suited to the age and interests of their guests. Lodging units are clustered together, which makes them ideal for groups. Furnishings are simple—more like those at a real ranch than those at most guest ranches. The majority of the rooms can sleep up to four. Six units have fireplaces.

The family-style dining room, one of the ranch's newest facilities, has a friendly feel. An adjacent sitting room has the only TV on the premises. In a nearby detached building there's a game room with table tennis, pool, and electronic games.

From mid-November to early January, deer and turkey hunting takes precedence over more typical guest ranch activities.

17

Guest Ranches

One of the best ways to experience the Southwest is on a guest ranch. Leave your city clothes behind and head to the land of cowboys. You don't have to ride a horse to enjoy a guest ranch. All that is required at most is a fun-loving spirit and a hearty appetite.

Summertime is the peak season at Texas guest ranches; winter is the prime season in Arizona. Some ranches are open year round, but their programs slow down during off-season.

All guest ranches have supervised rides only. Insurance restrictions prohibit guests from riding on their own.

ARIZONA

Flying E Ranch
  Box EEE
  Wickenburg, Arizona 85358
  602/684-2690
  OWNER/OPERATOR: Vi Wellik
  16 units
  $75–$190 per person including all meals
  Minimum stay of 2 nights
  Personal check, no credit cards
  Children welcome
  No pets
  Open November to May

By the flip of a coin, Vi Wellik and her husband discovered Flying E Ranch in 1949, thereby changing their lives. The couple, both flyers, first noticed the ranch on a flight to Phoenix in their private plane. "It looked like a motel in the middle of the desert," reminisces Vi. Their curiosity was sparked. That night they flipped a coin to decide whether to go back. Not only did the Wellicks return, but they ended up buying the ranch years later, operating it as a guest ranch since 1960.

Guests, many of whom visit Flying E year after year, find friendly folks and a relaxing atmosphere at this small ranch. The clock by the pool sets the tone: instead of hands, it says "Who cares." This is the kind of place where you can do what you want to do when you want to do it.

Horseback riding is a good option, but you don't have to get near a horse if that's not your style. There's an extra fee for riding—$12 per day for one ride, $18 for two rides. With more than 20,000 acres of riding terrain, you've got lots of roaming room, starting from the ranch's locale on a 2,400-foot mesa. Rides, all wrangler-led, are separated into groups according to riders' abilities. When you aren't riding, you can soak in the pool and hot tub, play tennis (one court) or shuffleboard, and spin yarns with other guests. Vi (now a widow) is a restorationist and history buff, so she can entertain guests with local lore.

Meals are served family-style and feature good ole home-cooking. Breakfast cookouts and chuckwagon dinners are highlights. Non-riders get escorted to the serving site via hay wagon.

Guest rooms are in motel-style units spread out from the main living room/dining room. Set with traditional furniture (twin or king beds) and accented with Navajo rugs, they're comfortable and well-maintained. All have private baths. Rooms are electrically heated and cooled, and stocked with electric blankets for extra nippy nights. TVs with VCRs are available for rent.

Kay El Bar Ranch
Box 2480
Wickenburg, Arizona 85358
602/684-7593
HOST: Jane Nash
10 rooms (private baths)
$85–$94 single, $155–$175 double including all meals, 1 ride per day per person
Minimum stay of 2 nights

MasterCard, Visa; personal check
Children welcome
No pets
Open mid-October to May 1

One of the oldest guest ranches in Arizona, Kay El Bar is a National Historic Site. Its first guests checked in back in 1926. Shaded by magnificent salt cedar and eucalyptus trees, the ranch buildings consist of several hacienda-style adobes.

Accommodating only 20 guests at a time, Kay El Bar is lowkey, laid-back, and downright friendly. The breakfast bell, nestled among the trees, rings at about 8 A.M. Guests gather in the Western dining room where photographs of Hollywood cowboys line the walls. The morning ride goes out around 10 A.M. Depending on the crowd, it may come back mid-afternoon, or stay out all day, ending with a cookout. Those who choose not to ride can lounge by the pool, arriving at the cookout site just in time for barbecued chicken or fajitas.

At night guests gather in the main lodge room, a cozy sort of room with a fire crackling in the big stone fireplace, shelves upon shelves of books, and an array of games. Sometimes the hosts show an old Western movie on the VCR. When the mood is right, somebody may play a tune on the piano. Over to the side there's a stocked serve-yourself bar.

Eight guest rooms are in the main lodge. Their ranch-style furniture dates back to the 1920s dude ranch. Remington prints, cowboy lampshades, Indian rugs—the rooms have a nostalgic air. All have a private bath.

A separate two-bedroom, two-bath cottage with a living room and fireplace can be rented as a whole or as a two-room suite.

Rancho de los Caballeros

P.O. Box 1148
Wickenburg, Arizona 85358
602/684-5484
GENERAL MANAGER: Dallas Grant, Jr.
73 rooms
$84–$148 per person including all meals
Personal check, no credit cards
Children welcome
No pets
Open October to mid-May

In the Wickenburg area, renowned for its guest ranches, Rancho de los Caballeros reigns supreme, adding a touch of class to the Southwest. Its name means Ranch of the

Gentlemen on Horseback, paying tribute to the Spanish explorers who introduced horses to the Indian culture. Both a working ranch and a guest ranch, with 20,000 acres of hills and desert terrain, Los Caballeros has been welcoming guests since 1948. The overall style is casual yet tasteful; men are asked to wear sports jackets or Western shirts with vests or bolo ties in the evening, and women wear sports suits or dresses.

Horseback riding is the star event. With 60 or more horses, the ranch offers two rides a day. Guests pay an extra fee—$18 for morning rides, $12 for afternoon rides. A wrangler comes to your table in the dining room to sign you up.

Los Caballeros Golf Club is on the ranch grounds. Its 18-hole championship course is rated as one of the finest in Arizona. Guests pay $28 to play 18 holes, $22 for cart rental. The resort also has skeet and trap shooting, four tennis courts, a small pool, and miles of wide-open spaces. During appropriate seasons a children's program (ages 5-12) is offered at no extra charge. Counselor-led activities include riding, hiking, swimming, and games.

Near dinner time, guests congregate at Los Caballeros Saloon. Meals are served in the large dining room, ornate with Spanish-style decor. Lunch is a buffet; breakfast and dinner are ordered from the menu. Once a week the ranch goes all-out Western, with an evening cookout at South Yucca Flats. Dine on barbecued ribs and hot apple crisp, then sit back and enjoy the campfire entertainment.

Accommodations spread out over the grounds and come in a variety of choices. Sun Terrace Rooms, situated in one wing of the main building and in bungalows, are furnished with hand-painted beds, simple curtains and carpeting, and have small modern baths. Sunset Rooms, available in one-, two-, or three-room units, have patios and fireplaces. Bradshaw Mountain Rooms are the most modern and luxurious. They have one or two large bedrooms, a parlor with lots of comfortable seating, a fireplace, and a kitchenette. You can rent just a bedroom portion of a Bradshaw Mountain unit, or you can combine a bedroom with the living/kitchenette segment.

Tanque Verde Ranch
   Route 8, Box 66
   Tucson, Arizona 85748
   602/296-6275
MANAGER: Bob Cote
60 units
$140–$226 double including all meals, horseback riding
HIGH SEASON: mid-December to April
LOW SEASON: May to September
American Express; personal check
Children welcome
No pets
Open year round

   One of the best places to fulfill your fantasies of the Old West is at Tanque Verde Ranch. Imbued with the romance of history, it combines as much horseback riding as city folks can stand with a saddlebag full of other sports, and adds a nature program to boot.

   From Tucson you drive east on Tanque Verde Road until it dead-ends at the ranch. The road dips up and down past giant saguaros, and then leads straight into the Old West. Here in the foothills of the Tanque Verde, Rincon, and Catalina ranges, the elevation is 2,800 feet. To the east is Coronado National Forest. Saguaro National Monument (63,000 acres of the beautiful cacti) is to the south.

   The adobe ranch house, shaded with a ramada built of saguaro ribs, dates back to 1877 when Don Emilio Carrio started a cattle spread here. The lodge living room is decorated with Indian and Mexican crafts, along with some life-like mannequins of cowboys and Indians that give you a start, even the second time around. At the back of the house is an attractive modern dining room overlooking the pool. And so the tone is set—the feeling of history along with the comforts of home.

   If riding is at the top of your list, you won't be disappointed. Three rides go out daily, plus there are specially scheduled day-long, breakfast, and overnight rides. (From Thanksgiving through April, there's an optional children's program, ages 4-11; children under age 12 must ride with the children's program.) The ranch has 80 head of horses, which take guests over open desert, up rocky canyons, and into the mountains beyond.

When you're ready for more, there's swimming in two pools (indoor and outdoor), tennis (five excellent courts), and a health club (saunas, whirlpool, exercise room). Save some energy for nature hikes, both guided and on your own. The ranch has its own bird banding program, providing a close-up view of desert wildlife. Over 155 species have been banded since 1970.

Sixty casitas and patio lodges are scattered residential style over the grounds. Four types of rooms are available, ranging from standard to suites. Furnishings are among the best of Southwest guest ranches, providing regional flavor as well as comfort. All have air conditioning and phones, some have fireplaces, and most have patios. Giant saguaros as well as ocotillo, prickly pear, agave, and cholla are right outside your door.

Activities vary throughout the year, with the fullest program during high season. To avoid disappointment, find out ahead of time what will be available during your visit. Then head to Tanque Verde, ready to savor the Old West.

White Stallion Ranch

9251 W. Twin Peaks Road
Tucson, Arizona 85743
602/297-0252
OWNERS: The True Family
28 rooms (private baths)
$80–$105 per person including all meals, horseback riding
Personal check; no credit cards
Children welcome
No pets
Open October through April

White Stallion Ranch spreads over 3,000 acres, set on beautiful desert and mountain terrain 17 miles northwest of downtown Tucson. Both a working and guest ranch, it's been owned and operated by the True family since 1964.

Year-round, the Trues raise quarter horses (also some longhorn cattle), but in the winter season they go all out to show guests a slice of the West. Over the years visitors have arrived from 50 or so countries (look for the collection of flags representing the guest list). Many return year after year for what White Stallion has to offer—four horseback rides a day, informal rodeos, nature walks, homecooked meals, and a family atmosphere.

The Trues own about 45 horses, and one of their specialties is matching riders with the right horses. Some rides are designated as slow and scenic, others as fast. Trails lead from flat desert up into the mountains. Children five and older are allowed to ride on their own; younger children ride with their parents.

Some guests never ride, preferring to soak up the Western atmosphere. There's a Saturday afternoon rodeo (roping, bulldogging, and a steer who does tricks), hayrides and cookouts, and a weekly barbecue with the whole meal cooked in an outdoor Indian oven.

Areas for relaxing include the comfortable and spacious main lodge (TV room, pool room, library, self-serve bar) open round the clock, an outdoor pool, and an enclosed redwood hot tub (one of the most popular places on the ranch). There are also tennis courts, horseshoes, and shuffleboard. One unusual feature is the ranch's wildlife zoo—fallow deer, mouflon bighorns, emu, pheasants. Spread out over a wide expanse, the zoo attracts lots of attention from adults as well as children. Nature walks are a weekly feature, led by a wildlife biologist.

Accommodations are comfortable and fairly simple. Three units are in the main lodge; the other 25 are scattered over the grounds. All have private baths. Most have a double and twin bed and can be rented either as a bedroom or suite. The newest unit is a suite sleeping seven. Several small units have been specially designed for singles, enabling them to stay at a cost savings. Catering to groups as well as singles and families, White Stallion can arrange transportation to and from the airport.

TEXAS

Mayan Dude Ranch
Box 577
Bandera, Texas 78003
512/796-3312
HOSTS: The Hicks Family
60 units
$70–$75 per person per day; $420–$455 per week including all meals and riding
Reduced rates for children and teens
American Express, Diners Club, MasterCard, Visa
Children welcome

No pets
Open year round

It doesn't take long to settle into a cowboy frame of mind at the Mayan, a sprawling ranch with plenty of space to ramble and a tone of informality conducive to relaxing. The Hicks family has been welcoming guests since the early 1950s, and they have it down pat. Along with hearty cowboy grub they serve up a big helping of hospitality and fun.

It all starts with orange juice and coffee delivered to your door in the morning (probably by one of the Hicks offspring). Then you choose whether to have breakfast on the trail or in the dining room. (We're talking about a real breakfast here—thick bacon, homemade sausage, hash-brown spuds, grits, biscuits.)

Morning trail rides lead into the hills or down by the cool green Medina River. Guests are entitled to two rides per day, led by well-trained guides. Don't worry about knowing how to ride—the Mayan Dude Ranch prides itself on teaching you. When you aren't riding, there's swimming in the large pool with a slide, tubing in the river, fishing, hiking, and playing tennis. During the summer there's a full roster of group activities—contests, theme nights, and hayrides.

Off-season is less scheduled but still includes riding, cowboy breakfasts, barbecues, and hayrides. Families, groups, seminars, and conventions make up the guest roster.

Accommodations are in rock cottages or in one of three lodges (6 to 16 rooms). It's hard to go wrong here, and there's lots of variety. Some of the cottages are designed for large families. No matter how rustic any of the exteriors are, the interiors are spacious and Western-plush. If views are important to you, be sure to ask for an appropriate lodging. Units are sprinkled throughout the woods, creating a sense of space.

One of the most attractive features of this ranch is the outdoor deck adjacent to the dining room. It's the perfect place to relax as you watch the sun set beyond the hills.

So popular is the Mayan that reservations, especially for the summer, need to be made well in advance.

Silver Spur Guest Ranch
  P.O. Box 1657
  Bandera, Texas 78003
  512/796-3639
HOSTS: The Winchell Family
11 rooms (private baths)
$65 per person daily; $390 per week including all meals,
  horseback riding

Reduced rates for children and teens
Minimum stay of 2 nights
MasterCard, Visa; personal check
Children welcome
No pets
Open year round

For would-be dude ranchers who place a high premium on horseback riding, Silver Spur is the place to head in the Texas Hill Country. Guests have a chance to ride four or more hours a day, following trails through the ranch's 275 acres and in the Hill Country State Park nearby. Silver Spur's setting differs from that of area dude ranches. Here the terrain is craggy and open, conveying a feel of the Old West. The ranch's junior Olympic pool is especially beautiful; set on a hillside, it overlooks the surrounding countryside.

The 11 guests rooms, accommodating up to 54 people, are in stone cottages (arranged as duplexes) and on the second floor of the modern ranch house. All rooms have king-size beds, private bath, color TV, and air conditioning. Some rooms have double beds in addition to the king bed.

The family-style dining room and a large party area are on the first floor of the ranch house. Cowboy fun at the Silver Spur means hayrides, cookouts, and barbecues. For a change of pace, there's hiking, volleyball, and horseshoe pitching.

During hunting season, mid-November through early January, the Silver Spur turns into a hunting lodge; whitetail deer, wild turkey, and javelina are the most sought-after game.

18

Hideaways

A hideaway is a stand-alone lodging, a gem of a place that you and your companions have all to yourself. Some are tiny, accommodating no more than two. One, a modern-day mansion, is suitable for up to eight people traveling together. (For additional choices, see chapter on B&B Reservation Systems.)

ARIZONA

Flying V Ranch
 6800 N. Flying V Ranch Road
 Tucson, Arizona 85715
 602/299-4372, 299-4900
OWNERS: Reed and Tillie Shields
13 units
Studio: $50 (accommodating 2)
Two-bedroom cottages: $95 (accommodating 4)
Personal check; no credit cards
Children welcome
Pets with approval
Open year round

You have to be looking for it to find it. Even a few hundred yards away, you'd swear it's not there. But Flying V Ranch has been around since about 1903, and it will probably take more than modern development to get rid of it.

Once, the ranch consisted of over 1,000 acres. In the early 1980s the Shields family sold all but 75 of the acres, and now Flying V has a major hotel (Loews) and a golf and racquet club (Ventana Canyon) as neighbors.

Access is through Loews's parking lot. Turn down the little dirt road and drive to the two huge eucalyptus trees. And there you have it—a hideaway, near the city yet far removed. Flying V sits on the floor of a brook-ridden canyon in the foothills of the Catalina Mountains. Its name comes from the huge natural V formed by the mountains behind it, rising to a height of 9,000 feet. Downtown Tucson is about 16 miles south.

Reed Shields couldn't bear to see his childhood home deteriorate, so he has lovingly restored the main lodge and the surrounding cabins, one by one. Originating as a working ranch in the early 1900s, Flying V began operation as a guest ranch in 1927; Reed's parents bought it in 1947 and continued the tradition.

The main lodge, wonderfully rustic, exudes the romance of history. Over 4,000 books are stacked around, some with stories of the Old West. (Ask to see the 1930s brochures inviting Easterners to visit the Flying V. Its best tag line is, "Dude, Go West and Be Wrangled.") The lodge's big native stone fireplace has some unusual components mixed into the design. Look for the Indian metates, the axeheads, and the grinding stones.

Guest quarters consist of one- and two-bedroom stone and stucco cabins, some with screened porches, others with decks overlooking a creek. Furnishings are modern and fairly simple. Kitchens are well-equipped, baths are adequate, and units are air-conditioned and heated. Some have a phone and TV. The largest (1,000 square feet, accommodating up to six), has a huge kitchen with dishwasher and a big sitting area, plus two bedrooms.

Outside under the trees, there's a small but delightful swimming pool. The grounds are sprinkled with orange and grapefruit trees. (Reed encourages guests to pick their breakfast.)

Don't expect a range of services here. This is a retreat, a place to kick back and relax, hike up the canyon, browse through the books, and lounge by the pool. Horseback rides can be arranged through an outfitter. Most important, the hosts are hospitable and flexible.

NEW MEXICO

Dasburg House and Studio
  P.O. Box 1813
  Taos, New Mexico 87571
  505/758-2031
MANAGER: Theo Roth
House accommodating 8; studio accommodating 4
House: $300–$400 per night (3-night minimum)
Studio: $135–$180 per night (3-night minimum)
Lower daily rates for 4-7 night stays
Personal check accepted; no credit cards
Children welcome
No pets
Open year round

From 1933 to 1979, artist Andrew Dasburg—described as "the greatest draughtsman of landscape since van Gogh"—lived and painted in Taos. Today both his house and studio have been converted into deluxe guest lodgings.

Situated about three miles from downtown Taos, the two structures sit on a five-and-a-half acre site. Sheep graze in the nearby fields, and in the distance rise the Sangre de Cristo Mountains. Whatever the time of year—from ski season to getaway summers—the houses are a good alternative to traditional lodgings. For several couples vacationing together, the cost of staying in either of these stand-alone houses is comparable to first-class hotel rooms or condos. Two hours per day of maid service are included in the rate.

The Dasburg House, listed as a Registered Cultural Property by the New Mexico State Historical Registry, was built in the early 1800s. The pueblo-style adobe structure is classic in design, with viga-supported ceilings, thick adobe walls, and kiva fireplaces. The interior is Southwest Plush, with thick carpets and stylish furniture accented with Navajo rugs and Indian crafts.

Both the house and the studio have a full kitchen. If your idea of a vacation is staying out of the kitchen, you have the option of hiring a French chef.

The main house, sleeping up to eight, has three bedrooms (two with twin beds, one with queen size), a library with a queen-size sleeper sofa, and three-and-a-half baths. There's also a living room, dining room, and two porches—both with mountain views. Other features include six fireplaces (two in bedrooms), whirlpool, wet bar, washer and dryer, and ski rack.

The studio, accommodating four, has one bedroom with queen-size bed, living room with queen-size sleeper sofa, and one-and-a-half baths. Fireplaces are in the living room and bedroom. The kitchen is spacious and well-equipped, and there's a washer and dryer off to one side.

La Jacona Ranch

Route 5, Box 250
Pojoaque
Santa Fe, New Mexico 87501
505/455-7948
MANAGER: Cheryl O'Connor
5 guest houses
$82–$120 double, mid-May to September
$64–$105 double, rest of the year
Rates based on 2-day minimum; extra $15 charge for 1 night
   only
Personal check; no credit cards
Children welcome
No pets
Open year round

About 20 miles north of Santa Fe, far from the scores of tourists that the popular city attracts, five guest houses on the grounds of a former estate offer a tranquil retreat. Here amid the pines, cedars, and cottonwoods, you feel more like a house guest visiting well-to-do friends in the country than a paying customer.

The cottages are scattered over the grounds, residential-style. In front of the main house where the manager lives there's a tiny pond, set with stepping stones and draped with willows.

La Jacona's adobe-style one-, two-, and three-bedroom cottages are well furnished, sporting modern decor splashed with southwestern accents. While all of the expected ingredients are present (kiva fireplace, viga and plank ceilings), there's the sense that the decorator had an individualistic streak, creating interiors with their own personality instead of adopting a total "Santa Fe" look. Kitchens, festooned with decorative tile, have such extras as toasters and coffee makers. Bedrooms, while not overly spacious, are pleasant and comfortable.

Not only is Santa Fe less than half an hour away, but Taos is about 50 miles to the northeast. Even closer are several Indian pueblos and the village of Chimayo, renowned for its weavers. For winter vacationers, Santa Fe Ski Basin is about 30 minutes away.

TEXAS

Austin Cottage and Guest Suites
  406 Austin Street
  P.O. Box 488
  Jefferson, Texas 75657
  214/938-5941
OWNER: Cindy Edwards-Rinkle
2-bedroom guest house; 2 suites in separate building
$75 for 2, $104 for 4 including continental breakfast
MasterCard, Visa; personal check
Children over 13 welcome
No pets
Open March to mid-December

Located within Jefferson's historic district, just a block from downtown, is a little red cottage where you can hide away in between jaunts to nearby attractions. Austin Cottage is romantic, decorated with quilts and chintz, white wicker furniture, and country crafts.

A restored 1890s batten board cottage, it has two bedrooms, living room, sun room, and fully equipped kitchen. There's a TV, board games, and a front porch that invites you to sit and rock. Out back is a brick patio where you can eat breakfast—a continental-style affair featuring homemade breads. Rented in its entirety, the cottage is perfect for two couples traveling together.

Two suites in a separate building are also good options. While their construction is new, the suites have a historical feel, built with French doors, windows, and woodwork salvaged from earlier structures. Each has a private bath, sitting and dining area, small kitchen (refrigerator but no stove), bedroom, and bath. Nonie's Niche has a king-size bed and twin hideabed; Texie's Favorite has two double-size antique iron beds.

Gant Guest House
936 Bowie Street
P.O. Box 112
Columbus, Texas 78934
409/732-3864, 732-2190
OWNER: Laura Ann Rau
2 bedrooms
$45 for 1 person–$75 for 4 people including continental
   breakfast
MasterCard, Visa; personal check
Children over age 12
No pets
Open year round

In Columbus, site of one of the oldest settlements in Texas, you can stay in a tiny restored German cottage dating back to the 1870s. In recent years the house was moved from nearby Alleytown to its present site—a quiet street in this town of 4,500 residents.

An itinerant German painter probably stenciled the walls and ceilings of this home. His work, hidden by years of soot, was uncovered by the present owner when she set out to restore the gem-like house. So charming is his stenciling that the Texas Society of the DAR copied the entire room to put in the DAR Museum in Washington. Antique furniture, some native to Texas, fills the rooms. A cradle and rocking chair add to the authenticity of the setting.

Two small bedrooms with double beds and a hall sitting room with a daybed accommodate up to five people in one party. Don't worry about having to rough it: there's a modern kitchen (cooking is allowed), small bath with tub-shower, central air conditioning and heating, and a TV. Breakfast is put in the refrigerator prior to your arrival, enabling you to eat when you choose.

A few blocks away are antique and gift shops, conducive to lazy afternoon exploring. Or you can retreat to the side porch and enjoy your hideaway.

Guest House
506 W. Austin
Jefferson, Texas 75657
214/665-8774 or 665-8922
OWNER: Karen Collins
2 bedrooms (shared bath)

$75 double including continental breakfast, $5 for each additional person
MasterCard, Visa; personal check
Children welcome
No pets
Open year round

In slow-paced Jefferson, a Texas town that values its history, the little cottage on Austin Street is an excellent getaway, well-suited for a family or for two couples vacationing together.

Country Cozy is the style. The living room is comfortable and casual, with willow-wood furniture, country-style décor, and wooden floors. A quilt hanging on the wall and an old-fashioned telephone in the corner add to the feeling of quaintness.

The front bedroom has a double bed; the one behind it has a double and a single bed. Although the kitchen is decorated with an ice box and a 1930s stove, no cooking is allowed. Continental breakfast, highlighted by homemade pumpkin bread, magically appears each morning.

Guest Quarters on the Grounds of the Barton House
Main Street
Route 2, Box 411
Salado, Texas 76571
817/947-5718
OWNERS: Robert and Doris Denman
1-room cottage
$45 single or double
Personal check
No children
No pets
No smoking
Open year round

There's no phone and no TV at the Guest Quarters. You aren't served breakfast and you can't take your children or pets. But what you get is a cozy cottage in a slow-paced village, set with historic homes and country-craft shops. Salado is a friendly sort of town, a place where people would rather talk to their neighbors than race off to the city. The fact is, many Saladans once lived in a city and have chosen the country town instead.

The diminutive guest house, situated a few hundred yards from the Denmans' historic home, was once a doctor's office. Built in the 1870s, it's a one-room cottage with a small front porch. Interior walls are lined with pine. Furnishings are primitive-style antiques—a 19th-century rope bed (but with a modern-day mattress), pine wash stand, and a family heirloom chest. The tiny bathroom is modern, and so is the air conditioning.

Next door, the Denmans' daughter and son-in-law operate the Inn at Salado (see Village Bed and Breakfasts).

Montgomery House
   1419 Milam
   P.O. Box 112
   Columbus, Texas 78934
   409/732-3864
OWNER: Colleen Willrodt
2-bedroom house
$45 per bedroom including continental breakfast
MasterCard, Visa; personal check
Children over 12 welcome
No pets
Open year round

Life moves slowly in Columbus, a historic town in southeast Texas. One of its oldest structures is the Montgomery House, an elegant little home built in 1867. Set on a residential street in this preservation-minded town, the Empire-style cottage is an attractive alternative to more traditional lodgings.

From high ceilings to original wooden floors, cornices to stained glass, there's a look of quality and refinement here. The two bedrooms are furnished in Victorian pieces. The bathroom, located at the end of the hallway, has a water closet, footed tub, and marble lavatory.

Continental breakfast is served in the dining area. For convenience, there's a refrigerator and toaster oven that guests can use, as well as a TV.

19

Historic Hostelries

Step back into another era at a historic lodging. Listen to its stories, and soak up its charm. But be advised: all of these hostelries have more to their credit than age. Comfort and service, along with historic ambience, had to pass muster to be included.

Some of the lodgings are members of Historic Hotels Reservations, a non-profit organization dedicated to promting historic lodgings in the West. Member hotels in this chapter are Hassayampa Inn, Plaza Hotel, and Taos Inn. Member hotels in other chapters are La Fonda Hotel, Santa Fe; The Lodge, Cloudcroft; and La Posada de Albuquerque, Albuquerque.

You can make reservations by calling 800-626-4886 (U.S.), 800-228-4326 (CO), or 303-759-1918. Telephone hours are 8:30 A.M. to 5 P.M., MST.

ARIZONA

Hassayampa Inn
  122 E. Gurley Street
  P.O. Box 2356
  Prescott, Arizona 86302
  602/778-9434
GENERAL MANAGER: Jay Anthony
67 rooms
$42–$62 single, $52–$72 double; $95–$110 suites

American Express, Diners Club, MasterCard, Visa; personal
  check
Children welcome
No pets
Open year round

Hassayampa Inn was truly a grand hotel when it opened in
1927. A product of its age, it was flamboyantly elegant. As a
social leader, it was one of the first hotels in Arizona to cater
to automobile travelers.

In 1985 the restored grande dame assumed her rightful place
in society. Listed on the National Register of Historic Places,
the Hassayampa offers a sense of history coupled with style.
The lobby is adorned with tiled floors, oriental rugs, antique
piano, and potted palms, but the focal point is the beamed
ceiling, decorated with Spanish and Indian motifs. During the
renovation the ceiling was meticulously restored, working
from photographs of the original. Several small rooms off the
lobby lend themselves to intimate tête-à-têtes.

Ride up the attended elevator, original to the building, to the
second and third floor guest rooms. More than half of the
rooms feature Castilian walnut furniture inset with Spanish
tiles—the same pieces that decorated the rooms in 1927. TVs,
air conditioning, and heating are modern-day additions.

With color schemes of deep blue and mauve or peach and
green, the high-ceilinged rooms are fresh and inviting. Beds
are dressed in comforters, dust ruffles and pillow shams, coor-
dinating with draperies and wallpaper designs. Several suites
are available, including one with a large whirlpool tub. All
have sofa hideabeds in the parlors.

The Peacock Room is a convivial dining spot, serving three
meals a day. Dinner entrees range from $10 to $14.

Hotel Vendome

230 S. Cortez Street
Prescott, Arizona 86303
602/776-0900
INNKEEPER: Janie Stamp
21 rooms (private baths)
$35–$55 single or double; $65–$80 suites
HIGH SEASON: summer
American Express, Diners Club, Discover, MasterCard, Visa;
  personal check
Children welcome
Pets with approval
Open year round

This small wood-and-brick hotel, built in 1917 and restored in 1983, sits near the center of downtown. It's a simple, pleasant lodging, making no pretense of being elegant. The tiny lobby doubles as an informal bar. Guests can sit at the cherry wood counter and enjoy coffee and doughnuts or wine served from a Cruvinet.

Behind the front desk is a charming reminder of the hotel's vintage. It's a two-way signaling system pre-dating house phones, enabling guests to buzz the front desk, or the front desk to buzz guests in their rooms. The system still works— ask for a demonstration.

Guest rooms stretch along central hallways on the first and second floor. All have a tailored, uncluttered look, with solid blue or beige bedspreads and mini-blinds in place of curtains. Rooms have either one queen or two twin beds. Two-room suites are a good choice for families, with a sofa bed in the parlor. Bathrooms, which have also been nicely renovated, have either a clawfoot tub with shower or an oversized sunken tub. Lighting is good, with open bulb fixtures reminiscent of theatrical dressing rooms. Cable TVs, phones, and ceiling fans in lieu of air conditioning are in every room.

Monte Vista Hotel

100 N. San Francisco Street
Flagstaff, Arizona 86001
602/774-9086, 779-6971
INNKEEPER: Matt Casado
41 rooms
$40–$60 single, $45–$65 double; $110 suite
American Express, MasterCard, Visa; no personal check
Children welcome
No pets
Open year round

The sign in the lobby says "Check Guns at Desk." A bedroom upstairs is named for Zane Grey, who stayed here while working on one of his Western novels. There's a bright red Victorian couch in the lobby, and an authentic Western bar off to the side. The restored Monte Vista Hotel, dating back to 1927, sits in the heart of downtown Flagstaff. Vacationers can explore nearby attractions (Grand Canyon, Walnut Canyon, Sunset Crater), using the romantic hotel as a hub.

Pink and white hallways, fresh and cheerful, lead to guest rooms on the second through fourth floors. Brass beds and lace curtains, ceiling fans and antique-style wall phones—the rooms are picturesque and plush. Bathrooms are accented with gleaming brass fixtures. Such modern amenities as TVs keep you in touch with the 20th century. Rooms are not air-conditioned but are pleasantly cool even in the midst of summer.

Downstairs there's an upscale dining room (open Wednesday through Sunday evenings) and a coffeeshop serving breakfast, lunch, and dinner.

NEW MEXICO

Hotel St. Francis
  210 Don Gaspar Avenue
  Santa Fe, New Mexico 87501
  505/983-5700
  800/666-5700
GENERAL MANAGER: Michael Cerletti
83 rooms
$40–$90 rooms; $125–$140 suites
MasterCard, Visa; personal check
Children welcome
No pets
Open year round

In a town dating back to 1610, a hotel built in 1924 is a relative newcomer, but this 1920s-style hotel, renovated in 1987, adds charm and flavor to the cultural capital of the Southwest.

A wide front porch set with white wrought iron furniture opens onto Don Gaspar Avenue, only a block from the Plaza. The hotel's high ceilinged lobby has the look of elegance, with classic white columns, Queen Anne furniture, oriental rugs, and Saltillo tile floors. In keeping with the mood, afternoon tea is served in the lobby and on the veranda.

In Francisco's Restaurant, waitresses dressed 1920s-style serve guests while classical music plays in the background. Specializing in Northern Italian dishes as well as seafood, Francisco's has one of the most interesting menus in town, and food is reasonably priced. Entrees range from $10 to $14, with such choices as stuffed sole; cioppino; veal medallions with truffles, mushrooms, and fontina cheese; and quail Zinfandel (with a sauce of Zinfandel wine and juniper berries).

There's a hint of romance throughout the hotel. Hallways leading to guest rooms on the second and third floor are wide and grand, with white walls and deep blue carpets. Guest rooms, although small, are delightfully decorated, featuring white iron and brass beds, period furniture, and matched-fabric bedspreads and curtains. Beds are dressed in pillow shams and dust ruffles. Bathrooms, also small, are adorned with marble. Some guest rooms have free-standing marble lavatories, adding to the beauty of the room as well as the convenience.

Plaza Hotel
230 on the Old Town Plaza
Las Vegas, New Mexico 87701
505/425-3591
OWNER: Katherine Slick
37 rooms
$45 single, $50–$60 double; $65–$70 suites
American Express, Carte Blanche, Diners Club, MasterCard,
    Visa; personal check
Children welcome
Pets accepted with $25 deposit
Open year round

In 1879 the railroad came to Las Vegas, making it the first large town in the territory to be reached by rail. Of course a railroad town needed a hotel, so in 1881 local businessmen headed by Don Benigno Romero formed the Plaza Hotel Company. Their three-story hotel, hailed as "the Belle of the Southwest," opened in 1882.

In its earliest days, notorious outlaws such as Billy the Kid were among the Plaza's patrons. Then in 1913 the hotel brushed shoulders with Hollywood: popular silent-film star Romaine Fielding selected the Plaza as his studio headquarters, renaming it Hotel Romaine (the lettering can still be seen on one facade of the building). Later, cowboy actor and director Tom Mix came to town. Scenes for several of his movies were filmed in Las Vegas and included shots of the renamed Plaza Hotel.

An agricultural depression hit the area in the mid-1920s, and the hotel suffered along with the rest of the town. The decline of the one-time "Belle" continued until 1982 when Wid and Katherine Slick joined with then-owners Lonnie and Dana Lucero to restore it.

Listed on the National Register of Historic Places, the Plaza Hotel is a lodging with charm. Its 37 guest rooms are spacious and airy, with high ceilings and twice as much square footage as the original rooms. Antique furnishings include a superior collection of armoires, not only convenient for the traveler but also conducive to camouflaging TVs. Touches such as fringed lamps and lace curtains add a dash of nostalgia. Baths are also well-decorated. Happily, modern-day comfort has not been overlooked. Rooms are air-conditioned, and of course there are telephones.

Just off the lobby, set with antiques but not opulent in style are a western saloon and a pleasant dining room. Dinner selections range from hamburgers to veal piccata, with entrees priced up to $13.

Las Vegas has other historic sites to see, beginning with a walking tour of the Plaza area. There's also the Rough Riders Memorial and City Museum featuring Rough Rider memorabilia, Indian artifacts, and city history. Area outdoor activities include horseback riding, fishing, hay rides, and pack trips into the Pecos Wilderness.

Taos Inn

P.O. Drawer N
Taos, New Mexico 87571
505/758-2233
800/TAOS-INN
OWNERS/MANAGERS: Bruce Ross and Feeny Lipscomb
40 rooms
$45–$65 single, $50–$85 double
American Express, MasterCard, Visa; personal check
Children welcome
No pets
Open year round

In keeping with its history, Taos Inn is a center of activity in this popular tourist town. The Plaza is only a block away, and within a few blocks are dozens of galleries, shops, and restaurants. The hotel's lobby, originally a small plaza centered by the town's well, is still a local gathering spot. Artists, drawn to this site since the early 1900s, frequent the hotel as part of a "Meet the Artist" series instituted by the hotel's current owners.

The design of the hotel is unique, for the lodging is composed of several houses that once faced the tiny plaza. In 1936 Helen Martin, widow of popular Doc Martin who practiced medicine in the town for many years, bought the surrounding houses (the Martins had lived in one of them), enclosed the plaza and converted the composite into a hotel. In 1982 the hotel was lovingly restored, resulting in an inn that exudes a sense of history combined with modern-day comfort. Now on the National and State Registers of Historic Places, it is a noted Taos landmark.

About half of the inn's 40 guest rooms are on the first and second floors of the main building. Only a few steps behind it is the Sandoval House with six rooms. An additional 16 rooms are within a one-story complex surrounding a courtyard to one side of the Sandoval House.

Each of the inn's rooms is somewhat different, but all are steeped in Southwest decor, from handloomed Indian bed-spreads (made by the Zapotecs especially for the inn) to hand-crafted Taos furniture. Most rooms have kiva fireplaces, crafted by a local adobe sculptress and decorated with Indian designs. Rooms in the Sandoval House, while smaller than the rest, have high ceilings and interesting configurations. All guest rooms have comfortable seating, TVs, and phones. Bathrooms, average in size, are festively adorned with tiles and have tub/showers. Some rooms have vanities with lavato-ries, adding to the convenience. Most rooms have fans; only three have air conditioning.

The small two-story lobby has an informal feeling—con-ducive to relaxing amid southwestern surroundings. In its center is a tiled fountain, once the town's well. To one side of the lobby is the Adobe Bar, originally the Tarleton house. Popular with Taos residents and visitors alike, it features a host of specialty drinks—how about a Mercedes Margarita, Chile-tini, or Almond Blossom?

Adjoining the lobby on the opposite side is Doc Martin's Restaurant, situated in a structure which was once the good doctor's home and office. (His birthing room is now a cozy dining area seating four.) But history only counts for so much in a dining establishment—in truth, the best reason to visit Doc Martin's is for the outstanding cuisine. Specializing in regional dishes and emphasizing fresh indigenous foods, the restaurant serves such entrees as fresh chicken breast grilled and served with homemade chicken sausage, blue corn po-lenta, and fresh tomato salsa. The wine list is one of the best in the state.

Breakfast is no ordinary meal at Taos Inn. Choose from carne adovada (pork loin marinated in a mixture of red chili and spices, then grilled and served with eggs, rice, and beans), huevos rancheros, blue corn griddle cakes, or a half dozen more specialties.

The inn's "Meet the Artist" series is a semi-annual event, running from mid-May to mid-June, and from mid-October to mid-December. On Tuesdays and Thursdays during the series, Taos artists talk about their work. Studio tours, demonstrations, slide shows, videos, music or readings are part of the presentation. Contact the inn for upcoming sche-dules. Reservations are required for some sessions.

A popular in-town lodging for skiers, the inn offers ski packages. The shuttle bus to Taos Ski Valley stops at the front door. Also on the grounds are a small swimming pool, open during the summer, and a hot tub, open year round.

TEXAS

Excelsior House
211 W. Austin
Jefferson, Texas 75657
214/665-2513
MANAGER: Carole Wetsel
14 rooms and suites (private baths)
$30–$40 single, $35–$45 double; $50–$55 suites
Personal check; no credit cards
Children accepted but not encouraged
No pets
Open year round

One of the oldest hotels in Texas, the Excelsior is a precious jewel, set in one of the state's most history-minded towns. Public rooms are richly elegant, and the 14 guest rooms, each with a distinctive design, have charm and grace.

Outside the hotel's doors stands an idyllic village, begging to be explored. The historical museum next door exhibits European and American treasures—art, furnishings, and crafts. The Black Swan Restaurant, serving outstanding fare reminiscent of New Orleans, is across the street. Within one block you can board a horse-drawn surrey for a ride around Jefferson, tour a historic railroad car, or shop for antiques.

In 1961 the Jessie Allen Wise Garden Club bought the 1850s Excelsior and set about restoring it. Not only did they create a lodging of beauty, but also they and their project became a catalyst for a community attitude of restoration, resulting in Jefferson's emergence as a major tourist attraction. The garden club still owns and operates the hotel; volunteers give tours twice daily.

While the hotel is unimposing on the exterior, the interior holds many surprises. The ballroom is studded with antiques, some original to the hotel. There's an 1850s piano which was floated up the river from New Orleans, hand-painted French chandeliers, and an Italian marble fireplace trimmed in pewter and gold.

In the dining room overlooking the New Orleans-style courtyard, guests as well as other diners revel in the famed

Excelsior breakfast, a feast of orange blossom muffins, country ham, and scrambled eggs. (Reservations are required.).

Guest rooms, although inexpensively priced, offer priceless memories of a trip into another era. The Lady Bird Room was furnished by friends of the Johnsons, honoring the woman who once went to school in Jefferson. The Sleigh Bed room is true to its name, featuring a handsome carved bed resembling a sleigh. The Presidential Suite is the most expensive room in the house, and would be a bargain at double the price. A magnificent canopied bed, large sitting area, and decorative fireplace set the tone of elegance.

Reservations for the hotel should be made three to four months in advance, especially for weekends during spring and fall.

Landmark Inn

U.S. Highway 90 West
P.O. Box 577
Castroville, Texas 78009
512/538-2133
Managed by Texas Parks and Wildlife Department
8 rooms (some with shared baths)
$25 single, $30 double
Personal check; no credit cards
Children welcome
No pets
Smoking in designated areas
Open year round

Colonists from the provinces of Alsace and Lorraine settled Castroville in 1844. From their homeland they brought their language, customs, and architecture. Remnants of all three exist in modern-day Castroville, a town of about 2,000 residents. One of the best preserved examples of Alsatian architecture is the Landmark Inn, a charming eight-room lodging which is the focal point of the Landmark Inn State Historic Site operated by the Texas Parks and Wildlife Department. The hotel, built in 1849 as a stagecoach stop, is open for touring. So is a historic stone grist mill and an exhibition depicting life in early Castroville.

This is the place for history lovers as well as those who like to get off the beaten track. Don't expect TVs, telephones, a restaurant, or even air conditioning, for the Parks Department's goal is to preserve the historical nature of the structure.

Your first sight of the inn is of a quaint two-story curbside building. Save your judgment until you walk around to the back; the tiny white hotel overlooks beautiful grounds and a graceful garden, planted with shrubs and flowers representative of the town's early days. All rooms in the main building (5 upstairs, 1 downstairs) open onto the gardens. Guest rooms, simple in decor, are furnished with antiques. (Don't worry—authenticity doesn't go as far as the mattresses, which are modern.)

The old bathhouse has been converted to two tiny bedrooms, one above the other. Each has a double bed and private bath. While the one on top (number 8) is often booked by honeymooners, people who tend toward claustrophobia or those who are large (whether tall or plump) should avoid it.

Tol Barret House

Route 4, Box 9400
Nacogdoches, Texas 75961
409/569-1249
HOSTS: Charles and Ann Phillips
Accommodations in 3 houses
$55–$70 double including cook-your-own breakfast
Reduced rates for stays of longer than 1 night
Personal check
Children accepted only at Gatehouse
No pets
Open year round

Hidden away in the pine forests of East Texas, there's an 1840s pioneer-style farmhouse ready to welcome guests, especially those with a bent toward history. Once the house was occupied by Taliaferro "Tol" Barret, the man credited with drilling the first producing oil well west of the Mississippi. Today the house reflects the Barrets' lifestyle. The front yard is still swept clean of grasses, and early Texas flowers such as widow's tear and lantana still bloom. Mrs. Barret's "sittin" room, furnished with American Empire pieces, looks much as the lady of the house might have left it. Listed in the National Register of Historic Places, the house has been beautifully restored by two knowledgeable preservationists, Charles and Ann Phillips. Between the two of them, they have rebuilt, restenciled, and redecorated the house as well as its furnishings—all indigenous to the period.

Connected to the house by a covered walkway is the kitchen and loft, constructed from wood of the same vintage as the house. This is the structure that the Phillips have turned into a B&B accommodation, truly one of the most distinctive in the Southwest.

Downstairs in the country-style kitchen guests cook their own breakfast. The larder is stocked with such specialties as venison sausage and homemade bread, along with standard fare such as eggs and cereals.

The bedroom upstairs is straight out of the pages of a history book. Four under-the-eaves rope beds (with feather mattresses), handmade quilts, handcrafted furniture, braided rugs, and wooden floors make for a cozy and comfortable retreat.

But that's not all the Phillips have to offer. Their own home, a restored 1820s pioneer house, is about a quarter of a mile down the road. Like the Tol Barret house, it's surrounded by trees—seemingly remote from neighbors. Guests lodge on the second floor, ascending from the back porch via a private stairway to two bedrooms, central sitting area, and bath. Furnishings are charmingly romantic, circa pioneer days. The original pole rafters still arch overhead.

Also on the property is the Gatehouse, a small 20th-century house with two bedrooms. While it is no competition with the other two houses as far as charm is concerned, the Gatehouse is good for families with children, affording a farm-like setting.

The Tremont House
   2300 Ship's Mechanic Row
   Galveston, Texas 77550
   409/763-0300
   800/874-2300 US
GENERAL MANAGER: Roy Chen
113 rooms
$60–$120 single, $70–$130 double; $250 suites
HIGH SEASON: April to mid-September
LOW SEASON: January to March
American Express, Diners Club, MasterCard, Visa
Children welcome

No pets
Open year round

One of the finest hotels in all the Southwest is The Tremont House, situated in Galveston's Strand National Historic District. Conceived and owned by oilman/real estate developer George Mitchell and his wife Cynthia, the hotel is a loving, thoughtful creation. The Mitchells are a prime force behind Galveston's movement toward historic preservation; the hotel is one of their ten historic restoration projects.

The Tremont House is a delightful rendition of glittery turn-of-the-century Galveston.   Interiors are sophisticated and stylish. Unlike hotels where the public areas get all the attention and guest rooms seem to be an afterthought, at this hotel the rooms themselves are the best part. Decorated in chic black and white, the high-ceilinged rooms have white enamel-and-brass beds, lace curtains, black and white rugs on hardwood floors, and baths with hand-painted Italian tile. Eleven-foot high windows open onto ironwork balconies.

Luxury is the pervading tone—terry cloth robes, heated towel racks, oversized towels, imported chocolates at turn-down. Service is exemplary—attentive and hospitable. Complimentary valet parking, a full-time concierge, and 24-hour room service are all part of a Tremont House stay.

The original Tremont House, built in 1839, was for many years the largest and finest hotel in the Republic of Texas. From its balcony, Sam Houston delivered his last public address. The hotel's guest register included presidents, foreign ministers, and entertainers. Rebuilt in 1872 after a fire seven years earlier, the hotel again played host to the rich and famous. But after the devastating 1900 hurricane, the Tremont, like the city itself, never recovered. It was demolished in 1928.   Today its namesake, located a few blocks from the original hotel site, is in the beautifully restored Leon and H. Blum Building, constructed in 1879.   Styled to recreate the atmosphere of the old Tremont, it is intimate yet grand. At the center of its design is a four-story rectangular atrium. About half of the guest rooms overlook the atrium; interior bridges connect the upper level hallways across it. Within the atrium is the Toujouse Bar, featuring a rosewood bar built in 1888, white wicker chairs, and potted palms. Off to the side is The Merchant Prince restaurant, named for Leon Blum, who was Galveston's "Merchant Prince," with a million-acre empire stretching across Texas.

About the guest rooms being the best part of The Tremont House: The Merchant Prince is also a strong contender for that distinction. A jewel of a restaurant, it has a splendid menu featuring nouvelle American cuisine. The execution is as good as the promise. The restaurant is well worth a visit, wherever you stay (entrees from $10 to $17).

20

Hunting/Fishing Lodges

Wild game is abundant in the Southwest, and its waters teem with fish. Hostelries in this chapter are ones that function primarily as hunting and fishing lodges.

NEW MEXICO

The Lodge at Chama Land and Cattle Company
P.O. Box 746
Chama, New Mexico 87520
505/756-2133
GENERAL MANAGER: Leo Smith
11 rooms (private baths)
$1,750–$6,400 for 1-week hunt (rate dependent on type of game)
$275 per day including meals, guide, transportation for fishing
Special arrangements for non-hunting/fishing companions
$155–$195 double including all meals during non-hunting season
Personal or business check; bank draft; traveler's check; no credit cards
Children over 12 welcome
No pets
Open year round; hunting seasons mid-May to mid-March

Chama Land and Cattle Company, set in the San Juan Mountains of northern New Mexico, is a working ranch with over 36,000 acres. The ranch spreads over beautiful terrain ranging from oak foothills and meadows of aspen and spruce to alpine country of up to 10,000 feet.

On its land, hidden away from public view, is an exclusive, luxurious lodge catering to hunters and anglers as well as business groups. Repeat visitors account for three-fourths of its clientele.

Elk hunting is at the heart of the lodge's operation. The ranch has one of the largest elk herds on privately owned land in the country. Ninety percent of its hunters take 6 x 6 bull elk or better; the rest take 5 x 5s. Each hunter has a private guide. Travel is by four-wheel-drive vehicle, horseback or on foot. Hunts last about three or four days. Other game hunted include mule deer and black bear.

Fishing is in mountain lakes stocked with rainbow, German brown, brook, and native cutthroat trout. Comments in the guest register tell the story. "Better fishing than in Alaska," wrote one guest.

The stone lodge is a sprawling ranch-style house set on a hill a short distance from the highway. (There's a security gate at the entrance, so be sure you're expected.) The main room, appropriately named the Trophy Room, is truly handsome, centered with a 22-foot stone fireplace and decorated with original western art. Stuffed elk, deer, and bear—all native to the area—as well as wildlife from other parts of the world set the tone. Owner Grady Vaughn is a collector and has assembled an impressive display.

Eleven guest rooms line the adjoining hall. Large and luxurious, each has its own theme, with wildlife as the focal point. Leather and wood, Indian pottery and woven work make the rooms distinctive. The huge junior suite has a kiva fireplace and rugs made by the famous Ortega weavers in Chimayo.

The hot tub room, adjoined by a sauna, is truly luxurious. Dining is in the Trophy Room. All of the food is made from scratch, and meals are served with a flair. An open bar is included in the rate.

During winter months, the lodge is a great place for mountain vacationing, especially if you like cross-country skiing, sleigh rides, and observing wildlife.

Moreno Ranch Hunting Lodge
P.O. Box 135
Eagle Nest, New Mexico 87718
505/377-6581, 377-6555

OWNERS: The Butler Family
Accommodates up to 15 hunters
$3,500 for elk hunt
$2,000 for mountain lion hunt
$1,500 for bear hunt
$100 per day for non-hunter accompanying hunter
Rates include lodging, meals, guide; hunts last up to 6 days
Children and pets not appropriate
Open only during hunting seasons: October to December
    (specific dates vary) for elk; April to May and August to
    September for bear; January to February for mountain lion

Moreno Ranch is a family-owned 50,000-acre cattle ranch situated between Raton and Taos. Adjacent to Kit Carson National Forest in an area renowned for its elk, Moreno boasts some of the best elk hunting around.

Labeling its program "executive hunts," the ranch arranges for guides to take hunters to the best areas via four-wheel-drive vehicles (one guide is provided for every three hunters). Ninety-six percent of the hunters take an elk; 60 percent take at least a 5 x 5. Deer, bear, mountain lion, turkey, and grouse are also hunted during appropriate seasons. The price of a hunt includes room, meals, open bar, trespass permit, guide, four-wheel-drive vehicle, and skinning and quartering of game. Extra fees are charged for a state hunting license. Hunters who take a trophy elk (5 x 5 bull or better) pay a $1,500 trophy fee.

Lodging is in several bedrooms in a modern rambling ranch house. Meals are hearty—steaks, prime rib, turkey, home-made sausage. Guests have lots of room to relax, including the sprawling game room with pool table, video movies (more than 700), card tables, and open bar.

Although Moreno Ranch's accommodations are not open during the summer, the Butler family offers trout fishing in three stocked mountain lakes (May 1 to September 15). There's a $50 charge per person, with a six-fish limit. No state license is required.

Oso Ranch and Lodge

P.O. Box 808
Chama, New Mexico 87520
505/756-2954
MANAGERS: Benny and Jessie Salazar
6 rooms (private baths)
Rates start at $750 for 5-day hunting package
$100 per day for non-hunters
American Express, MasterCard, Visa; personal check

No pets

Open varying dates from September to December, depending on hunting seasons

A year-round sports lodge, Oso Ranch becomes a hunting lodge during appropriate seasons. Elk, mule deer, mountain lion, and black bear are the predominant game.

Oso Ranch (oso is the Spanish word for bear) offers two types of hunts: "fully outfitted," and "lodge." The "fully out-fitted" version includes a guide, transportation while hunting, game care, lodging, meals, and hunting permits. New Mexico license and hunting fees are extra. An outfitter arranged by the ranch takes hunters out via four-wheel-drive vehicle or horse-back. "Lodge" hunts include private land hunting permits, transportation to and from the hunting area, and assistance in retrieving game when needed, but no guide service. Lodging and meals are also included in the price.

Oso Ranch has approximately 1,500 acres of hunting country. In addition to its own land, the ranch has hunting rights to thousands of acres of private land. The rolling countryside, dotted with juniper, pine, and spruce forests, varies in elevation from 7,000 to 10,000 feet.

Hunting package rates range from $750 for a "lodge" five-day buck mule deer hunt, with no trophy fee, to $2,500 for a "fully-outfitted" five-day bull elk hunt, with a $500 trophy fee. Elk hunts have to be booked one year in advance. The ranch will arrange for taxidermy, meat storage, and freezing upon request.

Fishing at Oso Ranch is a year-round sport. Its private lakes are stocked with rainbow trout. Anglers can also fish in private streams (cut-throat, brown, and brook trout, Kokonee salmon) and in the Chama, Little Navajo, and Brazos rivers. There is no extra charge for fishing.

For a description of Lodge facilities, guest rooms, and meal service, see Sports Lodges.

Vermejo Park Ranch
P.O. Drawer E
Raton, New Mexico 87740
505/445-3097
PRESIDENT: Jim Charlesworth
6 cottages accommodating up to 56
1 lodge accommodating up to 12
$1,200–$7,000 for up to 5-day hunt including meals, guides, transportation
$160 per day including meals, fishing privileges

$100 per person including meals for summer vacationing,
   non-hunters/anglers
Personal check; no credit cards
Children welcome during summer season
No pets
Open October to December for hunting, June to mid-September for fishing and summer vacationing

Vermejo Park Ranch is one of the largest blocks of privately owned land in the country. Its 392,000 acres in the Sangre de Cristo Mountains date back to an 1840s land grant encompassing two million acres. The ranch, owned since 1973 by the Pennzoil Company, is an outdoor recreation resort and a working cattle ranch. As a hunting and fishing destination, it offers expansive private grounds far removed from the masses.

The nucleus of the resort is about 40 miles from Raton, partially over private road. In the early 1900s a wealthy businessman from Chicago owned the ranch, building a mansion for himself and several houses for guests. Today's guests stay in six of the houses (the mansion, exquisitely furnished with antiques, is only used on special occasions) or in a wonderfully rustic Costillo Lodge 28 miles from the headquarters. Accommodating up to 12 guests, the lodge is usually reserved for groups.

In 1911, elk were re-established at Vermejo Park after having been killed off from the entire area in the early 1890s. Today Vermejo claims to be home to New Mexico's largest elk herd. In 1986 its hunters had an overall 85 percent success rate at Vermejo, and over 70 percent of all bulls taken scored 6 x 6 or larger. Heavily populated with wildlife, the ranch also offers hunts for mule deer, antelope, bear, mountain lion, buffalo, and Merrium turkey. All hunts include a private guide, four-wheel-drive vehicle, hunt license, and game skinning and quartering.

During the summer season, anglers can fish in ten lakes and 25 miles of creeks. Cutthroat, brook, rainbow, and brown trout, along with Coho salmon, are the featured catches. Fly fishing schools are scheduled several times during the season. There's a limit of 12 fish per day.

Outdoor enthusiasts can enjoy the ranch in the summer. Activities include horseback riding, hiking, and skeet shooting.

Lodging is truly different from anywhere else in the Southwest. The setting is magnificent. Here you're in a mini-village surrounded by miles and miles of wide-open wilderness. The guest houses are indeed houses, with a variety of floor plans and are set apart from each other, village-style. Furnishings are modern but not particularly luxurious or atmospheric. Bedrooms have either double or twin beds.

Meals are served in a separate house, Casa Minor, which has a glass-enclosed sun porch affording views of the open terrain and a full service bar where guests socialize. The cuisine tends to be meat-and-potatoes, hearty but not gourmet. While lunch is served in the dining room, most guests ask for box lunches. Guests staying at Costillo Lodge have their own dining facility.

Casa Grande, the one-time owner's mansion is truly grand, with hand-carved ceilings, interior marble columns, oriental rugs, and a 1904 Steinway. Its remote location makes you feel as if you've stumbled upon an undiscovered castle. Be sure to ask for a tour.

TEXAS

The Farris 1912
201 N. McCarty Avenue
Eagle Lake, Texas 77434
409/234-2546
PROPRIETORS: William and Helyn Farris
16 rooms (most with shared baths); 4 suites (private baths)
HUNTING SEASON: $90–$95 per person including all meals
OTHER SEASONS: $30–$35 single, $40–$48 double including continental breakfast
American Express, MasterCard, Visa
Children over 12 welcome
No pets
Open for hunting season November to January; closed part of July, also December 24-25

The Farris 1912 wears two faces. From November through January it caters to hunters drawn to the Eagle Lake area by excellent duck and goose hunting. During the rest of the year the historic hotel, known as "Eagle Lake's birthplace," is a getaway destination.

Guests have the use of a private lake, whether their preference is fishing or observing wildlife. Attwater Prairie Chicken Refuge, a 3,400-acre sanctuary dedicated to the near-extinct birds, is six miles from the Farris.

So popular is the area for bird hunting that the hotel's winter-time roster includes international as well as national guests. This is no ordinary hunting lodge. Casual elegance is the theme, and public areas are richly decorated with antique furniture, lace curtains, silver candelabra, mirrors, and floral carpets. A sign by the back door advises, "Hunters, Unload Guns! No Muddy Boots in Hotel, Please." In a small separate building is a gun-cleaning facility as well as refrigerated storage.

All meals are provided during hunting season, hence the higher prices. As on a cruise ship, food is omnipresent, with an "eat-all-you-want" philosophy. No gratuities are charged, expected, or permitted at any time for lodging or food services.

Continental breakfast is the only meal served during the rest of the year. For groups and private parties, food service can be arranged.

Accommodations are on the second floor of the main hotel (16 rooms) and in the 1920s guest house next door (4 suites). Hotel guest rooms, cheerfully but simply furnished, have double or twin beds. Two have private baths. The VIP room has an antique spool bed as well as one twin bed. Number 14 is especially pretty, one of the most feminine in design. All rooms open onto a sprawling mezzanine, a popular gathering spot with couches, easy chairs, and game tables.

Suites in the guest house have private entrances, bath with shower, parlor, wet bar, refrigerator, and TV.

21

Lakeside

Lodgings in this chapter have more to offer than lake views. All have facilities that give you access to a lake, whether you want to boat or fish. (In other words, you don't have to arrive with your own boat in tow to feel like you've had a lake vacation.)

OKLAHOMA

Shangri-La
  Route 3
  Afton, Oklahoma 74331
  918/257-4204
  800/331-4060 US, 800/722-4903 OK
GENERAL MANAGER: Dennis McDonald
619 units
$89–$310 single or double
American Express, Carte Blanche, Diners Club, MasterCard,
  Visa; personal check
Children welcome
Pets with approval
Open year round

On the shores of 59,000 acre Grand Lake O' the Cherokees is a resort with enough recreational features to keep most vacationers happy, plus so many restaurants that you can try a different one every day.

Shangri-La spreads over 660 acres. Choose your favorite sport and it's probably there: golf (36 holes), tennis (10 courts), boating, outdoor and indoor swimming, horseback riding (three miles from main lodge), racquetball, biking, and jogging. The huge recreation center is unusually well-equipped—everything from a health spa to bowling alleys. At the marina you can arrange water skiing, fishing boats and/or fishing guide service, pontoon boats, cruisers, and scenic cruises. Rates are less expensive than at many resorts. Greens fees, including cart, range from $25 to $35. Tennis is $8 per court per hour. Ski boats are $45 for four hours. Fishing boats are $75 for eight hours; bass boats with a guide are $80 for four hours.

Lodging options are extensive, with rooms in the main lodge, an 11-story tower, and several condo complexes. Personal favorites are the main lodge (the least expensive and close to most of the activities) and Shangri-La Estates (condos tucked away beneath the trees near the golf course—definitely the most romantic). Interiors are spacious and modern.

Dining areas are imaginative, providing diverse environments to suit different moods. Tahitian Terrace serves Chinese food in an enclosed courtyard arranged around a banyan tree. Cellar Clubroom has pizza and spaghetti. The elegant Garden Room is a gourmet retreat. The Angus Room is well-suited for families. Golden Eagle is a 1940s-style supper club. There are total of six restaurants; four are open on most nights.

Three Buoys Houseboat Vacations
Lake Eufaula
400 Lake Shore Drive
Eufaula, Oklahoma 74432
918/689-9152
800/843-2503 US, 800/722-0779 OK
GENERAL MANAGER: Vic Lohr
67 boats
$895–$1,595 per week; 3 and 4 days available from $395
American Express, MasterCard, Visa
Children welcome

Pets not advised ($100 extra charge)
Open year round

Hey, wait a minute. Aren't houseboats out of place in a book about accommodations? In general, perhaps so—but Three Buoys Houseboat Vacations are more like renting a private villa than boating. Yes, this lodging does float, but that just means that you can change the scenery whenever you choose.

A houseboat vacation has lots of possibilities, from partying with friends to sailing alone with somebody you love. Three Buoys provides the environment for a total vacation experience; you're the pilot of your own accommodations. Porters meet you in the parking area to carry your luggage on board. An activities director helps you plan your vacation. Radio contact is maintained throughout your trip, and a chase boat comes to call if you need assistance.

Best of all, the houseboats themselves are truly luxurious. Designed especially for Three Buoys, they're equipped with everything needed for navigating, sleeping, cooking, and relaxing, plus they have such extras as an AM/FM cassette stereo, with speakers both inside the cabin and on the top deck. There's even an irresistible waterslide off the back.

You have a choice of two sizes of houseboats: a 44-foot Sunseeker and a 40-foot Sportcruiser. Sunseekers are definitely more spacious. Both boats can sleep up to ten, but groups of that size would be more comfortable on the larger boat. Each boat has one private stateroom, a loft sleeping area, and couches that convert into beds. Kitchens are as well equipped as many home kitchens, with service for ten and a good selection of cookware. Out on deck there's a gas grill. Extra conveniences on a Sunseeker include a changing room with sink (in addition to the bath), wet bar, and microwave. Sunseekers have central air conditioning plus a booster unit; Sportcruisers have an air conditioning unit only.

Even if you don't know the difference between the bow and the stern, Three Buoys makes you comfortable about operating your "floating villa." A captain comes on board to teach you the ropes, giving you plenty of time to ask questions. Overall, the company takes away the hassle and makes it easy for you to enjoy yourself.

The setting for this care-free vacation is Lake Eufaula in eastern Oklahoma. Nicknamed the Gentle Giant, the lake is the 15th largest man-made lake in the U.S., with 650 miles of shoreline. And gentle it is, making it ideal for a relaxing cruise. You can sunbathe on the top deck, anchor in secluded coves, or play captain for as long as you want. Fishing is for bass, crappie, and catfish. If you yearn for more activity, you can stop at Fountainhead Resort for golf, horseback riding, tennis, and dining. Several restaurants around the lake are directly on the water.

(Lake Eufaula was the site visited in researching this book. Three Buoys has a similar operation on Lake Havasu, situated on the Arizona/California border.)

TEXAS

Del Lago Resort
  600 Del Lago Boulevard
  Montgomery, Texas 77356
  409/582-6100
  713/350-5023
  800/558-1317 US, 800/833-3078 TX
  GENERAL MANAGER: Alberto Cobian
  310 rooms
  $60–$80 single, $70–$90 double
  American Express, Diners Club, MasterCard, Visa; personal
    check
  Children welcome
  No pets
  Open year round

Undeniably, Del Lago is a conference center. In fact, hotel check-in is within the conference building instead of the hotel tower. But Del Lago is also a resort, offering couples and families a lakeside vacation complete with marina, golf course, tennis courts, and health spa.

Situated on the shores of Lake Conroe northwest of Houston, the resort has a 300-slip marina as its focal point. Of course some guests arrive with their own boats, but those who don't can rent sailboats, ski boats, bass boats, or low pontoons. (Ask about reserving a boat when you book your stay; weekend rentals need to be arranged at least four days ahead.)

The 18-hole championship golf course is one of the resort's most popular features. Opened in 1982, the Jay Rivere/Dave Marr-designed course has lush fairways. Tennis is also important at Del Lago. The 13 hard surface courts are all lighted, and there's a good pro shop. The spa is outstanding, with a well-equipped exercise room, racquetball courts, sauna, steam, whirlpool, tanning, and massage. All sorts of classes and clinics are geared toward health and fitness, from water exercise to foot massage to nutrition. Use of the spa (it's also a private club) is $10 a day; extra fees are charged for some services.

There's always something special going on at Del Lago—fishing tournaments, family bike rides (bikes are available for rent), festive theme night buffets. Some events are just for children—beach parties, games on the green, movie nights. Weekend packages are often offered, featuring golf, tennis, or just getting away.

The 20-story hotel tower, right on the lake shore, has rooms well-suited for families. Sleeping and sitting areas are separated, and there's a pull-out couch and a kitchenette (not sufficient for major meals, but fine for snacks).

Cafe Verde serves all three meals; poolside food service is available on a seasonal basis. Fiddler's lounge, overlooking the marina, has pool tables and a big screen TV. On weekends, there's live entertainment at Tiffany's.

Horseshoe Bay Country Club Resort

Box 7766
Horseshoe Bay, Texas 78654
512/598-2511
800/531-5105 US, 800/252-9363 TX
VICE PRESIDENT: Ron Mitchell
75 rooms; 50 condos
$90–$325 double
IN SEASON: mid-February to mid-November
American Express, Diners Club, MasterCard, Visa
Children welcome
No pets
Open year round

On the shores of Lake LBJ in the gently rolling Hill Country west of Austin, Horseshoe Bay is a residential resort community with special beauty. Spread over 4,000 acres, it can boast the best of country life plus city sophistication. Deer roam freely, and the pace of life is slow, but at your fingertips is exceptionally fine dining and a cornucopia of recreational facilities, including the largest Robert Trent Jones designed golf complex in the world.

At the heart of the community is Horseshoe Bay Country Club Resort, a private club with extensive facilities, open only to members and temporary members (the status accorded lodging guests). Enhancing the already beautiful landscape are gardens and fountains, waterfalls, and statues. In all, the resort has an idyllic air—restful and aesthetically pleasing.

Golfers can choose from three courses, all with unusually scenic terrain—a combination of cliffside lake views, cedar- and mesquite-studded countryside, and ravines and streams. The newest of the three courses, Applerock, was named Best New Resort Golf Course in the U.S. for 1986 by *Golf Digest*. Greens fees range from $35 to $40; cart rental is $17 for 18 holes. (Arrange a tee-off time a week in advance.)

The main lodge and guest accommodations are centered around the marina. Boat and ski rentals and fishing guides are all available. It's advisable to reserve a boat prior to arrival.

The tennis complex, set on 18 acres and surrounded by oriental gardens, has 14 Laykold courts. Four courts are covered. The resort also has several outstanding swimming pools; a two-tier pool, fed by waterfalls cascading off bedrock granite outcrops, overlooks the golf course. Horseback riding is over scenic trails traversing the countryside.

Many of the guest lodgings, arranged in several low-rise buildings, are directly on the marina. Several styles are available, ranging from one- to three-bedroom units. Refreshingly, the units don't resemble standard condo designs: space is used innovatively, interiors are large, furnishings are modern and upscale, and kitchens and baths have lots of extras.

Dining is a top-rated feature of a stay at Horseshoe Bay. The Captain's Quarters is formal, with a richly varied menu and an exclusive atmosphere. Coat and tie for men, evening attire for women is the code. Other dining choices include two informal restaurants, romantic in style as well as in their lakeside setting.

Lakeway Inn
  101 Lakeway Drive
  Austin, Texas 78734
  512/261-6600
  800/LAKEWAY
MANAGER: Dan O'Malley
138 rooms; 100 villas
$105–$125 room; $170–$360 villa single or double
American Express, Discover, MasterCard, Visa; personal
  check
Children welcome
No pets
Open year round

On cliffs overlooking Lake Travis about 20 miles west of Austin, Lakeway Inn is at the center of a huge resort and residential community. There's a wealth of recreational choices here: two 18-hole championship golf courses, a marina with lots of boats for rent (fishing, sailing, ski, pontoon, and deck boats), 32 tennis courts (renowned World of Tennis Club), horseback riding on 25 miles of trails, and several swimming pools.

Lodging is in rooms and suites spread out in low buildings near the main lodge, or in two- to four-bedroom villas adjacent to the World of Tennis complex (about a five minute drive from the lodge).

Single bedrooms or bedrooms joined by parlors (you can rent one to three segments of a unit) are very spacious, modern in decor, and have private balconies with great lake views. Many have big stone fireplaces. Villas have fully equipped kitchens and fireplaces. Each cluster of villas has its own tennis court, supplementing the tennis complex a few hundred yards away. There's a dining room and lounge at the main lodge and at the World of Tennis.

Here are some sample fees for recreation: greens fees for 18 holes of golf, $30–$36; cart rental, $20 for shared usage; tennis at Lakeway Tennis Center, $10 all day, per court, per player; World of Tennis courts, $12 per hour; fishing boat, $18 per hour; fishing boat with guide, $140 per day; ski boat, $72 per hour; pontoon boat, $54 per hour; sailboat, $18 per hour; horseback riding, $15 per hour.

For children ages 5 to 12, there's a supervised day camp during the summer (fee of $15 a day).

22

National Park Lodging

The Southwest is blessed with six national parks, all adding dimension and beauty to the region's offerings. Two of the parks have lodgings within their boundaries. Here are the best choices.

BIG BEND NATIONAL PARK

Chisos Mountains Lodge
Big Bend National Park, Texas 79834-9801
915/477-2291
MANAGER: Ron Houchin
34 units
$41.50–$59 for 1-4, motel or lodge unit
$53–$69.50 for 3-6, stone cottages
American Express, Carte Blanche, Diners Club, MasterCard, Visa; personal check
Children welcome
Pets accepted
Open year round

In the heart of the Chisos Mountains you'll find a motel and several stone cottages that can put you in close touch with the national park. Walk out your door to mountains you can almost touch. Dine at the lodge and look upon a magnificent panorama of mountains caressed by clouds. Hiking, river rafting, and horseback riding are the top attractions in this magically beautiful park—wild, rugged, and untamed. Lodging is limited (most visitors camp in the three campgrounds), so make reservations as far ahead as possible. For fall, spring, and major holidays, book lodging at least a year in advance.

The 28 motel units are arranged in a long low modern building. Each room has two double beds, a bath with tub and shower, and individually controlled air conditioning and heating. Don't expect luxury, but they are comfortable enough. Pay phones are within a few steps. The one-room stone cottages are more picturesque, tucked away within the trees. They have one to three double beds, baths, and small porches.

Chisos Mountains Lodge Dining Room and Coffee Shop serves throughout the day. Dinner choices, priced from $7 to $12, are American fare—roast turkey, ham steak, pork chops, steaks. Whatever you order, it's guaranteed to taste great; the mood is convivial and the setting is hard to beat.

GRAND CANYON

Bright Angel Lodge and Cabins
Grand Canyon National Park Lodges
P.O. Box 699
Grand Canyon, Arizona 86023
602/638-2401
GENERAL MANAGER: Bill Bohannon
89 units
$25–$65, single or double; Bucky Suite, $135
American Express, Carte Blanche, Diners Club, MasterCard, Visa; personal check
Children welcome
Kennels for pets (pets not allowed in lodgings)
Open year round

Bright Angel Lodge dates back to 1896, when it began as cabins and tents on the very edge of the Grand Canyon's South Rim. The name comes from Bright Angel Creek, so christened by John Wesley Powell—the first white explorer through the inner gorge of the Grand Canyon.

Today the lodge is a conglomeration of lodging types. At the low end of the scale are simple rooms with no baths or half baths. The most expensive unit, Bucky Suite, is an 1890s cabin built by the Rough Riders. Sitting right at the canyon's rim, it is a delightful old cabin with two rooms, king-size bed, two double hideabeds, fireplace, full bath, phone, and two TVs.

Rim cabins built in 1935 are the best choice. Views don't come any better than this, and the price is right—$50 to $65. These two-room stone and log cabins are roomy, and although their furnishings are simple, they are more than adequate. Don't expect artwork on the walls, but with your view through the windows, it's hard to ask for more. Some of the rim cabins have stone fireplaces. All have a bathroom (shower and tub), phone, and TV.

The cabins labeled "historic" have little to recommend them except their location within a few hundred feet of the Grand Canyon.

Standard rooms, priced at $34, are situated in rambling one-story buildings connected to the main lodge by breezeways. A typical room has two double beds, dresser, and two chairs, with pine walls and shag carpet. The private bathroom has a clawfoot tub.

In the main lodge there's a casual restaurant serving sandwiches and burgers, plus steak and seafood entrees priced from $6 to $12. The lobby is the headquarters for booking bus tours and mule rides.

Hotel management suggests that you make reservations four to six months in advance. On the other hand, they note that it is sometimes possible to get a room by calling at the last minute. Grand Canyon National Park Lodges accept reservations as far as "two years minus two days" in advance.

El Tovar

Grand Canyon National Park Lodges
P.O. Box 699
Grand Canyon, Arizona 86023
602/638-2401
GENERAL MANAGER: Bill Bohannon
78 rooms
$86–$110 single or double; $135–$200 suites
American Express, MasterCard, Visa; personal check
Children welcome
Kennels for pets (pets not allowed in lodgings)
Open year round

The grandest place to stay at the grandest of all canyons is El Tovar. Situated on the South Rim, it looks down on the 190-mile-long chasm carved by the Colorado River.

Built in 1905, the lodge-style hotel was named for Don Pedro de Tovar who in 1540 became the first European to visit the Hopi Indians. Centuries later Hopi craftsmen built the lodge, using native limestone and logs shipped from Oregon. El Tovar was renovated in 1984, and while it still retains its historical character, rooms are stylishly furnished. From Queen Anne chairs to brass lamps, they have a look of distinction. Colors tend to be neutral. Most rooms are spacious and have two double, two queen, or one king bed. Baths are larger than average and have showers and tubs. Some rooms have canyon views; four suites are designated as "guaranteed view" accommodations.

The front porch, set with rockers, is welcoming. The lobby, handsome and dark with its deep-hued log columns and hunting lodge design, bustles with activity. A cocktail lounge is off to one side. So is the restaurant, lodge-like in architecture yet wearing a formal air. Stone fireplaces stand tall at each end. The menu features fowl, beef, and seafood, with entrees priced from $10 to $22.

One of the most pleasant areas in the hotel is the mezzanine lounge overlooking the lobby. Reserved for hotel guests, it serves continental breakfast and light meals, offering a relaxed atmosphere above the activity below—but for good views of one of the world's grandest natural sites, head to the cocktail lounge or dining room down below.

Grand Canyon Lodge North Rim
North Rim, Arizona 86052
602/638-2611
RESERVATIONS: TW Recreational Services, Inc.
P.O. Box 400
Cedar City, Utah 84720
801/586-7686

200 units
$42.70–$55.70 double
American Express, Carte Blanche, Diners Club, MasterCard,
    Visa; personal check
Children welcome
No pets
Open mid-May to mid-October

In the spruce and fir forests on the Grand Canyon's north rim, far from the crowds of the South Rim, there are four types of lodgings. All are near the rim itself.

Cabins are built of logs, while the motel is wood frame. Frontier cabins are the smallest, with one double bed, one single bed, and a bathroom with shower. Pioneer cabins have two rooms, each with two twin beds, and a small bath. Motel rooms are furnished with two double beds and a bath with shower. Western cabins are the top of the line, with two double beds, carpeting, private porch, individual heating, full bathrooms, and telephone.

The Grand Canyon Lodge, built of native stone and logs, has one of best porches in the world, for it directly overlooks the magnificent canyon. There are no guest rooms here, but the dining room serves all three meals. Dinner entrees range from $8 to $14. (Be sure to make reservations.) You can also arrange to buy a picnic lunch.

By air, the North Rim is 15 miles from the more commonly visited South Rim; by road, it's about 200 miles. The pace is slower here. There's time to feel the serenity, to drink in the grandeur. You can hike, ride mules, or drive to see more of the canyon's splendor. Mule trips range from one to eight hours. Hiking trails are from .5 to 10 miles long. North Kaibab Trail is the only one that leads into the canyon. Hiking to Roaring Springs, 3041 feet below the rim, and back to the trailhead takes from six to eight hours.

Phantom Ranch

Grand Canyon National Park Lodges
P.O. Box 699
Grand Canyon, Arizona 86023
602/638-2401
MANAGER: Bill Bohannon
2 dorms; 11 cabins
$16 per person in dorm; $50 for cabin, single or double
American Express, Carte Blanche, Diners Club, MasterCard,
    Visa; personal check
Children welcome
No pets

Open year round

It's an eight mile hike to Phantom Ranch from the South Rim—down, down, down the walls of the incredibly beautiful canyon. At the end of the trail is a lodging that would look welcoming whatever its location, but here at the end of a long trek, tucked within the cottonwoods alongside Bright Angel Creek, it's paradisiacal.

The ranch is made up of 11 rustic cabins scattered among the trees, two dormitories with ten bunks each, and a dining hall. The cabins, sleeping two to ten people, are furnished with queen-size beds.

Meals are served family style. Breakfast is priced at about $8, stew dinner at $12, and steak dinner at $22. You can also buy a box lunch for the hike out of the canyon.

Mule trips to the canyon floor include a stay at Phantom Ranch. (Riders must not be pregnant, shorter than 4'7", or weigh over 200 pounds, and must be able to speak and understand English.) A mule trip that includes meals and one overnight at the ranch costs $188.

Be advised that to stay at the ranch on the night of your choice, you need to plan ahead six to nine months. Also be aware that temperatures at the bottom of the canyon differ greatly from those on the rim. Average summer temperatures are from 110 to 115 degrees Fahrenheit. In winter, the mercury may drop to -15 degrees Fahrenheit.

23

One of a Kind

Each lodging selected for Best Places is distinctive, having qualities that set it apart from the crowd. But the accommodations listed in "One of a Kind" are so distinctive they defy being categorized.

ARIZONA

Inn at Castle Rock
  112 Tombstone Canyon Road
  P.O. Box 1161
  Bisbee, Arizona 85603
  602/432-7195
OWNER: Jim Babcock
17 rooms (some with shared baths)
$30–$40 single or double including breakfast; $15 per person
  for groups
MasterCard, Visa
Children welcome
Pets accepted
Open year round

To say that Inn at Castle Rock is unusual is an understatement. It's eccentric, kooky, and wonderful. Wedged into a steep hillside in Bisbee, Arizona, the inn looks straight at its namesake rock across the street. The lodging dates back to 1919 when it was built as a boarding house for miners.

(Bisbee was founded in 1880 after the discovery of the Copper Queen Lode.)

In the early 1980s Jim Babcock transformed the building into guest accommodations. One of his projects was incorporating into the inn the 70-foot mine shaft where Apache Springs—the town's first source of water—bubbles forth. Water from the springs broke into the shaft as the mine was being dug years ago. Today fish swim in the deep hole while guests socialize in the lounge that surrounds it. The rest of the inn is unconventional in design as well. Built on several levels, it has lots of nooks and crannies, porches and overlooks. A sitting area situated on probably the second floor (it's hard to tell) has the feeling of a large tree house. Down below there's a patio surrounded by plants, steep trails leading to hillside terraces, and an abundance of fruit trees.

Guest rooms are not only different one from the other, but different from guest rooms anywhere. Many are decorated with Jim Babcock's art work—individualistic pieces mirroring the artist's energy and imagination. Like the art, the rooms themselves are extensions of Jim's personality. (Not only is he a painter, but also a writer, musician, gardener, and one-time geologist.)

The Micronesia room has memorabilia from Fiji and Samoa, with mat-covered walls and ceiling. Another room with an oak poster bed is draped in batik. Gold Strike, centered with a brass bed, is one of the prettiest. Overall, rooms are small, casual, and fun: well worth a visit.

Miners Roost Hotel
  Main Street
  Jerome, Arizona 86331
  602/634-5094
INNKEEPERS: Betty and George Daech
7 rooms (6 with shared baths)
$35–$55 double including breakfast for Friday and Saturday
  stays only
MasterCard, Visa
No children
No pets
Open year round

Before you ever get to your room at Miners Roost (probably sometime between getting out of your car and walking into the hotel), you'll swear that you'll never read an accommodations guidebook again. Admittedly, Miners Roost Hotel is different. But look at it this way—you may never have a chance to stay anywhere like this hotel again.

Jerome itself is an unusual town. It hangs from a mountain on the winding and incredibly beautiful road between Prescott and Flagstaff. ("Hangs" is not an exaggeration. Just wait till you get there.)

Once a copper mining town, Jerome wore the title of "Wickedest City in the West." By 1929 its population had swelled to 15,000. But by 1953 the mines had closed, and the town dwindled to fewer than 100 residents. In 1967 Jerome was declared a National Historic Landmark, and in the intervening years it has gradually developed into a tourist destination, with craft shops, art galleries, and a handful of restaurants. The population is now all the way up to 400.

One of the restaurants in town is Betty's Ore House Café and Bar. The café is a 60-seat restaurant serving hamburgers and blue plate specials. The bar is about one-third the size of the restaurant. It's the kind of place where you throw peanut shells on the floor and watch TV.

Betty is the innkeeper. The inn is upstairs, over the bar and restaurant.

The building that holds all of these businesses dates back to 1899. In a town that has suffered major fires, landslides, and near-desertion, it is a real survivor. Betty and George Daech have done an excellent job of converting the second floor into a charming lodging.

The parlor at the top of the stairs is popular for socializing. The seven guest rooms stretch along the upstairs corridor. Cleopatra is decorated in brilliant red; Montana in blue. Rooms have twin, double, queen, or king beds. All have period furnishings. Six of the rooms share two hall baths. The Bartlett has two twin beds and a private bath.   No TVs or phones intrude upon your stay at Miners Roost, for this is truly a trip into another era.

On Friday and Saturday night stays, guests eat a full breakfast downstairs in Betty's Café. On Sundays through Thursdays, Miners Roost changes from a B&B into a B, offering bed only. (The restaurant doesn't open until 11:30 A.M. on weekdays.)

NEW MEXICO

Bear Mountain Guest Ranch
P.O. Box 1163
Silver City, New Mexico 88062
505/538-2538

OWNER: Myra McCormick
16 units (private baths)
$48 single, $79 double including all meals
Cash preferred; no credit cards
Children welcome
Pets acceptable
No smoking in public areas
Open year round

Nature is the star attraction at Bear Mountain Guest Ranch. Owner Myra McCormick has been operating the ranch since 1959. An expert nature guide, she cordially invites guests to get to know her part of the world. More than 200 species of birds have been spotted in the Bear Mountain area. Mountain chickadees, Mexican Jays, brown towhees, and Gambel's quail are among the frequent visitors.

Myra's specialties are birding, wild plants, archaeology, and ghost towns. Scattered throughout the year are special events at the ranch, such as archaeological digs and birding expeditions. She also assists guests in planning area excursions—spelunking, white water rafting, canyon exploring, rockhunting, fishing, and sightseeing.

Guided tours to archaeological sites of the Mimbres Indians, a culture that flourished between 1000 and 1150 A.D., can be arranged upon request. The Mimbres produced sophisticated pottery, "the most unique of any," says Myra, explaining that their work was decorated with black-on-white geometric designs and human and animal figures.

Bear Mountain Guest Ranch is about four miles outside of Silver City. Ringed by distant mountains, it sits on grassy meadowland studded with junipers.

The hacienda-style ranch house was built in the late 1920s as a home for emotionally disturbed children. The main lodge room is welcoming with its native stone fireplaces, casual sitting areas, and huge array of magazines. Off to one side is the sun porch dubbed by Myra as "the bird-watching room."

Ranch guests have a choice of rooms in the main house or in three cottages nearby. Furnishings are casual and simple, reminiscent in style of the 1920s-'30s. Windows are free of curtains in order not to obstruct nature's beauty. One cottage has four bedrooms, each with a private bath, and a large central area. The other two cottages have one bedroom each.

Meals are served family-style in the main house. Everything is cooked from scratch using natural foods. Since the cottages have kitchens, guests in these units have a choice of eating in the main house or cooking for themselves.

The ranch hosts Elderhostels at scheduled times throughout the year, so be sure to arrange your stay as far ahead as possible.

Sunrise Springs Resort
   Route 14, Box 203
   La Cuienega
   Santa Fe, New Mexico 87505
   505/471-3600
   800/772-0500
OWNER: Megan Hill
36 rooms (private baths)
$40–$80 single, $55–$95 double
HIGH SEASON: July to October
American Express, Diners Club, MasterCard, Visa
Children welcome
No pets
Open year round

Sunrise Springs Resort is much more than a place to stay or even a destination to visit. It's an experience—a place dedicated to the body, mind, and spirit.

Located about 15 miles from downtown Santa Fe, the resort is in the tiny community of La Cienega, spreading over nearly 70 acres dotted with cottonwoods and willows. Simple in its beauty and yet complex in its diversity, Sunrise Springs is the creation of owner and artist Megan Hill. Since 1981 the resort has been evolving, expressing various facets of its creator. Everywhere you look there's a surprise, visual or intellectual.

It all started with a natural spring-fed pond, once used as a stage coach stop. Now there's an outstanding restaurant, spa facilities, numerous recreational features (junior Olympic pool, tennis courts, quarter-mile track used for bicycling and roller skating), botanical gardens, professional wellness services (from nutritional counseling to deep tissue massage), life enhancement services (whole brain learning, guided visualization and relaxation, plus a host of others), and computer resource center. At the "Excellerated Learning Forum," or "be-kind-to-your-mind center," as a staff professional dubs it, guests are guided through sessions utilizing alpha chambers (specially-equipped chairs), with the goal of promoting relaxation via soothing music and video tapes.

Guests can choose their own experience at Sunrise Springs, for there is no regimentation. Your stay can be as simple as spending the night and walking along nature trails, or you can stay as long as a month for life enhancement programs. During ski season, special packages include accommodations, breakfast, massage, use of hot tubs and saunas, and transportation into Santa Fe to connect with the shuttle to Santa Fe Ski Area.

Medically supervised wellness packages offered for four, seven, or ten nights feature more than 40 choices of services. The range is wide, divided into four major categories: professional wellness counseling (such services as blood and hair analysis and Swedish massage), body imaging and movement (beauty services, yoga, sports), life enhancement (sample topics are "Making Friends with the Inner Child" and "Discovering Inner Gifts"), and computer familiarization (desktop publishing, guided computer tutorials).

Most guest rooms are in two buildings situated on opposite sides of the quarter-mile track. Decorated in bright cheerful colors, each room is an aesthetic delight, with painted modern furniture, comfortable chairs, plants, and lots of light. All of the rooms have private patios or balconies, TVs, phones, and such amenities as hairdryers. Each of the two buildings has a lounge with fireplace, making them well-suited for groups.

The Blue Heron restaurant, serving three meals a day, is well deserving of a special trip whether you stay at Sunrise Springs or not. Of course the food is prepared with a bent toward health, but it isn't "health food" as the term is usually used. Even the breakfast menu is special, with such treats as trout served with eggs and grilled sesame potatoes, or blue corn cakes with maple syrup. Dinner entrees include rack of lamb served with rosemary sauce and baked salmon topped with cilantro lime sauce. Sunday brunch is a headliner event, with such creations as lemon chicken, roast baron of beef, pasta salad, fresh baked breads, assorted sushi, and pastries. There's a full bar, serving fine wines as well as a myriad of juices. Not only are many of the restaurant's ingredients supplied by the organic gardens on the premises, but also the resort's gardeners are involved in research and education. For example, they work with Indians to gather rare seeds.

An artistic display on one wall of the Blue Heron seems to symbolize Sunrise Springs. It's a collection of mirrors, each with a different shape. Stand in one spot and look into them one by one. Each reflects a different facet of you, the viewer. And so does Sunrise Springs.

24

Ranch Lodges

Each of these lodgings is distinctive, offering you a different view of ranch life. All are off the beaten track, which adds to their appeal. (See also Guest Ranches.)

ARIZONA

Price Canyon Ranch
  P.O. Box 1065
  Douglas, Arizona 85607
  602/558-2383
OWNERS: Scotty and Alice Anderson
5 units
$75 per person including meals and horseback riding
Reduced rates for those under 18; 2-day minimum
Personal check; no credit cards
Children welcome
Pets accepted
Open year round

For such a small lodging, Price Canyon Ranch offers immense variety. Price Canyon is situated between Douglas and Apache on the slopes of the Chiricahua Mountains, elevation 5,600 feet. The flat but bumpy dirt road that leads to the ranch is one of the longest seven miles around, but at the end of the road are the hospitable Andersons, ready to introduce you to their way of life. A working ranch, Price Canyon invites vacationers to experience ranch life by pitching in with the chores—everything from branding and rounding up cattle to repairing fences. In between the work, veteran rancher Scotty Anderson leads horseback rides across the desert and into the mountains.

Those with special interests go to the ranch for bird watching, rockhounding, cave exploring, hiking, and archaeological study (the ranch sits on a pre-Columbian Indian site). Hunters may arrange guided hunts for deer, bear, and javelina. Those seeking adventure may arrange guided one- to 12-day pack trips (for 4 to 20 people). The ranch also has a summertime youth riding program.

Groups can rent a spacious "people barn" with kitchen and bath facilities as well as living, sleeping, and recreation space. Ten camper and trailer sites are also on the premises. The ranch can accommodate three or four families or 30 individuals. Lodging is in the Anderson's home, a nearby bunk house, and an apartment. Not only are each of these different, but also they range in vintage from the 1870s ranch house to the new apartment. All are pleasant and comfortable. Explain your needs to the Andersons and they'll match you with the best unit.

Meals are served family-style, featuring good ole home cooking, with fresh vegetables, beef raised on the ranch, and hot apple pie.

You don't have to know how to ride horses to stay at Price Canyon. Scotty and his hands are experienced teachers. And there are 400 miles of trail to practice on. There's also a small catfish pond and a spring-fed swimming pool on the property.

TEXAS

Prude Ranch
  P.O. Box 1431
  Fort Davis, Texas 79734
  915/426-3347
OWNERS: The Prude Family
35 motel rooms; also cottage rooms, bunk houses

$39–$54 double; $42–$58 triple or quad
Group rate: $30 per person including 1 night's lodging, 3
    meals; $46 per person including 2 night's lodging, 5 meals
American Express, MasterCard, Visa; personal check
Children welcome
Pets accepted
Open year round

There's nothing fake about Prude Ranch. It's not a Hollywood type of guest ranch, with city folks pretending to be cowhands. Nope, it's the real thing—a working ranch, high on Texas-style hospitality and low on prices. The Prude Family has been welcoming guests since 1911. The ranch itself is even older, dating back to 1898. Three generations of Prudes operate the ranch today, and the pint-sized fourth generation is in training.

The ranch raises its own horses and has 60 or more ready to ride whenever guests choose. Guided rides cost $6 per hour. Set within the Davis Mountains at an elevation of 5,500 feet, the ranch has trails traversing miles of scenic terrain. When guests want some other form of recreation, there's a heated indoor pool (large and attractive), lighted tennis courts, mountain hikes, and miles of open space.

Meals are served in a large Western dining room. The fare is hearty, and since the ranch produces some of its own meats (beef, pork, sausage), it's high on quality. A typical dinner, served cafeteria style, includes barbecued chicken and beef, potato salad, beans, homemade bread, and cherry cobbler.

The nicest accommodations are those designated as "motel" but bearing little resemblance to the image conjured up by the word. With four side-by-side units to a building, they are true Western in flavor—real wooden walls, a solid wooden rocker, cowboy prints on the wall. Happily, there's air conditioning and a ceiling fan, but no TV or phone. The porch is the best part, providing a setting for putting your feet up and doing some serious mountain gazing. One of the best things about the ranch is that the Prudes aim to please. Special arrangements for groups are easy to make—just ask. Group lodging choices include "family rooms" (pre-dating the motel units), bunk houses, camp sites, and RV hook-ups.

There's often something special going on at Prude Ranch, such as the Davis Mountains Fitness Camp, Texas Duck

Races, Prude Ranch Triathlon, or "Snowbird" week, so be sure to check the schedule. Summer camps (for ages 7-14) are the focal point from mid-June through July.

Y.O. Ranch Hilton

2033 Sidney Baker Street
Kerrville, Texas 78028
512/257-4440
800/531-2800 TX only
GENERAL MANAGER: Charles Jensen
200 rooms
$40–$82 single, $60–$102 double; $120–$135 suites
American Express, Carte Blanche, Diners Club, Hilton,
  MasterCard, Visa
Children welcome
Pets acceptable
Open year round

In the heart of the Texas Hill Country, the Y.O. Ranch Hilton is cowboy plush. Stride into the lobby (one of the most distinctive in the Southwest) and you know you're in cattle country: chandeliers are fashioned from branding irons, there's a life-size bronze of a cowboy wrestling a longhorn, and hand-carved chairs are covered in rawhide.

Although the motel-style lodging is set within the town of Kerrville, it bears close kinship to the famed Y.O. Ranch, located about 30 miles away. A working ranch, the Y.O. has one of the finest herds of Texas Longhorns in the country, plus exotic game. Hotel guests can use a direct phone line to the ranch to sign up for tours. Both the hotel and the ranch are owned by the Schreiner family, descendants of Capt. Charles Schreiner, who founded the 50,000-acre ranch.

Guest rooms have high-class comfort, with Queen Anne style furniture, Saltillo tile floors, and well-designed baths. Some have balconies overlooking the pool (there's even a giant Y.O. brand on the bottom). Suites are extra special here. The American Indian Suite is decorated with beaded and silver artifacts, arrowheads, and Indian portraits. The Longhorn has mementos depicting the history of the breed. Some suites have fireplaces.

Dine at the Sam Houston Room serving Texas specialties and exotic game, and be sure to visit the Elm Waterhole saloon. There's a hot tub adjoining the pool, a tennis court on the grounds, and a municipal golf course next door.

Ranch tours are offered Tuesday through Sunday. The $23 price tag includes lunch. Children 7 to 12 are half price; those under 7 are free.

Private game hunts are also offered at the Y.O. Ranch. Stocked with game animals from all parts of the world, it has herds of axis deer; aoudad, mouflon, and Corsican sheep; American elk; and Indian black buck antelope. Year-round hunting for both native and exotic game is available.

25

Romantic Getaways

*A romantic getaway is truly special—a place to hide away
with someone you love. Other good choices are sprinkled
through the pages of B&B Inns, Grand Old Mansions, Grand
Old Resorts, and Gourmet Getaways.*

ARIZONA

Grapevine Canyon Ranch
  P.O. Box 302
  Pearce, Arizona 85625
  602/826-3185
OWNERS: Gerry and Eve Searle
9 cabins
$55–$95 per person including meals
MasterCard, Visa; personal check
Children over 12 welcome
No pets
Open year round

For a getaway with a Western flavor, Grapevine Canyon
Ranch is hard to beat. It's tucked away in a secluded canyon
about 85 miles southeast of Tucson at the foot of the Dragoon
Mountains (elevation 5,000 feet). This is a place where you
ride horses if and when you want to, wander along trails by
foot and to ghost towns by car, or do nothing at all but hide
away.

Owner Gerry Searle is an experienced horseman, having trained, roped, and jumped horses since his childhood. One of his specialties is matching people and horses. He's also a cowboy artist, ex-stunt man, and accomplished yarn-spinner. Eve was a commercial pilot and flying instructor when she discovered Arizona and fell in love with cattle and horse country. Together the Searles have developed a guest-oriented ranch, building upon the remnants of an earlier working ranch. The couple welcomed their first guests in 1983. Tranquillity and solitude are the keynotes here, but that doesn't mean it's always quiet. The hosts are convivial, and they set the tone. Guests have the freedom to socialize or retreat, whatever their mood.

Accommodations are exceptionally nice. The cabin-suites and cabins, built in the mid-1980s, blend into the setting, enabling you to feel like you're part of nature's landscape. They feature large wooden decks overlooking the woods, comfortable sitting areas, large baths, and lots of creature comforts such as coffeepots and magazines. Cabin-suites have a king and two day beds; cabins have a queen or full bed and a hide-abed. All are air-cooled and heated.

Mealtime is important at Grapevine. Breakfast has four courses (biscuits and gravy, bacon, sausage, waffles, eggs— real cowhand stuff). Lunch is spaghetti or burritos or some other comparable snack. At dinner time, be ready for steaks, prime rib, Cornish hen, or rainbow trout sauteed in wine sauce. Meals are served family-style.

Horseback rides include half-day, full-day, breakfast cookout, and moonlight rides. (Rates start at $40.) There's also a heated pool, video and TV room with film library, and miles of hiking trails.

For a special dash of romance, you can order breakfast in bed, complete with champagne and roses, or dinner by candlelight served in your cabin (additional charge).

Stouffer Cottonwoods Resort

6160 N. Scottsdale Road
Scottsdale, Arizona 85253
602/991-1414
800/HOTELS-1
GENERAL MANAGER: Phil Heyl
170 suites
$55–$150 single, $65–$160 double
HIGH SEASON: January to May
LOW SEASON: June to mid-September

American Express, Discover, MasterCard, Visa; personal
  check
Children welcome
Pets with approval
Open year round

Scottsdale Road is lined with glamor—a mix of golden resorts, boutiques, and restaurants. In the midst of it all, Stouffer
Cottonwoods provides a tranquil hideaway, close to the glitter
yet removed, offering the best of both worlds.

There's a residential, club-like feeling about the place.
One-story villa suites are scattered over the 25 acres of
grounds, interwoven with flower-decked paths and draped
with cottonwoods. The pace is unhurried here. Tucked away
among the villas and courtyards, far away from the main road
left behind, is a large swimming pool that invites you to
lounge. The sunken tennis courts, backed by grassy banks,
have an intimate feeling. A jogging track with par exercise
stations encircles the grounds, leading past natural desert landscapes.

When you're ready for the cosmopolitan atmosphere for
which Scottsdale is renowned, it's a few steps away—literally.
Borgata Shopping Village, with an array of boutiques and galleries, is just across the parking lot. Special footbridges
through the hedges lead you to it.

The villas, designed for privacy, are hideaways within
themselves. Each has a patio. Decorated with a Southwest
scheme, they have wooden beamed ceilings and touches of regional art. Flagstaff villas are the smallest, somewhat bigger
than an average hotel room and furnished with one king or
two double beds, refrigerator, and vanity. Tucsons have a
living room with wet bar and a private spa on the patio.
Phoenix villas are the creme de la creme, with a large living
room and fireplace, kitchen, huge bath, bedroom with king
bed, and an enclosed courtyard with hot tub—truly a romantic
getaway.

Moriah Restaurant is upscale and elegant. The food is outstanding—southwestern in theme, connoisseur in execution.
There's also a wine bar.

NEW MEXICO

Hacienda del Sol
  Box 177
  Taos, New Mexico 87571
  505/758-0287
INNKEEPERS: Mari and Jim Ulmer
3 rooms (private baths)
$30 single, $48–$78 double including full breakfast
MasterCard, Visa; personal check
Children accepted on individual basis
Pets with approval
Smoking in designated areas
Open year round

Years ago when art patron Mabel Dodge Luhan was searching for a hideaway home for herself and her Indian husband, Tony, she chose the adobe house now known as Hacienda del Sol. D.H. Lawrence, Georgia O'Keeffe, Willa Cather, Thomas Wolfe, and Aldous Huxley all came to call. Today the 180-year-old house has a feeling of history, enhanced by the efforts of current owners Mari and Jim Ulmer. They enjoy introducing visitors to Taos, suggesting sights and talking about the area's history.

Don't despair when the Ulmers give you directions. Yes, Hacienda del Sol is indeed directly behind Lotta Burger, about one-half mile northwest of downtown. When you turn off Highway 64 onto the little dirt road leading to their front door, you'll probably have second thoughts about the reliability of your guide.

But once you step inside the courtyard, it's easy to forget the commercial development nearby. Situated on an acre lot, graced with centuries-old cottonwoods and ponderosa pines, the Hacienda adjoins Indian reservation land of more than 95,000 acres, offering an uninterrupted view all the way to Taos's Magic Mountain.

Inside the home, ancient vigas, kiva fireplaces, oak and brick floors, and handcrafted furniture please the eye. Throughout the Hacienda, there's a look of hominess. Instead of pristine rooms where everything matches and nothing is ever out of place, it's a place where house guests come and go with regularity, relaxing in the kitchen over a cup of coffee.

Mari is renowned for her breakfasts, served in the casual dining area adjoining the family-style kitchen. Freshly baked bread is always on the menu, along with such dishes as stuffed baked bananas.

A talented lady, Mari wears several hats in addition to baker and innkeeper. Not only is she a practicing attorney, but she's a writer as well. She's written a lay person's guide to the law, and her series of "Little Green Dragon" children's stories have been compiled into book form after appearing originally in *Wee Wisdom Magazine*. Look for the green dragon stained glass in the kitchen.

La Escondida is the smallest guest room, distinctive with its viga and plank ceiling, skylight, stained-glass window, and blue four-poster double bed. One of its doorways opens onto the front courtyard. The bath is across the hall. La Sala del Don, or "Tony's Room" according to the Ulmers, is a large room with kiva fireplace, queen-size Spanish bed, and queen sofa-sleeper. Windows open onto peaceful gardens with 100-year-old apple trees.

The most popular room is Los Amantes, or The Lovers Room. Not only is it romantically decorated (candles are always lit before guests arrive), but it's adjoined by the piece de resistance—a spa room centered with a black marble hot tub on a mahogany platform. There's even a skylight above the tub—what better place for star-gazing? Bedroom furnishings include a hand-carved bed, Spanish dresser (mid-1770s), Dutch chocolate chest, and German altar piece. French doors open from the bedroom onto the back courtyard.

TEXAS

Butterfields
P.O. Box 1098
Main Street (Highway 118)
Fort Davis, Texas 79734
915/426-3252
OWNERS: Joe and Janiece Moore
4 cottages
$60 double
American Express, MasterCard, Visa; personal check
No children
No pets
Open year round

In the tiny West Texas town of Fort Davis there's a hideaway just for couples. It's not tucked away within a forest or a canyon, mind you.   In fact, it's barely off the road—but it's perfect for a stop along the way in exploring West Texas.   Big Bend National Park is 100 miles south, McDonald Observatory is 15 miles north, and Fort Davis National Historic Site is less than a mile away.

Butterfields is four yellow one-room cottages situated behind a little gift and antique shop in downtown Fort Davis. Identical in design and decor, they are as welcoming as home. Plush country-style is the decorating scheme.   A cannonball pine bed, two recliner rockers, stone fireplace, and whirlpool tub make the rooms extra special.   Every cottage has a TV.

Open since 1983, the cottages are the creation of Joe and Janiece Moore, who bought the plot of land intending to build their retirement home.   But somewhere along the way they decided to open a gift shop (teddy bears, country crafts, jams and jellies).   One thing led to another, and before long they were designing cottages.

Their intention was to create lodgings that they would want to stay in themselves.   Because the Moores like to escape the telephone when they vacation, the cottages are sans phones. (Guests have use of their hosts' phone just a few steps from the cottage.)   Providing two comfortable chairs (you can easily fall asleep in them) was a high priority, and so was including such luxuries as whirlpool tubs.

No meals are served at Butterfields, but there's a country café half a block away.

Inn on the Creek
Center Circle
P.O. Box 261
Salado, Texas 76571
817/947-5554
INNKEEPERS: Suzi and Lynn Epps
7 rooms (private baths)
$65–$105 double including full breakfast
American Express, MasterCard, Visa; personal check
Children welcome
No pets
No smoking
Open year round, except Christmas Day

On the banks of tree-shaded Salado Creek there's a stately Victorian home with a back porch just made for creek-watching.   Inside, the Epps family are delightful hosts, making you welcome with bounteous breakfasts or even gourmet dinners (by prior arrangement).   At night there's a chocolate on your pillow, and if you wish, the hosts will help you plan your stay in the historic Salado area.

Suzi Epps is a registered architect, so when the couple decided to move an 1880s home from a nearby community, she was well qualified to oversee the project. For over a year they restored the old house, doubling its size in the process. The fine wooden trims of the original home were retained, and new trims were milled to duplicate them. This is a picture-perfect home, with exquisite decor where everything matches. Guests can choose from first, second, and third floor accommodations, all decorated with handsome antiques. A personal favorite is the Tyler Room, a swirl of peach with a white iron bed and wicker furniture.

The best room in the house is the third floor McKie Room. The canopied king bed is made of brass. There's a mirrored armoire, Queen Anne chairs, and an idyllic reading alcove overlooking the creek. Extras befitting its grandeur come with the room—chilled champagne and breakfast in bed.

Every room has a TV and phone. The hosts bubble with creativity, offering such special getaways as murder mystery or gourmet weekends.

La Borde House

601 E. Main Street
Rio Grande City, Texas 78582
512/487-5101
INNKEEPER: Che Guerra
8 historic rooms
$59 double including continental breakfast
American Express, MasterCard, Visa; personal check
Children welcome
Pets accepted
Open year round

Rio Grande City, population circa 9,000, sits on the Mexican border between Laredo and Brownsville. Agriculture is at the heart of its economy, especially melon and vegetable farming.

On Main Street just a few blocks from the center of town is one of the most charming inns in the Southwest. Definitely off the beaten track, it is well worth discovering. Bird-watchers, hunters, and history buffs have already found it, so be sure to call ahead. (Groups of travelers often book the entire inn.)

Local sights include Our Lady of Lourdes Grotto, a replica of the famed shrine in France. Falcon Lake recreation area begins about 30 miles north. Mexico is accessible via several nearby entry points.

La Borde House dates back to 1899 when Rio Grande City was the head of navigation on the river separating Texas and Mexico. The advent of the railroad led to the demise of the thriving steamboat trade, thereby altering the town's status. Many years later the river was dammed up to form Falcon Lake, and today the Rio Grande is barely one-eighth mile wide here. The two-story brick house was built by Frenchman Francoise La Borde. Plans were drawn in Paris, later to be refined by San Antonio architects. The resulting structure is a combination of Creole, Victorian, and South Texas styles, crafted by Mexican artisans. Restored in 1982 with meticulous attention to detail, the house is listed on the National Register of Historic Places. Downstairs there's a parlor that revives the glory days when riverboats docked nearby. Be sure to allow time to peruse the scrapbook and historical references, sufficient for many hours of reading.

Guest rooms are touched by magic, for how could something so beautiful be tucked away in a remote rural town? Each high-ceilinged room is a museum-quality exhibit of antique furnishings. Elaborately carved beds are the focal point. Recamara Roja, or Red Room, is a bordello-style room with a half-tester draped in red. (Once the room was home to a high-priced "lady of the evening.") The Audubon Room, decorated with Audubon prints, honors the naturalist who did some of his best birdwatching in the area. The Law Office, so-named because it was indeed the office of a lawyer, has a different look from all the others. More private than the rest, its entrance is from the courtyard. There's a big rolltop desk with pigeon holes, and a headboard formed from book-lined shelves.

The Maria Tejas is a personal favorite. Its magnificent tester bed has a canopy of soft apricot. Armoires, an ornate mirror, Victorian couch, and tall shuttered windows combine to create a turn-of-the-century atmosphere.

Throughout the inn, guest rooms are spacious. Baths (every room has one) range from tiny to large. Some have clawfoot tubs within the room itself, hidden away behind oriental screens. TVs but not phones are in the rooms. Central air conditioning and ceiling fans add to the comfort, as do the soft down comforters. Out back there's a charming courtyard and a restaurant named Che's that serves Mexican food.

Motel-style rooms, priced at $40, are also part of the hostelry, but if there's a historic room for rent, it's well worth the asking price (actually, it'd be a bargain at twice the rate).

McKay House
   306 E. Delta Street
   Jefferson, Texas 75657
   214/665-7322 in Jefferson
   214/348-1929 in Dallas
INNKEEPERS: Tom and Peggy Taylor
6 bedrooms (4 with shared bath, 2 with private bath)
$55–$70 double including full breakfast
MasterCard, Visa; personal check
Children with approval
No pets
No smoking inside house
Open year round on Friday and Saturday

This pristine 1850s cottage stands proudly in the heart of historic Jefferson. Across the street is the House of the Seasons, a grand old mansion which is one of the most popular visitor attractions in town. Within a five block radius are more than 30 structures bearing Texas Historic Markers. The McKay House itself is not only a historic Texas building but is also listed in the National Register of Historic Places.

Here on East Delta Street, life moves slowly, so slowly that it doesn't take long to get caught up in the tranquillity. The hosts at the McKay House are adept at creating the illusion of living in an earlier era. They greet guests with lemonade and teacakes, serving them on the front porch where relaxation means rocking in white wicker chairs or sitting in the porch swing. At bedtime, ladies find Victorian nightgowns hanging in the armoire. Men are not overlooked—they have long sleep shirts ready for the wearing. Breakfast is hearty country fare, served in the dining room which overlooks a courtyard.

In the main house are four guest rooms, all with 14-foot ceilings, fireplaces, and antique furnishings. The McKay Room, decorated in blue, has memorabilia symbolizing the law profession—in honor of the man to whom the house once belonged. The Quilt Room and the Spinning Room are aptly named, each decorated with warmth. Three bedrooms are furnished with double beds, one with twin beds.

Two guest rooms are in a detached building, reflective of a simpler lifestyle than the grand McKay house. The decor in this early 1900s house is as appealing and imaginative as that of the main house. A blackened pot hangs over the stone fireplace in one room. Both bedrooms have private baths.

26

Ski Lodges

New Mexico is the ski center of the Southwest. Some of its slopes are among the best in the American West. Lodgings in this chapter are within one mile of ski slopes. Staying in Santa Fe is also a good choice, providing easy access to Taos Ski Valley, Angel Fire, Sipapu, and Red River. Also, see lodgings in Ruidoso (Ski Apache) and Cloudcroft.

NEW MEXICO

Austing Haus Hotel
  Box 8
  Taos Ski Valley
  Taos, New Mexico 87571
  505/776-2649
  INNKEEPER: Paul Austing
  14 rooms
  SKI SEASON: $65 single, $75 double
  Group rates during off season: variable (see text)
  Mastercard, Visa
  Children welcome
  Pets accepted
  Open for skiing from Thanksgiving to mid-April; available for
    groups rest of year

Staying at Austing Haus is like visiting in the home of a friend. Innkeeper Paul Austing caters to those who want a quiet and cheerful atmosphere.

Priced lower than most of the accommodations at Taos Ski Valley one mile up the road, the inn is a service-oriented lodging. "If there is something you like that is not on the menu, by just asking it will be prepared for you," proclaims the menu at The Glass Dining Room.

This is not the place for those who want to party late into the night. Quiet hours start at 10:30 P.M. and last until 7 A.M. There are no telephones or TVs in the guest rooms, but there is a TV in the lobby—a comfortably furnished gathering spot. Another favored place is the loft hot tub room, a charming nook with views of the snow-covered mountains.

In 1984, Paul Austing and Chuck Jeanette proudly completed the 14-room lodge, a timber-framed construction with over 3,000 interlocking joints and 1,600 oak pegs. Built of Douglas fir and pine, it's lovingly referred to as "one giant piece of furniture." Beams are exposed both inside and out.

Guest rooms, situated on two levels, are especially spacious, furnished with queen-size beds and handmade furniture. (Austing was the craftsman.) Glass-walled hallways extend the length of the building, creating a feeling of proximity to the wooded terrain.

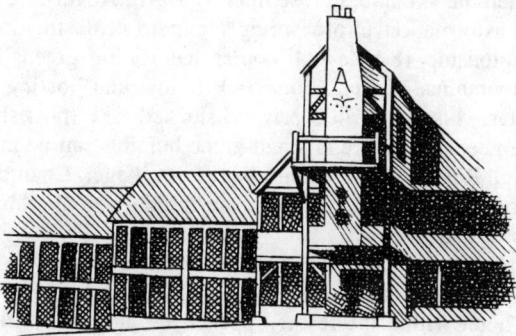

The lodge's dining room is light and airy, decorated with plants, stained glass, and quilts hung on the walls. Queen Anne chairs pull up to light-toned wooden tables. Entrees such as sole amandine and veal Cordon Bleu range from $11 to $17. Austing himself is the chef, serving up his specialties of roasted duck with black bing cherry sauce and frog legs Provencale.

During off-season, Austing Haus specializes in meeting the needs of groups, pricing services to meet their requirements. For example, groups have the option of cutting costs by acting as their own cleanup crew, both in the dining room and in the lodging areas.

The Legends Hotel
P.O. Drawer B
Angel Fire, New Mexico 87710
800/633-7463
PRESIDENT: John McIntosh
157 rooms
SKI SEASON: $95–$180 double
REST OF YEAR: $65–$90 double
American Express, MasterCard, Visa
Children welcome
No pets
Open year round

In the Rocky Mountains' Moreno Valley, 26 miles east of Taos, Angel Fire is a sprawling year-round resort village. Ski season gets top billing at Angel Fire, with its 2,180-foot vertical drop and 55 downhill ski trails. A sophisticated snowmaking system covers 60 percent of the terrain, making this resort a good bet whatever the yearly snowfall.

When the ski slopes close in early April, Angel Fire begins its transformation into a spring/summer/fall destination. Its championship 18-hole golf course has rolling greens backed by mountains. Tennis, horseback riding, and boating are all popular. Fishing is in a private, stocked lake (no fishing license needed). Big and small game hunting can be arranged through Resort Sports within the resort village. Chamber music concerts and community theater productions highlight the summer season.

Spread over 12,000 acres, Angel Fire is a composite of condos and single family residences. The Legends Hotel—the only hotel within the resort—opened in late 1987 (originally The Plaza, the new hotel is a complete renovation). Set right at the base of the ski slopes, The Legends is contemporary in design. A five-story atrium with swimming pool and hot tub overlooks the mountains. The Mill restaurant serves breakfast and lunch; Springer's is an elegant dining room. Annie O's, named for Annie Oakley, is the place to relax over drinks.

Guest rooms are unusually spacious. All have two queen-size beds. Studios, which can be rented separately or in combination with standard rooms, have cooking facilities (four-burner stove, oven, refrigerator) and a Murphy bed. Studios accommodate two people; suites, which are a combined studio and hotel room, accommodate six.

St. Bernard Condominiums
   Taos Ski Valley, New Mexico 87571
   505/776-8506, 505/776-2233 NM
   800/992-SNOW US
RESIDENT MANAGER: Kathy Janosko
13 condos
SKI SEASON: $1,800 per week (up to 6)
SUMMER SEASON: $1,400 per week (up to 6)
American Express, MasterCard, Visa; personal check
Children welcome
No pets
Open Thanksgiving to mid-April, June through August

The most luxurious accommodations in Taos Ski Valley are the St. Bernard Condos. Situated in a long three-story building, they overlook the valley itself.

The two-bedroom, two-bath units, accommodating up to six, are individually owned and decorated. Not only are they spacious, but they're also plush. Kitchens are fully equipped. Covered parking is adjacent to each unit.

During ski season, guests can use the hot tub at Hotel St. Bernard, located at the base of the slopes. There's also a ski room in the hotel for the exclusive use of St. Bernard Condo guests. The hotel's restaurant, headed by a French chef, serves dinner.

Ski packages including seven nights lodging, gourmet dinners at Hotel St. Bernard, ski lessons, and unlimited usage of ski lifts start at $713 per person, based on six people in a condo unit. For double occupancy, the rate goes up to $1,240 per person.

During the summer, St. Bernard is an excellent hideaway destination. Most of the ski valley is closed during summer months (don't count on finding any food service), but you can use a condo as a home base for enjoying the surrounding mountains and nearby sights in Taos. Right outside the doors is a picturesque stream, and the complex is enveloped in trees.

Twining Condominiums
   P.O. Box 696
   Taos Ski Valley, New Mexico 87571
   505/776-8648
MANAGERS: Kenneth and Wanda Burkett
20 units
SKI SEASON: $110–$235 double; $265 for up to 6

OFF-SEASON: $35–$55 double
Mastercard, Visa; personal check
Children welcome
No pets
Open late November to March, June to October

Only a three-minute walk from the base ski lifts of Taos, Twining Condominiums are comfortable and attractive. Their two-story exterior is distinctive, with dark-stained wood siding and balconies overlooking the snowy landscape.

Twining's management prides itself on providing well-maintained units where everything works. Spare parts are always kept on hand. (The claim took on added significance when a guest at a nearby complex was overheard complaining about an oven that refused to heat, despite repeated reports to the manager.) Built in 1981, the condos are among the newest accommodations on the mountain. Unlike other area complexes, units are not privately owned. Interiors are well-decorated, from stylish fabrics to signed prints by local artists. Fireplaces, built of artificial stone, are handsome. Much of the furniture is solid oak.

Two-bedroom units, which can accommodate up to eight people, have two floors of living space plus a loft. One of the two baths has a whirlpool tub; the second has a shower. Kitchens have full-size refrigerators and stoves, dishwashers, garbage disposals, lots of cookware, and table settings for 12. Studios, probably the most economical lodgings at the ski base, are one-room units accommodating two people. Like the larger units, they're well furnished, but they don't have fireplaces.

All units have color TV but not telephones. Daily maid service is included in the rate. So is wood for the fireplaces. An indoor hot tub is within the complex, and a licensed masseuse is on call.

Twining offers Learn-to-Ski Week packages which include seven days of lodging, six days unlimited use of all lifts (Sunday to Friday), and six days of morning ski lessons. Per person rates start at $544 (six people sharing a two-bedroom unit).

During off season, the condos are an economical place to stay while enjoying the Sangre de Cristo Mountains. The town of Taos is 19 miles away. No restaurants or shops are open in the ski valley during the off season, so be sure to buy groceries before starting up the mountain.

27

Spas

Spas are dedicated to refreshing the body, mind, and spirit. Each of the spas included in this chapter is unique, offering its own combination of invigorating ingredients.

ARIZONA

Canyon Ranch Spa
  8600 E. Rockcliff
  Tucson, Arizona 85715
  602/749-9000
  800/742-9000 outside AZ
FOUNDER AND OWNER: Mel Zuckerman
140 units
$155–$300 per day per person including meals, spa facilities
Packages of 4, 7, and 10 days available
HIGH SEASONS: January to mid-June, mid-September to mid-
  December
Discover, MasterCard, Visa; personal check
For men and women
Children over 13 welcome
No pets
Open year round

  Canyon Ranch is a place where people go, not to relax, but to change their lives—for re-creation in the literal meaning of the word. Geared to the health of the body and mind, it's a coed fitness resort and spa with an amazing array of facilities, classes, and services—all selected by the participant instead of dictated by the staff. People go to Canyon Ranch seeking different things—weight loss, stress reduction, body fitness, cessation of smoking. Through a combined program of exercise and nutrition, many find what they're looking for. Unlike some spas, this one attracts as many men as women, all seeking rejuvenation through a healthier lifestyle.

Set upon the Sonoran Desert on the edges of Tucson, the spa offers exercise options that take advantage of the area's beauty, such as hikes to nearby waterfalls and bike rides through Sabino Canyon.

The spa building itself pulsates with energy. Locker rooms are overflowing with amenities and are decorated with energy-evoking yellow, red, and orange. More than 30 classes are taught in this building, from water aerobics to yoga. Personal services are all-encompassing, including massage, herbal wraps, life change counseling, nutrition counseling, astrology, and biofeedback. Facilities include a weight room, gymnasiums, and racquetball courts. Three swimming pools and six lighted tennis courts are also on the grounds. The entire complex is woven together by paths flanked with desert landscaping.

At mealtime, guests dine in soothingly beautiful surroundings on such delicacies as lamp chops dijon, paella, and blueberry cheesecake. Menus come with a calorie count; guests themselves make the choice of what they eat. Whole grains, fresh fruits and vegetables, and the absence of refined flour and sugar, along with small portions, are at the heart of the cuisine. Meals are low in salt and have no additives or preservatives. No caffeine or alcoholic beverages are served at the ranch. To help guests continue healthy eating habits when they leave, there's a demonstration kitchen to teach food preparation the Canyon Ranch way.

Accommodations are in small buildings scattered over the resort's 28 acres. Standard rooms are fairly small. Executive kings have a sitting area, and casitas have a living room and kitchen in addition to the bedroom. Furnishings are modern and plush.

Tucson National Resort and Spa
2727 W. Club Drive
Tucson, Arizona 85741
602/297-2271
800/528-4856
GENERAL MANAGER: Richard McGuffie

167 units
$55–$200 single or double
Spa Packages: from $588 for 5 days including meals, extensive spa treatments
HIGH SEASON: January to May
American Express, Carte Blanche, Diners Club,
For men and women
MasterCard, Visa; personal check
Children welcome at hotel
No pets
Open year round

This resort wears many faces. Originally designed as a private golf club, its 27-hole USGA championship golf course hosted the Tucson Open for 15 years. As a family resort, it has a large attractive pool, tennis courts, two restaurants, and several lounges. As a getaway, it has beautifully designed rooms and suites. As a spa, it has few equals, offering a wide menu of services, professional attention, and flexibility in its program.

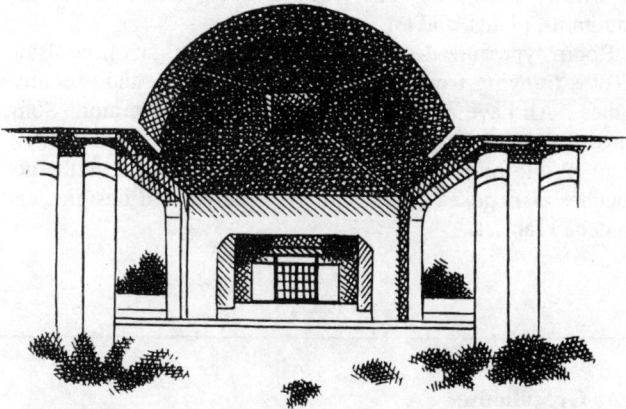

The once-private club opened to the public in 1986. The spa, situated downstairs in the main building, is extremely well-equipped. Of course there are herbal wraps and massages, loofah rubs and body facials, hydrotherapy pools and tanning beds. Special services on the women's side include Swiss showers (water ranging in temperature from 60 to 105 degrees comes from 14 shower heads and sprays from all directions, activating the capillary nerve endings in the skin and stimulating circulation) and orthion machines (back manipulation machines that help adjust the spine through gentle stretching and massaging with rollers). On the women's side there's also a panathermal (one of the few in the U.S.) that is designed to break down cellulite, along with a Finnish sauna.

The men's spa features a Scottish water massage (16 needle-spray shower heads and two high-pressure hoses controlled by an attendant, with varying pressure and temperature) and a Russian bath (special steam room that opens pores and reduces toxicity, hence reducing tension).

Both men and women have inhalation rooms (eucalyptus and other herbs that help open sinuses and allow freer breathing). Lounges are plush, quiet, and relaxing. Exercise classes include aerobics, water exercise, stress management, and creative movement. The weight and exercise room is adequately equipped. The spa program is extremely flexible, enabling you to enjoy just one of its services, sign up for a whole day of rejuvenation, or buy a five- to seven-day package which includes room, meals, and an abundance of spa services.

Situated about 15 miles north of downtown Tucson, the resort is surrounded by 650 acres of saguaro-studded desert. An appropriate setting for a spa dedicated to fitness and beauty, it is artfully designed. The lobby is a swirl of pink marble, fountains, plants, and art.

Room types are designated as villas (hotel size), poolside, casitas (ranging from hotel size to near-suites), and executive suites. All have a patio or balcony and a refrigerator. Some have fireplaces. Interiors are large, plush, and visually exciting. While rooms differ in decor, each is special with such touches as exposed beam ceilings, hand-painted designs, and matched fabrics.

TEXAS

The Greenhouse
P.O. Box 1144
Arlington, Texas 76010
817/640-4000
EXECUTIVE DIRECTOR: Cary Collier
39 rooms
$2,850 per person per week including meals and spa program
American Express, Neiman Marcus; personal check
For women only
No pets
Open year round except 2 weeks in winter, 4 weeks in
  summer; yearly schedule varies

The Greenhouse is an exclusive retreat. Women enter its doors to renew their vitality by getting in shape. Its program is based on beauty, fitness, diet, and pampering. Activities are suggested but not required. Each guest is treated as an individual, with a custom-designed program ranging from the number of calories she eats to the fitness activities she engages in.

The setting itself is conducive to beauty and serenity. The spa building resembles an elegant home, decorated with arched windows, fine furnishings, and artful accents. The hall from the formal drawing rooms leads to a beautiful indoor pool, surrounded by lattice arches and topped by a latticed skylight.

All of the spa's facilities including the guest rooms are within the same building, adding to the feeling of privacy. Rooms are residential in feel, spacious and tastefully decorated with bleached wood furniture, cool colors and soft carpets. Phones and TVs are in each. Suites, designed for friends visiting the spa together or mothers and daughters, are especially large.

A day at The Greenhouse begins with breakfast in bed. On the food tray there's a card with the day's activities, perhaps beginning with flex and stretch classes and including beauty treatments as well as fitness exercises. Lunch is by the pool. Dinner is formal. Evening entertainment might be a book review, a fashion show, or piano music.

Nutrition gets lots of attention at The Greenhouse, from instructive classes to the cuisine itself. Alcoholic beverages are prohibited and smoking is discouraged.

After a week of seclusion amid beauty, of facials and massages, exercise and nutritious food, women leave The Greenhouse relaxed and invigorated. Most return for another visit.

Lake Austin Resort
1705 Quinlan Park Road
Austin, Texas 78732
512/266-2444
800/847-5637 US, 800/252-9324 TX
DIRECTOR: Deborah Hart
40 units
$105–$160 per day including all meals, fitness program)
$623–$945 for week-long program
American Express, MasterCard, Visa; personal check
For men and women
Ages 14-17 must be accompanied by parent

No pets
Smoking discouraged; designated areas only
Open year round

On the shores of Lake Austin just outside Texas's capital city, there's a spa dedicated to fitness education and conditioning. Its atmosphere is unpretentious and friendly; its program is comprehensive, including exercise, nutrition, wellness classes, and beauty services. In a peaceful setting and with personalized attention, participants work to achieve their goals, especially weight loss and a more healthful life style. Personnel include a physical fitness staff, dietician, and registered nurse.

Spa goers have a choice of 20 daily workouts, including Hill Country walks, low to high power aerobics, and use of an 18-station Swiss ParCourse. Classes on such subjects as relaxation, skin care, and nutrition are integral to the spa's program. For relaxation as well as exercise, there's both an outdoor and indoor pool.

Lodging is in a low-rise building fronting the lake. Rooms have two double beds, TVs, and phones. The dining room is pleasant and casual. Women are served a 900-calorie-per-day menu; men, a 1200-calorie menu. The emphasis is on wholesome food, featuring fresh vegetables and herbs grown at the resort.

Pampering services, available at an extra charge, include skin analysis and facials, massages, and hair and skin treatments. Special spa packages are offered throughout the year.

The Phoenix Fitness Resort

111 N. Post Oak Lane
Houston, Texas 77024
713/680-1601
800/548-4700 US, 800/548-4701 TX
PRESIDENT: Chris Silkwood
15 participants
$2,100–$2,500 for week including meals, spa program
American Express, MasterCard, Visa; personal check
For women only, age 18 and over
No pets
Open year round

The Phoenix is a top-rated luxury spa dedicated to a woman's overall health and well-being. Founded in 1980, it addresses physical fitness, nutrition, and the emotions. "Women come for a new beginning," says a Phoenix representative. "Many want to get their lives in order." Weight loss may or may not be one of their goals.

The spa is set within the Houstonian, a multi-faceted facility comprising a hotel and conference center, health and fitness club, and center for preventive medicine. Despite its mid-city location, the Houstonian is a wooded retreat, interwoven with winding paths and a wealth of fitness and recreational facilities.

Spa participants, limited to 15, have a choice of two programs. Both include fitness (stretching, toning, low-impact aerobics, advanced weight equipment, water exercise, scheduled brisk walks); nutrition (1,000 calories per day menu; low in fat, sodium, and refined sugar); personal testing (body composition test; strength, flexibility, and cardiovascular testing; personal fitness consultation); lectures (lifestyle management, fashion, healthy cooking, nutrition, eating disorders); and a beauty program (massages, facials, manicure and pedicure, hair styling).

The higher-priced program, "Ultimate Week," has a more comprehensive beauty program than the "Fitness Week Plus." Beauty services are at the Christine Valmy salon within the fitness club. When spa goers aren't involved in regularly scheduled workouts, they have use of the Houstonian Health and Fitness Club's racquetball and tennis courts, lap pool, outdoor and indoor tracks, whirlpools, saunas, and Swedish showers.

The Ambassador House, once a private home, serves as a nucleus for the Phoenix. Spa participants dine together in its private dining room, relax at its private pool, and gather in the living room for lectures or socializing. Accommodations are on a separate floor of one hotel wing, accessible only to Phoenix guests. Aerobics classes are in a studio used by the Phoenix exclusively.

Phoenix staffers include a nutritionist, chef, psychologist, physiologist, and image consultant as well as a physical fitness team.

The atmosphere is casual at the Phoenix: no need to dress for dinner here. The schedule, while regimented, allows room for customization and flexibility. A woman is encouraged to participate in the full program, but primarily, the staff "wants her to get out of the program what she came for," says a spokeswoman.

28

Sports Lodges

Golf, tennis, and a host of other recreational offerings are in abundance throughout the Southwest. Accommodations listed in this chapter focus on one or more sports, gearing their program to sports enthusiasts.

ARIZONA

John Gardiner's Tennis Ranch on Camelback
5700 E. McDonald Drive
Scottsdale, Arizona 85253
602/948-2100
800/245-2051
GENERAL MANAGER: Paul Pastoor
41 casitas; 3- and 4-bedroom casas also available
$195–$295 single, $195–$480 double including breakfast and lunch, use of tennis courts
Tennis clinic weeks from $1,375 per person
American Express, MasterCard, Visa; personal check
No children except during junior clinics
No pets
Open October to mid-May

If you like tennis *à la* luxury, John Gardiner's Tennis Ranch is the place to go. Scottsdale with its glitzy resorts is a stone's throw away, but here on Camelback Mountain, the rest of the world seems distant.

Tennis is king at this private club resort, which hosts such tournaments as the annual invitational U.S. Senators' Cup. Take your choice of 24 championship courts. In keeping with tennis tradition, players wear white on the court. Tennis clinics scheduled weekly during the resort's season feature 21 hours of instruction, six hours of optional tennis tournaments, and complimentary court time. More than 30 pros provide instruction at a ratio of one pro to every four guests. Workouts include computerized ball machines and video tape replay. In between sessions on the court guests can relax in three swimming pools, saunas, and whirlpools, or have a massage.

Lodging is in casitas or casas, all privately owned, scattered over the resort's 50-plus acres. Casitas come in three segments, with a living room in the middle and a bedroom on each side. You can rent any part, or the entire unit. Some have sun rooms and private balconies. Decorated with a modern Southwest motif, all are luxuriously comfortable. Living rooms have fireplaces and kitchenettes. Each segment has a phone and TV. For the ultimate in tennis luxury, opt for a casa. Casa Rosewall (home of Ken Rosewall) has a rooftop court and private pool. Several three- and four-bedroom styles are available.

Dining is in the clubhouse, which by day wears a sporty look and at night takes on a formal air. (Guests are asked to wear evening attire.) Meals are served both indoors and outdoors, overlooking the valley below.

Ventana Canyon Golf and Racquet Club
  6200 N. Clubhouse Lane
  Tucson, Arizona 85715
  602/577-1400
  800/447-4787 US, 800/233-4569 AZ
GENERAL MANAGER: Lauri Treweek
46 units
$90–$215 1-bedroom suite; $150–$310 2-bedroom suite
  single or double
HIGH SEASON: mid-January to April
LOW SEASON: June to mid-September
American Express, Diners Club, MasterCard, Visa; personal
  check
Children welcome
No pets
Open year round

Dramatically set at the base of the Santa Catalina Mountains northeast of downtown Tucson, this resort is a private club that welcomes guests to its 46 suites. During your stay, you may use all of the club facilities—most notably, the 27-hole golf course designed by Tom Fazio, 12 lighted tennis courts (one is a stadium court), junior Olympic pool, and exercise and weight room.

The Club Salon has a full range of personal care services for men and women—hair cutting and styling, manicures and pedicures, facials, and massages. There are also men's and women's spa areas with whirlpool bath, steamroom and sauna. Golf and tennis packages are offered year round. Designed for either two or six nights, they include accommodations, golf or tennis, and continental breakfasts.

Whether you take advantage of the club's recreational facilities or merely use this lodging as a hub for vacationing in the Tucson area, the accommodations themselves are guaranteed to please. Fresh and modern, they are also spacious (800 to 1500 square feet) and well-decorated. Space is used innovatively throughout. The TV, set within the wall, swivels between the bedroom and living room. Some of the two-bedroom units have lofts. Rooms feature lots of extras, such as double-size whirlpool tubs, stocked minibars, and terry robes. Kitchens have everything you need, including a dishwasher, toaster, and can opener.

Special services at Ventana Canyon include room service, bike rental, child care nursery, and evening baby sitting.

In the Clubhouse Dining Room you can look out at the mountains (excellent views) while you dine on such dishes as fresh seafood, roast duckling, or steak. Entrees range from $11 to $18. The wine selection is commendable, primarily featuring California wines, and prices are reasonable.

NEW MEXICO

Oso Ranch and Lodge
  P.O. Box 808
  Chama, New Mexico 87520
  505/756-2954
MANAGERS: Benny and Jessie Salazar
6 rooms (private baths)
$100–$135 double including meals, bar, fishing
American Express, MasterCard, Visa; personal check
No pets
Open year round

On the banks of the Chama River about two miles south of Chama is a lodge geared to outdoor enthusiasts all year long. Whatever the season, there's river and lake fishing (ice fishing in the winter). Summertime is horseback riding and hiking; winter is snowmobiling and cross-country skiing. Hunting for elk, deer and bear is the emphasis in the fall.

Originally build as a private lodge, Oso Ranch covers 800 acres of rolling country dotted with juniper, pine, and spruce. Guests accommodations are in the large log building that doubles as a dining room and social center.

The main lodge room is upscale rustic, decorated with hunting and fishing trophies, Indian and western art, and a large stone fireplace. Guests can enjoy the wide-screen TV, pool table, video-taped movies, and a library of western history.

Meals are served family-style. The fare is good country food—soups, stews, biscuits, grilled meats. Use of the bar, self-service style, is included in the rate.

One hall leads to the six guest rooms, with a choice of twin, queen- or king-size beds. The door of each room is a work of art—a suede and leather creation depicting an animal indigenous to the area.

Not only are the rooms comfortable, but they are thoughtfully decorated. The work of local artists hangs on the walls, and quilts cover the beds. Each room has its own decorating theme; for instance, the one with a rainbow trout on the door has such accents as a rod, creel and tackle box mounted on the wall and a display of fishing flies. Some rooms have ceiling fans. All have TVs.

Without a doubt, fishing is the most popular activity at Oso Ranch. Anglers have a choice of the Chama, Little Navajo, and Brazos Rivers and private streams for rainbow, brook, or brown trout and Kokanee salmon. The ranch also has a private lake stocked with rainbow trout.

Horseback riding, arranged by Oso Ranch through an outfitter, is on ancient Indian trails along the mesas and rim rock. Pack trips can also be arranged.

The Cumbres and Toltec Scenic Railroad with departures from Chama is a popular day trip. The train runs daily from mid-June to mid-October.

Quail Ridge Inn and Tennis Ranch

Taos Ski Valley Road
P.O. Box 707
Taos, New Mexico 87571
505/776-2211

800/624-4448
MANAGER: Peter French
116 units
$62–$85 single or double hotel rooms; $135–$200 suites, accommodating 4-6; including continental breakfast
HIGH SEASON: mid-November to mid-April
American Express, MasterCard, Visa; personal check
Children welcome
No pets
Open year round

Adobe casitas hug the ground at the foot of the Sangre de Cristo Mountains, blending unpretentiously into the landscape. The town of Taos is four miles to the south; Taos Ski Valley is 15 miles north. Quail Ridge Inn offers travelers the essence of Taos, from its southwestern architecture to its recognition of local art.

A year-round resort, the inn brims with activity whatever the season. Tennis is one of its strongest attractions, with eight Laykold courts (two enclosed in a bubble), a tennis pro, clinic instruction, and tournaments. (No court fee for hotel guests.) Quail Ridge's landscaped pool and deck, added in 1987, is one of the most attractive in New Mexico. In addition to the 20-meter pool itself, there's a large hot tub, children's pool, and locker room.

When snow blankets the nearby mountains, Quail Ridge is transformed into a ski lodge. Shuttle buses connect the inn to Taos Ski Valley. One of the advantages of this lodging's location is that skiers can easily combine a sports vacation with trips into Taos. Non-skiers traveling with ski companions can also find plenty to do in town while the rest of the group is on the slopes.

Accommodations include hotel rooms (queen-size bed, queen-size sleeper sofa), studios (Murphy bed, sitting area, full kitchen, patio or balcony), one-bedroom suites (hotel room plus studio), and two-bedroom suites (two hotel rooms plus studio). Every room has a kiva-style fireplace, as well as TV and telephone (local calls are free). Individually owned, the units are well-decorated. Kitchens are fully equipped with countertop appliances and cookware as well as full-size refrigerator and stoves, dishwashers, and garbage disposals.

Continental breakfast is included in all room rates. Carl's French Quarter Restaurant also serves dinner, featuring such specialties as trout amandine, shrimp creole, and veal Marsala. Prices range from $10 to $17.

One of the true delights of this inn is sitting on an adobe-style patio, gazing at the distant mountains by day or the star-sprinkled sky by night.

TEXAS

John Newcombe's Tennis Ranch
  P.O. Box 469
  New Braunfels, Texas 78130
  512/625-9105
  800/262-NEWK US, 800/292-7080 TX
  RANCH OPERATIONS MANAGER: Jamie Bell
  22 units
  $200–$250 per person, 2-day all-inclusive package
  $455–$595 per person, 5-day all-inclusive package
  American Express, MasterCard, Visa; personal check
  Children welcome
  No pets
  Open year round

John Newcombe's Tennis Ranch is the place for people who want to eat and breathe tennis. Clinics, exhibitions, and tournaments, plus unlimited court time, is the program. Pros and guests are at a ratio of one to four. Not only are the pros at your side on the courts, but they're around for Happy Hour, mealtime, and plain ole relaxing—always ready to talk about their favorite sport.

In operation since the mid-1960s, the tennis ranch is the creation of one of the sport's all-time greats. Reflective of its founder's viewpoint, the tennis ranch emphasizes laughter and fun as well as skills and strategy. Several of the top staffers are, like Newk himself, native Australians.

The adult program is geared to every level of player, with the overall goal of increasing enjoyment. Both weekend and five-day packages are offered. (Special rates for non-playing spouses and friends.) Weekend sessions, operating year-round, include seven-and-a-half hours of instruction, video replays, and round-robin tournaments, plus convivial evening entertainment. Five-day clinics are for players who want to work on stroke production and strategy. Advanced clinics feature intensity drills, court movement, and singles and doubles play.

Junior camps get lots of emphasis; there's even a Competitive Edge Academy for talented juniors who live and train at the ranch throughout the school year.

Accommodations are in one- and two-bedroom condos overlooking (you guessed it) the tennis courts. Some units are privately owned. All have fireplaces, TVs, full kitchens, washers and dryers, and deluxe furnishings.

Meals are served buffet style in the ranch dining room. Food is plentiful, not gourmet—just hearty and good. Dress is casual, whatever the time of day.

In addition to the 28 Laykold tennis courts (several are enclosed) there's a large swimming pool and a heated hot tub. Although the ranch tends to be a self-contained world while you're participating in its program, Hill Country scenic attractions and historic New Braunfels are nearby if you want a change of scene.

Rancho Viejo Resort
P.O. Box 3918
Brownsville, Texas 78520
512/350-4000
800/531-7400 US, 800/292-7263 TX
GENERAL MANAGER: Ted Trapp
120 units
$50 single, $65–$75 double rooms; $135–$195 villas
American Express, MasterCard, Visa
Children welcome
Pets accepted with $50 deposit
Open year round

About ten miles north of Brownsville is Rancho Viejo, both an incorporated town and a resort. The resort sprawls over 1,400 acres, a composite of two 18-hole championship golf courses, guest villas, private homes, and expansive palm-dotted grounds.

Once the site of a citrus orchard, the resort has retained some of its history. Casa Grande, the original hacienda, is now a fine supper club where roving troubadours entertain.

Golf is the headliner at Rancho Viejo. El Diablo and El Angel courses draw vacationers year round, especially in the winter when sun-starved Midwesterners head south. The courses are open only to members, resort guests, and golfers who belong to reciprocating clubs. The greens fee is $25; cart rental is $18. Once you check into Rancho Viejo, you can put your wallet aside. Guests sign for services, even at the two restaurants which, like the golf courses, are not open to the public.

In addition to golf, there's a great swimming pool with a huge waterfall and swim-up bar, and two tennis courts. Mexico is about a 20-minute drive; the beaches of South Padre are about 30 minutes away. Brownsville has an excellent zoo dedicated to rare and endangered species, and the Confederate Air Force Museum in Harlingen has a collection of American World War II combat aircraft.

Residential-style lodging is sprinkled across the resort's grounds. It's spread out, so plan to drive to the dining rooms and recreational facilities; courtesy vans will also pick you up upon request.

Villas, available in two- and three-bedroom styles, have modern furnishings, fully equipped kitchens, and washers and dryers. Executive suites are two-story condo-style units.

29

Town Inns

Akin to hotels, town inns have special character and charm. Most are historic; one is just beginning to write its history.

ARIZONA

Copper Queen Hotel
  11 Howell Avenue
  P.O. Box Drawer CQ
  Bisbee, Arizona 85603
  602/432-2216
OWNERS: Rick and Virginia Hort
44 rooms
$30–$63 single, $34–$64 double
MasterCard, Visa; personal check
Children welcome
No pets
Open year round

Sit on the upstairs porch of the Copper Queen Hotel and look down on the bustling town below. Straight ahead is a mountain—so near you can almost touch it. On both sides of the hotel is the historic town of Bisbee, stair-stepping up the sides of Mule Pass Gulch. It doesn't take much imagination to pretend that you're in a turn-of-the-century mining town. Bisbee was once the largest copper mining town in the world. Today's residents like to point out that Bisbee was never a boom town but was built to last. At one time it had two opera houses in addition to a host of brick buildings, many of which still stand. The Copper Queen Hotel was built in the early 1900s. Right around the corner was Brewery Gulch, site of forty or so bars where the miners caroused.

Refurbished in the mid 1980s, the Queen has charm and lots of character. The saloon looks like a Western scene come to life. On one wall hangs a painting of a reclining nude, with a winged cherub nearby.

Up the stairs are 44 guest rooms with differing sizes and decor. In one room, burgundy curtains are tied back with lace. The wallpaper, also burgundy, repeats the theme, and the bed is covered with a colonial white spread. The bathroom is small but well-decorated. Some rooms have either a tub or shower; others have both. If TVs are important to you, be sure to ask for a room that has one. Note that guest rooms are not air-conditioned but do have ceiling fans.

Unexpectedly for a historic hotel, the Copper Queen has a swimming pool. Other amenities include a sidewalk café and a picturesque dining room. Waitresses wearing long blue skirts serve such dishes as baked orange roughy, veal Oscar, and Southern fried chicken. Entrees are priced from $7 to $13.

NEW MEXICO

Inn on the Alameda
  303 E. Alameda
  Santa Fe, New Mexico 87501
  505/984-2121
  800/552-0070, ext. 289, outside NM
  GENERAL MANAGER: Patty Jennison

36 rooms
$75–$95 single, $85–$105 double including continental breakfast
HIGH SEASON: June to October
American Express, MasterCard, Visa; personal check
Children welcome
Pets accepted
Open year round

A small, conveniently located hotel offering personal service—that's Inn on the Alameda. Only two blocks from the Plaza, this pueblo-style adobe lodging is a quiet retreat, secluded from the hubbub and yet within easy walking distance of many area attractions.

The inn opened in 1986. Throughout its grounds there's a look of freshness. Guest rooms are spacious and airy, definitely reflecting their Southwest locale but with a modern flair. Much of the furniture is handmade, such as aspen-pole beds, flagstone tables, and mirrors framed in hammered tin. Wood is an important accent, from pine-plank ceilings to latilla chairs. Most rooms have a private patio or balcony. Air conditioning (not necessarily standard in this part of the country), cable TV, and phones are in each unit.

Rooms have either one king- or two queen-size beds. A mini-suite and full suite are also available. Bathrooms are above average for the area, with theatrical-style bulb lighting, Neutrogena amenities, and full-length mirrors.

Breakfast comes with the room rate. It's served buffet style in the library, which doubles as the lobby. Typical fare is coffeecake, croissants, blueberry muffins, raisin rolls, bagels, fresh fruit, freshly squeezed juice, and freshly ground coffee. Room service is available from 7 A.M. to 11 A.M.

Out in the courtyard, there's an enclosed blue-tiled whirlpool shaded by apricot trees—truly a romantic nook.

But the best thing about Inn on the Alameda is its service. The general manager visits with guests at breakfast, and the desk clerk is sincere when she asks, "What can I do to help you?" Due to the inn's smallness, staff people wear several hats. The same person may carry your luggage and pour your drink at the bar.

Two book stores (including one for children), a travel agency, and a manicure salon are on the premises. Hotel parking is free.

La Fonda De Taos
   Taos Plaza
   P.O. Box 1447
   Taos, New Mexico 87571
   505/758-2211
OWNER/MANAGER: Saki Karavas
24 rooms
$33–$75 single, $55–$75 double; $85 suites
American Express, MasterCard, Visa; personal check
Children welcome
Pets accepted
Open year round

Whether you stay at La Fonda or not, be sure to step inside
this Spanish-style hotel which dates back to 1938. It's the
only lodging right on the Plaza; outside its doors there's always activity, for the Plaza is the town's focal point.

La Fonda's lobby is a gallery of local art, covered from
floor to ceiling with art works. From the red kiva fireplace to
the Spanish costumes encased in glass, there's lots to see despite the room's small size. Off to one side there's a tiny
room crammed with more art, most notably a collection of
paintings by D.H. Lawrence. You have to pay a dollar to enter the "gallery," which also functions as an office.

"This is the only showing of the D.H. Lawrence controver-
sial paintings since his exhibition was permanently banned by
Scotland Yard, where his show opened at the Warren
Galleries, London, in 1929," reads a plaque at the hotel's entrance. After Frieda Lawrence's death (her husband was already deceased), the paintings were sold to art collector/inn-
keeper Saki Karavas. Art critics have described Lawrence's
paintings of nude men and women as sensuous yet crudely
executed. All are signed "Lorenzo." Mixed in with these
paintings are other art works as well as an assortment of
Karavas's personal memorabilia. One of the landscapes was
jointly painted by Lawrence, his wife Frieda, and Dorothy
Brett. Of special interest is a letter from Albert Einstein to
Saki Karavas's father, dated April 2, 1943.

La Fonda's 24 guest rooms are arranged on several levels,
connected by hallways that overlook the lobby. While there's
no pretense of plushness, they are cheerful and lively. Everything that doesn't move has been touched by a paintbrush.
Doors are bright blue, and decorated with Indian symbols. In
rooms overlooking the plaza, even the window panes have
been decorated with bright designs.

Bathrooms (many have a step up to conceal plumbing) have a combined tub and shower. Even here there's a strong dash of color, with burgundy tiles and blue towels.

At the top of the stairs that lead down to the lobby, there's a large rambling sitting area with leather-upholstered couches, beamed ceiling, and a TV. (No TVs in guest rooms.)

No restaurant is within the inn itself, but just outside its doors are lots of dining choices.

La Posada de Santa Fe
330 E. Palace Avenue
Santa Fe, New Mexico 87501
505/983-6351
800/531-6424 outside NM
GENERAL MANAGER: Dottie Vreed
110 rooms
$60–$97 rooms; $97–$250 suites and casitas, single or double
American Express, Carte Blanche, Diners Club, MasterCard,
   Visa; personal check
Children welcome
No pets
Open year round

Spread over six acres in a garden-like setting three blocks from the Plaza, La Posada de Santa Fe is an assortment of rooms, suites, and casitas built adobe-style. The inn dates back to 1882 when Abraham Staab, a German emigrant, had a mansion built for his bride.

Today the Staab House Restaurant is central to the inn. In warmer months, the adjoining patio, overhung with huge trees, is popular for dining. Nearby there's a small pool under the aspens. The well-tended grounds of La Posada are integral to its appeal. Pathways wind through the blue spruce, aspens, and apple trees to the individual units.

While each room is different, all reflect their Southwest heritage. Viga and plank ceilings, Mexican tile, and adobe fireplaces set the tone. Rooms tend to be dark, but the overall feeling is one of charm. Be forewarned that rooms are not air-conditioned. TVs and phones are in every unit.

Traditional rooms, available in one- or two-bedroom versions, have kitchenettes. Suites comprise a living room and bedroom; some have fireplaces, wood-burning stoves, and private patios. Casitas (one-, two-, or three-bedrooms) have living rooms and kitchenettes. Many have fireplaces, wood-burning stoves, and patios.

Sagebrush Inn
  Box 557
  S. Santa Fe Road
  Taos, New Mexico 87571
  505/758-2254
  800/428-3626 outside New Mexico
  GENERAL MANAGER: Roger Mariani
  63 rooms; 20 condos
  $35 single (4 rooms only), $55–$95 double
  American Express, Carte Blanche, Diners Club, MasterCard,
    Visa; personal check
  Children welcome
  Pets with approval
  Open year round

Long a Taos landmark, the Sagebrush Inn offers tradition, aesthetics, and comfort—all at an affordable price. Located about three miles south of downtown Taos, it's removed from the crowds, yet easily accessible to area attractions. During ski season, shuttle buses link the Sagebrush to Taos Ski Valley twice a day.

The pueblo mission-style inn was built in 1929, catering to well-to-do travelers in transit between New York and Arizona. Painter Georgia O'Keeffe lived in the inn for six months, creating some of her art works in a third-story room.

There are two distinct looks to the inn. In the original portion, guest rooms open onto one of two courtyards, one centered with a pool. Authenticity isn't simulated here; the huge vigas used for ceiling support came from trees felled in the nearby mountains, and the adobe walls—stuccoed on both the interior and exterior—are 24 inches thick.

At the back of the property, overlooking miles of sagebrush-studded fields backed by the Sangre de Cristo Mountains, is Sagebrush Village, a condo complex with 20 units. While the architecture is in keeping with the original inn, there's a definite look of modernity here, both in the exteriors and interiors.

If historic flavor is important to you, an inn room is the best choice. If spaciousness and privacy are your prime considerations, request a condo. Rooms in the original section are delightfully decorated, with kiva fireplaces, hand-painted accents on the walls, Navajo rugs, pottery lamps, and tin light fixtures. All have TVs and phones. Some have walk-in showers (no tubs), so be sure to ask if having both a shower and a tub matters to you.

Two sizes of condos are available, priced from $75. The larger units ($95 for two, $5 extra for each additional person) sleep up to six people. They have a living room with a pull-out couch and a Murphy bed, bedroom with king-size bed, two full baths, mini-refrigerator, and kiva fireplace. The massive Spanish-style furniture in the condos is handsome, creating a different look from the inn rooms. The bedroom portion of the larger units opens onto a patio or balcony, offering unobstructed views of wide-open fields and distant mountains.

Back in the main inn, the lobby lounge is a popular gathering spot both for locals and guests. Richly decorated with art works, most with a southwestern flavor, it's dark and atmospheric. Most nights there's live entertainment. Off to one side are two dining rooms specializing in New Mexican and continental fare. Also on the grounds are two tennis courts, two hot tubs, and a swimming pool.

TEXAS

La Posada
1000 Zaragoza
Laredo, Texas 78040
512-722-1701
800-531-7156 US, 800-292-5659 TX
GENERAL MANAGER: Al Ramirez
272 rooms and suites
$55–$125 single, $65–$125 double; $150–$300 suites
American Express, Carte Blanche, Diners Club, Discover,
    MasterCard, Visa; personal check
Children welcome
No pets
Open year round

Laredo is almost Mexico. Nuevo Laredo across the Rio Grande is its sister. Together the two offer historic sites, shopping for Mexican wares, and horse and greyhound racing, all with a wonderful Mexican flavor.

Near the river the narrow streets of Laredo weave around plazas and squares. Agustin Plaza, overlooked by San Agustin Church with its 1700s stained-glass windows, is the best known. Across from the church and fronting the plaza is La Posada, a sprawling, lively hotel with arches and courtyards, pools and palm trees.

Unusual for a hotel, La Posada is built around a tiny museum. The Museum of the Republic of the Rio Grande commemorates the short-lived nation that existed for 283 days in 1840. Constructed of native stone and adobe, it opens onto Zaragoza Street as does La Posada.

Part of the hotel dates back to a 1916 school. Another part was once a convent. Still another wing is of much younger vintage, built in the mid 1980s. Together the complex has two swimming pools, one casual and one fine-dining restaurant, two lounges, and guest rooms ranging from simple to grand.

Rooms tend to be large. Most rooms have beamed ceilings; furnishings are modern traditional. The concierge floor in the new west wing has the nicest rooms, plus pampering services and a concierge who endears himself to guests. (At last visit, some of the older rooms had recently been redecorated; others were slated for refurbishing.)

Hotel guests have privileges at Laredo Country Club with golf, tennis, racquetball, swimming, and a sauna. La Posada provides transportation, and you can charge recreation fees to your hotel room.

One of the Laredo's three bridges to Mexico is a few blocks from the hotel; the trip across the border is a ten-minute walk. Several tour companies offer day trips to Nuevo Laredo, with departures from La Posada.

Via the Tex-Mex Express train, you can have a combined Laredo/Gulf Coast vacation, with accommodations at La Posada in Laredo and the Hershey Hotel in Corpus Christi (see Family Resorts).

La Posada
100 N. Main
McAllen, Texas 78501
512/686-5411
800/531-7156 US, 800/292-5659 TX
GENERAL MANAGER: B.J. Ulcak
164 rooms
$45–$150 single, $55–$150 double
American Express, MasterCard, Visa
Children welcome
No pets
Open year round

Deep in the Rio Grande Valley only a few miles from Mexico, La Posada is a gentle hacienda that lives up to its name of "the resting place." Its architecture is Spanish colonial—a wonderful composite of arches, fountains, and courtyards. From the outside, La Posada has a residential look, quite a trick for a 164-room lodging. Graceful palm trees and brilliant bougainvillaeas drape the three-story white stucco building topped by a red tile roof.

The hotel's history goes back to 1918 when a group of McAllen businessmen decided that the city needed a hotel. The site they selected was then a city park. Casa de Palmas was the hotel they built—a hacienda-style structure with a central patio. It became the business, social, and civic center for the entire Rio Grande Valley.

In 1973 the old hotel burned. Almost immediately, La Posada was built on its foundation, replicating the original hotel's architecture. Today a beautiful swimming pool is at the center of the courtyard—a great place to relax and get in tune with the surroundings.

At this writing, La Posada was closed for major refurbishment of public areas and guest rooms. Reopening was projected for spring of '88. La Posada in Laredo has the same ownership as McAllen's La Posada.

Yacht Club Hotel
700 Yturria Street
P.O. Box 4114
Port Isabel, Texas 78578
512/943-1301
OWNER: Lynn Speier
24 rooms
$30–$54 double including continental breakfast
American Express, Diners Club, MasterCard, Visa
Children welcome
Pets with approval
Open year round

Across the bridge on South Padre Island, gleaming new condo towers are the norm. But in the fishing village of Port Isabel, the Yacht Club Hotel puts you in touch with history. The atmosphere is vintage 1920s, guest rooms are comfortable, and the seafood restaurant is one of the best in the area. Beginning in 1926, the Spanish stucco structure was built as an exclusive private club, catering to the most prominent families in the Rio Grande Valley. Then in 1934 it opened as a fine hotel. But over the years it declined, eventually closing in 1969.

Today's hotel is a total refurbishment: new interiors, modern plumbing, and blessed air conditioning. The overall effect is of a Spanish hacienda. Out back there's a secluded swimming pool bordered by hibiscus. The main dining room, an addition to the original structure, is bright and airy yet in keeping with the Spanish theme.

Guest rooms are small but pleasant, decorated in rich green and white with matching bedspreads and drapes. Baths are completely modern. TVs but not telephones are in each room. Suites are a good choice, with entirely separate bedrooms and sitting rooms. Continental breakfast comes with the price of a room. The staff is friendly, setting the tone for guests to socialize.

Wherever you stay, there's hardly a better place to dine on shrimp, trout, and red snapper than at the Yacht Club Restaurant. Port Isabel calls itself the Shrimp Capital of the World, and the hotel maintains a high dining standard.

30

Village B&Bs

Some of the most charming lodgings in all the Southwest are these Village B&Bs. While the accommodations themselves are above average, it's the hosts of these B&B homes that set them apart. One host can tell you about her town's history (she's the offical town historian); another introduces you to regional art. Some are gourmet cooks; others are willing tour guides. All brim with hospitality and personality.

ARIZONA

Graham's Bed and Breakfast
   150 Canyon Circle Dr.
   Village of Oak Creek
   Mailing address: P.O. Box 912
   Sedona, Arizona 86336)
   602/284-1425
INNKEEPERS: Bill and Marni Graham
5 rooms (private baths)
$75–$115 single or double including full breakfast
Personal check or cash preferred; MasterCard, Visa accepted
Children over 12 welcome
No pets
Smoking only on balconies
Open February to the first week of January

A two-story western contemporary home sits at the base of Bell Rock in the Village of Oak Creek, about six miles south of Sedona. Graham's Bed and Breakfast is a pleasant, professionally run lodging, hosted by resident owners who enjoy getting to know their guests.

One-time Californians Bill and Marni Graham built the home as a B&B in 1985. Designed to take full advantage of its setting amid Red Rock Country, the house has lots of glass in the living areas and balconies off each guest room. Even the decor brings the outdoors in. For example, the downstairs terra-cotta-colored rug reflects the red of mountains visible through the windows.

Since the house itself is new, the Grahams have imbued the guest rooms with their personal history. Heritage Suite is done up in red, white, and blue, honoring Marni's father and his lifetime in the service. Southern Suite—a collage of soft blues and greens furnished with an antique love seat, four-poster twin beds, and a marble washstand—is a tribute to Bill's mother, who was raised in the South.

Every room has a marble bath and shower, balcony, air conditioning, and an assortment of books. The San Francisco Suite is the prettiest. Furnished with a custom-made California king bed, peach lacquered bureau and desk, and a specially made chaise lounge, the suite is the Graham's salute to their years in the Bay Area. This suite has a double whirlpool tub and views of the countryside.

In the afternoons, refreshments including wine or juice are served. A full breakfast is the bill of fare every morning; the menu changes daily. Guests eat together in the dining room.

In the back yard there's a nice pool and spa. Other favored activities are shopping at the nearby boutiques and art galleries, playing golf at the Village of Oak Creek's 18-hole course (one-half mile from Graham's), jeep rides through the countryside, and day trips to the Grand Canyon (two-and-a-half hours away).

NEW MEXICO

American Artists Gallery House
  P.O. Box 584
  Taos, New Mexico 87571
  505/758-4446
INNKEEPERS: Ben and Myra Carp
3 rooms (private baths)

$55–$65 double including full breakfast
Personal check accepted
Children accepted
No pets
Open year round

Only a few minutes from Taos Plaza, at the end of a tiny side street, there's a B&B dedicated to helping guests experience Taos—its history, its geology, and especially its art.

Ben and Myra moved to New Mexico from New York, bringing with them their love of art. Back East they operated a mail order art business. Today they continue to represent artists with whom they have dealt for years, complementing the work of national artists with some of the best art created locally. Throughout their home the Carps have a variety of art pieces—sculptures, oils, etchings, lithographs. While the house itself is small, art is in abundance, even in the gardens and courtyard.

Guests eat breakfast together at this B&B, dining on such specialties as French toast stuffed with nuts and cheese, or Myra's "New York Experience" with smoked trout, smoked salmon, and bagels. (All of the delicious menus are vegetarian, except for fish dishes.) Eating together provides a forum for discussing individual interests and sharing Taos experiences. The Carps are willing tour guides, specializing in taking guests to artists' studios and on geological trips and walking tours.

The rooms are named Gallery East, Gallery West, and Gallery Rose. Each has a kiva fireplace, private bath, and king or twin beds. All have private entrances from the portico. In Gallery Rose you awake to a view of the Sangre de Cristo Mountains, fronted by sculptures in the nearby garden. Bathrooms are beautiful, decked out in hand-thrown tiles. When you're ready to relax between jaunts to nearby attractions, you've got the cozy living room, sun room, bricked portico, and outdoor hot tub to choose from.

Brooks Street Inn
  P.O. Box 4954
  Taos, New Mexico 87571
  505/758-1489
INNKEEPERS: Susan Stevens and John Testore
7 rooms (5 with private bath)
$35–$70 single, $40–$75 double including breakfast
MasterCard, Visa; personal check
Children welcome
No pets

Smoking in designated areas
Open year round

Down a quiet residential street within walking distance of Taos Plaza is Brooks Street Inn—a gracious B&B operated by convivial hosts. The main house, which doubles as a four bedroom guest lodging and the home of the innkeepers, is a rambling adobe-style residence built in the mid-1950s. Behind it is a separate guest house with three guest rooms, each offering privacy and aesthetic charm.

There's a look of freshness and attention to detail at Brooks Street. Guest rooms have the look of the modern Southwest, with the work of local artisans woven into the overall design. The photography of graphic designer-turned-innkeeper Sue Stevens adds flair as well as a personal touch. The main house gleams, with its beamed ceilings, polished wooden floors, carved wooden doors, and large stone fireplace. Rooms are named after local trees. The guest room named Aspen features willow furniture and a cozy reading alcove. Its bath is especially spacious for a B&B. Spruce and Manzanillo share a bath and are good choices for families. A closet in Spruce has been converted into a cozy reading banco, adding to its spaciousness as well as visual interest.

Out in the guest house, individual rooms have such touches as skylights or a kiva fireplace. Birch, centered with a white poster bed, is decorated in rustic antiques.

Breakfast at Brooks Street, served buffet style, is headlined by Lithuanian and Czech pastries, including especially good bacon buns and coffeecakes. Fresh fruit and juices are always part of the bill of fare. Guests gather at the large kitchen counter or eat outside on the patio.

For travelers who like to visit with their hosts, Brooks Street is an excellent choice. In winter the gathering spot might be in front of the fireplace. In the summertime, the big back yard is great for relaxing. Sue and John, who moved from Chicago to start a B&B, are a bright, talented young couple who enjoy interacting with their guests.

El Paradero en Santa Fe

220 W. Manhattan
Santa Fe, New Mexico 87501
505/988-1177
INNKEEPERS: Ouida MacGregor and Thom Allen
12 rooms (6 with private bath)
$38–$65 single, $46–$90 double including full breakfast
MasterCard, Visa; personal check
Children over age three welcome

No pets
Open year round

In a quiet residential neighborhood in Santa Fe, El Paradero is a remodeled 1800s adobe farmhouse where B&B guests can relax in a tranquil setting. There's no pretentiousness about the place, just a convivial atmosphere and comfortable surroundings.

The living room sets the tone, a casual gathering spot with Mexican-crafted chairs, Indian rugs, and local art. Nine guest rooms are on the rambling ground level of the house, stretching along a courtyard. Three have private baths, and six share three "community" baths along the hallway. The most luxurious accommodations are in the main casa, all with private baths. They're pure Southwest, with Saltillo tile floors, Talavera tiled baths, and hand-woven rugs. Rooms can accommodate up to four. Several have fireplaces. Private phones are available at an extra charge.

If you like big country breakfasts, then put El Paradero high on your list. You'll feast on homemade breads and cherry jam made from the fruit of the tree out back. Guests gather between 8 A.M. and 9:30 A.M. in the large breakfast room.

La Posada de Taos

309 Juanita Lane
P.O. Box 1118
Taos, New Mexico 87571
505/758-8164
INNKEEPER: Sue Smoot
5 rooms (private baths)
$38–$71 single, $46–$79 double
Personal check; no credit cards
Children welcome
Pets accepted
Open year round

Taos Plaza is easy walking distance—only two-and-a-half blocks away. Within the walls of La Posada de Taos, guests find comfortable lodging and a convivial host.

Each morning Sue Smoot serves a hearty breakfast. The menu is always a surprise; main dishes include Mexican and "Anglo" quiches. Guests who opt to skip breakfast the first morning are prone to join their fellow B&Bers the second day, for by then they've heard tales of all they missed the first time around. Sue is a New Yorker who came to Taos to open an inn. Shortly before that she had earned a degree in architecture—knowledge that she would put to good use in restoring an 80-year-old adobe. Interiors throughout La Posada de Taos reflect her skill, especially her innovative use of space.

Each of the five guest rooms is distinctive, decorated with furnishings collected from around the world. Beautler Suite is the largest, furnished with one double and two twin beds. Its spacious bathroom has a whirlpool tub and shower. Lino, one of the smaller rooms, is light and airy. It has a white iron double bed, wood-burning stove, and enough books for a mini-library. While the adjoining bath is tiny (as are many in Taos), it is charmingly decorated with Mexican tile.

La Casa de La Luna de Miel, or the Honeymoon House, is a romantic hideaway. This tiny cottage, only about 50 feet from the main house, has a cozy loft double bed topped with a sky-light. Downstairs is a miniature kitchen, designed by architect Smoot with such ingenious touches as a pull-out table and a specially created drying rack. The mirror over the vanity was created by a local tinsmith. A fireplace adds to the cottage's allure.

Guests at La Posada de Taos can relax in the living room—centered with a fireplace and decorated with Southwest hangings. There's also a graveled courtyard set with plants and flowers. Ample parking is provided on the grounds.

TEXAS

Cotten's Patch Bed and Breakfast Inn

703 E. Rusk
Marshall, Texas 75670
214/938-8756
INNKEEPER: Jo Ann Cotten
3 rooms (1 private bath, 2 shared baths)
$55 to $65 double including continental breakfast
Mastercard, Visa; personal check
No children
No pets
Open year round

Cotten's Patch could well qualify for the definition of "a doll house lodging." Every furnishing, every decorating detail has been chosen with care, creating a romantic getaway in a slow-paced East Texas town.

Built in the late 1800s, the house has been exquisitely re-stored. Comfort and coziness are the keynote, though the decor is eclectic. Trompe l'oeil decorating touches add to the visual appeal—from stenciling on the pantry door to a "rug" and "tree" created by stenciling on the back porch. Quilts, lace, handmade wares, and country-style bonnets proliferate. So do antiques and wicker furniture. A collection of dolls spills from the landing.

The downstairs bedroom has a private bath; the two upstairs rooms share a bathroom. The screened-in front porch is a good place to watch the world go by, small-town style. Continental breakfast includes coffee and juice, fruit, and freshly baked coffee cake.

The Gilded Thistle
1805 Broadway
Galveston, Texas 77550
409/763-0194
INNKEEPER: Helen Hanemann
3 rooms (2 with shared bath)
$100–$125 double including full breakfast
MasterCard, Visa
Children welcome (preferred during the week)
No pets
Open year round

In all the world, there's only one Helen Hanemann. The best reason to stay at The Gilded Thistle is to hear her stories and join in her laughter. Of grandmotherly age, Helen has more energy than most persons half her years. Delightfully, her wit transcends age altogether, acting as a catalyst to make guests enjoy themselves.

Hers was the first B&B home in Galveston, opening in 1982. The house itself dates back to 1893. Built in Queen Anne style, it has inherent charm with its curly pine and cypress trimwork, oak fireplaces, and wrap-around verandas. This is a home of warmth as well as character. Teddy bears fill the couches, spill from the shelves, and sit coyly on the beds. Helen may try to introduce you to all of them, pointing to the latest additions that came from guests themselves. In addition to bears, Helen has a wonderful collection of seashells which figure into her overall decorating scheme. Many of the home's furnishings are family heirlooms. Decorative touches came from friends, each connoting the friendship that Helen engenders.

The house is cozy and tidy. Guest rooms, all with double beds, are on the second floor. The master bedroom, the only one with a private bath, has a couch and fireplace. The Umbrella Room is oriental in theme, decorated with Chinese umbrellas. The Treetops Room looks straight into the uppermost branches of trees. Every room opens onto the romantic wrap-around porch, set with chairs and lots of plants.

Helen is the kind of hostess who believes in ironing pillow cases, dressing the beds with decorative sheets, and keeping the silver polished. Her breakfasts should keep hunger pangs at bay until at least mid-afternoon, for she serves homemade breads, eggs, several breakfast meats, and fresh fruit. Snacks are kept on trays within easy reach.

If you want to talk history, Helen is willing and able. A descendent of early West Texas settlers, she can tell you stories of the Texas Rangers. It is said that one of her ancestors, a captain with the Rangers, discovered Carlsbad Caverns while on patrol with his troop.

The Gilded Thistle, located within East End Historical District, is nine blocks from the beach and is convenient to numerous area attractions.

High Cotton Inn Bed and Breakfast
   214 S. Live Oak
   Bellville, Texas 77418
   409/865-9796
INNKEEPERS: George and Anna Horton
5 rooms (shared baths)
$40–$55 single, $50–$65 double including full breakfast
Personal check
Children accepted; ages 1 $1/2$ to 3 not encouraged
No pets
Open year round

What better place to escape the humdrum than at High Cotton? Anna Horton always wanted to live in the country. Today she and her husband operate a country-style B&B in a two-story Victorian with wrap-around porches and period furnishings.

The mood is informal at High Cotton, making it a great place to relax. Much of High Cotton's charm is tied up in the hosts themselves, genuinely nice people whose natural enthusiasm and zest for living can't help but spill over to their guests. They revel in serving bounteous breakfasts, with a repertoire too lengthy to list (locally cured bacon, yard eggs, yeast biscuits, grits, rum cake—you get the idea). When the Hortons aren't welcoming guests, they're apt to be out in their cookie kitchen baking up goodies marketed under the name High Cotton Country Cookie and Candy Company. Be sure to try the caramel crisps and the oatmeal raisin spice cookies.

So fond are the Hortons of cooking that they're always looking for an excuse to stir something up. Thanksgiving Dinner at High Cotton may well be the definition of "feast." Make reservations for that meal far in advance. But you don't have to wait for Thanksgiving to dine at High Cotton. Call ahead and the Hortons will cook a dinner just for you, priced at $10 per person. The menu is cook's choice.

Excellent for small groups as well as couples, High Cotton has five guest rooms and two-and-a-half baths, all on the second floor. No detail of decorating has escaped the hosts' notice. Family antiques and memorabilia are the focal point. Uncle Buster's Room has a beautifully carved bed. A beaded gown worn by George's grandmother is displayed in the upstairs parlor. Even the medicine cabinet has a story to tell, with antique gloves and spats on display.

For recreation, there's a pool out back. There are also two porches to rock on, and a dozen or so antique shops nearby. The hosts can arrange golf (nine-hole course) and horseback riding.

The Inn at Salado
N. Main at Pace Park
Salado, Texas 76571
817/947-8200
INNKEEPERS: Larry and Cathy Sands
5 rooms (2 with shared bath)
$45–$80 double; $275–$325, entire house accommodating 18
   (including breakfast)
MasterCard, Visa; personal check
Children over the age of 10 welcome
No pets
Open year round

In the historic village of Salado, about halfway between Austin and Waco, there's an 1870s house well-suited for groups and families as well as other travelers. Situated right on Main Street, the five-bedroom Inn at Salado is dedicated solely to guests. The owners/innkeepers who live nearby are hospitable hosts, meeting guests upon arrival and serving a bounteous breakfast.

There's a warm, relaxed feel about the house. Games spill from the living room shelves. Quilts and lace, country antiques and fireplaces set the tone. Out back there's a tree-shaded patio. Groups have use of the kitchen, equipped with a microwave and dishwasher as well as the expected appliances.

Guest rooms (three are suites) are on the first and second floor. Named for people who have had an influence on Salado, they chronicle the village's history. The General Custer Suite (he camped on the nearby creek) has a homey sitting area and accommodates four. The Reverend Baines Room (a relative of Lyndon Baines Johnson) is furnished with a magnificent antique bed. Three rooms have private baths; two share a bath.

Just outside the inn's doors are country shops, antique stores, and art galleries.

The Matali
1727 Sealy
Galveston, Texas 77550
409/763-4526
INNKEEPER: Dan Dyer
3 rooms (2 with shared bath)
$68–$85 double including full breakfast
American Express, MasterCard, Visa; personal check
Children over 12
No pets
Open year round

The trim blue house with red shutters sits on the corner of Sealy and 18th Street. Through the little iron gate, up the front porch steps, you enter a B&B of charm and conviviality. Once it was the home of Isabella Offenbach Maas, sister of the famed German composer Offenbach. Isabella, a noted opera singer, fell in love with Galvestonian Samuel Maas and left her native Germany to marry him. In 1886 they built the home on Sealy Street. A whimsical "Isabella" dressed in black lace now stands on the interior staircase to welcome visitors.

For vacationers interested in getting the most out of a trip to Galveston Island, the Matali is a good choice. Right outside the front door you can hop aboard a trolley car for a tour of the island city. The innkeeper has bikes for you to ride, and if you'd like, he'll arrange a sunset horse-drawn carriage ride through the historic East End. When you're ready for fun in the sun, Matali guests have privileges at an oceanfront hotel's pool with swim-up bar, whirlpool, and tennis courts. If you want help planning your itinerary, the innkeeper/owner is happy to act as consultant. In fact, guests often linger around the breakfast table for an hour or more, discussing all the things they might do once they break away from the tranquility of the Matali.

Downstairs there's a music and game room that begs you to stop awhile. An old Victrola stands waiting for the next guest to put on a record. Wine and cheese often appear at your side as if by magic.

The house, listed on both the national and state historic registers, is ornamented with gingerbread trim and stained-glass windows. Inside there's a wealth of artistic woodwork: a carved cypress staircase, curly pine wainscotting, ceiling rosettes, and ten-foot sliding doors made of cypress and long leaf pine.

Guests have a choice of three second-floor bedrooms. (The first guests to check in get a private bath. Neither of the two baths is adjoined to a bedroom, but is just down the hall.) The Fisher Room (named for a previous owner) is beautifully decorated and has a double bed. It can be joined to the peach and white-colored Offenbach with its twin beds, wicker furniture, and stenciled floor. All of the rooms have a private porch, but the one adjoining the Maas Room is especially nice. In addition to central air conditioning, each room has a ceiling fan.

Throughout the house there's a profusion of memorabilia that enhances the historic ambience. Old photos, Victorian dolls, and swatches of lace transport you to a gentler era.

The Oxford House
563 N. Graham
Stephenville, Texas 76401
817/965-6885, 968-8171
INNKEEPERS: Bill and Paula Oxford
4 rooms (private baths)
$50–$65 double including continental breakfast
MasterCard, Visa; personal check
Children age 10 and over
No pets
Smoking in designated areas only
Open year round

In 1898 Judge Oxford built a fine Victorian home in Stephenville. In 1986 his grandson Bill opened the house as a B&B—a gem of a house steeped in local as well as family history. Bill's wife Paula has an obvious love for history, and throughout the house she has interwoven memorabilia into the design. As you sip afternoon refreshments, ask her about the home's history and you'll probably get a grand tour. The pump organ is a family heirloom transported to Texas by wagon. The violins belonged to the good judge himself. So did the law books. The hats and gloves belonged to his third wife.

The guest room at the top of the stairs has interior columns and gingerbread trim, plus a stained-glass window. There's a clawfoot tub in the bath along with a big basket of towels. Another room is decorated in peach, featuring a Texas-made Victorian-era bed. A third room has a sleigh bed and a fainting couch that converts into a single bed.

The Oxfords and their children live elsewhere, but they go out of their way to make you feel welcome. Breakfast is continental, with homemade breads and fruit.

In Stephenville you can visit the Historical House Museum Complex. Other nearby sites include Dinosaur Valley State Park, Fossil Rim Wildlife Ranch, and the historic village of Granbury.

Wise Manor
312 Houston Street
Jefferson, Texas 75657
214/665-2386
OWNER: Katherine Wise
3 guest rooms (1 private, 1 shared bath)
$45 double including breakfast
Personal check
Children accepted
No pets
Smoking permitted
Open year round

If you want to learn about the history of East Texas, especially the charming town of Jefferson, check into Wise Manor and settle down for a talk with town historian Katherine Wise.

Her Victorian peach-colored cottage proudly bears a Texas Historical Marker. Katherine has lived in the two-story home since 1929, and in the interim has been a significant force in the restoration effort which has transformed tiny Jefferson into a top visitor attraction.

The entire house is decorated with antiques and family memorabilia, resulting in an atmosphere of charm and comfort. Guests have the choice of a downstairs bedroom with a private bath and clawfoot tub, or of two upstairs rooms that share a bath. Double beds are in each bedroom; the larger upstairs room has an additional single bed and a TV.

Breakfast is served family-style, featuring croissants and a fruit compote.

31

Itineraries

These itineraries are our favorite things to see and do in or near some of the towns where an establishment in the book is located. All towns that appear in **bold** *have an establishment described in the book.*

EAST TEXAS

East Texas is pine forests, lakes, and meadowlands. Caddo Lake, mysterious with its moss-draped trees and maze of bayous, offers excellent fishing. The Big Thicket National Preserve is luxuriant with centuries-old trees, brilliant wildflowers, and flora found nowhere else in Texas.

The Alabama-Coushatta Indian Reservation, the oldest in Texas, is within the preserve. Not only is the Living Indian Village open to visitors, but mini-tours of the Big Thicket originate here.

East Texas is a good place to touch the history of Texas. Back in the 1800s, steamboats from New Orleans plied Caddo Lake. Over 200 a year docked in **Jefferson,** which became the largest city in the region. Today with a population of less than 3,000, Jefferson is a journey back to a slower era. Antebellum homes open for touring, antique shops, and Old South restaurants line the streets of this picturesque village. Riverboat excursions go to Caddo Lake or on moonlight serenade cruises. (Advice: Don't zip through Jefferson. Spend at least one night and take time to soak up its charm.)

Nearby **Marshall**, population 25,000, has a multitude of historic houses of its own. Most are open only during special weekends, but a driving tour puts you in touch with the spirit. Several are B&B lodgings.

Marshall can serve as a hub for enjoying other East Texas attractions, especially the Texas State Railroad. With 25 restored antique coaches, the train runs 25 miles through the heart of East Texas, connecting Rusk and Palestine.

Further south, **Nacogdoches** with a population of 28,000 is one of the most historic towns in Texas. Sites to visit include Old Stone Fort, built in 1779 as a Spanish trading post, and Millard's Crossing with restored 19th century buildings.

To the northwest, **Tyler** is a bustling business center with 70,000 residents. Tyler's best known visitor attraction is the municipal rose garden—more than 38,000 rose bushes in 500 varieties (peak season April-Oct.). The annual Rose Festival is in October. Historic homes are located in the Azalea District and in Charnwood. Tyler State Park, north of the city, is excellent for fishing, boating, and hiking.

HOUSTON AREA

Exuberant **Houston** has many dimensions—historic sites and sophisticated new architecture, glamorous malls and romantic turn-of-the-century shopping villages, ethnic eateries and gourmet restaurants.

A leader in the arts, Houston has a complete performing arts repertoire and an exciting variety of museums. Architecturally-grand Wortham Center, opened in 1987, is the home of the Houston Grand Opera and the Houston Ballet. The Alley Theater has a resident professional theater company presenting plays on two stages. Jones Hall is the home of the Houston Symphony Orchestra.

The Menil Collection museum, opened in 1987, is a rich display of art from primitive to ultra-modern. The Museum of Fine Arts has works from around the world, including a large collection of Remington westerns. The nearby outdoor sculpture garden has more than 30 works by such artists as Matisse, Calder, and Ellsworth Kelly. Bayou Bend is a museum within a museum. The house itself, set on spacious grounds, was the home of a prominent Houston philanthropist; inside is a fine collection of American art and furnishings.

Other attractions include the Museum of Natural Science and Planetarium, the Houston Zoo, Sam Houston Park (restored houses set in a park alongside the city's skyscrapers), and San Jacinto Battleground and Monument commemorating the site where Texas won its independence.

Astroworld/Waterworld is great for family entertainment. So is Fame City, a stylish indoor entertainment mall. The city's Children's Museum has participatory exhibits such as a video recording studio, computer center, and Texas frontier town. The Great Southwest Equestrian Center has thousands of acres of riding space, plus a large arena where horse shows are held on most weekends.

Johnson Space Center south of Houston is one of the most popular attractions in Texas. Self-guided tours lead to exhibits in seven buildings spread through the NASA complex.

GALVESTON

More than just a beach destination, **Galveston** has historic sites and cultural attractions, casual and fine dining, and lots of family entertainment.

Once Galveston was the largest and richest municipality in Texas. By the late 1800s it was dubbed "the New York of the Gulf." In 1900 a hurricane devastated the city, forever altering the course of its development.

Proud of its heritage, Galveston has a strong commitment to preservation. Visitor attractions range from a restored sailing ship to a historic railroad museum. City-wide, over 500 structures bear Texas Historical Commission Medallions. The East End Historical District is lined with wonderful old Victorian homes. Castle-like Bishop's Palace, built in 1877, is ranked by the American Institute of Architects as one of the nation's 100 most outstanding buildings. The renovated 1894 Grand Opera House, once played by Sarah Bernhardt and Anna Pavlova, hosts modern-day performances.

In downtown Galveston, the Strand National Historic Landmark District takes you back to the turn of the century with its gas streetlights and shops straight out of the pages of a Victorian novel. Put a coin in the nickelodeon, watch taffy being pulled at the candy store, shop for antiques and hand-made gifts.

The Railroad Museum (more than a collection of railroad cars), has displays that also transport you to an earlier era. A few blocks away is Galveston's own tall ship Elissa, a square-rigged merchant sailing ship that you can climb aboard and explore. Sea-Arama Marineworld, Seawolf Park (World

War II submarine to tour), and The Colonel paddlewheeler (daytime and evening cruises) add variety to an already rich menu of visitor attractions.

Well-designed for tourists, Galveston has a sightseeing train, trolley rides, horse-drawn carriages, and audio walking tours. Pick your favorite and explore the city.

Of course you'll also find all of the expected beachside activities. Anglers can choose from pier, surf, deep-sea, and bay fishing.

A city that celebrates year-round, Galveston has numerous festivals. The most popular are Mardi Gras, Dickens On the Strand (early December), Historic Homes Tour (May), and Jazz Festival (November). Reservations for accommodations should be made far in advance.

BLUEBONNETS TO PRAIRIE CHICKENS

Wherever you travel, whatever you see, it's hard to find anything more beautiful than a far-flung blanket of bluebonnets. Artists paint the scene again and again, but the reality far surpasses any representation. East of Houston there's a nugget of countryside where bluebonnets grow in profusion, blooming each spring and luring thousands of motorists along Bluebonnet Trails.

Whatever the season, this part of Texas has idyllic pastoral landscapes, historical interest, and country charm. It's the sort of countryside with a village every 15 miles, each one inviting you to stop awhile.

Washington-on-the-Brazos State Historical Park is a good place to start. Here is where the Texas Declaration of Independence was signed in 1836. From 1842 to 1846, Washington served as the capital of the Republic of Texas. The Star of the Republic Museum commemorates this portion of the Lone Star State's history.

Historic **Navasota**, a town of 6,000, is nearby. In addition to its own sites to tour, there's a winery to visit near Bryan.

To the south is **Chappell Hill**, once called "The Athens of Texas." The home of two colleges in the mid 1800s, Chappell Hill was an intellectual center. Today there are fewer than 400 people in the community, but homes from its grand era still stand. More than 25 structures have historical markers.

Bellville is bigger than Chappell Hill. It even has a town square. Antique shops abound in Bellville. So does rural charm.

On down the road in **Columbus**, population 4,000, there are historic homes to see, interesting shops to browse in, and a restored opera house. Called the City of Live Oaks, it's nostalgic and romantic.

Weimar, about 15 miles west of Columbus, is a country town with a look of the West. Weimar Country Inn, plus antique shopping and kolache-eating, are the best reasons to visit.

And now about prairie chickens. **Eagle Lake** is only 17 miles south of Columbus, and yet it has an entirely different look. Gone are the massive live oaks; instead, you gaze upon miles of grassland. Rice farming is the predominant industry. Duck and goose hunting is the most popular sport. Nearby is Attwater Prairie Chicken Refuge, a sprawling expanse dedicated to saving the declining prairie chicken population.

One of Eagle Lake's most prominent landmarks is The Farris 1912 hotel. During hunting season, November through January, The Farris caters to hunters.

Other towns of interest to visitors include Winedale with its music festivals, Round Top with a reconstructed historic village, and Egypt with a restored plantation.

AUSTIN AREA

Texas' capital city is renowned for its beauty. The pink granite State Capitol Building stands tall at one end of downtown. Nearby is the University of Texas with over 45,000 students. At the other end of the central business district is Town Lake, a gem of a lake with a beautifully landscaped shoreline. In mid-town is Old Pecan Street/Sixth Street, Austin's version of Bourbon Street, lined with restaurants, clubs, and shops.

Austin attractions include the LBJ Presidential Library and Museum, the O. Henry Home, and the Elizabet Ney Museum—once the studio of Texas' first eminent sculptress. The Laguna Gloria Art Museum displays 20th century art in a Mediterranean villa set on the shores of Lake Austin.

Children, whatever their age, will enjoy Barton Springs within Zilker Park. The spring-fed natural swimming pool is nearly as long as a football field. The nearby Rose Gardens and Oriental Gardens are well worth visiting.

Lake Travis, west of the city, is one of seven Highland Lakes, popular for fishing and boating. To the northwest, outside of Johnson City, LBJ Ranch is popular for touring.

About 40 miles north of Austin is the village of **Salado**, once a stagecoach stop on the Old Chisholm Trail. Life moves slowly in Salado. There are a handful of historic sites to see and a pleasant assortment of country shops to browse in—all to be enjoyed at a leisurely pace.

Southeast of Austin is **Bastrop**, another slow-paced town with a bent toward history. The oldest weekly newspaper in Texas is published in Bastrop. More than 130 sites are listed on the National Register of Historic Places. Bastrop State Park with boating and hiking is one mile from town.

When you're ready to sit back and absorb the essence of the Hill Country, head back to Austin to the Oasis Cantina. Dining terraces are tucked into a cliffside overlooking Lake Travis. The Mexican fare is wonderful, the mood is convivial. But the best part comes at sunset. A bell rings to announce its advent. Oooohs and ahhhs, as if in chorus, emanate from diners scattered throughout the multi-level terraces. At the great moment, just as the bright red ball slips below the horizon, the audience applauds. You may never happen to be at the Oasis again, but wherever else you are, sunset will take you back.

TEXAS HILL COUNTRY

Tranquil lakes and whitewater rivers, cedar-studded hillsides and craggy limestone cliffs—that's the beauteous Hill Country. Wildlife, especially white-tailed deer, is abundant. Seven Highland Lakes, popular for fishing and boating, stairstep their way northwest of Austin. The scenic Guadalupe River—popular for tubing, canoeing, and rafting—winds through the Hill Country. Other natural attractions include colorful caverns, most notably Natural Bridge and Inner Space.

Communities sprinkled through the Hill Country have individual character. **Fredericksburg** delightfully retains its German heritage. Historic buildings reflect the life of the early settlers, and restaurants serve locally made sausages and pastries. The one-time Steamboat Hotel houses the Museum of the Pacific War, a tribute to native son Fleet Admiral Nimitz.

New Braunfels, also settled by Germans, gives visitors a taste of Texas history combined with outdoor fun. Tour the Museum of Texas Handmade Furniture and the Sophienburg Museum (great introduction to local history). Slide down the Tube Chute at Prince Solms Park. Visit the winery at Gruene and stay to dance in the oldest dance hall in Texas. Spend an afternoon at Schlitterbahn, a water amusement park with the Cliffhanger Tube Chute, Schlittercoaster, and water slides. Wurstfest in November is the headliner event.

On the eastern edge of the Hill Country, the town of **San Marcos** is at the headwaters of the crystal clear San Marcos River. Tubing, canoeing, and kayaking are popular pursuits. At Aquarena Springs, you glide along in a glass-bottom boat.

To the west, **Kerrville**, on the banks of the Guadalupe, is a center for arts and crafts, music festivals, and summer youth camps. Sights to see include the Cowboy Artists of America Museum and the Hill Country Museum. The Kerrville area is a great hub for a family vacation, with lots of opportunities for outdoor recreation.

The tiny town of **Bandera** on the jade-green Medina River is at the center of Texas guest-ranch country. Its countryside, beautiful with rocky limestone cliffs, spring-fed streams, and stately trees, is also popular for hunting.

DALLAS/FORT WORTH METROPLEX

The metroplex is an intriguing mix of personalities, combining to form a dynamic destination. Sophisticated **Dallas** is to the east, **Fort Worth** with its distinctly Texan flavor is to the west, and fun-loving **Arlington** is in between. **Irving**, situated between Dallas/Fort Worth International Airport and Dallas, is the home of Las Colinas—a master-planned community with attractions of its own.

Dallas, a center for finance, fashion marketing, and technology, brims with cultural, shopping, and nightlife choices. The Dallas Museum of Art—focusing on 19th and 20th century American and European painting and sculpture—is the first facility to open in the city's downtown arts district. Set within the West End Historic District is West End Marketplace—a festive complex of shops, restaurants, and nightclubs.

Other sites include Old City Park with 25 historic buildings for touring, Fair Park with multiple museums, John F. Kennedy Memorial, and Southfork Ranch.

Fort Worth proudly wears the title of "Cowtown." The Stockyards Historical District is where you'll find its cowboy heritage on display. Western shops, restaurants, and saloons line the streets in an area that was once a major stop on the Chisholm Trail.

But there's another side to Fort Worth's personality. Renowned for its art collections, the city has an outstanding museum district. The Kimbell Art Museum is home to many European masterpieces. The Amon Carter Museum features the work of Frederic Remington and Charles Russell as well as other American artists including Georgia O'Keeffe and Winslow Homer. The Forth Worth Art Museum focuses on 20th-century works. The Museum of Science and History, the largest such museum in the Southwest, has an Omni Theater presenting simulated adventures such as hang-gliding and scuba diving.

And there's more—tranquil, beautiful Japanese Gardens, Log Cabin Village, Sundance Square (a restored Victorian-style shopping district), and the Water Garden in Fort Worth's downtown.

Arlington is a family entertainment center, with Six Flags Over Texas, Wet 'n Wild, and Texas Rangers Baseball. International Wildlife Park and Traders Village ("the Disneyland of Flea Markets") are nearby.

Irving's Texas Stadium is the home of the Dallas Cowboys. Visitors can tour nearby Valley Ranch to see the Cowboys training area and the cheerleaders' dance studio. In the community of Las Colinas, Mandalay Canal Walk is a mini-version of San Antonio's Riverwalk. Shops line the banks of the canal, and water taxis take visitors to area sights. "The Mustangs of Las Colinas" is one of the largest bronze sculptures ever created. Also within Las Colinas is the Dallas Communications Complex, a thriving film studio. Its National Museum of Communications has vintage recordings and broadcasts for viewing and listening.

GRANBURY COUNTRY
OPERA TO DINOSAURS

In the bustling Dallas/Fort Worth metroplex, life moves at a brisk pace. When you yearn for a simpler style, head to **Granbury**. The square at the center of town is the place to begin discovering this Victorian-style town. Hood County Courthouse on the square was restored in 1969, sparking interest in local restoration projects. Now antique stores, craft shops, and country-style restaurants surround the square.

Granbury Opera House, built in 1886, has outstanding productions, drawing audiences from throughout the Dallas/Fort

Worth metroplex. Old Hood County Jail, a western-style jail
built in 1885, is open for tours.

Near Granbury are Dinosaur Valley State Park, where you
can step inside dinosaur tracks (there's also a visitor center)
and Fossil Rim Wildlife Ranch with over 800 exotic animals
spread over cedar-studded hills.

SAN ANTONIO

The gateway to south Texas is **San Antonio**, one of the
most colorful cities in the U.S. Joyfully it retains its Spanish,
Mexican, and Texas heritage.

The Riverwalk, or Paseo del Rio, gently winds its way
through the heart of the city, flanked by European-style shops
and cafes. On the river itself riverboat taxis and sightseeing
barges cruise along. A few blocks away is the Alamo, the
shrine of Texas liberty.

There's much to see and do in San Antonio. On the
outskirts are four Spanish missions, established by Franciscan
friars early in the 18th century. At the heart of the city is
Hemisfair Plaza, the site of the 1968 Texas World's Fair and
now a top visitor attraction. Its Institute of Texas Cultures
highlights the 26 ethnic and cultural groups that shaped the
state.

Sea World, the 250-acre oceanarium kin to Sea World of
California and Sea World of Florida, is high on the list of
attractions.

El Mercado, a Mexican marketplace with shops and
restaurants, is a great place to savor the city's Mexican flavor.
La Villita Historic District is a charming walled village
adjacent to the Riverwalk. The site of a Spanish settlement
two centuries ago, it now has galleries, cafes, and shops in
restored buildings.

The McNay Art Museum, housed in a former private
mansion, has a collection of impressionist and post-
impressionist works. One gallery in the Museum of Art is
devoted to Mexican folk art. The Witte Museum focuses on
natural history.

Attractions especially good for children include Bracken-
ridge Park, San Antonio Zoo (one of the largest bird collections in the U.S.), Hertzberg Circus Museum, and Plaza
Theater of Wax with a spooky Theater of Horrors.

Find time for the performing arts in San Antonio. The
beautifully restored Majestic Theater is a work of art in itself.

Especially enjoyable are performances in open-air Arneson River Theater, overlooking the Paseo del Rio.

Only 14 miles west of San Antonio is a town with an entirely different history. **Castroville** is an Alsatian community settled in 1844. The immigrants built their homes of native limestone and cypress. About 100 of the houses still stand, some inhabited by descendants of the original settlers. The Alsatian culture permeates the community, not just in architecture but in customs. Castroville is a charming, slow-paced town—a good place to go antique hunting, with time out to sample the local bakeries.

CORPUS CHRISTI AREA

Texas' largest city on the Gulf of Mexico, **Corpus Christi** sparkles with activity. Not only does it have a large landscaped marina at its front door, but it serves as the northern gateway to Padre Island, most of which is a national seashore.

Corpus Christi Bay—dotted with sailboats, yachts, and excursion boats—is the city's focal point. You can rent sailboards, jet skis, and aqua cycles over at People Street T-Head. Nearby Water Street Market has several excellent seafood restaurants. Water taxis can give you a tour of the harbor or take you from Shoreline Boulevard to Corpus Christi Beach.

Also near the harbor are two museums well worth visiting. The Art Museum of South Texas has changing exhibits of fine art; Corpus Christi Museum is especially good for children with hands-on exhibits, a wonderful Barnum and Bailey room, and nature displays.

Across the bay on Mustang Island is **Port Aransas**, famed as a fishing destination. Anglers can take day-long trips into the Gulf for sailfish and marlin, or fish for trout, redfish, and drum from the jetties and pier.

Corpus Christi is a good hub for exploring nearby attractions. Aransas Wildlife Refuge, winter home of the whooping crane, is 60 miles north. Slow-paced Rockport, 30 miles northeast, is the site of an outstanding historic house, Fulton Mansion. Known as an artist community, Rockport has art studios and galleries open to the public. King Ranch, the world's largest working ranch, is 40 miles southwest (visitors permitted from 9 A.M. to 4 P.M.).

The Tex-Mex Express train links Corpus Christi to Laredo, offering a diversified combination of destinations. You can take a one-day round trip, or stay overnight in Laredo. (See La Posada in Laredo.)

SOUTH PADRE ISLAND

A two-mile-long bridge stretches across Laguna Madre connecting **South Padre Island** to the Texas mainland. A sliver of an island, it averages one-half mile in width along its 34 mile length. Port Mansfield Gulf Channel, opened in 1964, separates South Padre from the rest of Padre Island.

The town of South Padre, incorporated in 1973, is geared to tourism. Its shoreline is lined with gleaming highrises. North of town, the road continues for seven miles, paralleling a wildly beautiful undeveloped stretch of beach.

The beach is the star attraction at South Padre. The sand is white, the water is turquoise, and the climate is semi-tropical, making it a year-round destination. Vacationing here means sunning, swimming, surfing, strolling, shell-collecting, and sand-castle building—fun in the sun at a leisurely pace. Fishing is also a favored pursuit, with excellent bay and surf fishing as well as deep-sea excursions.

Back on the mainland, **Port Isabel** is a fishing village with a feeling of history. Its lighthouse is a state historic site.

Laguna Atascosa National Wildlife Refuge 20 miles northwest is excellent for bird-watching.

Matamoros, Mexico, only 25 miles south of South Padre, is a popular day trip, offering a glimpse of Mexico and shopping for Mexican crafts.

RIO GRANDE VALLEY

The Rio Grande Valley, paralleling the river that separates Texas and Mexico, is lush with palm trees and citrus groves. In this part of the country Hispanic and Anglo cultures mix, providing lots of local flavor.

Brownsville, Texas' southernmost city, is connected to Matamoros, Mexico, by a toll bridge. Sights within Brownsville include Gladys Porter Zoo, a 31-acre preserve with rare and endangered animals in natural surroundings.

McAllen is eight miles from Reynosa, Mexico. The McAllen International Museum has exhibits of Mexican folk art as well as local history.

West of McAllen is the historic town of **Rio Grande City**, retaining some of its early architecture. Following the river northward leads to Falcon Dam and International Reservoir, owned jointly by the U.S. and Mexico. Huge Falcon Lake is famed for fishing, especially for black bass and catfish.

North of the semi-tropical valley is **Laredo**, across the border from Nuevo Laredo. More kin to Mexico than any other major city in Texas, it has a colorful history dating back to the 1700s. Seven flags have flown over Laredo: Spain, France, Mexico, Texas, the Confederacy, the U.S., and the short-lived Republic of the Rio Grande, with Laredo as its capital.

FAR WEST TEXAS

A land of rugged beauty, west Texas is craggy mountains and a wide open desert, sprinkled with remnants of the past such as frontier forts and Indian trails. So beautiful is the region that it has two national plus several state parks.

Big Bend National Park is a dramatic blend of the Chihuahuan Desert and the Chisos Mountains. Long before you get to **Big Bend**, you leave civilization behind. According to legend, Chisos was an Apache word meaning ghost, and indeed, there is a mystical feel in these mountains. Driving through the park whets your appetite to see more. Hiking, back-packing, horseback riding, and white water rafting are excellent ways to envelop yourself in the grandeur.

Views from the South Rim are unbeatable. Here you are indeed on a rim. The vertical drop is 2,500 feet. Before you stretches a panorama so wide and so deep that no camera lens can capture it. Old Mexico is straight ahead. Surely no one else has ever been here. Before you is an untouched wilderness.

West of the park is tiny **Lajitas**, a slip of a town isolated in the midst of the starkly beautiful terrain. Once there was a military fort where the western-style town now stands.

The road between Lajitas and Presidio is an experience in itself. With grades as steep as 15 percent, the road roller-coasters over mountains, through canyons (you can almost touch the sheer walls), and across fields strewn with giant red boulders. Surely a sculptor shaped those mountains; surely an artist painted them in brilliant reds and white. All the while the Rio Grande flows below, sometimes with vigor, sometimes serene and slow. There's little sign of civilization here. You share the road with only a few others.

About 80 miles to the north are the gentler Davis Mountains. For the pioneers who settled the West, they offered a refuge. Fort Davis National Historic Site puts you in touch with this part of history.

Guadalupe Mountains National Park, opened in 1972, contains four of Texas' highest peaks. El Capitan, a sheer 1,000-foot cliff, is distinctive against the desert landscape. For daytrippers, McKittrick Canyon with beautifully varied vegetation is well worth visiting. A trail leads through the floor of the sheer-walled canyon. Guadalupe is primarily a backpacker's park, interlaced with miles and miles of trails. (The best place to stay here is in a backpacker's tent, high in the mountains, cuddled up with someone you love.)

Other sites to visit in Far West Texas are Monohans Sandhills State Park (4,000 acres of wind-sculpted sand dunes), Hueco Tanks State Historical Park (860 acres of caves and towering rock formations surrounded by desert), the Caverns of Sonora (delicate beauty), and McDonald Observatory near **Fort Davis** (visitor center open daily). At the observatory, visitors can look through the giant telescope only on the last Wednesday of each month; write ahead to make arrangements.

EL PASO TO SILVER CITY

In far west Texas where the wide open desert meets the foothills of the Rocky Mountains, **El Paso**—known to early explorers as the Pass of the North—is a blend of American cowboy, Spanish conquistador, and Southwest Indian heritages. Desperados, gold-rushers, traders, and cattlemen all played a part in its history.

Just across the Rio Grande is Juarez, Mexico—the largest city on the Mexican border. Residents and visitors move easily between the two cities, intermingling their cultures. Two-thirds of El Paso's residents are Hispanic. Throughout the city there's a South-of-the-Border flavor.

The city sprawls over 240 square miles. Old Spanish missions, unique museums, a western ranch with hayrides, and bargain shopping make El Paso a good destination for family vacations.

Within the city is the Tigua Indian Reservation, home of one of the oldest identifiable ethnic groups in Texas and one of the oldest Indian communities in North America. A tribe that nearly disappeared in the 20th century, the Tiguas re-united in recent years and set about preserving their culture. At their living pueblo you can see native dances, craft demonstrations, and historical displays. The restaurant is especially popular, serving spicy Indian dishes and bread baked in beehive ovens.

Other visitor attractions include Indian Cliffs Ranch (outdoor Western exhibits and steak restaurant), Fort Bliss (U.S. Army Air Defense Center for rocket research and combat training, variety of museums open to the public), the El Paso Museum of Art, and several Indian missions. Sunland Park for horse-racing is five minutes from downtown.

Half of the fun of visiting El Paso is going across the border. Attractions in Juarez include shopping, dog racing, and bullfighting.

Heading into New Mexico, about 45 miles northwest of El Paso at the foot of the Organ Mountains, is **Las Cruces**—a city of 45,000 basing its economy on agriculture, industry, and education (it's the home of New Mexico State University). Right next door to Las Cruces is tiny **Mesilla**, one of the most historic towns in the Southwest. Founded in 1598 and once a major stop on the Butterfield Trail Overland route, it is famed as the site of the signing of the Gadsden Purchase.

Silver City is about 100 miles northwest of Las Cruces (you turn north at Deming, recently famed for the annual Deming Duck Race). The countryside changes from desert shrubs to forests. Silver City, on the southern edge of the Gila Wilderness, is headquarters for Gila National Forest. The Gila Cliff Dwellings National Monument is about 35 miles north of town.

In 1870 Silver City was an overnight boom town, for indeed silver had been discovered. In more recent years its economy has been based on ranching and copper mining.

OKLAHOMA CITY AREA

Oklahoma was born on April 22, 1889. A gunshot signaled the start of the Land Run for the Unassigned Lands. About 10,000 pioneers staked their claims and then set about building a new life.

In the intervening years, cosmopolitan **Oklahoma City**, the state's capital, has come a long way. At its heart is a rich heritage. Indian culture is prominent, though today's Indians tend to be dressed in business attire. In June, 1987, a new annual event made its premier—Red Earth—a gathering of Indian tribes to celebrate their traditions, featuring an arts and crafts festival and competitions in such events as Pow Wow dancing.

The Kirkpatrick Center Museum Complex is a treasure house. Indeed it is a complex, with the Omniplex Science Museum, the Air Space Museum, the Center of the Indian, the International Photography Hall of Fame, and a planetarium. Other city attractions include the the National Cowboy Hall of Fame and Western Heritage Center, the Oklahoma Museum of Art, and the National Softball Hall of Fame.

About 30 miles north of downtown is **Guthrie**, Oklahoma's territorial capital and the first capital of the state. A town of 10,000 residents, Guthrie is a community that values its history. Approximately 100 red brick buildings, constructed in the late 1880s, still stand—considered to be the largest collection of commercial Victorian buildings in the U.S.

In addition to picturesque shops and country-style restaurants, the spectacular Scottish Rite Temple is a top visitor attraction.

TULSA AREA

Tulsa is a sophisticated city—rich in the arts, international restaurants, and shopping. Its heritage is Indian; its riches came from oil.

The Gilcrease Museum, built on the estate of oilman Thomas Gilcrease, is a poignant portrayal of the American frontier—the Indian, the cowboy, the pioneer. With over 8,000 paintings, thousands of artifacts from various Indian cultures, and a collection of rare books and manuscripts describing life in the New World, the Gilcrease is considered to be the most outstanding museum of its type in the world. Artists include Frederick Remington, Charles Russell, George Catlin, Olaf Seltzer, Winslow Homer, and Albert Bierstadt.

The Philbrook Museum of Art, housed in the Italianate villa of famed oil baron Waite Phillips, features Italian Renaissance painting and sculpture as well as an art collection from around the world.

In Claremore, about a 30 minute drive to the northeast, is the Will Rogers Memorial Museum. Galleries in the sprawling hilltop museum display memorabilia of the cowboy philosopher. Video tapes of his life are shown several times a day.

Opera, ballet, symphony, and theater all have a full repertoire in Tulsa. Tulsa's Performing Arts Center is a few steps from The Westin Hotel, Williams Center.

Other area attractions include Oral Roberts University and the Fenster Gallery of Jewish Art. Families can enjoy Tulsa Zoological Park and Big Splash Water Park.

But whatever else you do, make time for Rodgers and Hammerstein's *Oklahoma*, presented in an outdoor theater on the outskirts of Tulsa. Named in 1985 by the American Bus Association as one of the "Top 100 Events in North America," this musical extravaganza is thoroughly delightful, full of energy and zest. You'll leave the theater singing.

OKLAHOMA'S OUTDOORS

Oklahoma, home of over 70 Indian tribes and settled by hardy pioneers, maintains strong ties to the land. A state of lakes, plains, and rolling hills, some of its best attractions are outdoor adventures.

Oklahoma's Tourism and Recreation Department does an excellent job of operating resorts, each with its own personality and set of attributes. Lake Texoma Resort in south-central Oklahoma is on a 93,000 acre lake. Fishing for striped bass is a major draw. Roman Nose Resort, situated in red shale hills 70 miles northwest of Oklahoma City, has hiking trails and a natural rock swimming pool. Western Hills Guest Ranch, about 50 miles east of Tulsa, is on a lake of nearly 20,000 acres. Its countryside is rolling wooded hills. Wildlife is abundant near this resort, set within Sequoyah State Park.

In the northeast corner of the state is Grand Lake O' The Cherokees, a 59,000 acre lake with 1,300 miles of shoreline. Fishing is excellent, with largemouth and white bass, catfish, and sunfish as the favored catches. **Afton** is the center of resort activity.

Lake Eufaula, south of Tulsa and east of Oklahoma City, is the grandest lake of all. Its nickname is the Gentle Giant. Covering 102,000 acres, the lake is surrounded by hickory and elm trees, maples and pecans. Fishing, boating, and hiking are all popular.

Overall, Oklahoma has 560 parks, lakes, outdoor resorts, and campgrounds. Outdoor sports range from golf to tennis, canoeing to hunting, horseback riding to rockhounding.

ALBUQUERQUE

Home to one out of every three New Mexicans, **Albuquerque** is a pleasing mix of the old and the new. Old Town dates back to 1706. A sprawling assortment of adobes, the district brims with shops and restaurants, along with streetside Indian vendors selling their crafts. Simultaneously, Albuquerque serves as the high-tech hub of New Mexico. Its cultural life is sophisticated; its entertainment diversified.

Throughout the city there's evidence of the three cultures that have shaped Albuquerque—Indian, Spanish, and Anglo-American. Attractions include the Indian Pueblo Cultural Center, depicting the history of the state's 19 Indian pueblos, the Albuquerque Museum with the largest collection of Spanish colonial artifacts in the U.S., and the Maxwell Museum of Anthropology with Southwestern crafts.

Sandia Crest, at an elevation of 10,678 feet, is a year-round attraction. Situated just north of downtown, it provides a panoramic view of the city. A paved road leads to the top. Sandia Peak, popular for winter skiing and summer sightseeing, is accessible by tramway, chairlift, or a one-and-a-half mile trail from Sandia Crest. The tramway, said to be the world's longest with a 2.7 mile ride, glides over deep canyons and lush wooded terrain. A restaurant is atop Sandia Peak.

Maps for driving tours of the city are available from the Albuquerque Convention and Visitors Bureau. Choices include a trip through the Sandia Mountains; a Native American culture tour (Petroglyph State Park, Coronado State Monument, Isleta—a living pueblo); science and technology (Museum of Natural History with participatory exhibits, National Atomic Museum); nature (Rio Grande Zoo, Rio Grande Nature Center State Park), and shopping in districts ranging from historic to cosmopolitan.

In October, the city's skies are dotted with hot air balloons as it hosts the Albuquerque International Balloon Fiesta. Throughout the year there are a variety of colorful Indian dances and festivals.

SANTA FE AREA

Santa Fe's history, its architecture, its culture—all combine to make it truly The City Different. Founded in 1610, **Santa Fe** served as capital of the Spanish Kingdom of New Mexico and the Mexican province of Nuevo Mejico. It has been state capital since New Mexico gained statehood in 1912.

Some of the oldest buildings in the country are in Santa Fe. Spanish-Pueblo architecture unifies the city, giving it a distinct identity and beauty.

Art galleries and one-of-a-kind shops, museums and historic sites offer a near-inexhaustible list of things to do and places to see. The Plaza, now as when it was laid out by the Spanish, is the center of activity. Art workshops and galleries stretch along Upper Canyon Road.

Top sightseeing choices include the Palace of the Governors, St. Francis Cathedral, the Mission of San Miguel of Santa Fe, the Wheelwright Museum of the American Indian, and the Museum of International Folk Art. South of town is Rancho de las Golondrinas, a charming replica of a Spanish colonial village, with exhibits of such crafts as candlemaking and blacksmithing.

The Santa Fe Opera is one of the top companies in the world. Situated a few miles north of town, the open-air theater is dramatic in itself, overlooking the mountains. Performances are from early July though August.

Not only is Santa Fe one of the most popular tourist centers in the nation, but within an hour's drive are numerous other points well worth exploring. Nearby Indian pueblos include Nambe, **Pojoaque**, Picuris, **San Juan**, San Ildefonso, Santa Clara, **Taos**, and **Tesuque**. Bandelier National Monument, site of a prehistoric Indian culture, is 46 miles northwest. Pecos National Monument, 27 miles to the east of Santa Fe, preserves the ruins of an ancient Indian pueblo.

Los Alamos National Laboratory is 35 miles northwest. The quiet country town of **Galisteo** is 23 miles south. The High Road to Taos leads to the craft villages of **Chimayo**, renowned for its weavers; Cordova with its woodcarvers; and Truchas, another center of weaving.

Outdoor enthusiasts have a broad range of choices in the area, especially whitewater rafting on the Rio Grande and fishing, hiking, and horseback riding in the Santa Fe National Forest.

Santa Fe Basin ski area, 16 miles northeast of the city, has 38 trails—20 percent beginner, 36 percent intermediate, and 44 percent advanced. Three chair lifts take skiers up the slopes. Facilities are geared to day-use only, with no accommodations at the ski basin.

Whatever else you do in the Santa Fe area, enjoy feasting on regional cuisine. Some of the best known restaurants include The Shed (lunch only), Coyote Cafe, and Rancho de Chimayo (see Gourmet Getaways). And yet the best dining may be in the little cafe you discover on your own.

TAOS

Taos is New Mexico in microcosm. It's an art colony and a living pueblo, with outdoor adventures, museums of the Southwest, regional cuisine, and personable lodging.

The setting is a high valley at the foot of the Sangre de Cristo Mountains. To the west is a far-reaching desert plain. To the north are the mountains.

The town of Taos is smaller than you might expect, with approximately 3,600 residents. Indian, Spanish, and Anglo influences are intertwined, creating a colorful collage. The central plaza is the focal point of activity. Art galleries (more than 80 in the Taos area), boutiques, and restaurants lure you along the streets.

Pueblo de Taos, set within the Tewa tribe's 95,000 acres, is three miles northeast. Approximately 1,800 Indians live in the simple terraced adobe buildings, the oldest continuously inhabited structures in the U.S. By choice, their lifestyle is simple, with no electricity or running water. (Fees are charged for entering the pueblo; additional charges for cameras.)

Numerous sites within Taos put you in touch with its history and character. The Kit Carson Home, occupied by the famed Indian Scout from 1843 to 1868, is filled with memorabilia from his era. The D.H. Lawrence Ranch is 15 miles north of town. San Francisco de Assis Church, constructed over a 35 year period beginning in 1710, is an excellent example of Spanish churches. The Millicent Rogers Museum displays North American and Hispanic art and artifacts.

Much of Taos County is within Carson National Forest, providing a scenic playground. Each season brings its own special flavor. Golden aspen leaves give way to winter, and its snows cover the nearby mountains and attract skiers. Springtime is for fishing and hiking. Summer is popular for all sorts of outdoor recreation, including whitewater rafting on the Rio Grande. The Taos Box is an exhilarating 17-mile run through Rio Grande Gorge. Raft trips begin at Arroyo Hondo north of Taos.

(See also Taos Area Skiing. For skiers, staying in Taos is a good option, enabling you to vary your ski menu with day trips to Taos Ski Valley, Angel Fire, Sipapu, and Red River.)

Two companies provide accommodation reservation services for Taos: Taos Central Reservations 800-821-2437 US, 505-758-9767 NM and Taos Valley Resort Association 800-992-SNOW US, 505-776-2233 NM.

TAOS AREA SKIING

Taos Ski Valley

Some of the best skiing in the American West is at Taos Ski Valley. Famed for its steep slopes, the ski resort resembles a Swiss village, with European-style lodgings clinging to the mountainsides. Founded in 1955, Taos is not a glitzy new resort. Instead, it has a look of genuineness, almost quaintness.

Although there are beginner slopes at Taos, the ski destination is best known for its expert runs, and first-time skiers are often intimidated by the terrain. The top elevation is 11,819 feet; vertical drop is 2,612 feet. Six double and one triple chairlift take skiers up the slopes. Of the 71 runs, 51 percent are expert, 25 percent intermediate, and 24 percent beginner.

Taos' ski school, with nearly 100 full-time instructors, prides itself on small classes and personal attention. Children's classes start at age three. The Kinderkaifig Program, ages three to six, is a combination of ski lessons and indoor activities.

Shuttle service connects Taos Ski Valley and Taos. Special shuttles go to area attractions. The ski valley is 19 miles from downtown Taos.

Ski season is from Thanksgiving until early April. Lodging packages—some with meals, lift tickets, and ski lessons—are available in the ski valley and in town lodges. You can make reservations at any area lodges by calling 800-992-SNOW (US), or 505-776-2233 in New Mexico.

Note: If you're staying in a condo on the slopes, buy groceries before ascending the mountain.

Angel Fire

Angel Fire, 26 miles east of Taos, is a sprawling village covering over 12,000 acres in the Moreno Valley. A composite of homes, condominiums, and recreational facilities, it's a year-round playground.

Despite an 18-hole golf course, six tennis courts, 37-acre fishing lake, and horseback riding, Angel Fire's number one priority is its ski program. With 55 trails—78 percent of which are beginner and intermediate—it's a good destination for families.

The top elevation is 10,680 feet; vertical drop is 2,180 feet. The longest run, "Headin' Home," is a three-and-a-half mile beginner run. Six lifts go up the mountain; lift lines are usually short.

Sixty percent of Angel Fire's mountain is covered by a snowmaking system. Ski season is from mid November through early April.

In addition to downhill, Angel Fire has cross-country skiing, complete with equipment rental and instruction. Snowmobiling is also popular. For the vacationer, there's snowmobile rental and instruction; for the racing enthusiast, there are monthly competitions.

Winter resort activities include hayrides, campfire cookouts, teen activities, sightseeing tours, and swimming in a heated pool. Little Angels daycare provides supervision for children ages six weeks to 11 years, with indoor activities and fun in the snow.

Numerous ski packages are available, some for families and others for adults.

NORTHEAST NEW MEXICO
FISH TO CATCH AND STORIES TO TELL

Back in 1864, Lucien Bonaparte Maxwell became the owner of probably the largest private estate in the U.S.—1.7 million acres stretching across northeastern New Mexico and into Colorado.

The land, then and now, is wild and rugged, encompassing timbered mountains and grassy valleys. One branch of the Santa Fe trail led from the Great Plains up over Raton Pass at an elevation of 7,834 feet. From the pass, you look upon the Rocky Mountains rising in the distance.

About 40 miles southwest of the pass, near the town of **Cimarron**, Maxwell built a fortress-style home. (Today it's part of Philmont Scout Ranch.) Later, he built a mansion, and Cimarron sprang up around it.

Over the years Cimarron developed a reputation for being a wild and wooly town; it was a reputation well-deserved. Outlaws like Billy the Kid, Clay Allison, and Black Jack Ketchum frequently came to call. (See St. James Hotel.)

Today's Cimarron is a quiet little ghost of a town. Lucien Maxwell's grist mill is now a museum, filled with four floors

of history. The old stone jail, the original town plaza and
other pre-1880s buildings tell the town's story.

The countryside, especially to the north and to the west of
Cimarron, is rich in wildlife, and the waters teem with fish.
Eagle Nest, at an elevation of 8,200 feet, is known for its trout
fishing.

To the south of Cimarron, about 60 miles as the crow flies,
is **Las Vegas**, another stopover on the Santa Fe Trail. (Two
branches of the trail entered New Mexico; the branch passing
through Las Vegas was called the Cimarron Cutoff.) By the
1880s Las Vegas had become a leading commercial center of
the West.

Today's Las Vegas has 14,000 residents. It's a town that's
proud of its history, preserving a downtown historical district
and residential sections with beautiful Victorian homes.
Fishing and hunting are popular pursuits.

CHAMA

Just south of the Colorado border, within the Rocky
Mountains at an altitude near 8,000 feet, **Chama** is a popular
center for outdoor recreation. A land of ponderosa pine
forests, rolling grasslands, lakes and rivers, it's an excellent
setting for fishing, hunting, and hiking. During the winter,
cross-country skiing, snowmobiling, and ice fishing are
favored activities.

The top visitor attraction is the Cumbores and Toltec Scenic
Railroad, running between Chama, New Mexico, and
Antonito, Colorado. The historic narrow gauge steam train
winds though 64 miles of Rocky Mountain country, running
daily from mid June to mid October. Make reservations as far
ahead as possible.

From Chama, the train stops at mid-way point Osier,
Colorado. You can either ride the train round-trip to Osier;
ride the train one way to Antonito and return by van; or ride
the train to Antonito, stay overnight, and return by train the
next day.

SOUTH CENTRAL NEW MEXICO
HORSE-RACING TO GOLF IN THE SKY

Lincoln National Forest spreads across the Capitan and
Sierra Blanca Mountains to the north and the Sacramento

Mountains to the south. Forests of fir, juniper, and pine—laden with snow in the winter—provide a cool retreat in the summer.

Ruidoso is both a winter and summer playground. Ski Apache, with 38 trails and eight chair lifts, is 16 miles northwest of town. (No accommodations on the ski slopes.) During the rest of the year the area is popular for hiking, camping, and fishing; nearby Bonito and Nogal Lakes are favored fishing spots. Ruidoso Downs, featuring quarter horse and thoroughbred racing from May through September, draws thousands of visitors.

Tiny **Cloudcroft**, at an elevation of 8,600 feet, is a getaway destination. In winter there's skiing at Ski Cloudcroft—25 trails and one chair lift. Snow-making covers 60 percent of the ski area. Cross-country skiing, snowmobiling, and ice skating are other winter escapades.

Summertime is golfing on one of the highest courses in the world. There's also horseback riding, hiking, and visiting nearby attractions, especially Sacramento Peak Observatory.

Carlsbad Caverns National Park is 76 miles southeast of Ruidoso.

PHOENIX AND VALLEY OF THE SUN

Set within the rolling Sonoran Desert, **Phoenix** is a magnet for vacationers. Its resorts are among the best in the world. Not only are there 85 golf courses and more than 1,000 tennis courts in the area, but you can horseback ride, soar, sail, balloon, ride a riverboat, fish, hike, and pan for gold. Sophisticated shopping and dining and a broad range of cultural activities enrich the menu.

Valley of the Sun is not a geographic term but is used to refer to the 20-plus communities around Phoenix. **Scottsdale** is the resort center, with numerous resorts spread along Scottsdale Road and E. Scottsdale Drive. **Carefree** is to the north. **Litchfield Park** is far to the west.

Sites to visit in the Greater Phoenix area are wonderfully diversified. The Desert Botanical Garden has an enormous collection of cacti, desert flowers, and unusual plants. The Arizona Living History Museum is a complex of buildings depicting the region's history—from a miner's camp to a Victorian mansion. The Heard Museum depicts Southwest Indian life, with such displays as Kachina dolls, Navajo weaving, and Zuni jewelry. The desert home of Frank Lloyd

Wright, now a school of architecture, is open for visitors. And at the Cosanti Foundation you can see urban planner Paolo Soleri's designs for futuristic cities.

Other attractions include Frontier Town in Cave Creek, Soleri's futuristic town Arcosanti in Cordes Junction, Fountain Hills World's Highest Fountain, Heritage Square in Phoenix, Phoenix Art Museum, and Arabian horse ranches in the Scottsdale area.

Phoenix is also popular as a hub for exploring other parts of Arizona. Day trips include Apache Trail, which winds through the desert and mountains to the town of Globe, Mongollon Rim with a face of multi-colored rock (Zane Grey country), Montezuma Castle and Well, Prescott, and Sedona. The Grand Canyon is a five hour drive.

Winter season is prime time in the Phoenix area. Summer rates at resorts are reduced as much as 50 percent.

The Phoenix and Valley of the Sun Convention and Visitors Bureau operates a toll-free number enabling you to make reservations at over 100 resorts and hotels in the area as well as at Grand Canyon National Park Lodges (800-528-0483 US, 800-221-5596 AZ).

PRESCOTT TO SEDONA

About 35 miles north of Phoenix you leave the flat desert and begin to climb. By the time you reach **Prescott**, the elevation is over 5,000 feet. Surrounded by forested mountains, the one-time capital of Arizona Territory is a quiet town of 20,000 residents.

Prescott hasn't always been quiet. Truth is, before the turn of the century it was a rip-roaring town. In 1863, gold was discovered in the central Arizona highlands. A year later, Prescott was born. Its Whiskey Row became the whooping-up place for gold-rushers.

At the Sharlot Hall Museum you can walk into the town's early days. A collection of historic buildings, it chronicles Prescott's history. (Sharlot Hall was a poet, historian, and preservationist. She was one of the first women elected to the Arizona Women's Hall of Fame.) A folk arts fair is held at the museum complex in the spring, featuring such crafts as spinning, weaving, wood-carving, and blacksmithing.

The Smoki Museum displays artifacts of the ancient Southwestern Indian. The Smoki People, organized in 1921, are white men and women dedicated to preserving the Indian way of life. The group has become famed for its production of Indian ceremonials and the Smoki Snake Dance.

Scenic drives proliferate around Prescott. One of the most scenic is over Mingus Mountain to **Jerome**. The pages of *Arizona Highways* come alive as the road twists and turns, then opens onto incredibly beautiful views.

Jerome is a near-ghost town, re-born. It clings, literally clings, to the mountainside. Walk along its streets to shops, a museum, and one of the most atmospheric B&Bs in the Southwest.

Then on to magical **Sedona**, set in beautiful Red Rock Country. There awaits a spectacle of red spires and buttes, pinnacles and mesas. The center of tourism is at the junction of US 89A and Highway 179. Within a few blocks is Tlaquepaque—a mini-village of arts and crafts shops, reminiscent of the area in Guadalajara for which it is named.

To the north of town winds Oak Creek Canyon, thickly wooded and wonderfully scenic. To the south is the Village of Oak Creek. Here the look is entirely different—equally beautiful, but with bare red rocks in prominence. West of town is mysterious Boynton Canyon, spectacular with its red monoliths and wind-sculpted formations.

There's much to do in Sedona. Jeep tours take you deep into Red Rock Country. Hiking, horseback riding, and fishing are also good options. Renowned as an art center, Sedona has a profusion of galleries and shops.

An interesting side-trip is to Montezuma Castle National Monument to see prehistoric cliff dwellings within a great limestone cliff.

FLAGSTAFF TO GRAND CANYON

Flagstaff, elevation 7,000 feet, is on the Coconino Plateau at the foot of the San Francisco Peaks. With a population of 35,000, it's a slow-paced sort of town, ideal as a hub for exploring the area's fantastic array of natural wonders.

Ten miles to the northeast is Sunset Crater National Monument. Continuing on US 89 for 27 miles takes you to Wupatki National Monument, the site of prehistoric Indian ruins.

East of Flagstaff on I-40, only seven miles from town, is Walnut Canyon National Monument. Wooded trails lead down into the canyon to Indian cliff dwellings tucked beneath limestone ledges. The visitor center is excellent, with hands-on exhibits.

Meteor Crater, measuring three miles in circumference, is 46 miles east of Flagstaff. To the southeast are Mary, Mormon and Ashurst Lakes, popular for fishing and boating.

Oak Creek Canyon is 12 miles south of Flagstaff on US 89A. To the north is Fairfield Snow Bowl, with winter skiing and summer sky-rides. The Museum of Northern Arizona and Lowell Observatory are also a short distance north of town.

The grandest sight of all, **Grand Canyon**, is 80 miles to the north. Driving along the rim, hiking down trails, riding mule-back, and flying over the canyon via helicopter—all give you different perspectives of the spectacular chasm. The South Rim is the center of tourist activity, with a full range of services. The North Rim, only 15 miles by air but about 200 miles by road, also has accommodations. The mood is more tranquil to the north; the setting is wooded and serene.

WICKENBURG

Folklore has it that back in the early 1860s, Henry Wickenburg vented his anger at his ornery ole mule by striking it with a rock. But Henry struck more than he bargained for—a lot more. When the rock hit ground (whether it ever reached its intended target, we'll never know), it split open to reveal a streak of gold.

Indeed, there was gold in them thar hills. The Vulture Mine proved to be one of Arizona's richest. Life was fanned to a frenzy in the gold rush days. You can still see the "jail tree" in downtown **Wickenburg**, used by lawmen to chain up bad guys. (That was before the town could afford an honest-to-goodness jail.)

Desert Caballeros Western Museum on Frontier Street depicts the town's early way of life. But the best way to get in tune with the Old West is to stay at a guest ranch.

TUCSON

Plan to spend a long time in **Tucson**. If you don't, you'll always regret it. There are sights to see, canyons to explore, mountains to hike in, horses to ride, golf courses to play on, outstanding restaurants to dine in. Tucson itself deserves as long as you can possibly spend. Then there are day trips to a score more places.

Once you're in Tucson, whatever choices you make, you can't help but be fascinated by the saguaro cactus. The Sonoran Desert is the only place that it grows. Many are as tall as 30 or 40 feet, some even taller. With multiple arms growing in every direction, each cactus is different. It's easy to understand why the Indians believed that the cacti dance. As soon as a human looks at them, they stop—freezing their arms in all sorts of contortions.

Although Arizona is the youngest state in the continental U.S., Tucson is the oldest continually inhabited settlement in the country. When Father Eusebio Francisco Kino, a Jesuit missionary from Spain, first visited the area in 1687, he found the land inhabited by Pima and Sobairpuri Indians.

One of the most famous sites in the Tucson area is Mission San Xavier del Bac. Father Kino founded a mission several miles from the present site. When Apaches destroyed the original San Xavier in the late 18th century, Franciscan fathers built the present one. A mix of Moorish, Byzantine, and Mexican architecture, the cool white structure is known as The White Dove of the Desert. Open for visitors, it is still an active mission.

Here's a taste of Tucson highlights:

Arizona-Sonora Desert Museum
A combination zoo, aquarium, botanical garden, and natural history preserve spread over 12 acres; rated as one of the top zoos in the country.

Old Tucson
Replica of Tucson in 1880s; built as a movie set in 1940 and still used for movie productions; also a western theme park with shootouts and street brawls, stagecoach rides, and Wild West entertainment.

Old Town Artisans
Adobe with more than 300 local artists exhibiting their work.

University of Arizona
Planetarium, Southwest Indian art, history museum, art museum, Center for Creative Photography.

Historical displays and sites
Arizona Historical Society (near University of Arizona); John C. Fremont House, Fort Lowell.

Saguaro National Monument
Two sections of park preserving the giant cacti—Rincon Mountain section east of town, Tucson Mountain section to the west; visitor center at Rincon Mountain section; hiking/nature trails in both areas.

Colossal Cave
Called the largest dry cavern in the world (no one has ever discovered its end); famed as a robber's hideaway; spectacular colors.

Mount Lemmon
The highest peak in the Catalina Mountains (9,157 feet); the drive up from the desert goes through six climatic zones, as in traveling from Mexico to Canada; picnicking, fishing in trout-stocked lake; skiing in winter, sightseeing via chair lift in summer (southernmost ski area in continental U.S.).

Sabino Canyon
Streams, waterfalls, hiking trails, picnicking; no vehicles allowed—access by tram.

Kitt Peak National Observatory
Largest collection of ground-based optical telescopes in the world; exhibits, films, guided tours.

SOUTHEAST ARIZONA

This is the land of Cochise and Geronimo, of gun-slingers and gold-rushers, of pioneer families and the U.S. Cavalry. It's the Old West, kept alive by landscapes and attractions well worth discovering.

The countryside is high-desert valleys and gentle green canyons, centered by the Dragoon Mountains. **Bisbee**, an old copper mining town tucked away in the Mule Mountains, is one of the most interesting towns in all of the Southwest. Turn-of-the-century buildings line incredibly steep streets on mountains' faces.

The copper mine closed in the mid-1970s, but Bisbee certainly didn't die. Instead it began attracting artists, city folk fleeing metropolitan life, and tourists. Today it's a delightful expedition into another era.

Tours of the Queen Mine are led by old miners, all with stories to tell. By the end of the tour, you're almost a miner yourself—equipped with a hard-hat, slicker, and lamp. Other sights to help you soak up the flavor are Brewery Gulch (once a row of saloons and brothels, now converted into shops), the Mining and Historical Museum, and the Lavender Pit Mine (named for a mine manager, not the color of the mine).

West of Bisbee is **Douglas**, a town with historic buildings including the early 1900s Gadsden Hotel. Be sure to step inside and see its stained-glass murals and the white marble staircase. Douglas got its start as the site of annual roundups for area ranches. The Mexican village of Agua Prieta is just across the bridge.

Throughout the countryside are places to explore—Chiricahua National Monument with natural rock sculptures and the remnants of early ranches (hiking trails); Old Fort Bowie, established to protect travelers going through Apache Pass; Cochise Stronghold, a granite fortress where Cochise sought refuge from the U.S. Cavalry; Tombstone with Boot Hill Cemetery and the OK Corral; and the ghost towns of **Pearce**, **Gleeson**, and **Courtland**.

32

Glossary

Adobe: sun-dried brick, made of mud and straw

Adobe-style Building: structure in which walls are built of adobe bricks, covered with mud plaster; roof built by suspending large beams (vigas) from walls, with latillas arranged on top of vigas, covered over by straw and then soil

Carne Adovada: pork cooked in red hot chili

Casita: Spanish word meaning "small house"; used as equivalent of villa

Fonda: inn or restaurant

Hacienda: an estate, especially one used for ranching; the main house on the estate

Huevos Rancheros: fried eggs covered with spicy red sauce, served on top of tortillas

Kiva: a large ceremonial chamber, wholly or partially underground, used by the Pueblos

Kiva Fireplace: molded fireplace, usually in corner of room; also referred to as "adobe fireplace" or "beehive fireplace" (The term is commonly used but considered to be a misnomer.)

Latilla: small wooden poles laid side by side atop main support beams (vigas) to form a ceiling

Metate: stone with bowl-shaped depression, used for grinding corn

Posada: lodge or inn

Pueblo: multiple dwelling, most typically built of adobe; an Indian village; also, a member of a group of Indian peoples living in pueblo villages

(First called "pueblos" by Spanish explorers, these dwellings as built by native Americans are many-roomed structures of two to seven stories, arranged so that the roof of one building was the "front yard" of the one above. Modern-day "pueblo" architecture mirrors this historic style.)

Rincon: Spanish word for corner or nook

Saguaro: giant cactus that grows in the Sonoran Desert in southern Arizona and the state of Sonora, Mexico; tall green columns with as many as 50 branches, attaining heights of up to 60 feet

Santos: Spanish word for saint; used to refer to handcarved wooden religious figures

Sopaipilla: puffy fried bread, thought to have originated in what is now New Mexico

Territorial-style: style of Adobe construction: typically a one-story flat-roofed adobe, symmetrical in design with a central hall, modified Greek revival trimwork, often painted white; in New Mexico, dating back to the mid-19th century

Viga: large exposed logs which form the support for a ceiling

33

Recommended Guidebooks

We recommend these books as excellent sources of informa-tion for sightseeing and restaurant suggestions. This chapter was exerpted from **Going Places: The Guide to Travel Guides** *by Greg Hayes and Joan Wright, to be published by The Harvard Common Press in October 1988.*

THE SOUTHWEST

American Jewish Landmarks: A Travel Guide and History, Volume 4: The West
by Bernard Postal and Lionel Kappman, Fleet Press, 1986, 320 pages, paper, $12.95
  This guide is part of a scholarly four-volume set, well suited to the interested traveler. It makes available an immense amount of history and sightseeing materials with thumbnail biographies of important individuals, details on sites and landmarks, facts on national and local Jewish institutions and a great deal more. The most extensive, well-researched book of its kind.

American Southwest in 22 Days. See *22 Days in American Southwest* below.

Ancient Cities of the Southwest: A Practical Guide to the Major Prehistoric Ruins of Arizona, New Mexico, Utah, and Colorado
by Buddy Mays, Chronicle Books, 1982, 132 pages, paper, $7.95

In this beautifully done book Hays offers thoughtful descriptions of each ruin located in the local and national monuments, tribal parks, primitive areas and national parks of four western states. Included are notes on location, access, and, where applicable, a rather dated summary of the hours, facilities, and interpretive services available. An excellent overview.

Bicycle Touring in the Western United States
by Karen and Gary Hawkins, Random House, 1982, 390 pages, paper, $9.95

The Hawkinses sure know how to write an enjoyable book. This title contains more than one hundred pages on equipment, preparation, planning, the hazards of the road, camping out. Starting from square one, they introduce you to the Abcs of touring, then plot some great tours through all of the western states: the Southwest, Great Basin, Rocky Mountains, and Pacific Northwest. Each tour is fully described down to the nearest grocery store. It would be nice to see an update, but most information is still perfectly usable. The states of the Southwest included are Arizona and New Mexico.

The Condo Lux Vacationer's Guide to Condominium Rentals in the Mountain Resorts
by Jill Little, Random House, 1986, 338 pages, paper, $9.95

The Condo Lux Vacationer's Guide to Condominium Rentals in the Southwest and Hawaii
by Jill Little, Random House, 1986, 330 pages, paper, $9.95

Each title profiles about 150 condominiums available for your next vacation rental. The profiles give you detailed information as to the number of guests that can stay, the number of rooms, whether there is air conditioning, linens provided, maid service, etc. If these guides are kept up-to-date, they will be a real help in surveying the vacation rental market. The books also contain information on a newsletter available to learn the latest news in the world of condominium rentals. Note that the Mountain Resorts volume includes New Mexico.

Earth Treasures: Volume 4: The Southwestern Quadrant
by Allan Eckert, Harper and Row, 1987, 740 pages, cloth (flexible), $16.95

If you are one of those people who has the urge to look for fossils, rocks, or minerals on those trips into the country, this volume is the one to have. Here are literally hundreds of specific locations to explore. The format of the book is to arrange each state by county, plot each interesting location on a county map, describe the locations and what types of collectibles are to be expected in that area. Via the index you can sort out all the various areas that might have your favorite type of rock or fossil. The guide is set up for every interested person not just the devoted rock hound. It can add a whole new measure of fun to your vacation life.

Fielding's Spanish Trails in the Southwest
by Lynn and Lawrence Foster, William Morrow and Co., 1986, 302 pages, paper, $12.95

One of three guides from Fielding that structure themselves around three famous trails of the western United States. This book should prove of considerable interest to history buffs as it is laced with many descriptions and quotations from those who were part of the creation of this famous trail. Entwined with the historical pieces is a good deal of detail on what to see, where to go, walking tours, hotels, restaurants, etc.

The Great American Runner's Guide: Western States Edition
by Edward Moore, Beaufort Books, 1985, 141 pages, paper, $6.95

Running for the traveler in the major cities in the west will be made easier by this well-done guide. The excellently drawn maps of suggested running paths include the location of all the major hotels nearby. There is also a helpful narrative on each run as well as addresses and phone numbers of nearby racquetball facilities and athletic goods stores. Covers major towns in the entire Rocky Mountain/Great Basin region plus Alaska (Anchorage only), Arizona, California, Hawaii (Honolulu only), and New Mexico (Albuquerque only).

Great Hot Springs of the West
by Bill Kaysing, Capra Press, 1984, 208 pages, paper, $9.95

A comprehensive guide to hot springs in Arizona,

California, Colorado, Idaho, Montana, Nevada, New Mexico, Oregon, Utah, Washington, and Wyoming. Locations, descriptions, whether you will need a bathing suit, price and phone numbers when there are any, and an appendix filled with good detail maps. Two hundred hot springs are described; nearly 1,700 can be located on the detail maps—the remainder all free—flowing and yours for the finding!

The Great Towns of the West
by David Vokac, West Press, 1985, 464 pages, paper, $14.95

This is a guide to out-of-the-way vacation spots, each one a "great town" in its area. The author, David Vokac, defines a great town as "an independent, unspoiled community rich in human-scale charms and scenic splendor." For each town that meets his criteria, he provides a good overview, including detailed notes on history, weather, etc., as well as some well-described possibilities for lodging of every sort, restaurants, camping, shopping, nightlife, sightseeing, special events, and just general enjoyment. This is a great idea book and includes towns in Arizona and New Mexico.

Hiking the Southwest: Arizona, New Mexico and West Texas
by Dave Ganci, Sierra Club Books, 1983, 384 pages, paper, $9.95

One of a series of small, pocket-sized guides for the hiker and the walker. It describes a myriad of trails of every length and contains a good, well-organized planning and preparation section. Each hike is carefully detailed, topographical maps referenced, and important points summarized. Good notes on natural history topics are also included in this excellent guidebook. Bear in mind that there may be the occasional trail that has been altered since the guide was written, since it is not updated with any frequency.

Hot Springs and Hot Pools of the Southwest
by Jayson Loam and Gary Sohler, Wilderness Press, 1985 (2nd edition), 192 pages, paper, $12.95

A good resource to available hot tubs/spas in motels and inns along your route as well as good descriptions of improved and unimproved hot pools throughout Arizona, California, Nevada, and New Mexico. Good location maps and interesting photos supplement this quality guide.

Indian Villages of the Southwest: A Practical Guide to the Pueblo Indian Villages of New Mexico and Arizona
by Buddy Mays, Chronicle Books, 1985, 105 pages, paper, $8.95

A thoughtfully prepared guide to 18 picturesque small Indian pueblos, all but one of which is located in New Mexico. A bit of history and thought-provoking discussion is combined with practical information on access, when non-Indians can visit, any admission charges or permission needed to enter, what types of photography are permissible, any available interpretive services, special ceremonies, and an overview of arts and crafts produced by the pueblo. An excellent resource.

Insight Guides: American Southwest
by APA Productions, Prentice Hall Press, 1985, 384 pages, paper, $15.95

One of the wonderful Insight Guide series. Produced by a Singapore company, each guide weaves an interesting text through a potpourri of spectacular photographs. But don't think they are simply picture books; there is a vast amount of information inside as well. They dedicate a good, meaty fifty pages or so to the history, geography, and people of each area. Then they will take you on a guided tour of all the major areas—the backcountry too—as well as providing special features on areas of unusual interest, parks, etc. Their "guide in brief" at the back does a commendable job with practical details, including respectable lists of lodging and accommodations.

The Interstate Gourmet: Texas and the Southwest
by Barbara Rodriguez and Tom Miller, Summit Books, 1986, 232 pages, paper, $6.95

Have you ever been whizzing down the interstate when the hunger pangs set in? What to do? It is almost too depressing to deal with—another greasy spoon or fast food joint. Eating is supposed to be fun. Well, the Interstate Gourmet series, of which this book is a part, is the answer to your prayers. Exit by exit this guide will tell you what is just down the road that's really worth the time. Directions, hours, and a great, informative review. A few of these selections might have gone out of business since the book was last revised, but the choices are almost endless. If your having a problem, hop in the car and drive down the road a few miles more. There's great food ahead! For the interstate driver, this book is simply a miracle.

Journey to the High Southwest: A Traveler's Guide
by Robert Casey, The Globe Pequot Press, 1988 (3rd edition), 450 pages, paper, $16.95

The classic guide to the Four Corners region and the Santa Fe area has gotten even better in this third, expanded edition. Let Casey take you on an exciting tour of the natural wonders, archaeological ruins, Indian reservations, parks, and historic sites of this magnificent region. This edition includes tour information to the Flagstaff, Arizona and Albuquerque, New Mexico areas, the new Anasazi Heritage Center near Dolores, Colorado, and a revised and greatly expanded shopping and buying guide for southwestern Indian arts and crafts. Great guides simply don't get much better than this.

Landmarks of the West: A Guide to Historic Sites
by Kent Ruth, The University of Nebraska Press, 1986, 309 pages, paper, $17.50

A popular guide since its issue in 1963, now recently updated. Beautifully designed, well-written, with a fascinating collection of new and old photographs and drawings, this is a thoroughly classy, completely intriguing guide to dozens of historic sites through the entire west—all the states west of the Mississippi River. For history buffs, this is definitely recommended reading.

Senior Guide: Day-Hiking in the Southwestern National Parks and Monuments
by James Campbell, WestPark Books, 1986, 220 pages, paper, $11.95

If you are a novice or fairly inexperienced hiker, senior citizen or not, Campbell has a lot of words of experience to share with you. Nearly half of the book is spent on an excellent discussion on planning, equipment and clothing needs, hiking hardware that is worth the weight, safe hiking strategies, and more. Campbell, an ecologist and former park ranger, shares his selection of the best day-hike trails throughout the national parks and monuments of the southwest. He grades each hike, gives you the elevations you will experience, distances, best seasons to go, plants and animals to look for, and other special considerations (such as the presence or absence of water!). Just a superb little book. Campbell is also working on future volumes on the Pacific Northwest, Rocky Mountains, and the Intermountain West. Fills a real need—and does it magnificently!

The Sierra Club Guide to the National Parks of the Desert Southwest
Sierra Club Books, 1984, 352 pages, paper, $14.95

Since the Sierra Club was founded by John Muir, who fought so hard to create the magnificent Yosemite National Park (among other battles), it should come as no surprise that their national park series, of which this book is a part, is of a quality that would make John proud. This guide book is just chock full of information on the park, its history, its facilities, its points of interest, its hiking paths, its natural history, its geology, beautiful photos. trips and tours to take, food, lodging, and much, much more. Very well done.

The Sierra Club Guide to the Natural Areas of New Mexico, Arizona, and Nevada
by John and Jane Perry, Sierra Club Books, 1985, 412 pages, paper, $10.95

The Natural Areas guides, of which this is a part, include the national parks of the region, but go far beyond to address the lesser-known public-domain lands (Bureau of Land Management and U.S. forests), wildlife refuges, and other wilderness areas. For each area there is a wealth of detail on its location, physical description, the wildlife of the area, the flora, recreational opportunities that await, and the resources and facilities available. With this well-organized, thorough guide you will have a multitude of outdoor vacations at your fingertips whether you have only a few days or want to spend a week. The nationally accepted signs for camping, hiking, hunting, fishing, boating, walking, horseback riding, etc. are used to give you quick visual clues to the appropriateness of a given area to your needs. A wonderful guide for those who love the outdoors.

The Sierra Club Naturalist's Guide to the Deserts of the Southwest
by Peggy and Lane Larson, Sierra Club Books, 1977, 288 pages, paper, $9.95

For those of you who are particularly interested in geology, natural history, and the flora and fauna of your particular region, this book in the Sierra Club Naturalist's Guide series represents a fine choice. The materials presented are well organized, well written, and fascinating to consider. Why not learn something more about the natural things you see around you on your next trip? It will enrich your experience. This is a first rate guide whether you are serious about your natural history or just like to look up the occasional fact.

Traveling Texas Borders: A Guide to the Best of Both Sides
by Ann Ruff, Gulf Publishing, 1983, 119 pages, $9.95

Interesting things to do along the Texas-Oklahoma and Texas-New Mexico borders.

Twenty-two Days in the American Southwest: The Itinerary Planner
by Richard Harris, John Muir Publications, 1988, 136 pages, paper, $6.95

Part of a series in which the intent is to let you lead your own tour (the assumption is that you will have your own vehicle) by providing you with clear, well-planned itineraries for classic three-week vacations. In addition, there are optional side trips to expand your trip even further. Or you can jump into the plan at any point if you are rushed. While there are occasional days where the plan is simply "R and R," these trips are nevertheless for energetic souls with some get-up-and-go. In spite of the assumption of a vehicle of your own, there is a distinct budget orientation with good picks for lodging and restaurants. The whole idea is to let the experts lead the way, but not pay someone to actually be there. It's a great idea for those who want that much direction in their vacation life. Note that the title is a new one for this book. You may also find it on the shelf as the American Southwest in 22 Days.

ARIZONA

Arizona Traveler's Handbook
by Bill Weir, Moon Publications, 1986, 450 pages, paper, $10.95

This is a very popular title in one of those rare series whose excellence never varies. The orientation is on the young (or young at heart) and adventurous (and usually car-less), but every traveler can glean tremendous value from this superbly crafted handbook. Each guide offers an incredible amount of background information on history, natural history, the people, arts and crafts, events, etc. If you read and study this section before you go, you will be a very well-educated traveler.

Sightseeing notes are offered in copious detail and there are always good maps of important areas. Food and lodging recommendations are not neglected, with numerous choices, usually well described, that generally cover the price range from budget to moderate. Updated every two years.

Arizona Hideaways
by Thelma Heatwole, Golden West Publishers, 1986, 126 pages, paper, $4.50

Choose your hideaway from this collection of romantic small Arizona towns. A good list of tiny towns in which to spend a tranquil day or two.

Arizona Off the Beaten Path!
by Thelma Heatwole, Golden West Publishers, 1982, 142 pages, paper, $4.50

A veteran reporter for the Arizona Republic takes you to her favorite out-of-the-way corners of Arizona. The descriptions of her adventures will tweak your interest and simple maps will pin the location down (though you will probably want some additional maps besides).

Arizona Outdoor Adventure
by Earnest Snyder, Golden West Publishers, 1985, 126 pages, paper, $5.00

Arizona ranges from a few hundred feet above sea level to more than 12,600 feet. Mountains, deserts, canyons, rivers: your choices for outdoor fun are many. Snyder will help you understand more of what you are seeing with interesting information on plants, animals, geology, rocks, natural environments, landforms, all sorts of neat stuff. If you care a bit about the science of it all, get this helpful guide to supplement your pleasure.

Arizona Trails: 100 Hikes in Canyon and Sierra
by David Mazel, Wilderness Press, 1985 (2nd edition), 312 pages, paper, $12.95

This is one of the many hiking guides from Wilderness Press. It is well-done, thorough, and easy to use. Trail descriptions are particularly excellent and all the specifics as to distances, directions, elevation change, etc. are noted. Includes a full-sized, separate topographical map of excellent quality. The "topogs" produced by Wilderness Press are particularly excellent, because the routes described in the guidebook are more clearly plotted than the average USGS map, usually in a bright color. An excellent book we heartily recommend.

Explore Arizona!

by Rick Harris, Golden West Publishers, 1986, 126 pages, paper, $5.00

Ghost towns, old forts, cliff dwellings, caves, hot springs, ruins, pottery, and lots more. Each adventure idea is accompanied by a useful location map and special notes (which will often remind you to look at, enjoy, and leave the artifacts alone for the next person to see as well). A good collection of ideas for the explorer.

A Guide to Architecture of Metro Phoenix

by Central Arizona Chapter A.I.A., Gibbs M. Smith, Inc., 1985, 200 pages, paper, $12.95

A fine, comprehensible guide to the fascinating architecture of Phoenix.

The Hiker's Guide to Arizona

by Stewart Aitchison and Bruce Grubbs, Falcon Press, 1987, 157 pages, paper, $9.95

One of the Falcon Press series, an excellent collection of hiking guides with a wide array of hikes of varied length. Reproductions of typographical maps are used and each hike is well discussed, rated, its special attractions summarized, and other USGS maps recommended.

Hiking the Grand Canyon

by John Annerino, Sierra Club Books, 1986, 320 pages, paper, $10.95

One of the small-format Sierra Club Hiking Totebook series. See the write-up under Hiking the Southwest above.

On Foot in the Grand Canyon: Hiking the Trails of the South Rim

by Sharon Spangler, Pruett Publishing, 1986, 194 pages, paper, $11.95

This is an interpretive guide, a hiker sharing her adventures with you. But there are enough practical facts here to help you plan your own hike as well—including appendices which will give you the word on water available, topographical maps you will need, basic geology, and some "day-hike" suggestions. Enjoyable and stimulating reading!

One Hundred Best Restaurants in Arizona
by John and Joan Bogert, A.D.M. Inc., 1987 (11th edition), 208 pages, paper, $3.95

Well, actually, there are now 172 places described in this popular guide. The emphasis is on inexpensive yet gourmet dining and the prices range from downright cheap to moderate. This guide is written the way we like it: anonymous dining done several times over (at least) without any perks. Chances are the authors experienced the same kind of evening you will. Couple this fact with a brightly written, informative text and you have one first-class book. Wonderful—and all the practical data is here too, including access for the disabled. Updated annually.

Outdoors in Arizona: A Guide to Camping
by Bob Hirsch, Arizona Highways, 1986, 128 pages, paper, $12.95

Here are plenty of camping ideas replete with beautiful color photos, location maps, and charts of practical facts of importance. A useful compendium.

Outdoors in Arizona: A Guide to Hiking and Backpacking
by John Annerino, Arizona Highways, 1987, 136 pages, paper, $12.95

Forty-eight suggested hikes, many with topographical map reproductions, from the author of Sierra Club's Hiking the Grand Canyon. Good ideas—and beautiful photos to help you decide more easily where you would like to go.

Roadside Geology of Arizona
by Halka Chronic, Mountain Press, 1983, 314 pages, paper, $9.95

A wonderfully fascinating book on geology "for the rest of us," and right along the highway too! Part of the excellent "Roadside Geology Guide" series (see Roadside Geology of New Mexico under "New Mexico" below).

Shifra Stein's Day Trips from Phoenix, Tucson, and Flagstaff: Getaways Less Than 2 Hours Away
by Pam Hait, The Globe Pequot Press, 1986, 190 pages, paper, $8.95

This book will provide you with a great variety of possible trips into the regions immediately adjacent to Phoenix, Tucson, and Flagstaff—each within a two-hour drive. The suggested journeys include a clear map, numerous things to do, suggestions of places to eat, and good ideas for just wondering about, enjoying the sights and sounds of the area you are exploring.

Ski Touring Arizona: Plateaus of Snow
by Dufald Bremner, Northland Press, 1987, 136 pages, paper, $11.95

Snow in Arizona? You bet! And some excellent skiing too. Offered here are over 40 ski tours for beginners and experts. Each is rated, distances noted, a good map provided, directions to the starting point given, other maps you might want to obtain, and a well-written discussion of each trip. Plus there are planning notes on equipment needs, winter hazard warnings, even suggestions for that most pleasurable of skiing ideas—moonlight touring. An excellently prepared guidebook.

The State Parks of Arizona
by John Young, University of New Mexico Press, 1986, 204 pages, paper, $11.95

A well-written orientation to the numerous state parks throughout Arizona. You will learn about the history of each park and things of interest locally. Helpful photographs accompany the enjoyable text. Specific information on campsites, motels, etc. is not included.

This is Tucson: Guidebook to the Old Pueblo
by Peggy Lockard, Pepper Publishing, 1988 (3rd edition), 294 pages, paper, $9.95

The award for the best guidebook in the state goes to this fine piece now in its third edition. Well-written, full of useful information and exceptionally good maps, it covers history, cultural activities, walking and driving tours of the historic districts, sightseeing, hiking, picnicking, seasonal events, tours of the surrounding areas, shopping, 65 restaurant reviews, and more. Every city should have such a superb guide available.

Travel Arizona: Full Color Tours of the Grand Canyon State
by Joseph Stocker, Arizona Highways, 1987 (5th edition), 128 pages, paper, $8.95

Sixteen interesting tours of from one to three days are offered for the automobile traveler. The text is informative and beautiful color photos in this large-format book are typical of those that made *Arizona Highways* magazine famous.   There is also a small section of suggested day hikes.

NEW MEXICO

Children's Guide to Santa Fe
by Anne Hillerman, Sunstone Press, 1984, 32 pages, paper, $4.95

A booklet filled with lots of good ideas for things to do with the kids. In spite of the publication date, most of this information should still be reasonably up-to-date—but do double check where appropriate.

Escortguide: The People's Connection to New Mexico
by Joan Adams, Escortguide, 1986 (3rd edition), 294 pages, paper, $7.95

Here is a different sort of book, a directory of all sorts of services, professional guides, bicycling or horseback excursions you can take, unusual sightseeing ideas, lesser known inns, ranches, and haciendas, and a whole lot more. Some of this information is more for the resident of New Mexico, but a great deal will be of benefit to the traveler. An excellent resource.

Guide to New Mexico's Popular Rivers and Lakes
by Stephen Maurer, Heritage Associates, 1983, 53 pages, paper, $4.95

Provides a run-down of New Mexico's eleven largest lakes, including maps and a description of available facilities (though, of course, more may have been added since this booklet was published). In addition, there are river profiles for rafting enthusiasts.

Hikers and Climbers Guide to the Sandias
by Mike Hill, University of New Mexico Press, 1983 (2nd edition), 234 pages, paper, $9.95

A first-class guide to the beautiful Sandias which lie east of Albuquerque. There are good sections on weather, plant life, geology, and important notes on hiking and climbing in these rugged mountains. The trails are described are numerous and vary from very short, easy walk/hikes to strenuous back-breakers. A separate, fold-out topographical map is included. Excellent.

How to See La Villa Real de Santa Fe: Walking Tour of Historic S.F
by Lou Ann Jordan, Sunstone Press, 1986, 32 pages, paper, $4.95

An interesting, large-format walking tour booklet done entirely by hand with illustrations and hand-lettered narrative of the historic sites.

Insider's Guide to Santa Fe
by Bill Jamison, The Harvard Common Press, 1987, 150 pages, paper, $8.95

Bill Jamison, a free-lance journalist living in Santa Fe, has created a fine, well-researched book covering every need of the traveler to this spectacular city. His book is divided into three parts. Part One is an excellent chapter on Santa Fe's heritage—the pueblos, the early Spanish settlers, the coming of the American armies in the early nineteenth century, and the Santa Fe art colony that has since evolved. Part Two explores the living museum that is Santa Fe—the plaza, the museums, the fiestas, the mountain trails, and more. Part Three is a great rundown of the "Best Places" to stay, eat, and shop. Just a superb job; definitely the best guide to Santa Fe we know.

New Mexico: A New Guide to the Colorful State
by Lance Chilton, et al., University of New Mexico Press, 1984, 640 pages, paper, $17.50

Six excellent authors have teamed together to create this massive, large-format guidebook as a tribute to the famous 1940 Federal WPA (Works Projects Administration) publication of similar title. Here are finely crafted essays on everything from history and politics to arts and literature. The bulk of the book is 18 well-conceived driving tours to every corner of the state. The maps are clear and the amount of interesting and useful information crammed into the descriptions of each tour is truly remarkable. There is also a helpful section of special events arranged in a month-by-month format. One of the great sightseeing guides anywhere and destined to be a classic.

New Mexico's Best Ghost Towns: A Practical Guide
by Phillip Varney, University of New Mexico Press, 1981, 190 pages, paper, $13.95

An excellent large-format guide to the many ghost towns of New Mexico. Varney has put together a great selection of photographs and a fine narrative that is sure to tweak your interest. Included are good directions, some location maps, specific topographical maps available for each area, and comments on how important such maps are to your safe exploration of these ghosts of history.

Roadside Geology of New Mexico
by Halka Chronic, Mountain Press, 1987, 255 pages, paper, $9.95

One family member refers to her experience of taking a geology class in college as the time she took "Rocks." Obviously she didn't have the pleasure of using this book in the great Roadside Geology series. Even if taking "Rocks" in college was the epitome of boredom, there is always that occasional thought as the car moves through a cut in the highway, "I wonder what those colored layers are?" Here is a geology book specifically directed at what you will see from your car window or what you can see if you will just pull over at the appropriate time and take a look. And it is written for the average person, too. No need to know all those big, multi-syllabic words. The book is organized by highway. You will find it totally fascinating. We recommend it highly. We may even give a copy to the rock expert in our family. We think she'll be surprised.

The Santa Fe Guide
by Waite Thompson and Richard Gottlieb, Sunstone Press, 1986 (revised edition), 64 pages, paper, $5.95

If you put a premium on size, this tiny guidebook will give you a solid overview of history, culture, things to see and do, weather information, and transportation. There is also a list of suggested restaurants, though it notes only type of food without further comment.

Sante Fe On Foot: Walking, Running and Bicycling Routes in the City Different
by Elaine Pinkerton, Juniper Junction, 1986, 125 pages, paper, $7.50

A wonderful book on interesting routes to walk, run, or bicycle. The fine text will not only provide you with route information and plenty of background historical material but a pleasurable reading experience as well.

Santa Fe Then and Now
by Sheila Morand, Sunstone Press, 1984, 96 pages, paper, $14.95

Here is an interesting book for those who would like to know how the sights they are seeing now looked 100 years ago. The author has lined up old and new photos side by side and located each place on a street map to let you take a look firsthand.

Six One-Day Walks in the Pecos Wilderness
by Carl Overhage, Sunstone Press, 1984 (revised edition), 60 pages, paper, $4.95

A convenient-size booklet carefully describes six strenuous hikes from 11 to 21 miles for the experienced hiker. Each has a fold-out hand-drawn map and elevation chart. Appropriate topographical maps are recommended and instructions on how to reach each area are included. Some great ideas, if you are ready to really step on out.

The State Parks of New Mexico
by John Young, University of New Mexico Press, 1984, 160 pages, paper, $11.95

A good overview of New Mexico's many state parks. Included are many black and white photographs, a few historical notes, and some of the unique qualities of each park.

Summer People, Winter People: A Guide to Pueblos in the Santa Fe Area
by Sandra Edelman, Sunstone Press, 1986 (revised edition), 32 pages, paper, $4.95

A helpful brochure with overviews of the various pueblos near Santa Fe. Included are the dates of special fiestas, dances, and ceremonies.

Tours For All Seasons: 50 Car Tours of New Mexico
by Howard Bryan, Heritage Associates, 1986, 120 pages, paper, $4.95

A veteran reporter and writer of a weekly column for the *Albuquerque Tribune* on New Mexico lore shares his best automobile tours with you. The dozens of possibilities are grouped by the season in which they are best to do—plus a section of trips you can do anytime. There are a great many good ideas to consider in this compact guidebook. Simple orientation roadmaps are included though you will certainly want to have better ones at hand.

OKLAHOMA

Guide to Oklahoma Museums
by David Hunt, University of Oklahoma Press, 1981, 147 pages, paper, $9.95

A comprehensive guide to the museums of Oklahoma as well as important historic sites and zoological parks. In all there are nearly 150 places described, including some of the most unusual museums such as oil museums, doll museums, and three national halls of fame: softball, wrestling, and cowboy. A fine but aging directory. Be sure to confirm all time-dated materials.

Outdoor and Trail Guide to the Wichita Mountains of Southwest Oklahoma
by Edward Ellenbrook, In-the-Valley-of-the-Wichitas House, 1984, 108 pages, paper, $6.50

A helpful guide to the Wichita Mountains, prepared with obvious love for and interest in this southwest corner of Oklahoma. The guide offers you a little history, a large selection of places to go (and how to get there), numerous trails and walks both long and short, guided tours of the Valley of the Wichitas, Red Rock Canyon, and the Rock of Ages, and other helpful facts on outdoor fun like hunting and fishing.

TEXAS

The Alamo and Other Texas Missions to Remember
by Nancy Foster, Gulf Publishing, 1984, 88 pages, paper, $9.95

This large format book will let you in on a good deal of the history, architecture, as well as the tours available at various missions in the state. You will also learn about the special events that are held each year. In addition, there are clear locator maps and nicely chosen photographs. A helpful guide to Texas' fascinating history.

Amazing Texas Monuments and Museums: From the Enchanting to the Bizarre
by Ann Ruff, Gulf Publishing, 104 pages, paper, $9.95

Where else can you find a guide to monuments erected to the strawberry, pecan, roadrunner, mosquito, and jackrabbit? Where else can you locate museums featuring things like 10,000 birds' eggs or Lee Harvey Oswald's can opener? Well, this is the one. Lots of tombstones too. A whole lot of sightseeing fun.

Austin: The Complete Guide to Texas' Capital City
by Richard Zelade, Texas Monthly Press, 1988 (2nd edition), 272 pages, paper, $9.95

One of a first-rate series of guides to the Lone Star state (you will find others below). Only Texas, the biggest guidebook of the lot, is thoroughly out-of-date at this juncture. The other regional guides are being kept regularly up-to-date and the word is now that the big, single-volume guide to the state will finally see a new edition in (probably) 1989. That aside, you will find this series offers an excellent summary of what each city or area has to offer: what to do, where to go, tours, annual events, night life, shopping, the arts, and, of course, hotels and restaurants. The latter emphasize the moderate and up range, at least in the big cities, but there are some less expensive options as well. The write-ups are informative and each guide is, overall, most enjoyable to read.

Authentic Texas Cafes
by Susan and Ed Kennard, Texas Monthly Press, 1986, 202 pages, paper, $8.95

A good rundown on the Kennards pick of the top 100 cafes in the state which are located in or near 87 different towns. Like they say, these are places "where good food is still more important than speed or gimmicks." A quality list.

Backroads of Texas
by Ed Syers, Gulf Publishing, 1988 (2nd edition), 176 pages, paper, $12.95

You will find Syers' 62 tours of the backcountry will planned, well written, and just plain fun. It's time to explore the ghost towns, boom towns, farm towns, cow towns, and all those places of interest in between. Comprehensive, compact, and definitely first class.

Beachcomber's Guide to Gulf Coast Marine Life
by Nick Fotheringham, Gulf Publishing, 1980, 124 pages, paper, $9.95

Let this popular naturalist's guide increase your enjoyment of the fascinating gulf coast. Instead of just puzzling over the shell you just picked up, you will be able to learn something about it, perhaps even identify it precisely.

The Best Country Cafes in Texas: The East
by John Forsyth and Meg Tynan, Texas Geographic Interests, 1983, 146 pages, paper, $7.95.

The Best Country Cafes in Texas: The West
by John Forsyth and Meg Tynan, Texas Geographic Interests, 1984, 128 pages, paper, $6.95

Forsyth and Tynan really have a knack for capturing the flavor of a place—gastronomic and otherwise. Their superb compilation of the hundreds of country cafes throughout the state has been a real service to the traveler and they have tried to keep their information fairly up-to-date by including a list of those cafes that have bit their final bullet and closed their doors. Since 1985 they have written a weekly restaurant review column for the Houston Chronicle and so, armed with all these new ideas, have stated that a single-volume update is "in the works." Watch for it.

The Best of Texas Festivals: Your Guide to Rootin' Tootin' Downhome Texas Good Times!
by Ann Ruff, Gulf Publishing, 1986, 100 pages, paper, $9.95

Here is just the ticket—a single resource, arranged in a month-to-month format, giving you all the inside scoop on 60 good time Texas festivals: a citrus fiesta, a peach jamboree, the fiddler's festival, and the hushpuppy Olympics. Here is all you need to know plus addresses and phone numbers if you need to know more.

Dallas Epicure: Peanut Butter Publishing
1986, 160 pages, paper, $7.95

This is one of a large series of menu guides to major cities of the United States. Updated frequently, they are a good way, for those so inclined, to select their own restaurants, to be their own judge rather than reading someone else's opinion. If you feel you can judge a restaurant by the quality of its menu, this is a good series to assist you. And there is enough practical information to facilitate its use as a guide.

The Dallas Morning News Guide to Dallas Restaurants: The Definitive Guide to the 150 Best
Chronicle Books, 1986, 160 pages, paper, $7.95

There are plenty of places to eat in Dallas and this book will tell you about some of the best of every type and price range. In addition there is a helpful section on the foods of Texas and a rundown on the 16 wineries that were in business in the Lone Star state in 1986—included is brief touring information and phone numbers in case you would like to put together a little tasting tour. Restaurant reviews are well done and all the necessary information is included.

Dallas: Your Complete Guide to a Vibrant Texas City
by Ellen Gunter, Texas Monthly Press, 1987, 265 pages, paper, $9.95

Part of the "Texas Monthly Guide" series. See *Austin: The Complete Guide to Texas' Capital City* above.

Eyes of Texas Travel Guide: Dallas/East Texas
by Ray Miller, Gulf Publishing, 1988 (2nd edition), 224 pages, paper, $10.95

Eyes of Texas Travel Guide: Fort Worth/Brazos Valley
by Ray Miller, Gulf Publishing, 1981, 200 pages, paper, $9.95

Eyes of Texas Travel Guide: Hill Country/Permian Basin
by Ray Miller, Gulf Publishing, 1982, 200 pages, paper, $9.95

Eyes of Texas Travel Guide: Houston/Gulf Coast
by Ray Miller, Gulf Publishing, 1987 (2nd edition), 224 pages, paper, $10.95

Eyes of Texas Travel Guide: Panhandle/Plains
by Ray Miller, Gulf Publishing, 1982, 200 pages, paper, $9.95

Eyes of Texas Travel Guide: San Antonio/Border
by Ray Miller, Gulf Publishing, 1979, 250 pages, paper, $9.95

This well-known series, listed above in its entirety, combines Miller's penchant for history with the facts and figures of modern Texas. Packed with photographs, these regional guides make great companion guides, excellent supplements to more standard travel guides.

Flashmaps: Instant Guide to Dallas/Ft. Worth
Fodor's Travel Guides, 1987, 72 pages, paper, $4.95

A small guide in a series where a premium is placed on space. Each title in the series slips easily into a purse or coat pocket. Yet summarized within is a substantial amount of information on many travel topics: restaurants, theatres, transportation, libraries, whatever. The "flashmaps" are single subject maps that locate each selection precisely. The style is utilitarian, detailed analysis non-existent with no thought of being comprehensive, but, within their limited format, these guides are very handy and quite useful. And they are updated annually so the facts are sure to be as current as possible.

Fort Worth and Tarrant County: A Historical Guide
edited by Ruby Schmidt, Texas Christian University Press, 1984, 101 pages, paper, $5.95

A very well-done assemblage of the history behind a vast array of historical buildings, homes, churches, cemeteries, schools, etc. in the Fort Worth area. Arranged alphabetically, those located in Fort Worth proper are accompanied by several hand-drawn maps. Nonetheless, you will want to get an additional map of the surrounding area to assist you in locating other important sites. Most sites you will have a historical marker to help you locate them, however, the historical notes in this guidebook go well beyond those included on the marker itself. The index also allows you to see at a glance all the page references for cemeteries, churches, etc., which will be helpful if you are particularly interested in one type of historical site.

Frontier Forts of Texas
by Charles Robinson, Gulf Publishing, 1986, 86 pages, paper, $9.95

A large-format travel guides that delivers the practical facts you will need along with fascinating accounts of those adventurous events of yesteryear. The stories cover the more than two dozen forts that have survived the years as well as those that were destroyed. Includes information on visitor facilities and local events at each of the still-existent forts.

A Guide to Bicycling in Texas: Tours, Tips, and More
by George Sevra, Gulf Publishing, 1985, 96 pages, paper, $9.95

A great collection of tours—one-day, inter-city, as well as more lengthy routes—spanning the entire state that will serve to prove to you, once and for all, that Texas is not just "flat and empty." There are also helpful lists of bicycle shops, sources of maps (though some good-sized detail maps are included in this large-format book), and local Chambers of Commerce in towns you plan to pass through and might like to stop and explore a little more.

A Guide to Historic Texas Inns and Hotels
by Ann Ruff, Gulf Publishing, 1985 (2nd edition), 132 pages, paper, $9.95

A popular guide from a popular writer, this large-format book offers you excellent descriptions of the best of the historic lodging spots. The practical facts are listed separately in the margin for easy access and each selection is accompanied by a line drawing or, sometimes, a photograph. Very well done.

A Guide to Texas Rivers and Streams
by Gene Kirkley, Gulf Publishing, 1983, 120 pages, paper, $9.95

A large-format guide to white water canoeing and kayaking, float trips, fishing, or just plain fun along Texas' many waterways.

Great Hometown Restaurants of Texas
by Mary Beverly, Gulf Publishing, 1984, 150 pages, paper, $9.95

This large-format guide is a lot of fun, with great write-ups on all sorts of intriguing spots where home style cooking is the rule. It includes all the practical data, too, so you won't get lost along the way, but be aware of its age.

Hiking and Backpacking Trails of Texas
by Mildred Little, Gulf Publishing, 1985 (2nd edition), 148 pages, paper, $9.95

Here is another finely done book that proves Texas to be something more than flat and empty. There is some beautiful country out there and Mildred Little has done a quality job in pointing the way. The state is divided into four regions in this large-format book. In each region trails are clearly located, adequate trail notes and distances included, and maps, sometimes, topographical ones, are provided as well. Among your choices you will find a good number of short day hikes.

Hill Country: Discover the Secrets of Texas Hill Country
by Richard Zelade, Texas Monthly Press, 1987 (2nd edition), 509 pages, paper, $9.95

This superb book, while part of the Texas Monthly series, is structured differently. Here are ten driving tours through the hills of central Texas—including areas near Austin and San Antonio. Each tour can be done in a day if you like, though they are up to several hundred miles in length and you will probably enjoy dawdling a bit more than that. Zelade will let you in on the history of the area and the points of interest both on and off the beaten track as you pass through towns like Dimebox and Enchanted Rock. You'll learn the best spots to stop when it's chow time and some tips on lodging along the way. Good directions, clear maps—just a wonderful guidebook.

Historic Homes of Texas: Across the Thresholds of Yesterday
by Ann Ruff and Henri Farmer, Gulf Publishing, 1987, 130 pages, paper, $18.95

Take a look at the homes built by the cattle and oil barons and the genteel women who came west in times gone by. Each is recognized by the Texas Historical Commission, many are on the National Register of Historic Places, and all are open to the public. Included is all the information you will need to find and enjoy each historic site. Also included are details for tours of other homes not normally open to the public.

Houston: Your Complete Guide to Texas' Largest City
by John Davenport, Texas Monthly Press, 1985 (4th edition), 175 pages, paper, $9.95

Part of the "Texas Monthly Guide" series. See *Austin: The Complete Guide to Texas' Capital City* above.

Insight Guides: Texas
by APA Productions, Prentice Hall Press, 1985, 384 pages, paper, $15.95

One of the Insight Guides series. See write-up on *Insight Guides: American Southwest* above.

A Marmac Guide to Houston and Galveston
by Dale Young, Pelican Publishing, 1988, 270 pages, paper, $7.95

One of Marmac Guides, a series which offers very solid, well organized views of major cities. You will learn the ropes of each city and some of its history and tradition. The hotels and restaurants are many, and each is first presented by geographic area, then alphabetically (for hotels) or by type of cuisine. The prices run the gamut, but moderate is the most common. The restaurant section is particularly comprehensive and well done. Additional sections cover shopping, sightseeing, museums, sports, nightlife, theater, various excursions, walking tours, and transportation. The format is easy to use and will serve you well. Updated every two years.

Places to Go With Children in Dallas and Fort Worth
by Joan Jackson and Glenna Whitley, Chronicle Books, 1987, 144 pages, paper, $7.95

Ideas, ideas, ideas. Over 350 possibilities in every category you can think of: art , culture, sports, science, nature, parks, history, and on and on. There are ideas here for every age group, including the grown-ups. Each resource is briefly described and all the particulars presented. Amusements parks, science stores, a culture center, and special eateries where kids are most welcome. You'll never run out of good ideas with this great resource guide.

Ray Miller's Texas Forts: A History and Guide
by Ray Miller, Gulf Publishing, 1985, 223 pages, paper, $13.95

Miller presents a lively history of the many forts, including the famous Alamo, that sprung up during the 19th century and were important points of focus during the Mexican War, the Indian wars, and the Civil War. Includes a large number of interesting photographs.

Ray Miller's Texas Parks: A History and Guide
by Ray Miller, Gulf Publishing, 1984, 232 pages, paper, $13.95

You will find the practical information you need on the numerous parks in the state system, but in addition you will get a large measure of the history behind what you see. Some specifics about each park may be dated—call ahead to see—but you will find this an excellent resource nonetheless.

San Antonio: An Indispensable Guide to One of Texas' Favorite Cities
by Ben Fairbank, Jr. and Nancy Foster, Texas Monthly Press, 1988 (2nd edition), 224 pages, paper, $9.95

Part of the "Texas Monthly Guide" series. See Austin: The Complete Guide to Texas' Capital City above.

Shifra Stein's Day Trips From Houston

by Carol Barrington, the Globe Pequot Press, 1988 (3rd edition), 180 pages, paper, $7.95

Part of the well-done Shifra Stein's Day Trip Guide series. See Shifra Stein's Day Trips from Phoenix, Tucson, and Flagstaff under Arizona above. This third edition was released after press time; price and number of pages are tentative.

Six Central Texas Auto Tours

by Myra McIllvain, Eakins Press, 1980, 220 pages, paper, $9.95

These driving tours, filled with historical notes and anecdotes, are all in the central Texas area around Austin. Some of the roadways in the area have changed since this book was published, but most of the copious detail should still stand you in good stead.

Texas Coast: Discover Delights Along the Gulf Coast of Texas

by Robert Rafferty, Texas Monthly Press, 1986, 289 pages, paper, $9.95

Part of the "Texas Monthly Guide" series. The emphasis in this book is the long Texas beach front from Port Authur to Brownsville and the "boating, fishing, fiestas, seafood, shopping, history and hilarity" you will find if you hit the right spots.

Texas—Family Style: Parent's Guide to Hassle-free, Fun Travel With the Kids

by Ruth Wolverton, Gulf Publishing, 1981, 120 pages, paper, $7.95

Though it is getting older now, this large-format guide will still be a source of lots of good ideas for what to do with the entire family.

Texas Golf: The Comprehensive Guide to Golf Courses and Resorts of the Lone Star State

by Frank Hermes, Taylor Publishing, 1987, 192 pages, paper, $7.95

Like the title states, your best compendium of golfing information in Texas.

Texas Parks and Campgrounds: Central, South, and West Texas

Texas Parks and Campgrounds: North, East, and Coastal Texas
by George Miller and Delena Tull, Texas Monthly Press, 1984, 141 pages, paper, $7.95

These two titles will give you a good rundown of the many state parks and campgrounds, including good notes of the attractions of the area, its ecology, facilities, fees (if any), and some succinct comments on hiking options as well. Call ahead to determine up-to-date information.

Texas Restaurant Guide
by Pat Pugh, Pelican Publishing, 1987, 243 pages, paper, $4.95

Pugh provides you with information and opinion on more than 450 restaurants in the big cities and cow towns alike. Both budget and high price selections are included along with all the necessary practical facts.

Tour Guide to North Texas
by Catherine Gonzalez, Eakin Press, 1982, 224 pages, paper, $8.95

Here are seven well-conceived driving tours of north Texas replete with good driving instructions, historical notes and anecdotes, and a variety of interesting photographs to help you choose the tours you will like best. Included are the Dallas area and the Red River country—north Texas, "a land of lakes, pines, and history."

Traveling Texas Borders: A Guide to the Best of Both Sides
by Ann Ruff, Gulf Publishing, 1983, 119 pages, paper, $9.95

A good detailing of the many things to do and see along Texas' vast border. Included are activities in Arkansas, Louisiana, Mexico, New Mexico, and Oklahoma. This large-format guide offers plenty of interesting suggestions.

Why Stop? A Guide to Texas Historical Roadside Markers
by Claude and Betty Dooley, Gulf Publishing, 1985 (2nd edition), 560 pages, paper, $14.95

There are more than 2,600 roadside markers in Texas with historical notes on all sorts of interesting subjects. Now, with this guide, you can read the markers without necessarily even stopping the car. Even if you stop, this will prove a very handy resource guide to keep on the back seat.

Appendixes

A: Size/Weather of Southwest

The American Southwest is huge. Not only is Texas the second largest state in the U.S., but New Mexico is the fifth largest, and Arizona is the sixth. Oklahoma is the Southwest's only "average size" state—with 69,000 square miles, measuring in as the 19th largest.

In all, the four states account for nearly 566,000 square miles of territory—the near equivalent of Spain, Portugal, France, and Italy combined. From the western border of Arizona to the eastern border of Texas it is about 1,200 miles by air, not by road. From northern Oklahoma to the tip of Texas it is about 800 miles.

Not surprisingly, the weather in the Southwest varies tremendously. Southern Arizona has mild winters, making it a favored winter getaway, and hot summers, which is why summer rates in some parts of the state are reduced as much as 50 percent. Even in summer, the mountains north of Phoenix are pleasantly cool, serving as a retreat for both visitors and natives.

In general, the peak tourist season in the other three states is in summer. Much of New Mexico is mountainous, from Chama and Raton in the northern parts of the state to Cloudcroft and Ruidoso in the south. In New Mexico, the Great Plains meet the Rockies, providing a dramatic contrast. Elevations range from 2,800 to 13,000 feet. In the winter, the mountains turn into winter playgrounds, beckoning skiers with long runs and incredibly beautiful terrain.

Oklahoma, whose highest point is not quite 3,000 feet, is characterized by forested rolling hills, sprawling lakes, and wide-spread plains. Texas' landscapes are widely varying. There are vast wide open spaces in west Texas punctuated by magnificent mountains, huge cattle ranches in the Panhandle and the South, piney woods in east Texas, gently-rolling Hill Country, and hundreds of miles of Gulf-coast beaches.

Moving from the east to the west, rainfall in the Southwest decreases, resulting in semi-tropical to desert climates. The variety of plant and animal life is remarkable. From the desert, with its low creosote bush and its giant saguaro, the landscape rolls to high mountains with Douglas fir, blue spruce, and quaking aspens. The whooping crane and road-runner, black bear and ringtailed cat, mountain lion and armadillo—all live in the Southwest.

Not only is the land varied, but so is the style of life. You can drive from a city of three million to a ghost town tucked into the high mountains, and on the way encounter miles and miles of uninhabited, uncluttered land. Here is the magic of the Southwest, inviting your soul to soar as you revel in the untouched, balanced by the civilized.

B: Southwest Look

Spanish explorers traveled over much of the American Southwest, dating all the way back to the mid 1500s. Until the middle of the 19th century, much of this land we call the Southwest belonged to Mexico.

By the mid 1800s, settlers began streaming in from other parts of the world—not just from the United States but from Europe and the Orient. Texas alone claims 26 ethnic groups as part of its heritage.

The Spanish, and later the Mexicans, left an indelible imprint on the Southwest. In some areas, especially in central New Mexico and in Oklahoma, so did the native Indians.

Today, Southwest style refers to the intermingling of Indian, Spanish, and Anglo cultures. In some regions it is unmistakably visible. Santa Fe and Taos exhibit it best, with their adobe-style architecture and Indian and Mexican crafts such as pottery and weaving. So distinctive is the look that modern artists have been inspired to make their own Southwest statement, resulting in daringly creative sculpture, woodcarving, and art.

In other parts of the Southwest, the Spanish influence—while still present—is more subtle. Whether your ordering enchiladas in Dallas or staying in a casita in Phoenix, you can sense it. Some parts of the Southwest have a very close kinship to Mexico. Two-thirds of El Paso's population is Hispanic. The Texas/Mexican border, from Brownsville to Laredo to Del Rio, is almost a country within itself—a beautiful blend of the two cultures. San Antonio celebrates its

Spanish heritage everyday—in its architecture, cuisine, and celebrations.

Oklahoma, home to more than 70 Indian tribes, is strongly linked to those who first called the land their home. In the summer, Oklahoma boasts the "world's largest native American celebration,"—Red Earth.

But the Southwest is more than Spanish architecture, Mexican food, and Indian crafts. The cowboy and the Old West are still here—alive and well. Fort Worth and Tucson are good places to experience it. So are the guest ranches in Arizona and Texas.

And sprinkled throughout are pockets of other cultures, adding grace and charm to the whole. The German settlements in New Braunfels and Fredericksburg are especially notable. So is Castroville with its Alsatian history.

C: Children Welcome

State	Place	Page
NM	La Posada de Taos	300
	Legends Hotel	268
	Otra Vez	101
	Pueblo Bonito	4
	Quail Ridge Inn & Tennis Ranch	281
	Rancho Encantado	184
	St. Bernard Condominiums	269
	Story Book Cabins	33
	Twining Condominiums	269
OK	Embassy Suites Hotel	96
	Lake Texoma Resort	188
	Roman Nose Resort	127
	Shangri-La	231
	Three Buoys Houseboat Vacations	232
	Western Hills Guest Ranch	128
TX	Austin Cottage & Guest Suites	207
	Bridgepoint	102
	Camp Warnecke Resorts	103
	Chain-O-Lakes	34
	Gant Guest House	208
	Inn at Salado	304
	Inn of the Hills River Resort	141
	John Newcombe's Tennis Ranch	283
	La Borde House	262
	Lajitas on the Rio Grande	191
	Lakeway Inn	236
	Menger Hotel	87
	Port Royal by the Sea	26
	Remington on Post Oak Park	78
	San Luis Hotel and Condominiums	27
	Seascape	104
	South Padre Hilton Resort	28
	Stoneleigh	63
	Wise Manor	307

D: Dining Room Open to the Public

State	Place	Page
AZ	Arizona Biltmore	174
	Arizona Inn	175

State	Place	Page
NM	La Posada de Santa Fe	290
	Legends Hotel	268
	The Lodge	180
	Los Pinos Guest Ranch	32
	Meson de Mesilla	147
	Plaza Hotel	215
	Pueblo Bonito	4
	Pyramid Holiday Inn	46
	Quail Ridge Inn & Tennis Ranch	281
	Ramada Hotel Classic	47
	Rancho Encantado	184
	Sagebrush Inn	291
	St. James Hotel	148
	Sunrise Springs Resort	248
	Taos Inn	216
OK	Doubletree Hotel at Warren Place	95
	Embassy Suites Hotel	96
	Lake Texoma Resort	188
	Oklahoma City Marriott	83
	Roman Nose Resort	127
	Shangri-La	231
	Tulsa Marriott	97
	Waterford Hotel	83
	Western Hills Guest Ranch	128
	Westin Hotel, Williams Center	98
TX	Adolphus	53
	Annie's Bed & Breakfast	117
	Best Western Sandy Shores	23
	Chain-O-Lakes	34
	Chisos Mountains Lodge	238
	Dallas Marriot Mandalay Hotel	55
	Del Lago Resort	234
	Driskill Hotel	48
	El Paso Airport Hilton	66
	El Paso Marriott	67
	Excelsior House	218
	Fairmont Hotel	56
	Fairmount Hotel	84
	Four Seasons Hotel Austin	49
	Four Seasons Hotel-Houston Center	72
	Four Seasons Resort and Hotel	163
	Gage Hotel	119
	Hershey Corpus Christi Hotel	140
	Hotel Crescent Court	57

State	Place	Page
TX	Worthington Hotel	71
	Wyndham Hotel Greenspoint	82
	Wyndham Southpark	52
	Y.O. Ranch Hilton	254
	Yacht Club Hotel	294

E: Handicapped Access

State	Place	Page
AZ	Arizona Biltmore	174
	Arizona Inn	175
	Hacienda del Sol Guest Ranch Resort	177
	Hotel Park Tucson	94
	Hyatt Regency Scottsdale at Gainey Ranch	154
	L'Auberge de Sedona	143
	Loews Ventana Canyon Resort	156
	Marriott's Camelback Inn	133
	Monte Vista Hotel	213
	Pointe at Tapatio Cliff	157
	Red Lion's La Posada	158
	Scottsdale Princess	160
	Sheraton Tucson El Conquistador	
	Golf and Tennis Resort	160
	Sky Ranch Lodge	125
	Stouffer Cottonwoods Resort	257
	Ventana Canyon Golf and Racquet Club	279
	Westin La Paloma	161
	Westward Look Resort	136
	The Wigwam	178
NM	Albuquerque Marriott	43
	Bear Mountain Guest Ranch	246
	Galisteo Inn	116
	Inn of the Mountain Gods	138
	Inn on the Alameda	287
	La Fonda	93
	La Posada de Albuquerque	45
	La Posada de Taos	300
	The Lodge	180
	Pyramid Holiday Inn	46
	Ramada Hotel Classic	47
	Rancho Encantado	184

State	Place	Page
NM	Taos Inn	216
OK	Doubletree Hotel at Warren Place	95
	Embassy Suites Hotel	96
	Lake Texoma Resort	188
	Oklahoma City Marriott	83
	Roman Nose Resort	127
	Shangri-La	231
	Tulsa Marriott	97
	Waterford Hotel	83
	Western Hills Guest Ranch	128
	Westin Hotel, Williams Center	98
TX	Adolphus	53
	Annie's Bed & Breakfast	117
	Best Western Sandy Shores	23
	Dallas Marriot Mandalay Hotel	55
	El Paso Airport Hilton	66
	El Paso Marriott	67
	Fairmont Hotel	56
	Fairmount Hotel	84
	Four Seasons Hotel Austin	49
	Four Seasons Hotel-Houston Center	72
	Four Seasons Resort and Hotel	163
	Hershey Corpus Christi Hotel	140
	Hotel Crescent Court	57
	Hotel Inter-Continental Houston	73
	Hyatt Regency Fort Worth	69
	Indian Lodge	129
	Inn on the Park	74
	Inn on the River	7
	La Colombe d'Or	75
	La Mansion Hotel Austin	50
	La Posada (McAllen, TX)	289
	Lancaster Hotel	77
	Loews Anatole Hotel	59
	Mansion on Turtle Creek	60
	Marriott's Hotel Galvez	24
TX	Omni Melrose Hotel	62
	Plaza San Antonio	88
	Port Royal by the Sea	26
	Radisson Gunter Hotel	89
	Radisson Suite Hotel	131
	San Luis Hotel and Condominiums	27
	Sheraton South Padre Island Beach Resort	28
	South Padre Hilton Resort	28

State	Place	Page
TX	St. Anthony Inter-Continental	90
	Stockyards Hotel	70
	Stoneleigh	63
	Stouffer Austin Hotel	51
	Stouffer Dallas Hotel	64
	Tremont House	221
	Westin Galleria and Westin Oaks	81
	Westin Hotel Dallas	66
	Westin Paso del Norte	68
	Wise Manor	307
	Worthington Hotel	71
	Wyndham Hotel Greenspoint	82
	Wyndham Southpark	52
	Y.O. Ranch Hilton	254

F: Murder Mystery Weekends;

State	Place	Page
AZ	Hacienda del Sol Guest Ranch Resort	177
	Hassayampa Inn	211
	Little America of Flagstaff	124
	Marriott's Camelback Inn	133
	Monte Vista Hotel	213
	Red Lion's La Posada	158
	Tucson National Resort and Spa	272
NM	Inn of the Arts Bed and Breakfast	38
	Monjeau Shadows	110
	St. James Hotel	148
TX	Adolphus	53
	Annie's Bed & Breakfast	117
	Crystal River Inn	6
	Hershey Corpus Christi Hotel	140
	Inn on the Creek	261
	La Colombe d'Or	75
	Omni Melrose Hotel	62
	Plaza San Antonio	88
	Townsquare Inn	120
	Wise Manor	307

G: Pets Allowed

State	Place	Page
AZ	Bisbee Inn	123
	Boulders	152
	Hacienda del Sol Guest Ranch Resort	177
	Hotel Park Tucson	94
	Inn at Castle Rock	244
	Marriott's Camelback Inn	133
	Price Canyon Ranch	251
	Red Lion's La Posada	158
	Sheraton Tucson El Conquistador Golf and Tennis Resort	160
	Sky Ranch Lodge	125
	Westward Look Resort	136
	The Wigwam	178
NM	Albuquerque Marriott	43
	Austing Haus Hotel	266
	Bear Mountain Guest Ranch	246
	Inn of the Governors	92
	Inn on the Alameda	287
	La Fonda	93
	La Fonda de Taos	289
	La Junta	187
	La Posada de Taos	300
	Plaza Hotel	215
	Pueblo Bonito	4
	Pyramid Holiday Inn	46
	Sunrise Springs Resort	248
	William E. Mauger Estate	39
OK	Doubletree Hotel at Warren Place	95
	Embassy Suites Hotel	96
	Harrison House	5
	Three Buoys Houseboat Vacations	232
	Western Hills Guest Ranch	128
TX	Best Western Sandy Shores	23
	Bridgepoint	102
	Chisos Mountains Lodge	238
	Dallas Marriot Mandalay Hotel	55
	El Paso Marriott	67

State	Place	Page
TX	Four Seasons Hotel Austin	49
	Four Seasons Hotel-Houston Center	72
	Gage Hotel	119
	Hyatt Regency Fort Worth	69
	Inn of the Hills River Resort	141
	Inn on the Park	74
	La Borde House	262
	La Mansion Hotel Austin	50
	Lajitas on the Rio Grande	191
	Plaza San Antonio	88
	Prude Ranch	252
	Rancho Viejo Resort	284
	Stoneleigh	63
	Westin Galleria and Westin Oaks	81
	Y.O. Ranch Hilton	254

H: Smoking Not Allowed

State	Place	Page
AZ	Bisbee Inn	123
	Graham's Bed & Breakfast Inn	296
	La Posada del Valle	36
NM	American Artists Gallery House	297
	Preston House	165
TX	Annie's Bed & Breakfast	117
	Browning Plantation	166
	Guest Quarters on the Grounds of the Barton House	209
	High Cotton Inn Bed and Breakfast	303
	Inn at Salado	304
	Inn of the Hills River Resort	141
	Inn on the Creek	261
	Inn on the River	7
	Landhaus Bed and Breakfast	112
	Lottie's Bed & Breakfast	113
	McKay House	264
	Pink Lady Inn	8
	Rosevine Inn	40
	Sunset on the Bay	29

I: Sports

ARCHERY

State	Place	Page
NM	Inn of the Mountain Gods	138

BADMINTON

State	Place	Page
TX	Inn of the Hills River Resort	141

BEACH

State	Place	Page
TX	Best Western Sandy Shores	23
	Bridgepoint	102
	Marriott's Hotel Galvez	24
	Port Royal by the Sea	26
	San Luis Hotel and Condominiums	27
	Seascape	104
	Sheraton South Padre Island Beach Resort	28
	South Padre Hilton Resort	28
	Sunset on the Bay	29

BOATING

State	Place	Page
NM	Legends Hotel	268
OK	Roman Nose Resort	127
	Shangri-La	231
TX	Horseshoe Bay Country Club Resort	235
	Lakeway Inn	236

CANOEING

State	Place	Page
NM	Inn of the Mountain Gods	138
OK	Roman Nose Resort	127
	Western Hills Guest Ranch	128
TX	Inn of the Hills River Resort	141

CROQUET

State	Place	Page
AZ	Arizona Biltmore	174
	Red Lion's La Posada	158
	Scottsdale Princess	160
	Hyatt Regency Scottsdale at Gainey Ranch	154
	Arizona Inn	175
	Hacienda del Sol Guest Ranch Resort	177
	Loews Ventana Canyon Resort	156
	Westin La Paloma	161
NM	Galisteo Inn	116
	Monjeau Shadows	110
	Chinguague Compound	107
	Bishop's Lodge	179
	La Jacona Ranch	206
TX	Indian Lodge	129
	Plaza San Antonio	88

CROSS-COUNTRY SKIING

State	Place	Page
NM	Legends Hotel	268
	The Lodge	180
	Monjeau Shadows	110
	Twining Condominiums	269

FISHING

State	Place	Page
AZ	Montezuma Lodge	31
	Price Canyon Ranch	251
NM	Chinguague Compound	107
	Legends Hotel	268
	Los Pinos Guest Ranch	32
	Moreno Ranch Hunting Lodge	225
	Oso Ranch and Lodge	226, 280
	Vermejo Park Ranch	227
OK	Lake Texoma Resort	188
	Roman Nose Resort	127
	Three Buoys Houseboat Vacations	232
TX	Lajitas on the Rio Grande	191
	Lakeway Inn	236
	Mayan Dude Ranch	200

GOLF

State	Place	Page
AZ	Boulders	152
	The Wigwam	178
	Arizona Biltmore	174
	Marriott's Camelback Inn	133
	Scottsdale Princess	160

State	Place	Page
AZ	Hyatt Regency Scottsdale at Gainey Ranch	154
	Poco Diablo Resort	135
	Loews Ventana Canyon Resort	156
	Sheraton Tucson El Conquistador Golf and Tennis Resort	160
	Tucson National Resort and Spa	272
	Ventana Canyon Golf and Racquet Club	279
	Westin La Paloma	161
	Rancho de los Caballeros	196
NM	Legends Hotel	268
	The Lodge	180
	Inn of the Mountain Gods	138
OK	Shangri-La	231
	Lake Texoma Resort	188
	Western Hills Guest Ranch	128
	Roman Nose Resort	127
TX	Lakeway Inn	236
	High Cotton Inn Bed and Breakfast	303
	Rancho Viejo Resort	284
	Horseshoe Bay Country Club Resort	235
	Four Seasons Resort and Hotel	163
	Y.O. Ranch Hilton	254
	Del Lago Resort	234
	Plaza San Antonio	88
	Lajitas on the Rio Grande	190

HIKING

State	Place	Page
AZ	Arizona Biltmore	174
	Boulders	152
	Bright Angel Lodge & Cabins	239
	Canyon Ranch Spa	271
	El Tovar	240
	Flying E Ranch	194
	Flying V Ranch	203
	Garlands's Oak Creek Lodge	115
	Grapevine Canyon Ranch	256
	Hacienda del Sol Guest Ranch Resort	177
	Kay El Bar Ranch	195
	L'Auberge de Sedona	143

State	Place	Page
AZ	Loews Ventana Canyon Resort	156
	Lynx Creek Farm	106
	Marriott's Camelback Inn	133
	Montezuma Lodge	31
	Phantom Ranch	242
	Pointe at Tapatio Cliff	157
	Price Canyon Ranch	251
	Rancho de la Osa	186
	Rancho de los Caballeros	196
	Sheraton Tucson El Conquistador Golf and Tennis Resort	160
	Tanque Verde Ranch	198
	Ventana Canyon Golf and Racquet Club	279
	Westin La Paloma	161
	White Stallion Ranch	199
	Wickenburg Inn	137
NM	Austing Haus Hotel	266
	Bear Mountain Guest Ranch	246
	Bishop's Lodge	179
	Chinguague Compound	107
	Dasburg House & Studio	204
	Galisteo Inn	116
	Inn of the Mountain Gods	138
	La Jacona Ranch	206
	La Junta	187
	Legends Hotel	268
	Los Pinos Guest Ranch	32
	Monjeau Shadows	110
	Twining Condominiums	269
	Vermejo Park Ranch	227
OK	Lake Texoma Resort	188
	Roman Nose Resort	127
	Western Hills Guest Ranch	128
TX	Chain-O-Lakes	34
	Chisos Mountains Lodge	238
	Guadalupe River Ranch	189
	Indian Lodge	129
	Lajitas on the Rio Grande	191
	Landhaus Bed and Breakfast	112
	Mayan Dude Ranch	200
	Prude Ranch	252
	Silver Spur Guest Ranch	201
	Tol Barret House	220

HUNTING

INDOOR POOL

State	Place	Page
TX	Marriott's Hotel Galvez	24
	Hotel Inter-Continental Houston	73
	Four Seasons Resort and Hotel	163
	Inn of the Hills River Resort	141

OUTDOOR POOL

State	Place	Page
AZ	Arizona Biltmore	174
	Arizona Inn	175
	Boulders	152
	Canyon Ranch Spa	271
	Copper Queen Hotel	286
	Flying E Ranch	194
	Flying V Ranch	203
	Graham's Bed & Breakfast Inn	296
	Grapevine Canyon Ranch	256
	Hacienda del Sol Guest Ranch Resort	177
	Hotel Park Tucson	94
	Hyatt Regency Scottsdale at Gainey Ranch	154
	John Gardiner's Tennis Ranch on Camelback	278
	Kay El Bar Ranch	195
	L'Auberge de Sedona	143
	Little America of Flagstaff	124
	Loews Ventana Canyon Resort	156
	Marriott's Camelback Inn	133
	Poco Diablo Resort	135
	Pointe at Tapatio Cliff	157
	Price Canyon Ranch	251
	Rancho de la Osa	186
	Rancho de los Caballeros	196
	Red Lion's La Posada	158
	Registry Resort	159
	Scottsdale Princess	160
	Sheraton Tucson El Conquistador Golf and Tennis Resort	160
	Sky Ranch Lodge	125
	Squaw Park Inn	37
	Stouffer Cottonwoods Resort	257
	Tanque Verde Ranch	198
	Tucson National Resort and Spa	272

State	Place	Page
AZ	Ventana Canyon Golf and Racquet Club	279
	Westin La Paloma	161
	Westward Look Resort	136
	White Stallion Ranch	199
	Wickenburg Inn	137
	The Wigwam	178
NM	Albuquerque Marriott	43
	Barcelona Court All Suite Hotel	44
	Bishop's Lodge	179
	El Rey Inn	126
	Galisteo Inn	116
	Inn of the Governors	92
	Inn of the Mountain Gods	138
	La Posada de Santa Fe	290
	The Lodge	180
	Meson de Mesilla	147
	Pyramid Holiday Inn	46
	Quail Ridge Inn & Tennis Ranch	281
	Rancho Encantado	184
	Sagebrush Inn	291
	St. James Hotel	148
	Sunrise Springs Resort	248
	Taos Inn	216
OK	Lake Texoma Resort	188
	Oklahoma City Marriott	83
	Roman Nose Resort	127
	Shangri-La	231
	Tulsa Marriott	97
	Waterford Hotel	83
	Western Hills Guest Ranch	128
	Westin Hotel, Williams Center	98
TX	Adolphus	53
	Best Western Sandy Shores	23
	Bridgepoint	102
	Browning Plantation	166
	Camp Warnecke Resorts	103
	Dallas Marriot Mandalay Hotel	55
	Del Lago Resort	234
	Driskill Hotel	48
	El Paso Airport Hilton	66
	El Paso Marriott	67
	Fairmont Hotel	56
	Four Seasons Hotel-Houston Center	72
	Four Seasons Resort and Hotel	163

State	Place	Page
TX	Greenhouse	274
	Guadalupe River Ranch	189
	Hershey Corpus Christi Hotel	140
	High Cotton Inn Bed and Breakfast	303
	Horseshoe Bay Country Club Resort	235
	Hotel Crescent Court	57
	Hotel Inter-Continental Houston	73
	Indian Lodge	129
	Inn of the Hills River Resort	141
	Inn on the Park	74
	Inn on the River	7
	John Newcombe's Tennis Ranch	283
	La Mansion del Rio	86
	La Mansion Hotel Austin	50
	La Posada (Laredo, TX)	292
	La Posada (McAllen, TX)	293
	Lajitas on the Rio Grande	191
	Lake Austin Resort	275
	Lakeway Inn	236
	Lazy Hills Guest Ranch	192
	Loews Anatole Hotel	59
	Mansion on Turtle Creek	60
	Marriott's Hotel Galvez	24
	Mayan Dude Ranch	200
	Menger Hotel	87
	Phoenix Fitness Resort	276
	Plaza San Antonio	88
	Port Royal by the Sea	26
	Radisson Gunter Hotel	89
	Rancho Viejo Resort	284
	Remington on Post Oak Park	78
	San Luis Hotel and Condominiums	27
	Seascape	104
	Sheraton South Padre Island Beach Resort	28
	Silver Spur Guest Ranch	201
	South Padre Hilton Resort	28
	St. Anthony Inter-Continental	90
	Stoneleigh	63
	Stouffer Austin Hotel	51
	Stouffer Dallas Hotel	64
	Warwick	79
	Westin Galleria and Westin Oaks	81
	Westin Hotel Dallas	65
	Westin Paso del Norte	68

State	Place	Page
TX	Wyndham Hotel Greenspoint	82
	Wyndham Southpark	52
	Y.O. Ranch Hilton	254
	Yacht Club Hotel	294

RACQUETBALL

State	Place	Page
AZ	Pointe at Tapatio Cliff	157
	Scottsdale Princess	160
	Canyon Ranch Spa	271
	Sheraton Tucson El Conquistador Golf and Tennis Resort	160
NM	La Posada de Albuquerque	45
TX	Driskill Hotel	48
	Adolphus	53
	Loews Anatole Hotel	59
	Plaza of the Americas	63
	Hotel Inter-Continental Houston	73
	Phoenix Fitness Resort	276
	Wyndham Hotel Greenspoint	82
	Inn of the Hills River Resort	141

RAFTING

State	Place	Page
TX	Lajitas on the Rio Grande	191

RIDING

State	Place	Page
AZ	Price Canyon Ranch	251
	The Wigwam	178

State	Place	Page
AZ	Grapevine Canyon Ranch	256
	Pointe at Tapatio Cliff	157
	Rancho de la Osa	186
	Marriott's Camelback Inn	133
	Hacienda del Sol Guest Ranch Resort	177
	Sheraton Tucson El Conquistador Golf and Tennis Resort	160
	Tanque Verde Ranch	198
	Westin La Paloma	161
	White Stallion Ranch	199
	Flying E Ranch	194
	Kay El Bar Ranch	195
	Rancho de los Caballeros	196
	Wickenburg Inn	137
NM	Legends Hotel	268
	Galisteo Inn	116
	Inn of the Mountain Gods	138
	Vermejo Park Ranch	227
	Bishop's Lodge	179
	Rancho Encantado	184
	Los Pinos Guest Ranch	32
OK	Shangri-La	231
	Lake Texoma Resort	188
	Western Hills Guest Ranch	128
TX	Lakeway Inn	236
	Mayan Dude Ranch	200
	Silver Spur Guest Ranch	201
	Chisos Mountains Lodge	238
	Guadalupe River Ranch	189
	Prude Ranch	252
	Landhaus Bed and Breakfast	112
	Horseshoe Bay Country Club Resort	235
	Lazy Hills Guest Ranch	192
	Chain-O-Lakes	34
	Lajitas on the Rio Grande	191

SAILING

State	Place	Page
NM	Inn of the Mountain Gods	138
OK	Western Hills Guest Ranch	128

State	Place	Page
TX	Lakeway Inn	236
	Lago Del Resort	231

SHUFFLEBOARD

State	Place	Page
TX	Inn of the Hills River Resort	141

SKATING

State	Place	Page
AZ	Rancho de los Caballeros	196
OK	Western Hills Guest Ranch	128
TX	Plaza of the Americas	63
	Westin Hotel Dallas	65

SKIING

State	Place	Page
NM	Legends Hotel	268
	Austing Haus Hotel	266
	Quail Ridge Inn & Tennis Ranch	281
	Twining Condominiums	269

SQUASH

State	Place	Page
AZ	Scottsdale Princess	160
OK	Waterford Hotel	83

State	Place	Page
TX	Loews Anatole Hotel	59
	Wyndham Hotel Greenspoint	82

SWIMMING HOLE

State	Place	Page
AZ	Garlands's Oak Creek Lodge	115
	Junipine Resort Condo Hotel	99
	L'Auberge de Sedona	143
	Tanque Verde Ranch	198
NM	Sunrise Springs Resort	248
OK	Shangri-La	231
	Three Buoys Houseboat Vacations	232
	Lake Texoma Resort	188
	Roman Nose Resort	127
TX	Lakeway Inn	236
	Guadalupe River Ranch	189
	Indian Lodge	129
	Landhaus Bed and Breakfast	112
	Inn on the River	7
	Del Lago Resort	234
	Camp Warnecke Resorts	103
	Chain-O-Lakes	34

TENNIS

State	Place	Page
AZ	Boulders	152
	The Wigwam	178
	Arizona Biltmore	174
	Pointe at Tapatio Cliff	157
	Marriott's Camelback Inn	133
	Registry Resort	159
	Scottsdale Princess	160
	Stouffer Cottonwoods Resort	257
	Hyatt Regency Scottsdale at Gainey Ranch	154

State	Place	Page
AZ	John Gardiner's Tennis Ranch on Camelback	278
	Poco Diablo Resort	135
	Arizona Inn	175
	Canyon Ranch Spa	271
	Hacienda del Sol Guest Ranch Resort	177
	Loews Ventana Canyon Resort	156
	Sheraton Tucson El Conquistador Golf and Tennis Resort	160
	Tanque Verde Ranch	198
	Tucson National Resort and Spa	272
	Ventana Canyon Golf and Racquet Club	279
	Westin La Paloma	161
	Westward Look Resort	136
	White Stallion Ranch	199
	Flying E Ranch	194
	Rancho de los Caballeros	196
	Wickenburg Inn	137
NM	Legends Hotel	268
	Inn of the Mountain Gods	138
	Bishop's Lodge	179
	Rancho Encantado	184
	Sunrise Springs Resort	248
	Quail Ridge Inn & Tennis Ranch	281
	Sagebrush Inn	291
OK	Shangri-La	231
	Lake Texoma Resort	188
	Waterford Hotel	83
	Westin Hotel, Williams Center	98
	Western Hills Guest Ranch	128
TX	Lakeway Inn	236
	Mayan Dude Ranch	200
	Guadalupe River Ranch	189
	Rancho Viejo Resort	284
	Loews Anatole Hotel	59
	Plaza of the Americas	63
	Stoneleigh	63
	Prude Ranch	252
	Worthington Hotel	71
	San Luis Hotel and Condominiums	27
	Seascape	104
	Horseshoe Bay Country Club Resort	235
	Hotel Inter-Continental Houston	73
	Inn on the Park	74
	Phoenix Fitness Resort	276

State	Place	Page
TX	Westin Galleria and Westin Oaks	81
	Lazy Hills Guest Ranch	192
	Four Seasons Resort and Hotel	163
	Inn of the Hills River Resort	141
	Del Lago Resort	234
	John Newcombe's Tennis Ranch	283
	Bridgepoint	102
	Sheraton South Padre Island Beach Resort	28
	South Padre Hilton Resort	28

TRAP AND SKEET SHOOTING

State	Place	Page
NM	Inn of the Mountain Gods	138

VOLLEYBALL

State	Place	Page
TX	Inn of the Hills River Resort	141

Index

Best Places Report

We appreciate any information you can supply about the quality of the lodging. Detailed information about the building, furniture, service, food, and setting is most important. Describe as many rooms as you can, including living rooms, dining rooms, other common rooms, and of course bedrooms. A note about activities and nearby sights would be helpful. Tell us what category you think the place belongs in and why. Finally, how did you hear about the place, and how long have you been going there?

We will be happy to send you a free copy of the next edition of the book if we use your suggestion.

To: *Chris Paddock*
      Best Places to Stay in the Southwest
      The Harvard Common Press
      535 Albany Street
      Boston, Massachusetts 02118

Name of hotel: _____

Telephone: _____

Address: _____

_____ Zip: _____

_____

Description: _____

_____

_____

_____

_____

_____

_____

Your Name: _____

Telephone: _____

Address: _____

_____ Zip: _____

_____

Best Places Report

We appreciate any information you can supply about the quality of the lodging. Detailed information about the building, furniture, service, food, and setting is most important. Describe as many rooms as you can, including living rooms, dining rooms, other common rooms, and of course bedrooms. A note about activities and nearby sights would be helpful. Tell us what category you think the place belongs in and why. Finally, how did you hear about the place, and how long have you been going there?

We will be happy to send you a free copy of the next edition of the book if we use your suggestion.

To: *Chris Paddock*
        Best Places to Stay in the Southwest
        The Harvard Common Press
        535 Albany Street
        Boston, Massachusetts 02118

Name of hotel: _____

Telephone: _____

Address: _____

_____ Zip: _____

_____

Description: _____

_____

_____

_____

_____

_____

Your Name: _____

Telephone: _____

Address: _____

_____ Zip: _____

_____

Best Places Report

We appreciate any information you can supply about the quality of the lodging. Detailed information about the building, furniture, service, food, and setting is most important. Describe as many rooms as you can, including living rooms, dining rooms, other common rooms, and of course bedrooms. A note about activities and nearby sights would be helpful. Tell us what category you think the place belongs in and why. Finally, how did you hear about the place, and how long have you been going there?

We will be happy to send you a free copy of the next edition of the book if we use your suggestion.

To: *Chris Paddock*
Best Places to Stay in the Southwest
The Harvard Common Press
535 Albany Street
Boston, Massachusetts 02118

Name of hotel: _____

Telephone: _____

Address: _____

_____ Zip: _____

_____

Description: _____

_____

_____

_____

_____

_____

_____

Your Name: _____

Telephone: _____

Address: _____

_____ Zip: _____

_____

Best Places Report

We appreciate any information you can supply about the quality of the lodging. Detailed information about the building, furniture, service, food, and setting is most important. Describe as many rooms as you can, including living rooms, dining rooms, other common rooms, and of course bedrooms. A note about activities and nearby sights would be helpful. Tell us what category you think the place belongs in and why. Finally, how did you hear about the place, and how long have you been going there?

We will be happy to send you a free copy of the next edition of the book if we use your suggestion.

To: *Chris Paddock*
    Best Places to Stay in the Southwest
    The Harvard Common Press
    535 Albany Street
    Boston, Massachusetts 02118

Name of hotel: _____

Telephone: _____

Address: _____

_____ Zip: _____

_____

Description: _____

_____

_____

_____

_____

_____

_____

Your Name: _____

Telephone: _____

Address: _____

_____ Zip: _____

_____

Best Places Report

We appreciate any information you can supply about the quality of the lodging. Detailed information about the building, furniture, service, food, and setting is most important. Describe as many rooms as you can, including living rooms, dining rooms, other common rooms, and of course bedrooms. A note about activities and nearby sights would be helpful. Tell us what category you think the place belongs in and why. Finally, how did you hear about the place, and how long have you been going there?

We will be happy to send you a free copy of the next edition of the book if we use your suggestion.

To: *Chris Paddock*
     Best Places to Stay in the Southwest
     The Harvard Common Press
     535 Albany Street
     Boston, Massachusetts 02118

Name of hotel: _____

Telephone: _____

Address: _____

_____ Zip: _____

_____

Description: _____

_____

_____

_____

_____

_____

_____

Your Name: _____

Telephone: _____

Address: _____

_____ Zip: _____

_____

Best Places Report

We appreciate any information you can supply about the quality of the lodging. Detailed information about the building, furniture, service, food, and setting is most important. Describe as many rooms as you can, including living rooms, dining rooms, other common rooms, and of course bedrooms. A note about activities and nearby sights would be helpful. Tell us what category you think the place belongs in and why. Finally, how did you hear about the place, and how long have you been going there?

We will be happy to send you a free copy of the next edition of the book if we use your suggestion.

To: *Chris Paddock*
        Best Places to Stay in the Southwest
        The Harvard Common Press
        535 Albany Street
        Boston, Massachusetts 02118

Name of hotel: _____

Telephone: _____

Address: _____

_____ Zip: _____

_____

Description: _____

_____

_____

_____

_____

_____

_____

Your Name: _____

Telephone: _____

Address: _____

_____ Zip: _____

_____

Best Places Report

We appreciate any information you can supply about the quality of the lodging. Detailed information about the building, furniture, service, food, and setting is most important. Describe as many rooms as you can, including living rooms, dining rooms, other common rooms, and of course bedrooms. A note about activities and nearby sights would be helpful. Tell us what category you think the place belongs in and why. Finally, how did you hear about the place, and how long have you been going there?

We will be happy to send you a free copy of the next edition of the book if we use your suggestion.

To: *Chris Paddock*
  Best Places to Stay in the Southwest
  The Harvard Common Press
  535 Albany Street
  Boston, Massachusetts 02118

Name of hotel: _____

Telephone: _____

Address: _____

_____ Zip: _____

_____

Description: _____

_____

_____

_____

_____

_____

_____

Your Name: _____

Telephone: _____

Address: _____

_____ Zip: _____

_____

Best Places Report

We appreciate any information you can supply about the quality of the lodging. Detailed information about the building, furniture, service, food, and setting is most important. Describe as many rooms as you can, including living rooms, dining rooms, other common rooms, and of course bedrooms. A note about activities and nearby sights would be helpful. Tell us what category you think the place belongs in and why. Finally, how did you hear about the place, and how long have you been going there?

We will be happy to send you a free copy of the next edition of the book if we use your suggestion.

To: *Chris Paddock*
     Best Places to Stay in the Southwest
     The Harvard Common Press
     535 Albany Street
     Boston, Massachusetts 02118

Name of hotel: _____

Telephone: _____

Address: _____

_____ Zip: _____ _____

_____

Description: _____

_____

_____

_____

_____

_____

_____

Your Name: _____

Telephone: _____

Address: _____

_____ Zip: _____

_____

Best Places Report

We appreciate any information you can supply about the quality of the lodging. Detailed information about the building, furniture, service, food, and setting is most important. Describe as many rooms as you can, including living rooms, dining rooms, other common rooms, and of course bedrooms. A note about activities and nearby sights would be helpful. Tell us what category you think the place belongs in and why. Finally, how did you hear about the place, and how long have you been going there?

We will be happy to send you a free copy of the next edition of the book if we use your suggestion.

To: *Chris Paddock*
      Best Places to Stay in the Southwest
      The Harvard Common Press
      535 Albany Street
      Boston, Massachusetts 02118

Name of hotel: _____

Telephone: _____

Address: _____

_____ Zip: _____

_____

Description: _____

_____

_____

_____

_____

_____

_____

Your Name: _____

Telephone: _____

Address: _____

_____ Zip: _____

_____